MW01630266

Lois M. Jones

Jazz Age Illustration

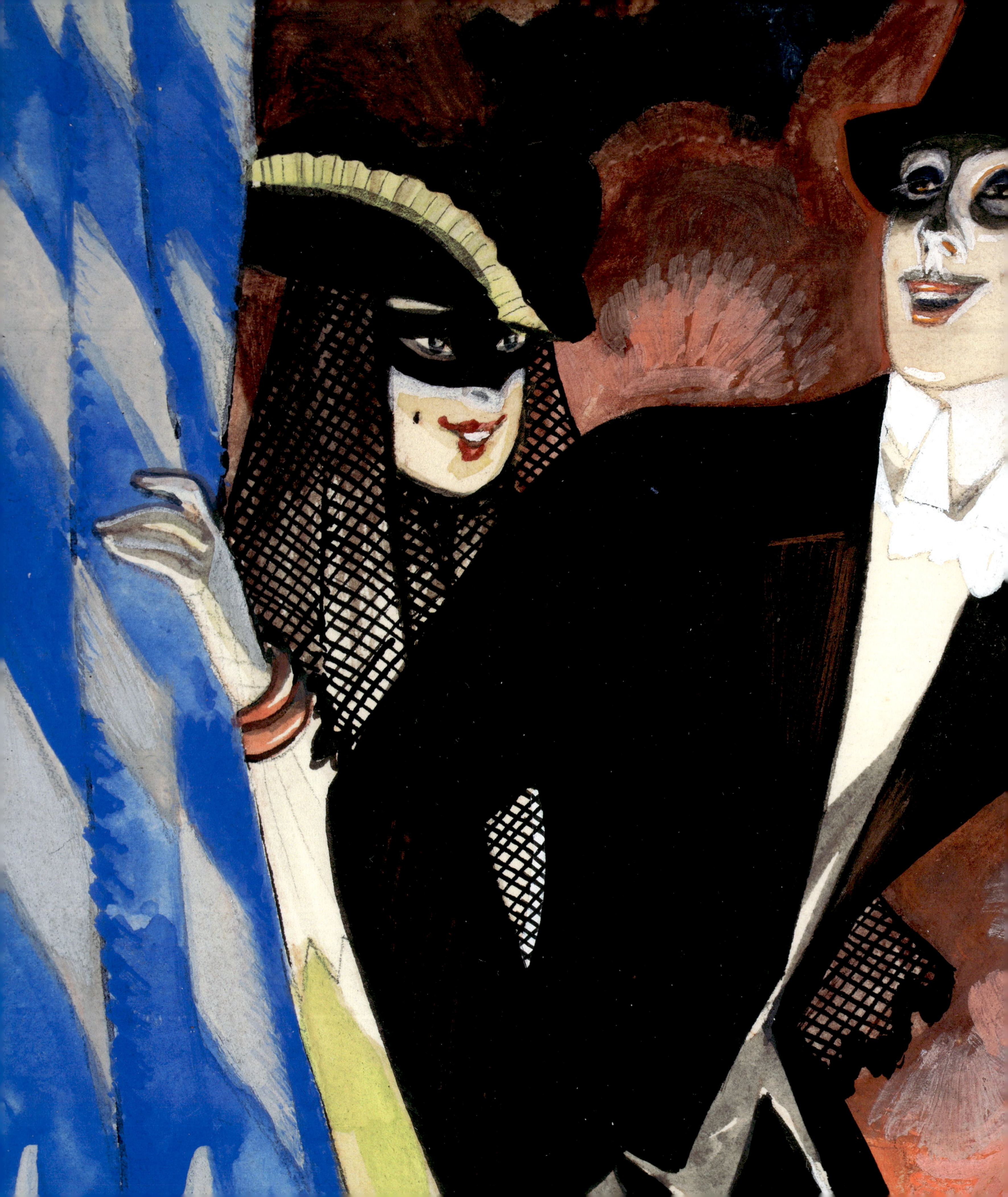

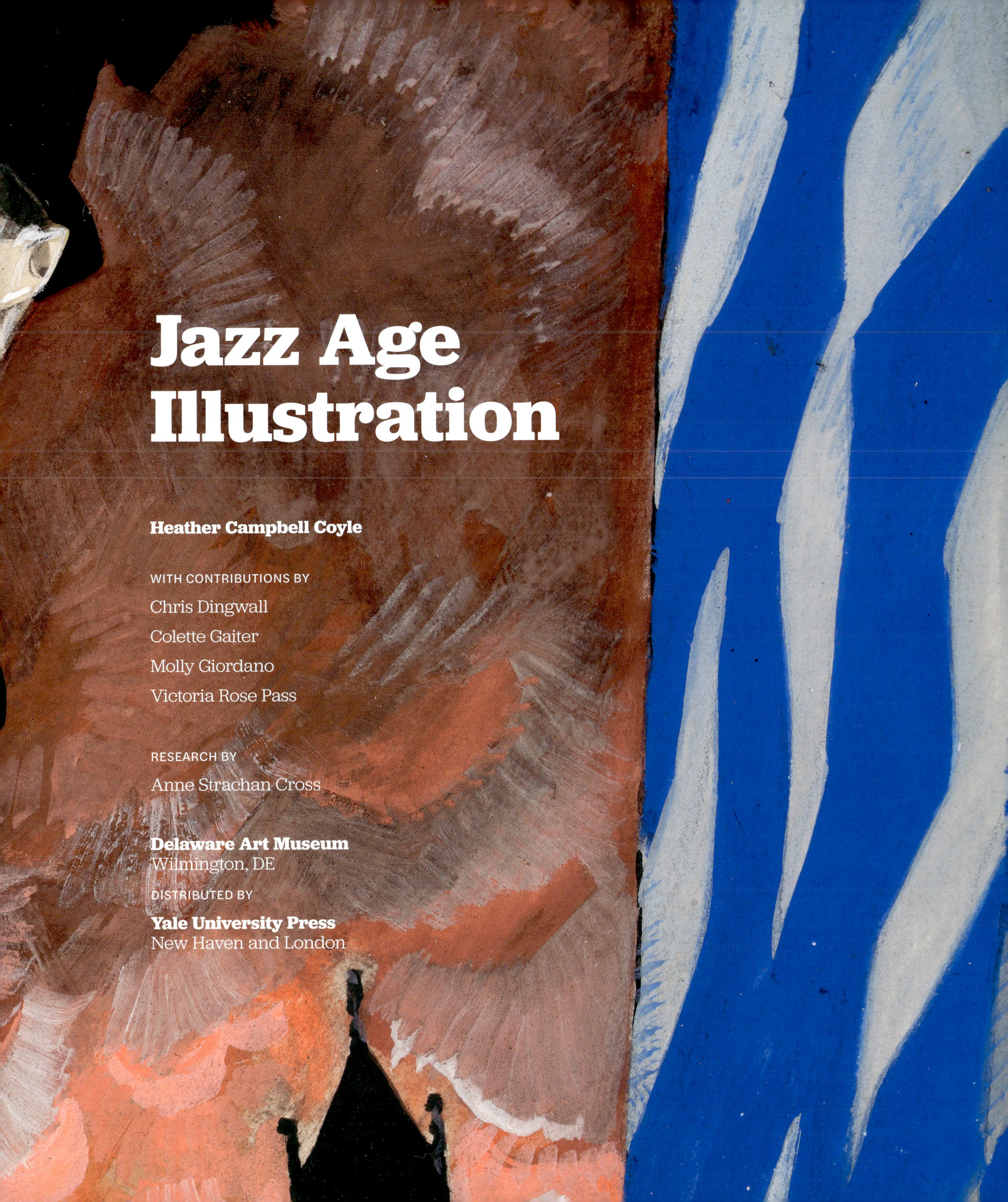

Jazz Age Illustration

Heather Campbell Coyle

WITH CONTRIBUTIONS BY

Chris Dingwall

Colette Gaiter

Molly Giordano

Victoria Rose Pass

RESEARCH BY

Anne Strachan Cross

Delaware Art Museum
Wilmington, DE

DISTRIBUTED BY

Yale University Press
New Haven and London

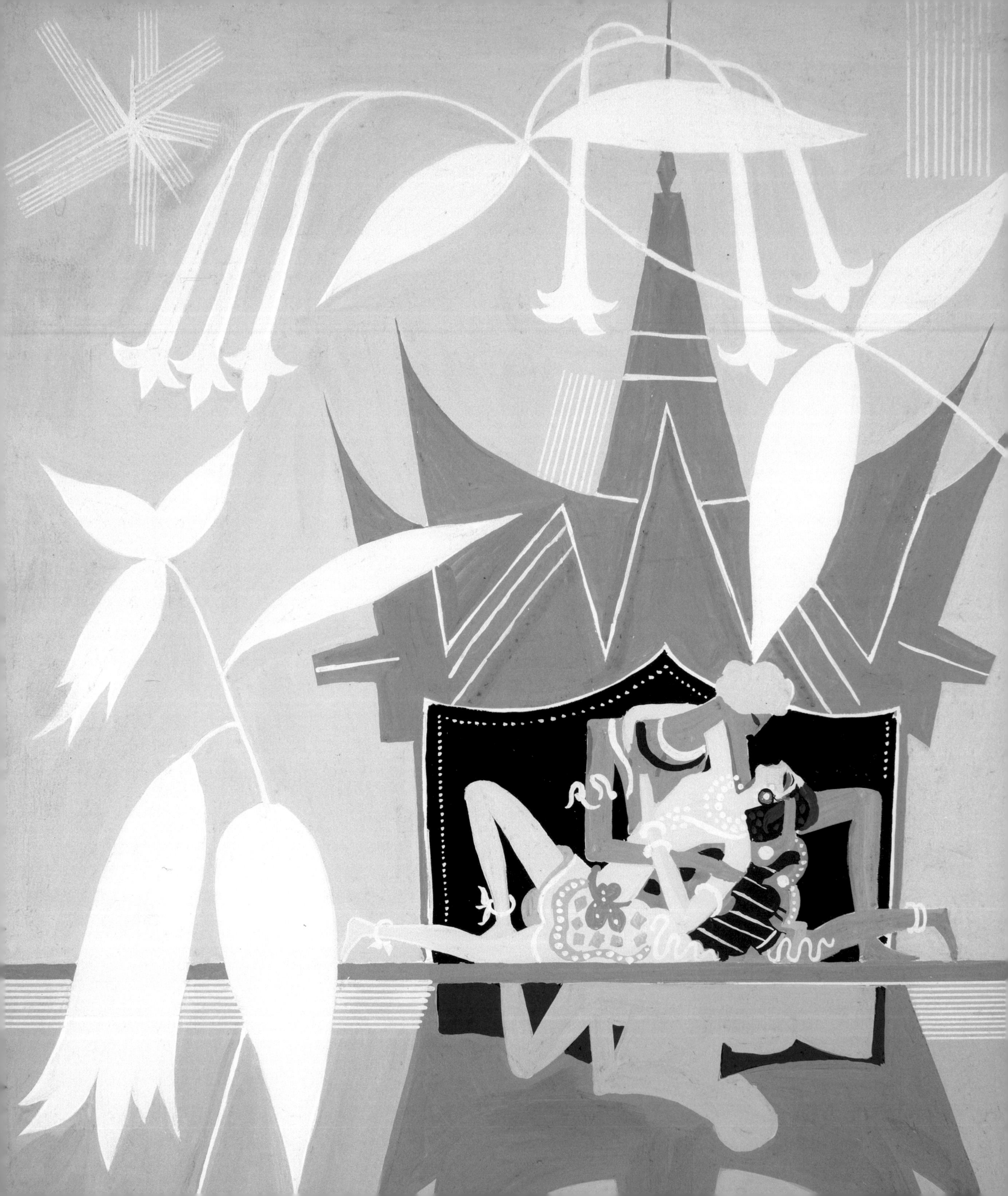

Contents

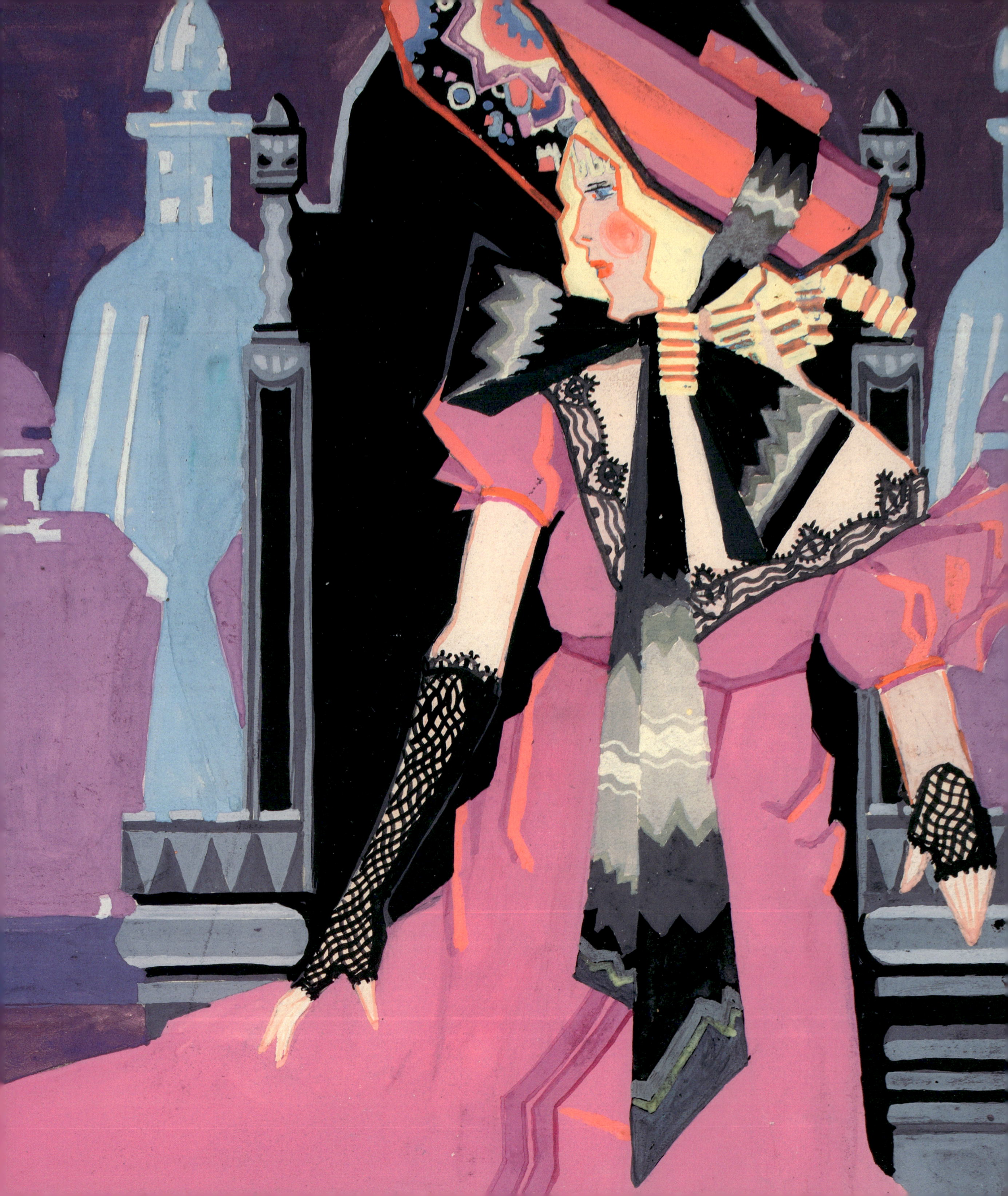

Director's Foreword

Illustration is at the heart of the Delaware Art Museum. The Museum was founded with a purchase of paintings and drawings by Howard Pyle, who lived in Wilmington and made our small city the center of American illustration through his practice and teaching. Pyle's students Frank Schoonover and N. C. Wyeth were among the Museum's earliest supporters, and their works entered the collection in the 1920s and '30s—during the Jazz Age.

At its core, *Jazz Age Illustration* is a project made possible by more than one hundred years of collecting at the Delaware Art Museum and featuring more than thirty recent acquisitions, many by women and African American artists. *Jazz Age Illustration* also reflects the Museum's commitment to building new narratives of art and illustration that are inclusive and engaging to all. This focus on community relevance and inviting input helped us reimagine our permanent collection galleries in 2021, which paved the way for this project.

This exhibition would not be possible without the generous support for collection-driven exhibitions provided by the Henry Luce Foundation. The Richard C. Von Hess Foundation funded the conservation, presentation, and long-term preservation of dozens of drawings and paintings for *Jazz Age Illustration*. The Wyeth Foundation for American Art supported the scholarship and design of this catalogue. *Jazz Age Illustration* also received critical support from the Rock Oak Foundation, in memory of Thomas C. Brokaw, the Roger and Sarah Bancroft Clark Foundation, Heritage Auctions, and the contributions of generous individuals.

A major exhibition requires a huge team effort, and all members of the Museum's staff contributed to *Jazz Age Illustration* in important ways. Curator of American Art Dr. Heather Campbell Coyle dedicated more than five years to this exhibition. I am particularly grateful for Dr. Coyle's thoughtful and decisive illustration acquisitions that strengthen both this exhibition and our permanent collection. Vital research, interpretation, and organizational assistance was provided by Anne Cross, recipient of the Lynn Herrick Sharp Curatorial Fellowship from the University of Delaware, a key partner for this exhibition and its programs.

I am delighted that *Jazz Age Illustration* will be shared with audiences at the Biggs Museum of American Art in Dover, Delaware, and the Norman Rockwell Museum in Stockbridge, Massachusetts. Exchanges with these partners have helped shape the exhibition and its catalogue, and I am grateful to their staff for embracing this project. I also extend my thanks to all the lenders, both institutions and individuals, whose generosity allows us to share a richer story of American illustration.

Ambitious exhibitions and publications are possible only with the confidence and engagement of the Museum's Board of Trustees. David Pollack, Board President from 2020 to 2023, enthusiastically supported *Jazz Age Illustration* from its earliest days, even as he guided the Museum through the pandemic. I am pleased to dedicate this exhibition to him.

Molly Giordano
Executive Director
Delaware Art Museum

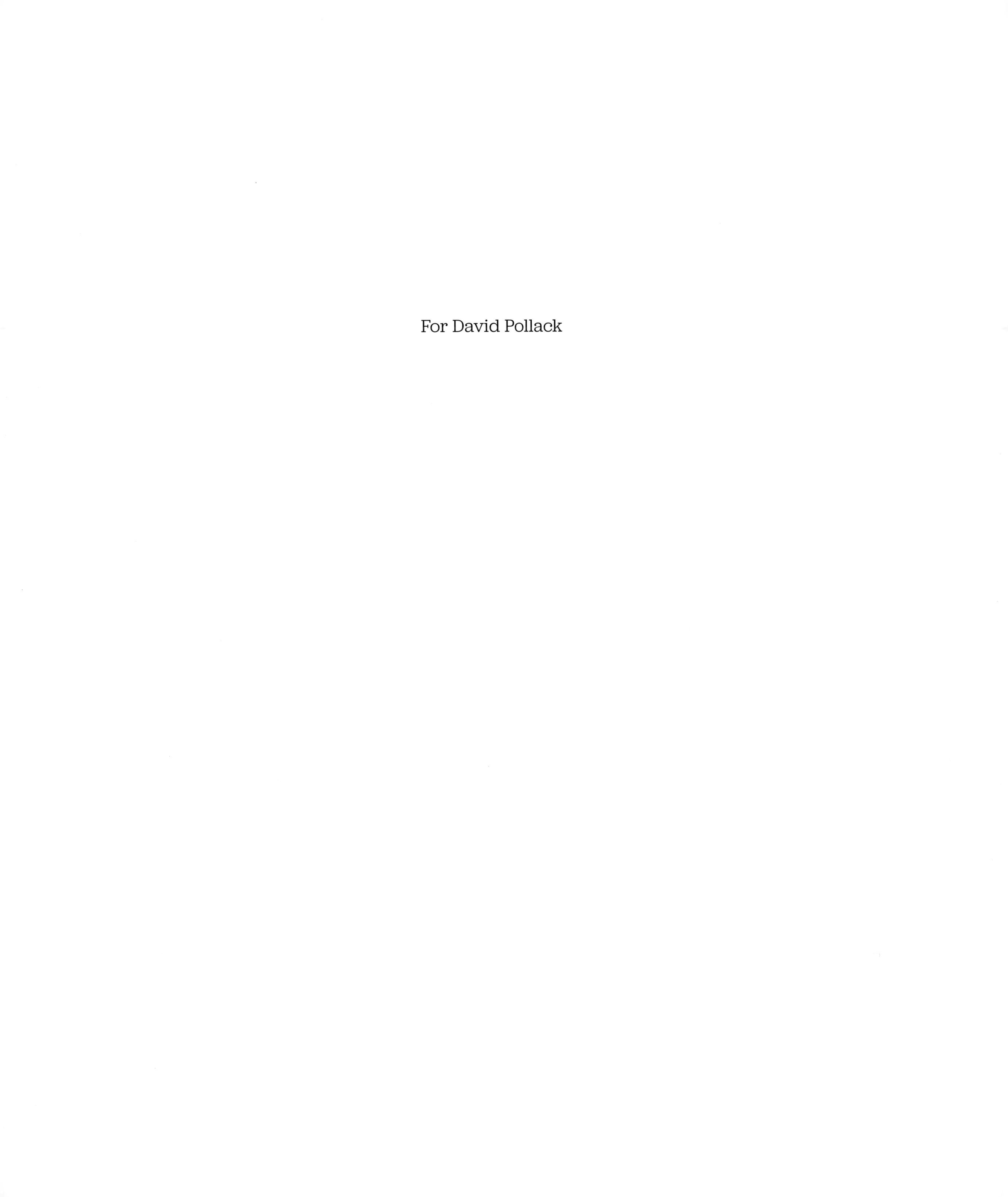

For David Pollack

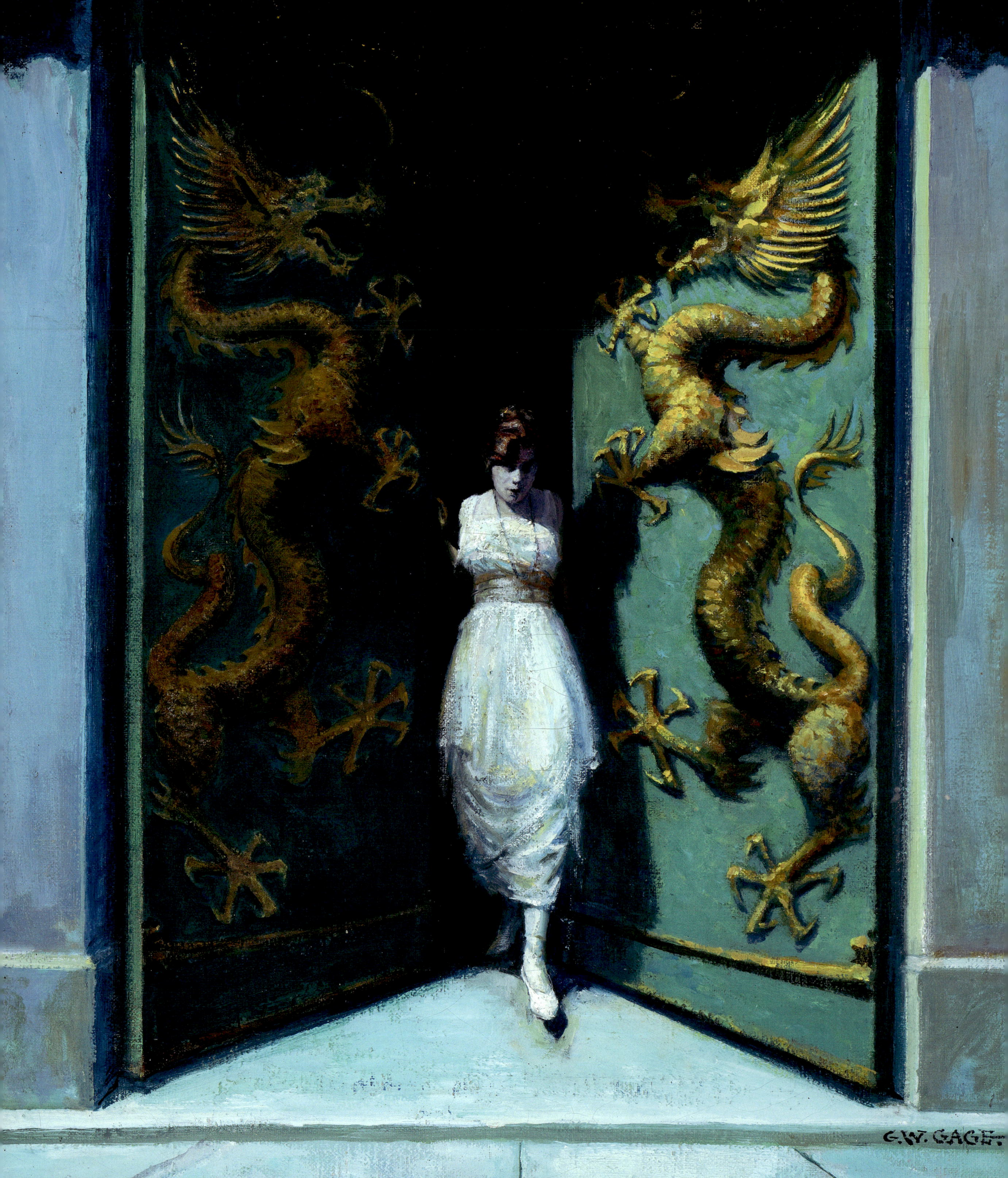
G.W. GAGE.

Introduction and Acknowledgments

Jazz Age Illustration is built around the Delaware Art Museum's deep collection of illustrations for mass-market magazines from the 1920s and '30s, but its aims are broader, bringing in examples from literary magazines, pulps, newspapers, books, and poster campaigns. The exhibition encompasses work from about 1919 through 1942, presenting an exciting time in American illustration when a considerable number of publications regularly circulated images created by thousands of illustrators, including women and artists of color whose work expanded the reach and range of published imagery. This period—going beyond the 1920s or even the mid-1930s—was chosen to allow for the display of more original art by African American artists.

With such a broad remit, *Jazz Age Illustration* cannot be comprehensive. Strong examples from the Museum's collection did not make the cut (I had over 800 works to choose from!), and some significant works were unavailable for loan. Countless originals remain unlocated, and even printed materials can be difficult to find. I am constantly learning about fascinating artists and publications that are new to me. Despite these limitations, I hope *Jazz Age Illustration* illuminates an exciting period and its vibrant visual culture. It is intended as a broad survey that provides an invitation and a prod to future research. Studying illustration allows us to paint a better picture of American visual culture. Focusing on Jazz Age illustration insists that we foreground Black cultural contributions and develop a more inclusive history of the American popular press.

This project was informed by excellent studies of key aspects of Jazz Age illustration. Caroline Goeser's *Picturing the New Negro: Harlem Renaissance Print Culture and Modern Black Identity* grounded my understanding of the Black press in the 1920s and '30s and strongly influenced the exhibition checklist, library acquisitions, and the first essay in this volume. I returned again and again to Amy H. Kirschke's in-depth studies of Aaron Douglas and *The Crisis* as I worked on this project. Years ago, Michele H. Bogart's *Artists, Advertising, and the Borders of Art* inspired me to seek a broader story of American art through published imagery. I probably wouldn't work on illustration if I hadn't read her book. My vision of mass-market American illustration was shaped by the essays in Dorey Schmidt's catalogue for *The American Magazine, 1890–1940*, an exhibition curated by Rowland Elzea at the Delaware Art Museum in 1979. Like all scholars of American illustration, I benefitted from the publications of Walter and Roger Reed and the ambitious *History of Illustration* compiled by Susan Doyle, Jaleen Grove, and Whitney Sherman. Over a decade ago,

I adored *Youth and Beauty: Art of the American Twenties* at the Brooklyn Museum, and I suspect that visit planted the seed for this show. More recently, I drew inspiration from displays of J. C. Leyendecker's work, including the powerfully researched *Under Cover: J. C. Leyendecker and American Masculinity* at the New-York Historical Society.

Jazz Age Illustration couldn't have started anywhere other than the Delaware Art Museum. Featured works were donated by artists' families, collectors, and the indefatigable Helen Farr Sloan and purchased by generations of curators. My colleagues Mary Holahan and Joyce K. Schiller did much of the heavy lifting in collecting and cataloguing the works that form the center of this show. Conversations with jazz drummer Jonathan Whitney back in 2019 provided the spark, and I am thankful to Molly Giordano, Erin Tohill Robin, Amelia Wiggins, and Margaret Winslow, who supported *Jazz Age Illustration* as the project expanded in scope. With help from Benét Burton, Meg Thomas coordinated the complex logistics of conservation, and Rachael DiEleuterio expanded the library collections to meet the needs of the project. As always, Carson Zullinger photographed nearly all the art and ephemera in Delaware, and Erin Tohill Robin organized loans from across the country. Jonathan Schoff and John Gibbons prepared and installed over one hundred works of art and dozens of archival items from the Museum's collection. I appreciate the Museum's Collections Committee members who responded with enthusiasm and alacrity to the many purchases we made with this show in mind. In particular, I am thankful for the constant encouragement of David Pollack, who identified acquisitions and loans for the show and shared my excitement over obscure artists and odd ephemera.

This exhibition would never have come together without two years of research, planning, and writing by Anne Strachan Cross. Annie located works for purchase and loan, organized a convening, and identified authors for this book. She kept *Jazz Age* going while I reinstalled the permanent collection and curated other exhibitions.

Jazz Age Illustration benefitted from the input of many advisors. During the depths of 2020, Stephanie Haboush Plunkett was the first person I reached out to, and I'm delighted that the exhibition will head to the Norman Rockwell Museum. I learned so much from serving on the Rockwell Museum's Advisory Committee for *Imprinted: Illustrating Race* alongside Stephanie, Robyn Phillips-Pendleton, and Laurie Norton Moffatt. Ideas shared by Michele H. Bogart, William H. Foster III, Nancy Goldstein, Theresa Leininger-Miller, and Cherene Sherrard-Johnson, among others, directly impacted the scope of *Jazz Age Illustration*.

Recognizing critical weaknesses in our knowledge and collections, in May 2023, Annie and I hosted a convening of scholars with expertise in the work of African American illustrators active in the Jazz Age. Participants included Mia Curran, Chris Dingwall, Brigitte Fielder, Colette Gaiter, Caroline Goeser, Jennifer Greenhill, Valerie Harris, Laura Helton, Elizabeth Humphrey, Theresa Leininger-Miller, Robyn Phillips-Pendleton, and Rebecca VanDiver. Their input at the convening and beyond shaped every aspect of this exhibition. I am particularly grateful to Chris and Colette, who wrote essays for the catalogue; to Jenny, who introduced me to the

Dolas family; to Theresa, who answered my sheet music questions; and to Robyn, who introduced me to Carlos Alejandro of the Cab Calloway Foundation. Carlos identified fantastic images of Calloway, including new favorites by Arthur Singer, whose son Alan Singer shared generously about his father's extraordinary career. Finally, I have loved learning about Jazz Age fashion from catalogue author Victoria Pass, who makes girdles fascinating.

I sincerely appreciate the personal assistance with loans and images from Gordon Wilkins and James Sousa at Addison Gallery of American Art; Laura Fravel at the Biggs Museum of American Art; Aileen McNamara and Allison Freyermuth at the Free Library of Philadelphia; Sarah Tignor at the Johnson Collection; Hannah Osborne at the Library of Congress; Dan Chudzinski at University of Findlay's Mazza Museum; Constance McPhee at the Metropolitan Museum of Art; V. Andrew Talley at the National Museum of African American History and Culture; Robyn Asleson, Erin Beasley, Dominique Lopes DelGiudice, Marissa Olivas, and Kim Sajet at the National Portrait Gallery; Angelina Lippert at Poster House; Stephanie P. Wiener at Princeton University Library; Summer Orndorff at Savannah College of Art and Design Museum; Dalila Scruggs at the Schomburg Center for Research in Black Culture at the New York Public Library; and Rebecca Hatcher at the Yale University Library. I am thankful for the private collectors who generously shared their knowledge and collections, including Lura Dolas, Theodore Dolas, Walter O. Evans, David Pollack, Roger Reed, and Brock and Yvonne Vinton.

Heather Campbell Coyle

Curator of American Art
Delaware Art Museum

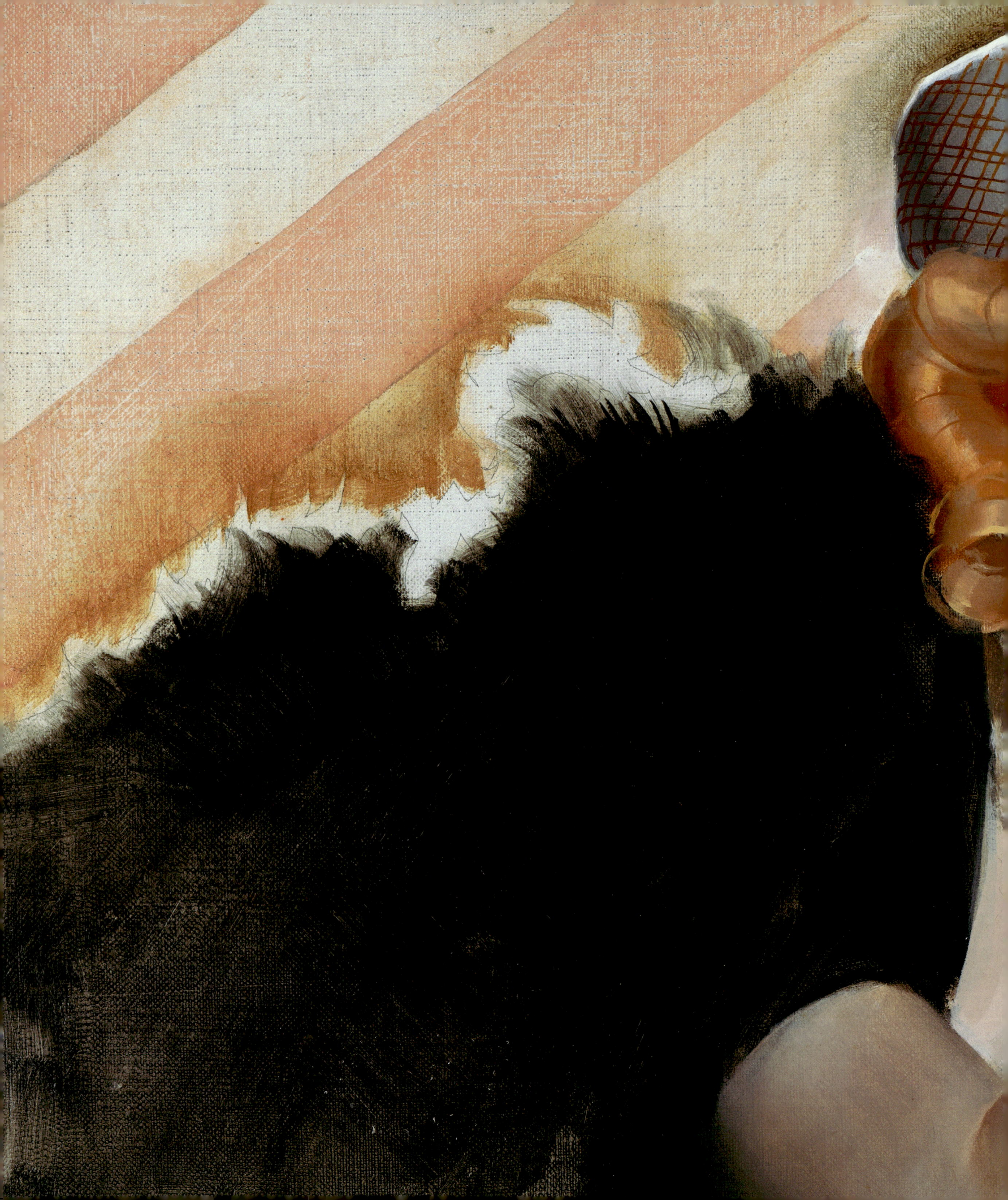

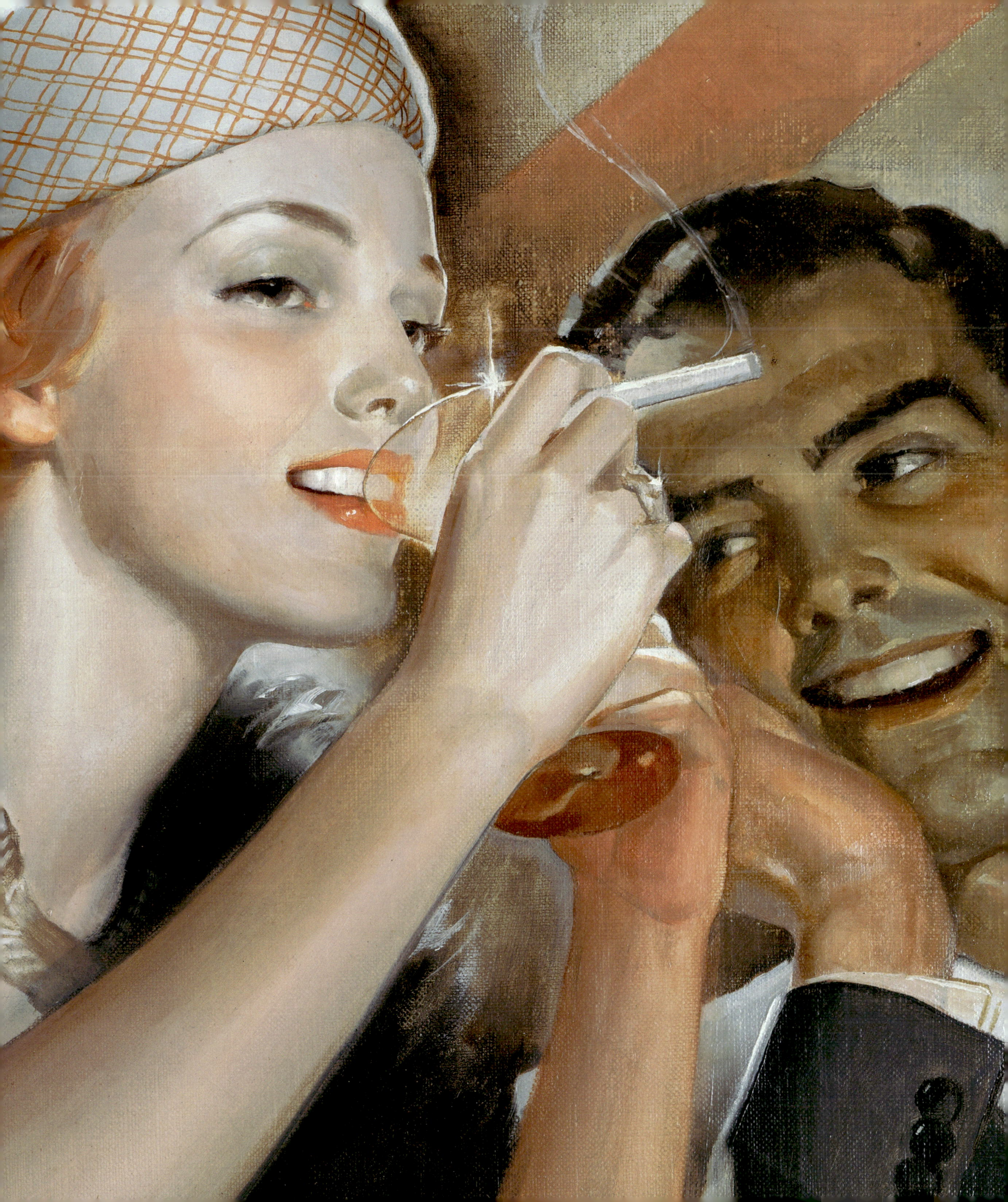

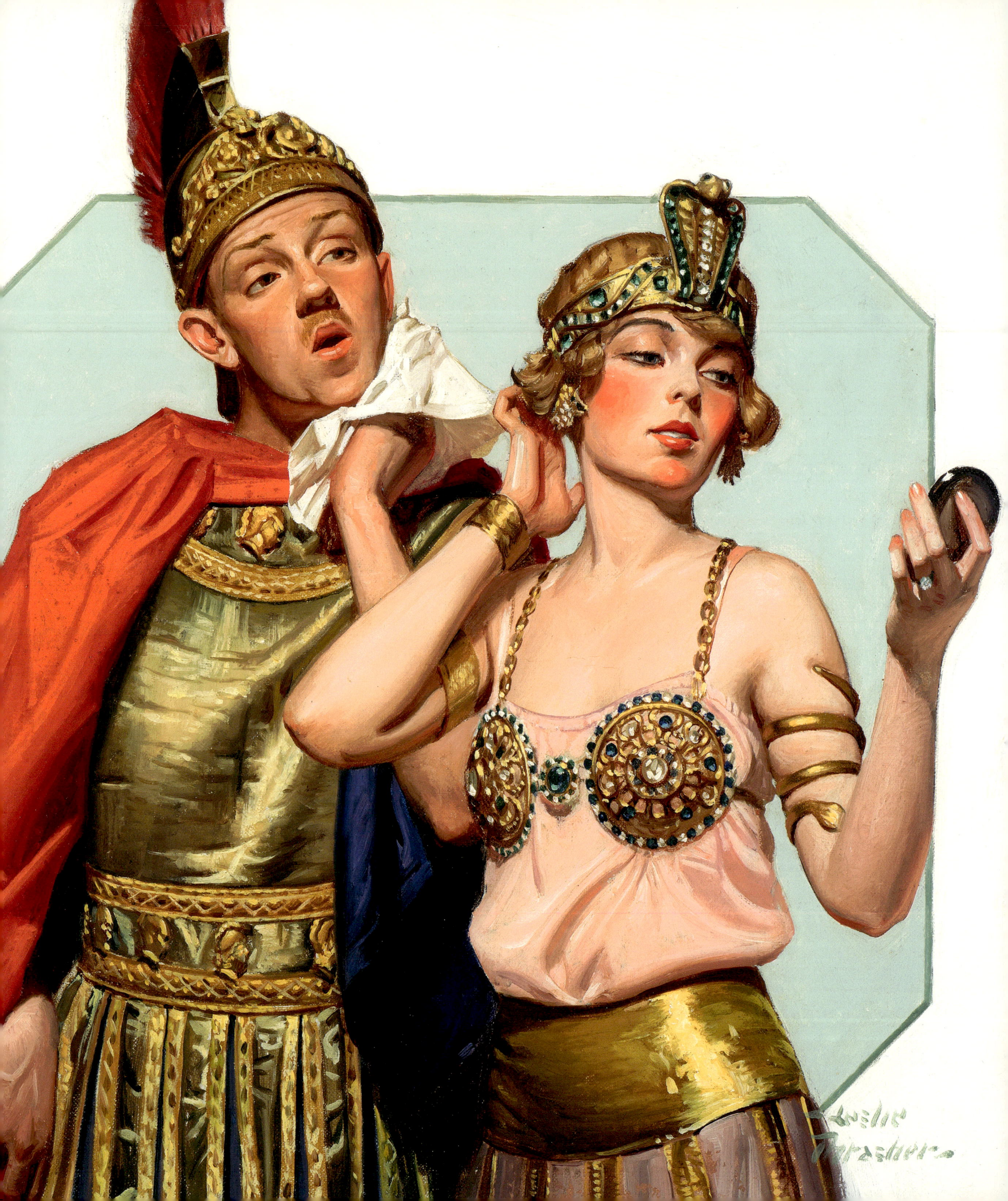
Leslie
Thrasher

Heather Campbell Coyle

High Notes of Jazz Age Illustration

Detail of pl. 1

A young man strains in his uncomfortable costume, mopping sweat with a handkerchief, while his companion consults her compact, checking her makeup and adjusting her bobbed hair (pl. 1). It's 1927 and Sandy Jenkins and Lil Morse are attending a costume party—a popular activity during the Jazz Age. They are dressed as Antony and Cleopatra, and he voices his exasperation with her primping by paraphrasing a line from Shakespeare's play: "I'm Dyin', Egypt, Dyin'." Lil's slinky costume, obvious makeup, and bobbed hair associate her with the flapper type, though she is not as wild as her style might imply. Lil works as a stenographer, and Sandy, an automobile salesman, is her high school sweetheart. They are recurring characters created by illustrator Leslie Thrasher for covers of *Liberty*, a general interest magazine that was one of many periodicals available on newsstands in the 1920s. Readers of this weekly followed the couple's courtship, marriage, and parenthood from 1926 through 1931.

Lil and Sandy's choice of costumes reflects the widespread fascination with ancient Egypt fostered by the discovery of King Tut's tomb in 1922, but her outfit, with its bejeweled brassiere over a modest chemise, was probably inspired by something closer to home—an advertisement for Palmolive soap illustrated by C. Coles Phillips (fig. 1). A middle-class woman like Lil (and an illustrator like Thrasher) would have encountered this advertisement in popular women's magazines like *The Ladies' Home Journal* and *Pictorial Review*.[1] Reflecting the target market of those magazines, the vision of Egypt promoted by Palmolive is remarkable for its whiteness. The woman's skin is as pale as her silk slip.

Laura Wheeler Waring presented a different perspective on Egyptian culture in her cover for the April 1923 issue of *The Crisis*, a magazine published by the National Association for the Advancement of Colored People (NAACP). Titled *Egypt—Spring*, the image features a black figure playing an ancient harp surrounded by stylized birds, vines, and flowers (fig. 2). A decorative border incorporates Egyptian motifs in an Art Deco manner. The harpist is rendered in solid black, indicating dark skin.

Alongside other African American writers and artists of the Harlem Renaissance, Wheeler Waring celebrated Egypt as an African culture.[2] Illustrators like Wheeler Waring and Aaron Douglas incorporated pyramids, sphynxes, papyrus flowers, and Egyptian-inspired attire into their work, and they activated the flattened forms and stylized anatomy of tomb paintings. Their efforts were encouraged by intellectuals like W. E. B. Du Bois, who was the cofounder of the NAACP and an editor of *The Crisis*. Celebrating ancient Egypt was part of a larger agenda that foregrounded Black

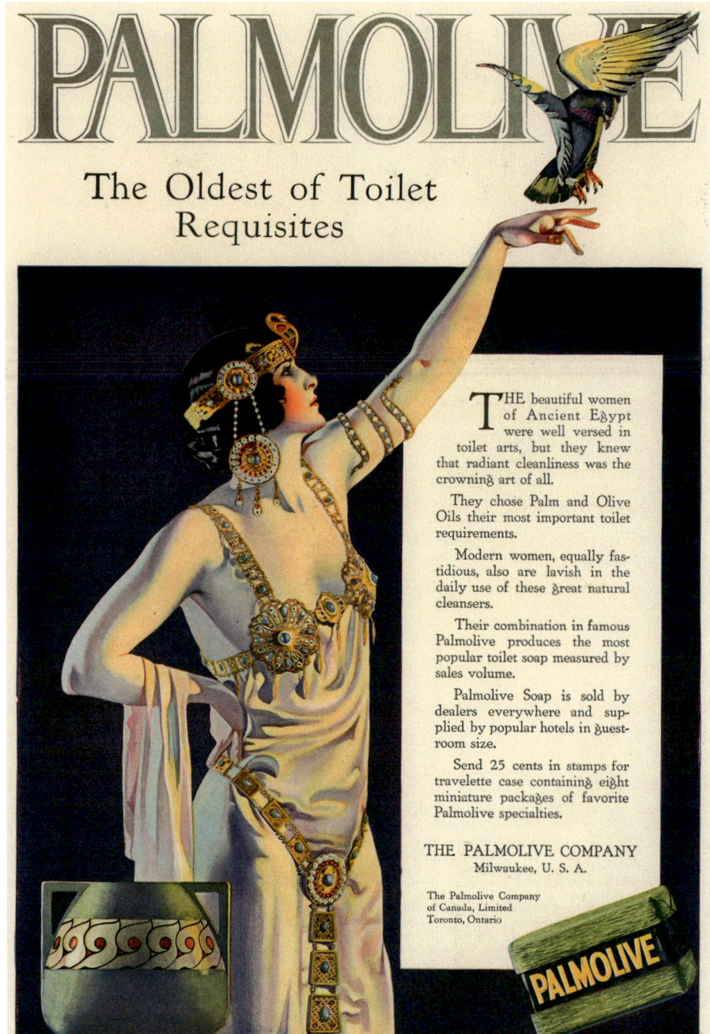

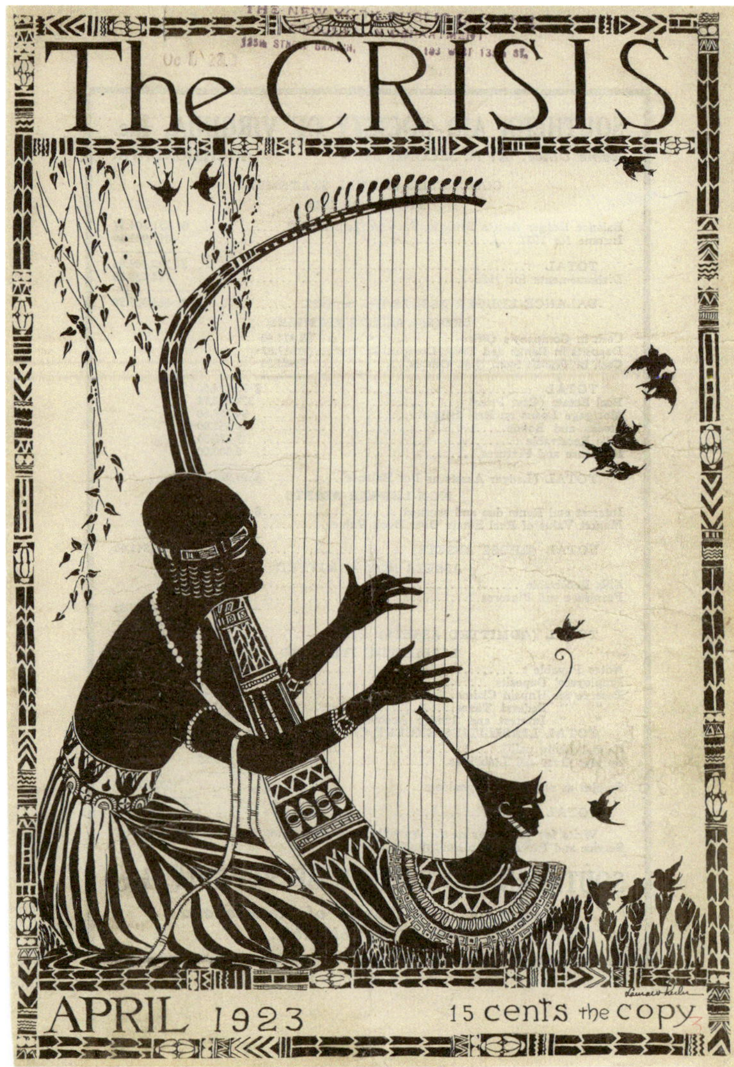

cultural contributions of the past and the present to inspire racial pride and counteract racism.[3]

The illustrations by Thrasher and Wheeler Waring differ in more than their approaches to Egypt. The artists made vastly different aesthetic choices. Thrasher rendered his characters with realist detail, while Wheeler Waring employed a modernist style, relying on silhouettes and stylized forms. During the Jazz Age, American illustration encompassed a wide range of artists, styles, and perspectives that reflected the nation's growing audiences for printed material. In this period before visual culture was dominated by photography, American illustrators contributed to popular weekly and monthly magazines, niche journals, daily newspapers, deluxe books, sheet music, calendars, and packaging for consumer products. More women and artists of color joined the ranks of illustrators, extending the range and reach of the illustrated press. It was a time of enormous expansion and influence for the illustrated press and significant social change in the United States.

Fig. 1 C. Coles Phillips (1880–1927), advertisement for Palmolive from *Pictorial Review*, May 1919. Printed matter. Delaware Art Museum, Helen Farr Sloan Library and Archives

Fig. 2 Laura Wheeler Waring (1887–1948), *Egypt—Spring*, cover from *The Crisis*, April 1923. Printed matter. New York Public Library, Manuscripts, Archives and Rare Books Division, Schomburg Center for Research in Black Culture

Arrival of the Jazz Age

The Jazz Age is defined here as encompassing the years from 1919 through 1942, bracketed by the involvement of the United States in the World Wars. The term "jazz" began to appear in newspapers in the early 1910s, referring to diverse activities from baseball to music and dance.[4] References to jazz music picked up steam in the middle of the decade, with advertisements and notices for jazz bands appearing in newspapers across the country.[5] When George Gould's Jazz Orchestra played in San Francisco in 1916, they were described as "San Francisco's newest and most sensational find, for the dance lovers. Mr. Gould renders a number of his own creations with that jazz syncopation rarely heard above the Mason and Dixon line."[6] In 1915 Gordon Seagrove published an article in the *Chicago Tribune* that introduced the new "craze."[7] Seeking to define jazz (but collapsing it with blues), he noted the African American origins of the music, and his article was illustrated with a racist caricature of a saxophonist.

As these early notices attest, jazz was rooted in Black cultural production. African American musicians in New Orleans developed a new sound, which spread throughout the nation. Jazz flourished in the urban communities created by the Great Migration of African Americans from the rural South to major cities. White critiques of jazz often reflected the relentless racism of the time: "The jazz is a relapse to the barbaric music of primitive peoples. . . . It is a jungle gift from the American negro," wrote a critic in 1919.[8] Jazz inspired expressive and athletic dances, like the Charleston, which violated traditional norms of social behavior, particularly for women, resulting in further censure from conservative cultural voices from both African American and white communities.[9] Nonetheless, jazz music spread rapidly through performances in urban nightclubs, musical theater, radio, sheet music, and records and was quickly appropriated by white musicians and composers.

By the end of the 1910s, the popular press trumpeted the start of "The Jazz Age," a moniker that flourished in newspapers aimed at white audiences.[10] In November 1919 a speech by Dr. John Allen Blair, a Presbyterian pastor in Philadelphia, was quoted in newspapers across the nation:

> Someone has said that Americans are worshipers of the great god Jazz. . . . It may be true that we are living in a jazz age. We are living in an age where everything goes. We are impatient under restraints. There is a moral looseness, a lack of steadiness. . . . Jazz epitomizes the spirit of the age. Jazz is the most popular dance and jazz is the most popular music.[11]

Many articles echoed the pastor's concerns about an era characterized by moral laxness and driven by youth. Some, like Blair, linked the new permissiveness to the experience of war, while others blamed the popularity of psychoanalysis and the frank conversations around sexuality that it encouraged. Enthusiasm for jazz and the nightlife surrounding it highlighted the generation gap. However, as Colette Gaiter suggests in her essay, this rejection by standard gatekeepers may have attracted younger consumers. In London, newspaper reporter Phillipa Martin lamented concisely, "Jazz and middle age do not mix well, and this is a Jazz age."[12]

Discussion of the Jazz Age was growing in 1922 when Charles Scribner's Sons compiled a collection of F. Scott Fitzgerald's short stories and titled it *Tales of the Jazz Age*, cementing the terminology. Designed by John Held Jr., the book's dust jacket depicts a white drummer and saxophonist entertaining young dancers while a couple—she smoking a cigarette and he holding a flask—toasts at the lower right (fig. 3). The women have all the hallmarks of flappers with their cropped hair, short dresses, and rolled stockings. Rendered in a cartoonish manner, images of couples spray across the cover in dynamic diagonals, and the lettering vibrates with energy. Jazz music had been incorporated into the lives of privileged white youth, and the Jazz Age was in full swing.

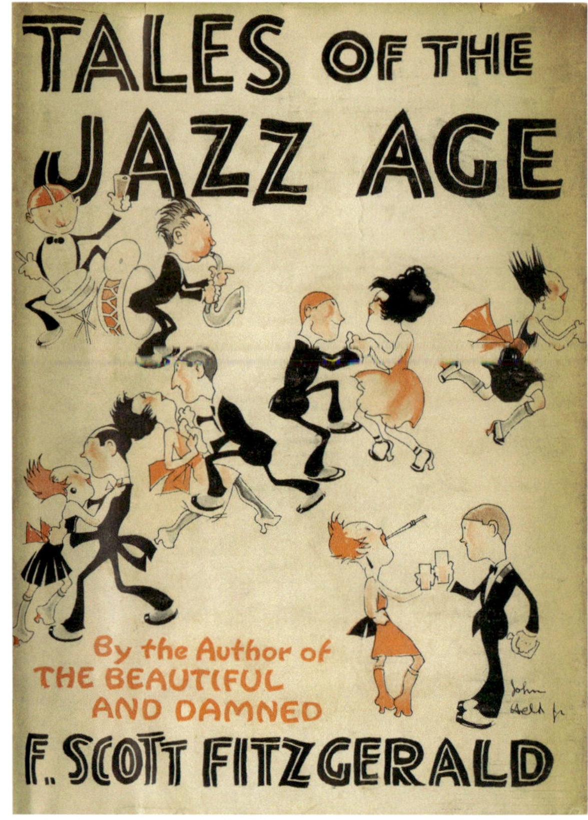

Fig. 3 John Held Jr. (1889–1958), cover from *Tales of the Jazz Age* by F. Scott Fitzgerald (New York: Charles Scribner's Sons, 1922). Printed matter. Cornell University Library, Rare Book and Manuscript Collections

A Changing Nation

The moralizing around jazz reflected discomfort with sweeping changes in American culture. For the first time, the 1920 census revealed that more Americans lived in cities than outside of them. In the following years, the American economy ballooned—the gross national product increased by 40 percent between 1922 and 1929—creating an affluent but unevenly distributed consumer culture. Economic growth benefited publishers and illustrators as national corporations turned to magazine advertising to reach audiences across the country. Advertising revenues allowed publishers to keep prices low and expand circulation, creating mass-market magazines with vast reach. Many new periodicals debuted in the decade surrounding World War I. These included general interest publications for middle-class readers, sophisticated "smart magazines" like *Vanity Fair*, humor and fashion magazines, specialty journals, and "little magazines" that presented avant-garde artistic and literary content. A growing African American middle class created an audience and advertisers for a dedicated Black press. In his study *Magazines in the Twentieth Century*, Theodore Peterson estimated that the circulation of periodicals nearly doubled between 1900 and 1923, and in the '20s, the most popular magazines, like *The Saturday Evening Post* and *The Ladies' Home Journal*, reached millions of Americans with each issue.[13]

Immigration and Labor

American cities had grown through the arrival of European immigrants and the relocation of Americans from rural areas seeking new opportunities and experiences. In the wake of the war, isolationism and nativism increased, and the nation was rocked by a Red Scare that targeted Catholics and Jews with accusations of being communists and anarchists. Italian immigrants Nicola Sacco and Bartolomeo Vanzetti went on trial in 1921 and were executed in 1927, an era when immigrants and African Americans were routinely blamed for urban violence, crime, and labor conflict. Impacted by the Red Scare, the Socialist Party of America and national labor unions (particularly the leftist Industrial Workers of the World) receded in power.[14]

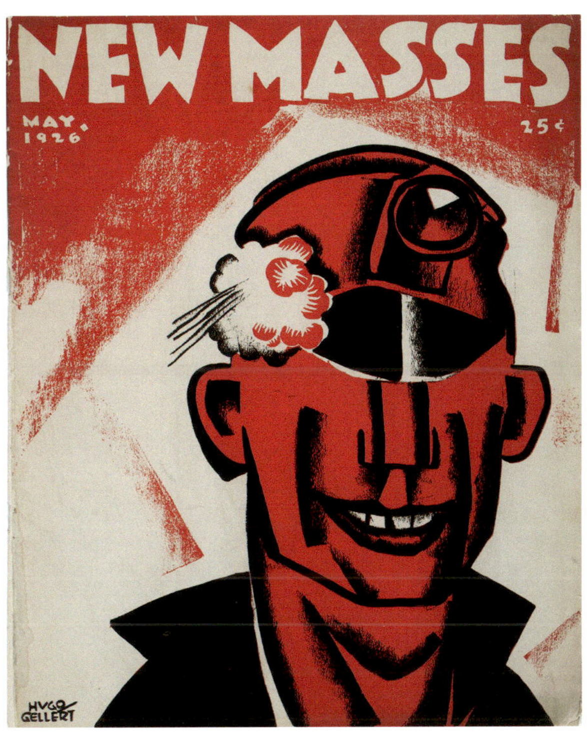

Fig. 4 Hugo Gellert (1892–1985), cover from *New Masses*, May 1926. Printed matter. Delaware Art Museum, John Sloan Manuscript Collection, Helen Farr Sloan Library and Archives

With the growth of massive corporations and changes in the federal tax structure, wealth became concentrated with the richest Americans as the 1920s wore on, encouraging new organizational efforts on the political left (pl. 2). The Workers Party of America was formed as the official Communist political party of the 1920s. They published the *Daily Worker* newspaper and, starting in 1926, the monthly periodical *New Masses,* which was notable for its support of modern art and design. Inspired by the example of *The Masses* in the 1910s, *New Masses* created space for Americans to publish radical writing and images.[15] Artists were not expected to toe a party line, and most of the magazine's contributors in the late 1920s were not members of the Communist Party. Regular artist-contributors included Hugo Gellert and Louis Lozowick, who provided sleek layouts and Machine Age decorations, as well as modernist cover designs (fig. 4). The *New Masses* published diverse writers and artists, including James Lesesne Wells, whose block print *African Family* appeared in August 1929 (pl. 3). The image was printed without relation to an article and depicted three African sculptures that Wells grouped to present a nuclear family. A printmaker and professor at Howard University, Wells found inspiration in the African art exhibited at the Brooklyn Museum.

The Great Migration and the Harlem Renaissance

Beginning in the late nineteenth century, many African Americans left the rural South and relocated to communities like Bronzeville in Chicago and Harlem in New York. In 1919 racial unrest broke out in American cities as Black soldiers returned from war to encounter racism and hostility in place of the appreciation for military service shown to white veterans. The years that followed saw the Harlem Renaissance, when African Americans crafted a vital literary and artistic culture in the 1920s and '30s. This efflorescence reached beyond the borders of New York, with vibrant Black communities developing in cities across the country. After World War I, the Black press expanded, providing venues for African American artists to share powerful imagery.

National publications, including *The Crisis*, *Opportunity*, *The Messenger,* and *Half-Century Magazine,* connected these communities intellectually and artistically and spread the New Negro movement, which encouraged racial pride, cultural achievement, and the refusal to submit to violence and Jim Crow segregation. *The Crisis,* the journal of the NAACP, had been founded in 1910 and reached a circulation of 100,000 by 1919. Each issue featured an illustrated or photographic cover and several interior images, primarily photographs, story illustrations, and editorial cartoons addressing major social concerns. In the early 1920s, cover artists included Wheeler Waring, John Henry Adams, Albert Alexander Smith, and Fred Waltz, though *The Crisis* regularly used photographs and reproductions of works of art on covers as well. Many, including photographic examples, presented attractive young women, and illustrated advertisements inside the periodicals targeted female consumers—the beauty industry was a key driver of Black prosperity.[16] Artists incorporated subjects and motifs from African art—from 1912 to 1914, the title block often featured a pharaoh's head and stylized wings—and cover images generally served the overall message of racial pride, demonstrating the accomplishments of Black artists and photographers.[17]

Three members of the editorial staff at *The Crisis*—Du Bois, Jessie Redmon Fauset, and Augustus Granville Dill—collaborated to produce *The Brownies' Book*, the first magazine aimed at African American children. The magazine was announced in the annual Children's Issue of *The Crisis* in 1919 and began publication the following January. Major publishers, including Harper's and Scribner's, had started children's periodicals in the late nineteenth century, but these rarely depicted children of color and occasionally reproduced racist caricatures. Aimed at middle-class families, *The Brownies' Book* was meant to educate African American children about their history and heritage. The editors promised more than uplift—"pictures, puzzles, stories, letters from little ones, clubs, games"—and provided fiction and fantasy featuring Black children.[18] Wheeler Waring's charming cover of the May 1920 issue captured this desire for middle-class children to see themselves reflected in stories and pictures (fig. 5).

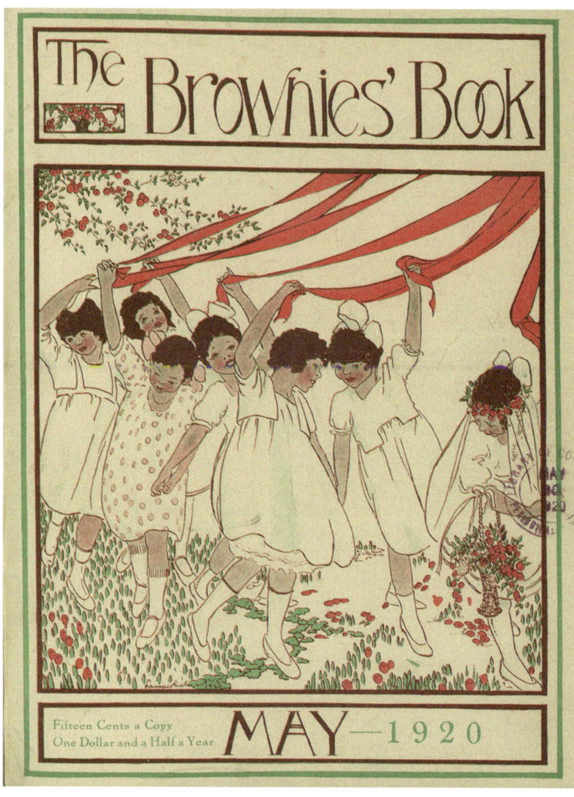

Fig. 5 Laura Wheeler Waring (1887–1948), cover from *The Brownies' Book*, May 1920. Library of Congress, Rare Book and Special Collections Division

Opportunity: A Journal of Negro Life began publication in 1923 as the organ of the National Urban League. As Caroline Goeser explained, *Opportunity*'s editor, sociologist Charles S. Johnson, sought a balance "between inquiry based on 'objective fact' and 'creative self-expression.'"[19] By the late 1920s, the journal featured dynamic illustrated covers, modern graphics, and interior illustrations and photographs alongside its articles, essays, and poems. Artistically adventurous, *Opportunity* was the first magazine to publish Aaron Douglas's work, and he produced striking covers (discussed below) for the periodical in his signature silhouette style.

While the magazine embraced modern imagery, *Opportunity* remained deeply political and published searing writing about contemporary issues. As racist violence and lynchings of African Americans continued, and the Ku Klux Klan revived in the 1920s, Black writers and artists composed texts and images to expose these horrors in national magazines. In 1934 James A. Porter illustrated a poem by Esther Popel for *Opportunity* (fig. 6), which memorialized a horrific murder: "A Kentucky mob, at a recent lynching, helped their victim say the 'Lord's Prayer' when he seemed to have forgotten the words, after which they hanged him and burned his body." In this illustration, which was not the version used in print, Porter juxtaposed the hanging, with its violent mob, at left, and the church steeple, at right. In the foreground, his expressive line pictured an agonized woman and children, presumably the family of the lynching victim. Poems, essays, illustrations, and political cartoons published in magazines added dimension to the NAACP's anti-lynching campaign in the 1920s and '30s.

These magazines joined the weekly newspaper *The Chicago Defender*, which was founded in 1905 and circulated nationally. The long-running comic strip *Bungleton Green* first appeared in *The Defender* in 1920, and in the late '20s, after cartoonist Jay Jackson joined the staff, the paper was filled with illustrated fiction, features, and comics.[20] In the spirit of the Harlem Renaissance, he created heroic characters, including the athlete-scholar-spy Speed Jaxon.

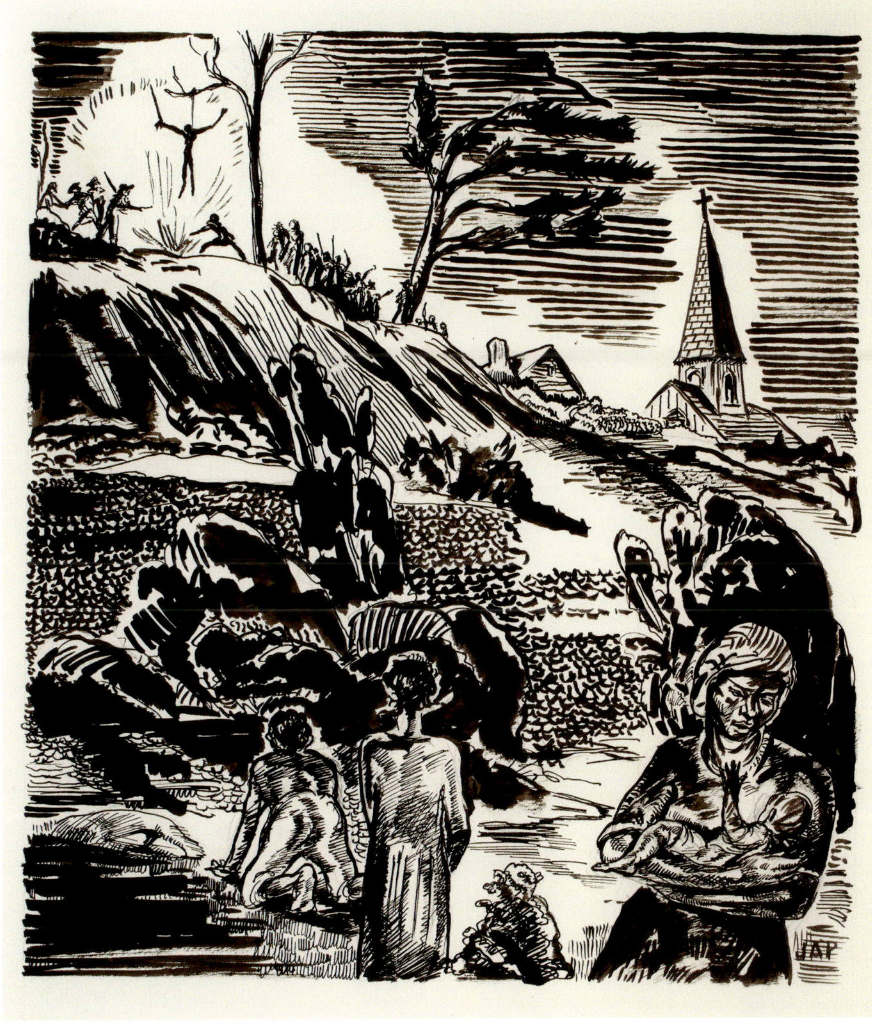

Fig. 6 James A. Porter (1905–1970), *Lynching in Kentucky*, alternate illustration for "Blasphemy—American Style" by Esther Popel, for *Opportunity*, December 1934. Brush, pen, and ink on cream wove paper, 11½ × 10¼ in. Delaware Art Museum, Acquisition Fund, 2021

In the Jazz Age, Black artists found steady work at African American newspapers. In 1929 Frederick C. Alston became the art director and cartoonist for the African American newspaper, the *St. Louis American*. He also exhibited the radiant Art Deco composition *Light of the World* in his hometown and sent drawings and paintings to the prestigious annual exhibition of African American art organized by the Harmon Foundation (pl. 4). In 1937 Jackie Ormes introduced *Torchy Brown in Dixie to Harlem* in the *Pittsburgh Courier*. The strip followed the adventures of a Mississippi teen who found fame performing at the Cotton Club in New York.[21] One of the first African American women to build a career as a cartoonist, Ormes was read nationally in the *Courier*'s fourteen city editions.

Women's Roles

The social revolution most notable in the illustrated press was the shift in the behaviors and attitudes of young women, marked by the emergence of the flapper. In 1920, with the ratification of the Nineteenth Amendment, women achieved the right to vote. This accomplishment symbolized broad social changes: more women were moving away from their family homes, taking jobs, playing sports, driving automobiles, and going out at night. They were wearing makeup and smoking cigarettes, and a sexual revolution was underway as some (mostly privileged) younger Americans reconsidered strictures around premarital sex. As Victoria Pass explores in her essay in this volume, popular publications enthusiastically recorded the fashions and frivolities that marked the flapper.

Lucile Murphy captured the era's concerns in *The Flapper—When She Is Good She Is Very Good—but—When She Is Bad She Is Horrid* (pl. 5). In the first panel of Murphy's cartoon, a pious young woman kneels in a pose that echoes the Virgin Mary in the window above her. In the second, she has transformed into a party girl in a revealing dress who antagonizes her worried parents by coming home at two in the morning. Similarly, in her *Flapper Filosofy* comics, Faith Burrows found humor in the moral failings of her subjects (fig. 7). In 1929 the captions to her drawings included: "Nowadays about all they can say is 'Sweet sixteen and never fell out of an aeroplane'" and "While her old grandmother is becoming spiritually prepared the modern daughter is becoming spiritually preserved." And Nell Brinkley's *Prudence Prim* showed its protagonist sneaking out, flirting with men, and driving fast cars (see fig. 53). As working newspaper artists, Burrows and Brinkley represented modern women through their bylines as well as their subject matter.

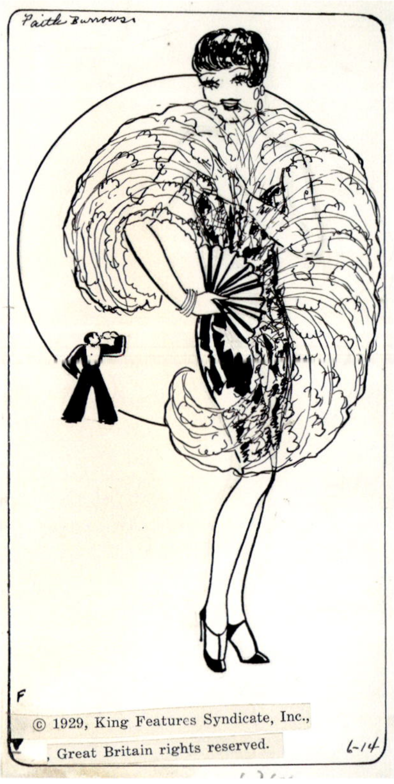

Fig. 7 Faith Burrows (1904–1977), *Nowadays about all they can say is "Sweet sixteen and never fell out of an aeroplane,"* for *Flapper Filosofy*, King Features Syndicate, *Cincinnati Enquirer*, June 14, 1929. Pen, ink, graphite, and wash on stiff paper, 6 7⁄16 × 3 1⁄4 in. Delaware Art Museum, Acquisition Fund, 2019

Even after the flapper's heyday, in 1938, a cigarette and a cocktail glass in a woman's hands spoke to her virtue (pl. 6). The caption for Michael Dolas's picture in *Cosmopolitan* reported: "Edie's love life was a revolving door."[22] In the mainstream press, most discussions of modern women were steeped in this kind of traditional morality: generally, the flappers, floozies, and femmes fatales who captivated readers were redeemed by marriage, punished for their moral failures, or exposed as nice girls who merely dressed in modern styles.

Entertainment

Even as radio and film threatened to divert attention and money away from books and magazines, new technologies worked their way into illustration.[23] In popular magazines, families gathered around radios, and romance stories unfolded on stage sets. Cartoonist Anne Fish illustrated *The Film Star* for her 1928 series "Careers for Our Girls" in *Cosmopolitan* (pl. 7). Dedicated to the motion picture industry, *Photoplay* magazine brought stories about film stars and movies to hundreds of thousands of Americans in the 1920s and '30s. The business of filmmaking had become familiar enough for readers to appreciate Jack Farr's cartoon, captioned "Keep shooting hell. . . . Heaven won't be ready till 10:30," when it appeared there in 1932 (fig. 8).

The Jazz Age also saw the growth of Broadway theater. Artists produced theater programs and posters, and Oscar Cesare illustrated reviews for the *New York Times*. Broadway musicals popularized songs that were published as sheet music with illustrated covers. In 1932 illustrator Russell

Fig. 8 Jack Farr (1889–1948), *Keep shooting hell. . . . Heaven won't be ready till 10:30*, for *Photoplay*, February 1932. Ink and brown wash on illustration board, $15\frac{1}{4} \times 20\frac{11}{16}$ in. Delaware Art Museum, F. V. du Pont Acquisition Fund, 1986

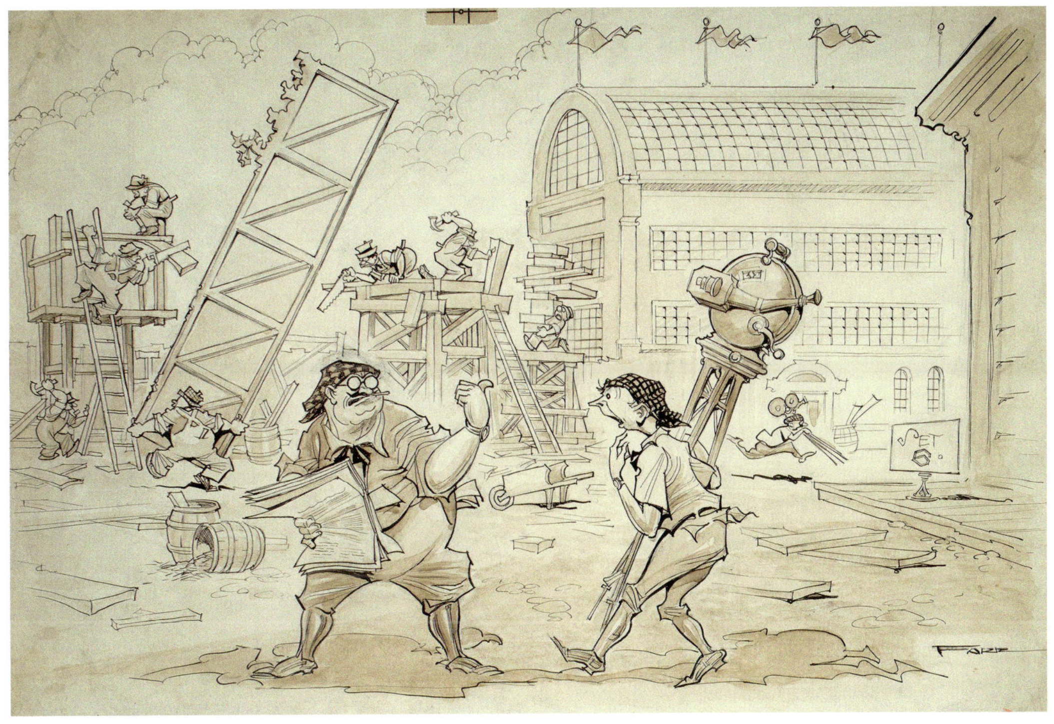

Fig. 9 Russell Patterson (1893–1977), *Man About Yonkers*, set design for *Ballyhoo of '32*, 44th Street Theatre, New York, September 6–November 26, 1932. Graphite, watercolor, and gouache on illustration board, $9 \times 20\frac{1}{8}$ in. Delaware Art Museum, Acquisition Fund, 2023

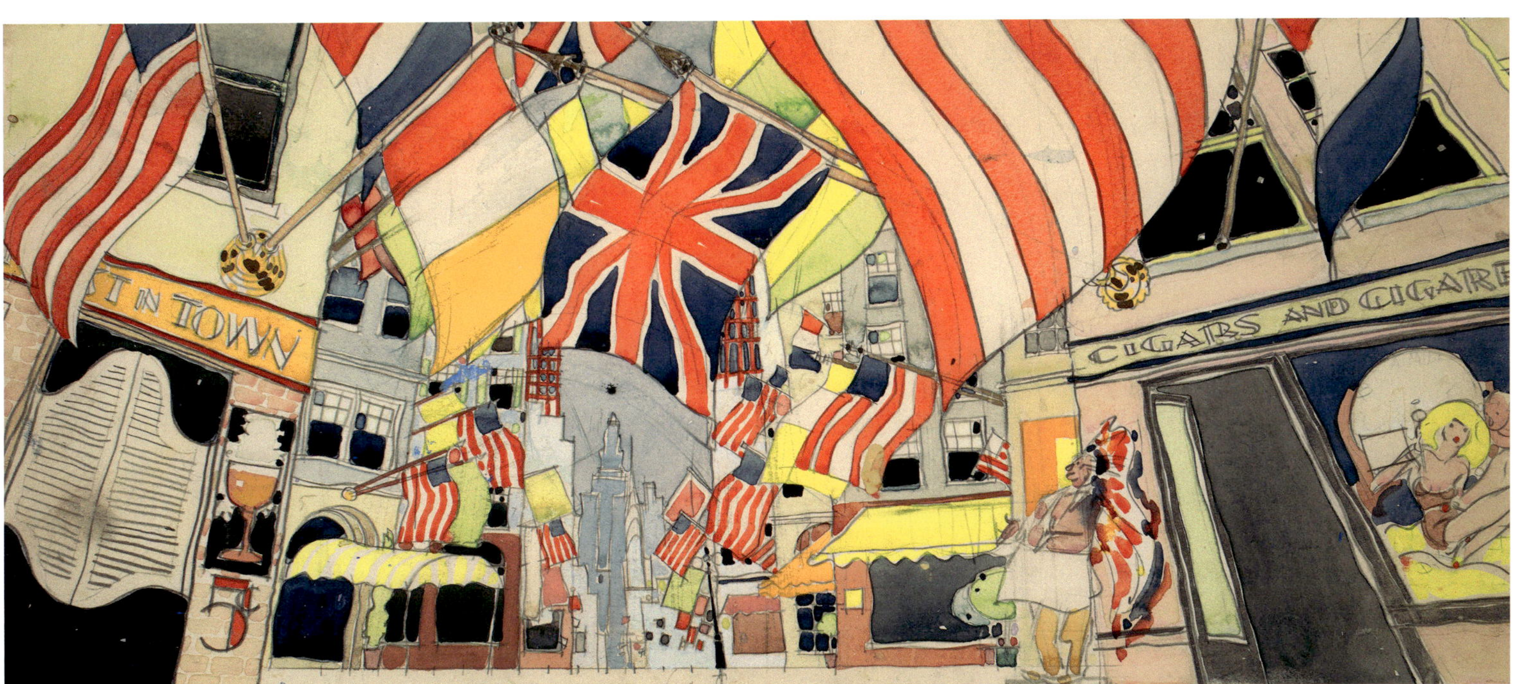

Patterson designed sets and costumes, as well as sheet music, for *Ballyhoo of '32*, a musical revue (fig. 9). His experience on Broadway in the early 1930s inspired his cover illustration of a sassy, striking showgirl for the magazine *Ballyhoo* (pl. 8).

Glamorous celebrities made great subjects for illustrators. As discussed by Chris Dingwall, Jay Jackson produced a stellar group of drawings of actor and singer Etta Moten that show her performing in front of a live audience, filming a movie, and singing for the radio (see pls. 45–47). Miguel Covarrubias, Al Frueh, and Al Hirschfeld produced celebrity caricatures for the popular press, and Hirschfeld was one of many artists to design movie posters.[24] Combining strong characterization and minimal line, Frueh's delineation of George M. Cohan embodied modern caricature (fig. 10). Carlo de Fornaro aptly described its operation: "Nothing remains but the angle of the hat, the swing of the cane, the hand in the pocket and the Cohan walk. But the portrait is unmistakable!"[25] As Wendy Wick Reaves described, celebrity caricature reached its apex in the 1920s and '30s.

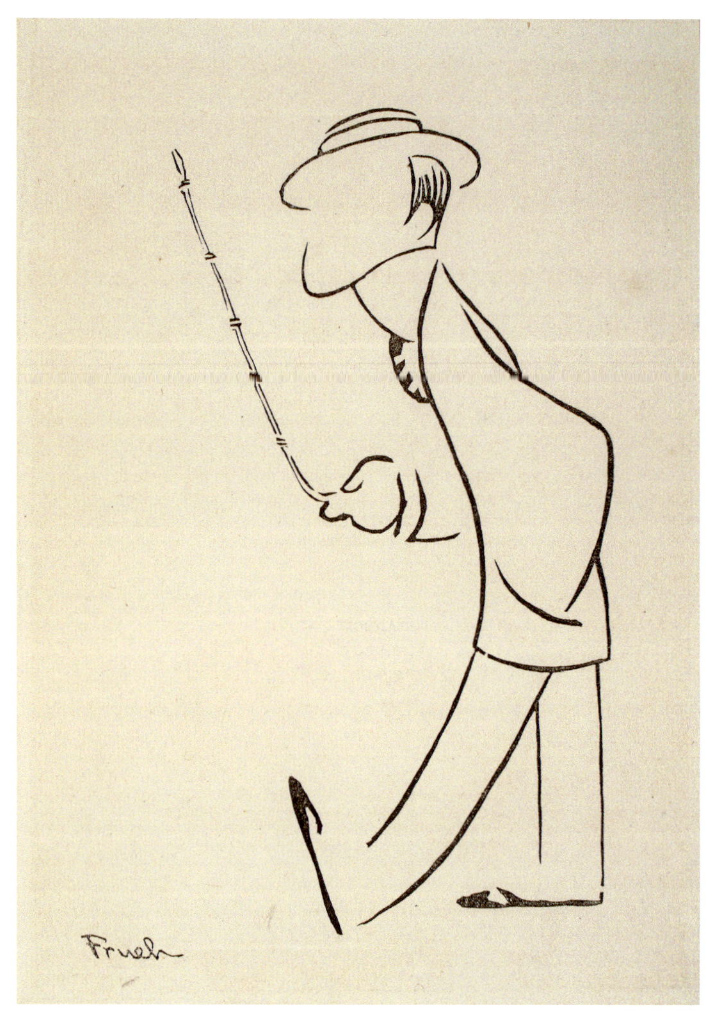

Fig. 10 Al Frueh (1880–1968), *George M. Cohan*, for *Stage Folk: A Book of Caricatures* by Alfred J. Frueh (New York: Lieber & Lewis, 1922). Linoleum cut, 12½ × 8¾ in. Delaware Art Museum, F. V. du Pont Acquisition Fund, 1986

Prohibition and Nightlife

Spurred in large part by anti-immigrant sentiment, the Eighteenth Amendment was ratified in 1919, and Prohibition started in 1920, making the sale of alcohol illegal in the United States. However, liquor was everywhere—in Greenwich Village tea rooms, Harlem nightclubs, and illustrated fiction and comics for the popular press. As Fitzgerald declared in a newspaper interview in 1922, "New York is going crazy! When I was here a year ago I thought we'd seen the end of night life. But now it's going on as it never was before prohibition. . . . Everybody is drinking harder—that's sure."[26] In 1926 illustrator N. C. Wyeth described a boozy ramble through Greenwich Village with restaurateur Don Dickerman. They downed Scotch highballs and "Silver Fiz" before heading to The Pirates' Den, Dickerman's themed nightclub outfitted with captains' walks, ropes, pistols, cutlasses, cages of parrots and monkeys, and servers dressed as buccaneers.[27]

In January 1933, almost a year before Prohibition's repeal, E. Simms Campbell, who was African American, captured the scene around Jazz Age Harlem in a centerfold map for the literary magazine *Manhattan* (fig. 11). Campbell's map shows the Cotton Club and Connie's Inn, which featured Black performers and catered to white audiences, and the Savoy Ballroom, which welcomed Black and white customers as long as they were great dancers. These Harlem hotspots hosted musicians including Louis Armstrong, Cab Calloway (pictured in the Cotton Club at lower left), Duke Ellington, Ella Fitzgerald, and Bessie Smith, who became celebrities in the Jazz Age. Campbell did not place the speakeasies but assured readers, "Since there are about 500 of them you won't have much trouble." His map reflected a widespread experience of the neighborhood, "a Harlem of racy music and racier dancing, of cabarets famous or notorious according to their kind, of amusement in which abandon and sophistication are cheek

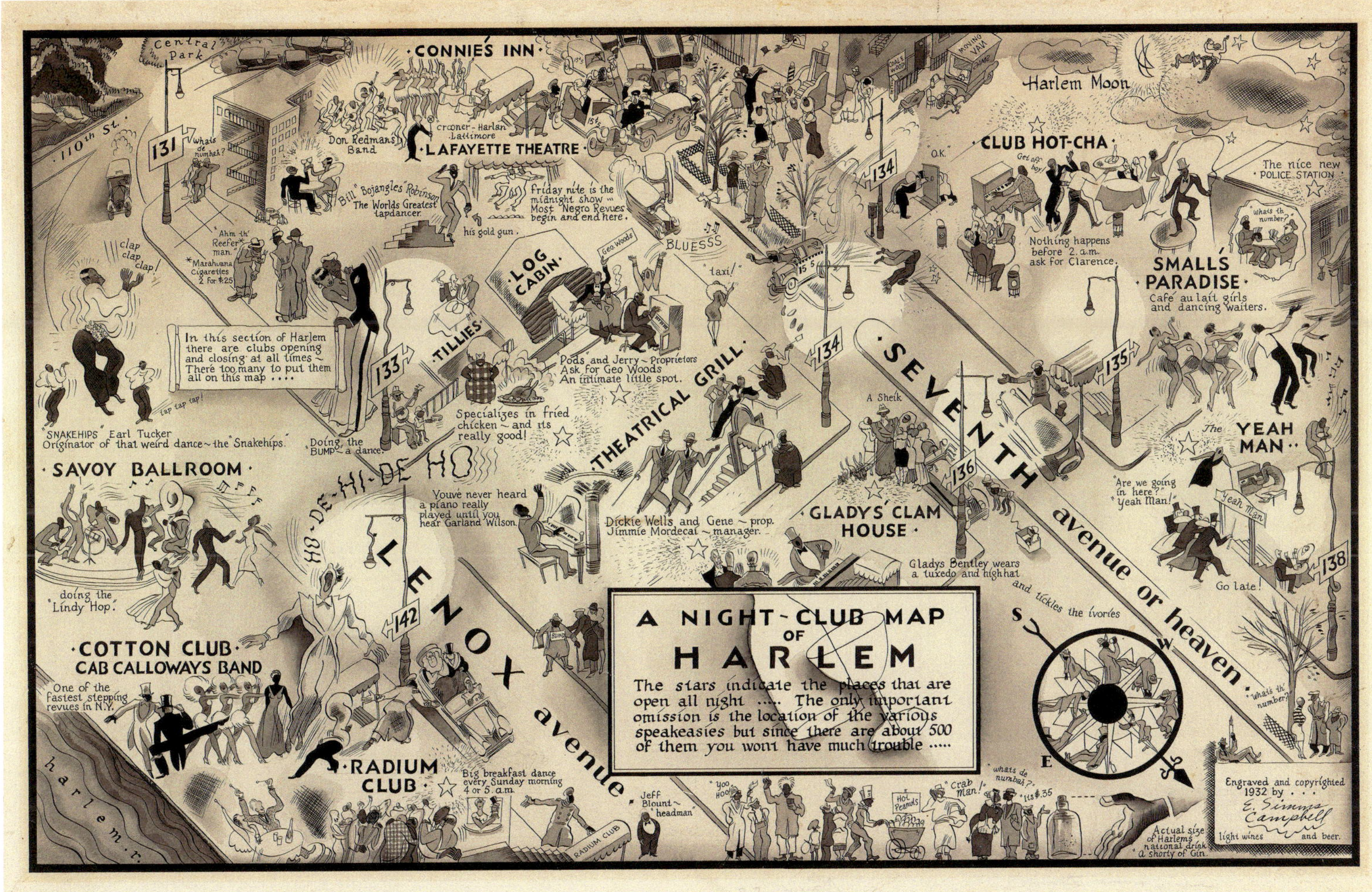

Fig. 11 E. Simms Campbell (1906–1971), *A Night-Club Map of Harlem*, 1932, for *Manhattan: A Weekly for Wakeful New Yorkers*, 1933. Pen and brush on board, 19¼ × 30 in. Yale University, Beinecke Rare Book and Manuscript Library

by jowl"—a Harlem that the writer Alain Locke designated "the exotic fringe of the metropolis."[28]

Nightclub performers like Calloway and Josephine Baker became international celebrities, touring internationally and headlining motion pictures. Their likenesses appeared in illustrations for programs, posters, advertisements, and features in the popular press. These promotional images ranged from minimalist caricatures to precise portraits, and some incorporated photographic and drawn elements. A vibrant tour poster from 1933 captured Calloway's energy and may have been based on a photograph by Carl Van Vechten taken earlier that year (fig. 12).[29] The photographer and the poster designer depicted Calloway when he was among the nation's most successful performers. In 1931, the year the bandleader turned twenty-four, his song "Minnie the Moocher" was the first single by an African American to sell a million copies. In the early '30s, Calloway and his orchestra performed twice weekly on NBC radio and regularly for the mostly white audiences welcomed at the Cotton Club.

As a teenager, Arthur Singer, who would later gain fame as a wildlife illustrator, snuck into the Cotton Club to see Calloway and Ellington

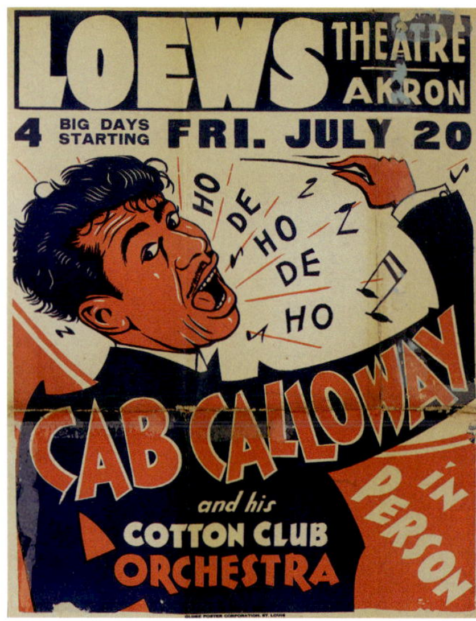

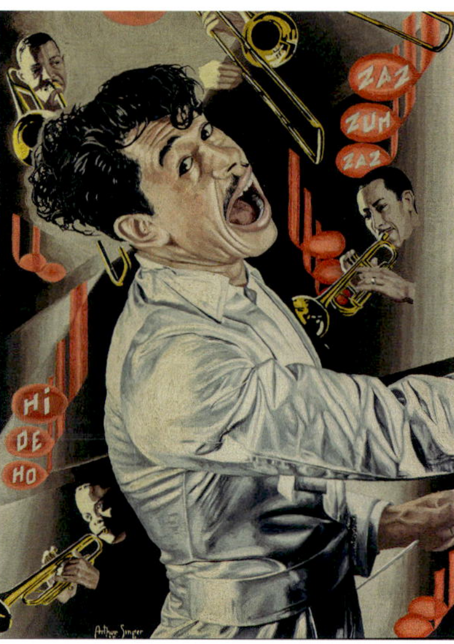

Fig. 12 *Cab Calloway at Loews Theatre, Akron, Ohio, July 20, 1933*. Lithograph, 28 × 22 in. Collection of the Smithsonian National Museum of African American History and Culture, Gift of Cabella Calloway Langsam

Fig. 13 Arthur Singer (1917–1990), *Zazzuhzaz*, 1935. Oil on canvas, 15¾ × 11¾ in. Collection of the Smithsonian National Museum of African American History and Culture, Gift of Cabella Calloway Langsam

perform, sketching and befriending the musicians. In a painting dated 1935, Singer, who commenced his studies at Cooper Union that year, riffed on the same photograph by Van Vechten (fig. 13). The young artist conveyed Calloway's presence in full color and surrounded him with thumbnail portraits of musicians playing trumpets and trombones, emphasizing his role as a bandleader.[30] Stylized musical notes read "hi de ho" and "zaz zuh zaz," referencing Calloway's famous scat singing. Photorealist in rendering, this was one of several modern, experimental portraits of the musician produced by the young illustrator.[31]

The Great Depression

Campbell's cartoon map of Jazz Age Harlem was published about a year before the end of Prohibition and well into the Great Depression. The stock market crashed in the autumn of 1929, sending the American economy into a tailspin. The stock sell-off signaled the start of the Depression, and soon millions of Americans were out of work. It's tempting to use that date to mark the end of the Jazz Age, and no less an authority than Fitzgerald did in his 1931 essay "Echoes of the Jazz Age."[32] Yet, in the '30s, jazz musicians thrived, women took on new roles, the New Negro movement continued, and Americans engaged with similar narratives in the popular press.

As markets and hemlines dropped, publishers and illustrators were deeply impacted by the loss of advertising revenue when corporations tightened their budgets. Some magazines closed or combined: Condé Nast folded *Vanity Fair* into *Vogue* in 1936. And a few periodicals, like the comic monthly *Ballyhoo*, launched to great (if brief) success. Pulp and confessional magazines flourished because their low prices depended on cheap materials and labor rather than advertising revenues.[33] Some illustrators designed covers for the pulps, while others turned to new outlets, working in the theater, painting murals, and creating products, packaging, pin-ups, and postcards.

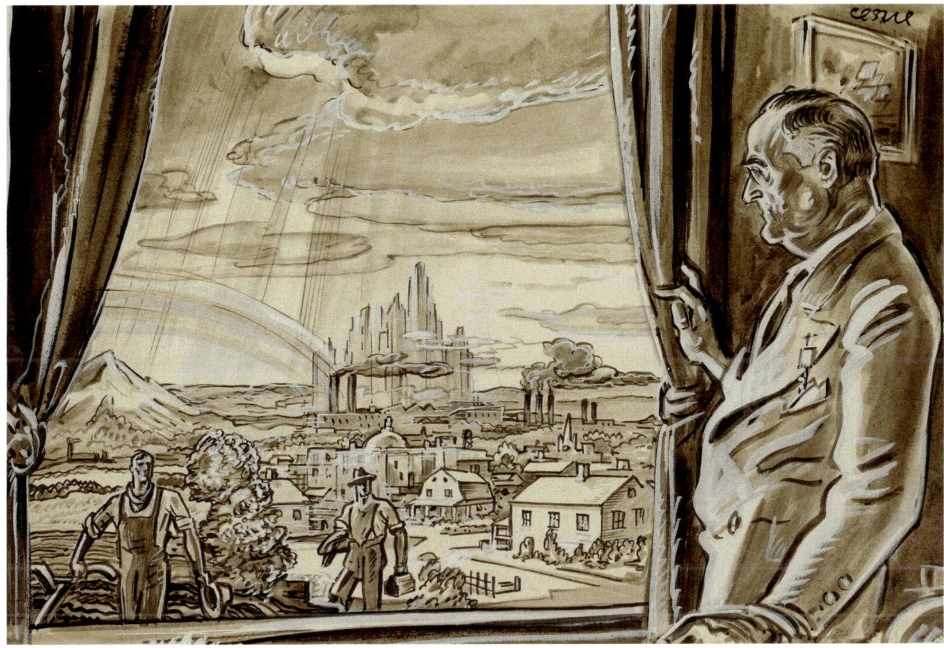

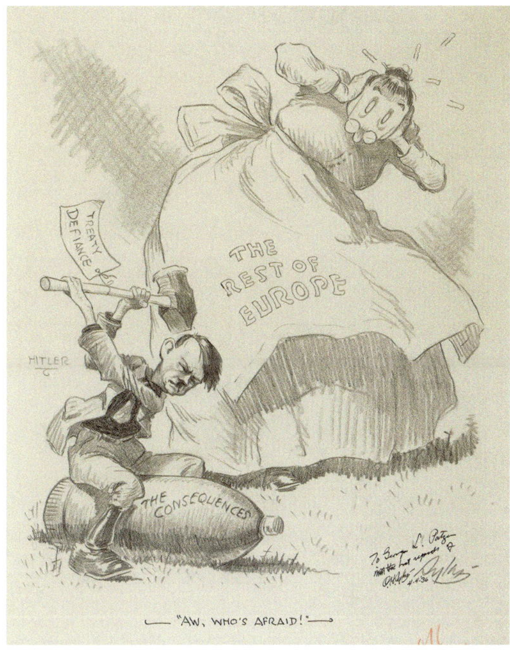

Fig. 14 Oscar Howard Cesare (1885–1948), *Is this Socialistic?*, for "Roosevelt Surveys His Course" by Anne O'Hare McCormick, *New York Times Magazine*, July 8, 1934. Ink and gouache on Bristol board, $12\frac{15}{16} \times 18\frac{3}{4}$ in. Delaware Art Museum, Gift of Valentine Cesare, 1992

Fig. 15 Charles Henry Sykes (1882–1942), *Aw, Who's Afraid?*, for *Rochester Democrat and Chronicle*, March 15, 1936. Crayon on paper, $20\frac{1}{16} \times 15$ in. Delaware Art Museum, Gift of Helen Farr Sloan, 1987

In all, however, there were fewer changes than might be expected in the subject matter and style of American illustration: pretty girls still graced the covers of most magazines, and contemporary romance remained an important subject in fiction. Plot devices shifted to mirror the new economic reality, and editorial cartoons chronicled the support for and challenges to President Roosevelt's New Deal programs, as well as the tensions building in Europe (figs. 14 and 15). Publishers called on illustrators throughout the 1930s to record the times, even as photography, movies, and television gradually changed the nation's visual culture. In the late '30s, photographs began to outperform illustrations on magazine covers—most famously with the tenure of Edward Steichen at *Vogue*.[34] This trend toward photography had been accelerating since the 1890s, and it would spell the end of what is often called the "golden age of illustration."

Jazz Age Aesthetics

Artists captured the energy of the Jazz Age with a variety of styles, from realist portraits to modern graphics. Each magazine issue featured illustrations by multiple artists, often working in different techniques, and newspapers presented a dizzying array of competing images from editorial cartoons to comics, fashion illustrations, and news photographs. Books, posters, and sheet music often allowed artists to communicate a more unified expression.

In keeping with the style of the previous two decades, American readers encountered a range of realist modes throughout the Jazz Age where the artist's mark-making was clearly present. J. C. Leyendecker, Frank E. Schoonover, and N. C. Wyeth worked in a painterly manner (see pls. 2, 19, 20, 48, and 49). Their major illustrations were produced in oil on canvas and evoked associations with fine art and the legacy of turn-of-the-century illustrators like Howard Pyle. For *The Crisis*, John Henry Adams made cover drawings of beautiful women with dense draftsmanship, and Laura Wheeler Waring sketched delicate vignettes for Jessie Fauset's prose.[35] The lively, expressive lines employed by May Wilson Watkins Preston, Arthur Davenport Fuller, Henrietta McCaig Starrett, and Kemp Starrett suited the breezy fiction they illustrated (see pls. 25, 38, 39, and fig. 16).

In the 1920s, a smoother aesthetic developed alongside these overtly artistic approaches. Popular younger artists like Norman Rockwell and Leslie Thrasher painted with nearly invisible brush strokes.[36] In reproduction, the watercolors of modern women by Coles Phillips appeared almost photographic, making them ideal for showcasing the details of contemporary fashions and consumer products. This stylistic shift paralleled technical changes. Artists increasingly drew their illustrations on smooth paper or illustration board, and ink, watercolor, and gouache became the most popular media for illustrators. Inexpensive and convenient, these materials suited the demands of the expanding publishing industry.[37] Precise styles reproduced best on the smooth paper used by leading publishers. These glossy pages earned the magazines the nickname "slicks" in the 1930s.[38]

Illustration board and ink were also ideal for cartoons and linear, stylized images. Smooth surfaces revealed the intricate curls of Lucile Murphy and Nell Brinkley and the minimalist comic stylings of John Held Jr. (pl. 9). With a precise, even-weighted line and spare composition, Held's technique is known as clear-line, an approach that was derived from Japanese woodblock prints and influenced poster design in the late nineteenth century. Clear-line had a resurgence among American illustrators like Held, Helen Dryden, and Russell Patterson in the 1920s.[39] The fashion was part of a larger revival of line drawing, described in 1922 by a critic in *Scribner's* as "an encouraging sign . . . which will emphasize the quality of good drawing and make very obvious the bad."[40]

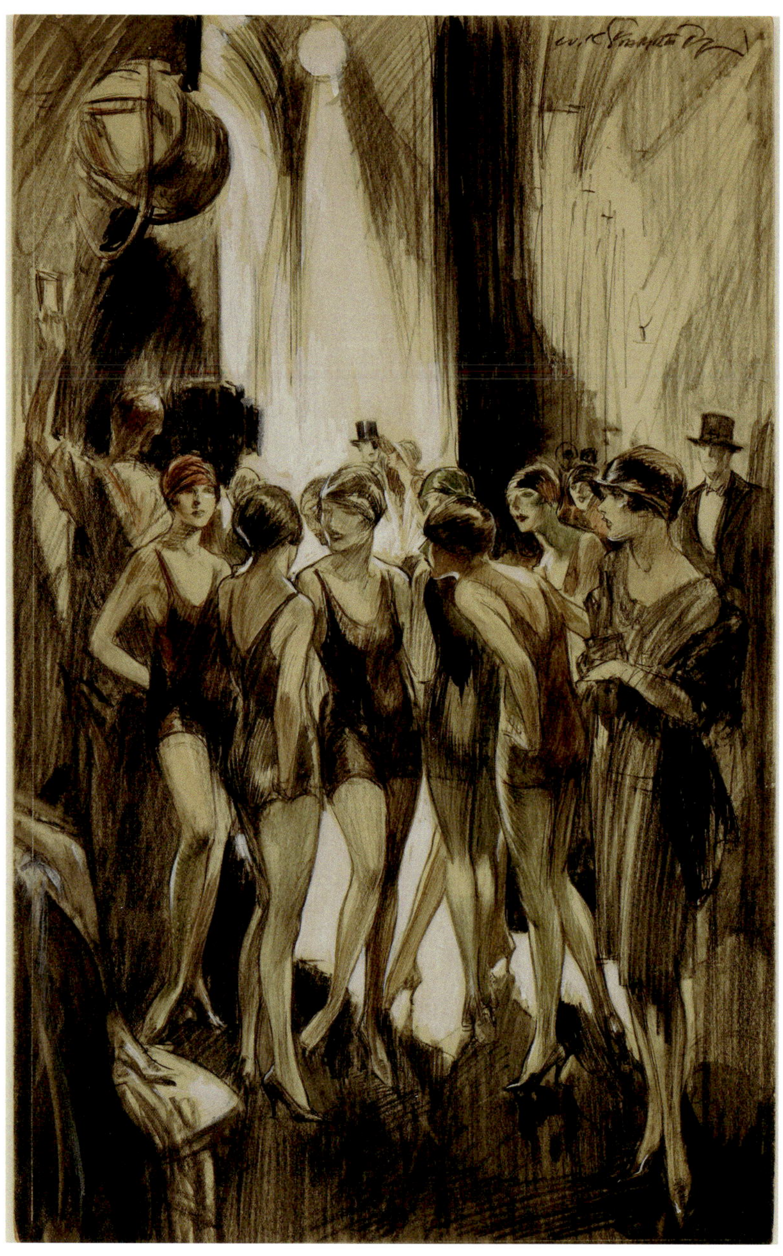

Fig. 16 William Kemp Starrett (1889–1952), *Backstage Scene*, n.d. Graphite, watercolor, and gouache on illustration board, sheet: 17¼ × 10⁹⁄₁₆ in. Delaware Art Museum, Gift of Helen Farr Sloan, 1987

Art Deco

Art Deco design became popular in the United States in the 1920s. Emerging in Paris in the previous decade, what we now call Art Deco incorporated the period's avid appropriation of non-Western art and the modernist tendency to simplify natural forms into geometric ones, creating designs with strong linear elements.[41] Like Cubism, which influenced it, Art Deco was developed in part through the study of African art brought to European museums through colonization. Art Deco designers were particularly enamored with Egyptian motifs. Art Deco aesthetics impacted the design of clothing, furniture, buildings, and consumer goods, as well as printed matter in the Jazz Age.

Helping to popularize Art Deco style in the 1910s and '20s, the Russian-born Romain de Tirtoff, called Erté, designed clothing for Parisian designer Paul Poiret, as well as opulent theater costumes and decorative magazine covers for *Harper's Bazaar*, attracting international attention (pl. 10). Cosmopolitan magazines like *Vogue* and *Vanity Fair* soon adopted the aesthetic for their own covers. Many of the artists most closely associated with Art Deco in the United States were European immigrants. Born in Warsaw, Poland, and educated in Paris, Witold Gordon settled in New York, where he produced murals for Radio City Music Hall in the early 1930s. During this time, he also made gorgeous monochrome illustrations for a deluxe volume on the travels of the fictional character Sindbad the Sailor (pl. 11). Around 1925 Beatrice Anderson, a young illustrator in Seattle, demonstrated the reach of Art Deco when she assembled a portfolio of work for magazine covers and advertisements. She executed her designs with bright colors and geometric volumes, creating elegant and highly stylized images that would have looked at home in *Bazaar* or *Vogue* (pl. 12).

Art Deco was also seen clearly in dynamic posters and sheet music covers. The 1933 poster for the Chicago World's Fair is dominated by the soaring central forms of the fair's Federal Building, reflecting the influence of Art Deco on architecture (pl. 13).[42] Sophisticated sans serif text and stylized clouds add to the elegant composition. Similarly, graphics for the 1939 World's Fair in New York celebrate the fair's modern aesthetics. In Nembhard Culin's poster, printed in 1937 to encourage investment in the fair, the park's central structures—the Trylon and the Perisphere—provide a geometric focus for the artist's innovative bird's-eye view and attenuated lettering (fig. 17).

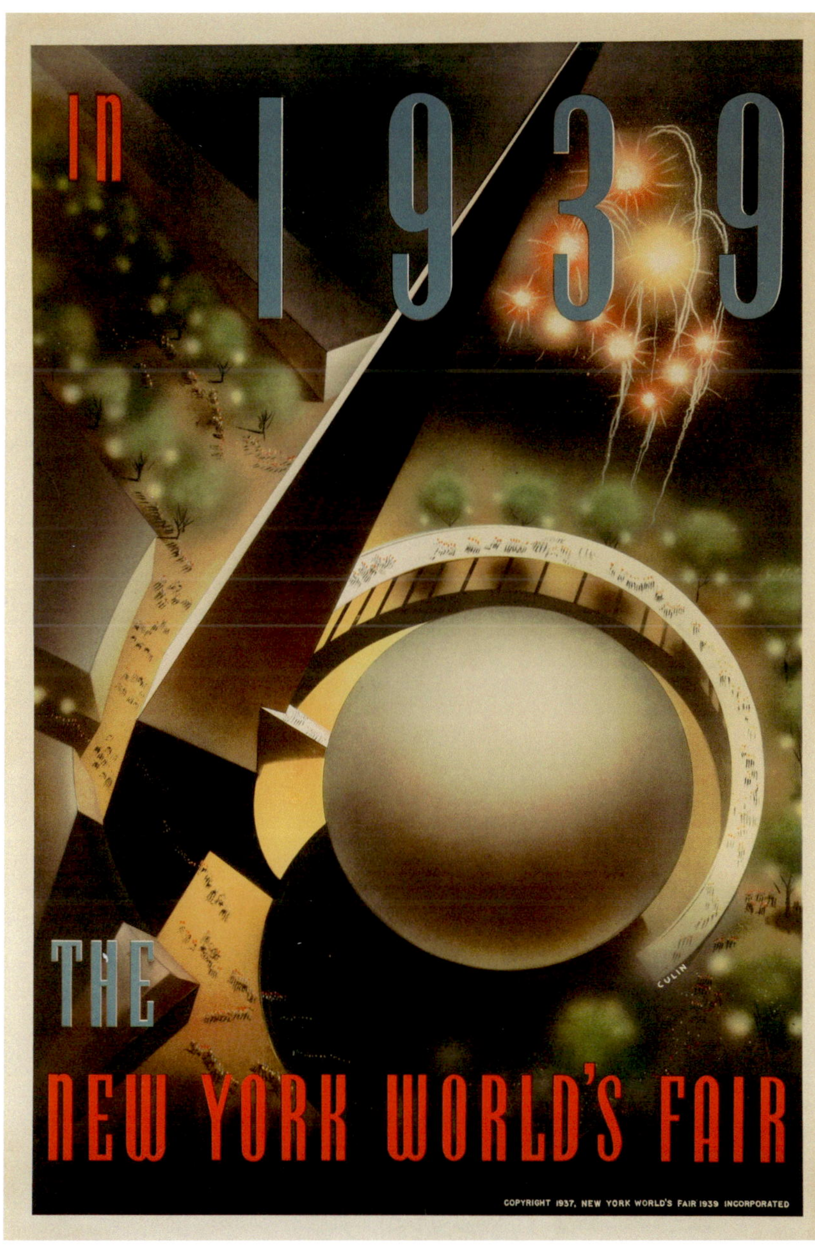

Fig. 17 Nembhard Culin (1908–1990), *In 1939 The New York World's Fair*, 1937. Offset lithograph, 38½ × 27 in. Courtesy of David Pollack

Another Art Deco masterpiece, Robert Pious's poster for the American Negro Exposition of 1940 focuses on two figures against a background that features skyscrapers and the stylized visage of Abraham Lincoln (pl. 14). The strong geometry, modern print, and rich complementary colors are characteristic of Art Deco. The bodies are smooth and idealized, with outlines that recall low relief panels on Art Deco buildings and poses that telegraph ancient Egyptian forms.[43] The figures hold a book, a gear, a scroll, and broken chains. Pious's design won a national contest to represent the exposition—an event, colloquially called the Black World's Fair, that celebrated seventy-five years of African American accomplishments since the end of slavery. Symbolically rich and stylistically modern, Pious's poster embodied the goals of the fair.

Art Deco design found another outlet in the work of Sydney Leff, one of the nation's most prolific illustrators of covers for sheet music.[44] His design for *Ain't Misbehavin'* captures the appeal of Harlem's nightclubs with a dynamic layout and bright, flat color (fig. 18). Rendered with sharp angles, four light-skinned African American showgirls dance while a red-lipped musician plays a saxophone. The sheet music was produced for Connie's Hot Chocolates, a revue that originated at Connie's Inn, where Thomas "Fats" Waller and Cab Calloway delighted white patrons with this song.[45] Leff's captivating cover for *Underneath The Harlem Moon* depicts a glamorous woman dancing under the stars (pl. 15).[46] Propped on the parlor piano, Leff's sheet music brought cutting-edge design into middle-class American homes.[47]

Art Deco and modern aesthetics were central to the Harlem Renaissance and are read as "Jazz Age" today. The style was most effective in non-narrative illustrations—like posters and covers—where eye-catching forms trumped any need for storytelling. However, realist rendering dominated American publishing throughout the 1920s and '30s. As Norman Rockwell became the nation's most famous illustrator, most magazine images were closer to realism than modernism. While there were a handful of publications closely associated with modernism, successful publishers employed a range of styles and artists during the Jazz Age.

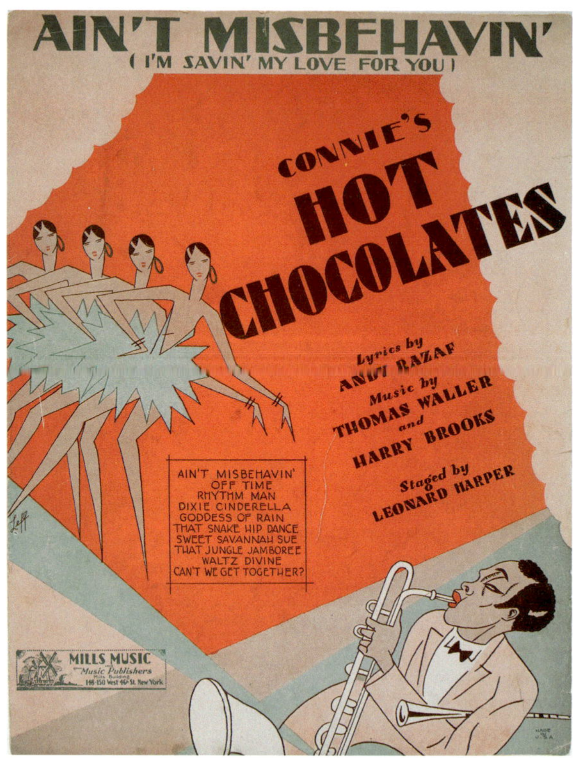

Fig. 18 Sydney Leff (1901–2005), cover from *Ain't Misbehavin'*, 1929 (New York: Mills Music). Printed matter. Delaware Art Museum, Helen Farr Sloan Library and Archives

The Harlem Renaissance in Magazines

In March 1925 Alain Locke served as guest editor for an issue of the social reform journal *Survey Graphic*.[48] With articles by Locke and W. E. B. Du Bois, and poems by Langston Hughes, Countee Cullen, and Claude McKay, this publication introduced readers to the literature, music, and ambition of contemporary Harlem. To illustrate the journal, Locke collaborated with photographers and artists, including the German-born artist and designer Winold Reiss.[49] The magazine opens with Reiss's meticulously drawn head of tenor Roland Hayes floating above the caption: "Whose achievement as a singer symbolizes the promise of the younger generation" (pl. 16).[50] Portraiture—drawn, painted, and photographic—had an important role in the New Negro movement, refuting racist stereotypes and crude caricatures by capturing the individuality and nobility of Black subjects. Reiss's detailed depiction of an accomplished musician worked toward that end. His other works included an image of actor Paul Robeson and a selection of "Harlem Types": a boy scout, a college lad, and a woman lawyer, among others.[51]

Reiss also produced a series of modernist drawings, including two *Interpretations of Harlem Jazz* for *Survey Graphic*. Incorporating influences from Cubism, African art, and cartoons, his jazz fantasies include off-kilter skyscrapers, smokestacks, workers, and dancers with arms and legs akimbo.[52] With overlapping images and bold patterns, the busy *Interpretations* paired well with the writing of Joel A. Rogers, who opined, "Jazz

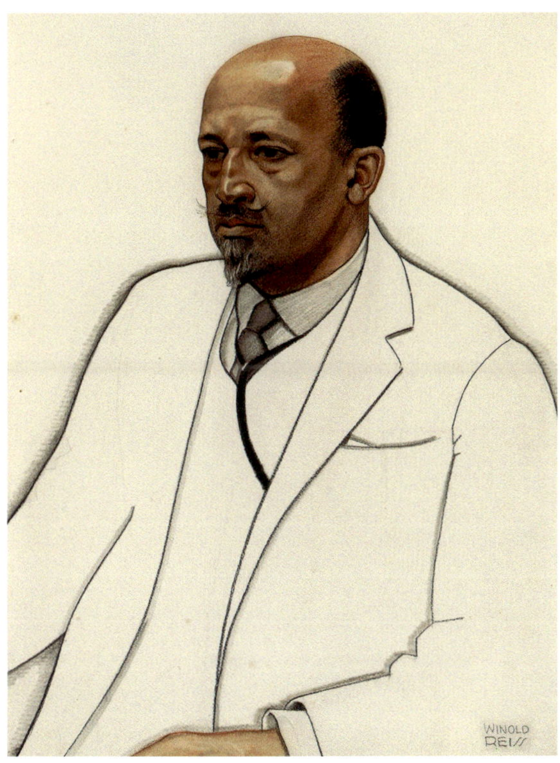

Fig. 19 Winold Reiss (1886–1953), *W. E. B. Du Bois*, ca. 1925, study for *The New Negro: An Interpretation* (New York: Albert & Charles Boni, 1925). Pastel on illustration paper, 29 15/16 × 21 5/8 in. National Portrait Gallery, Smithsonian Institution; purchase funded by Lawrence A. Fleischman and Howard Garfinkle with a matching grant from the National Endowment for the Arts

isn't music merely, it is a spirit that can express itself in almost anything. The true spirit of jazz is a joyous revolt from convention, custom, authority, boredom, even sorrow—from everything that would confine the soul of man and hinder its riding free on the air."[53]

At the end of 1925, Locke put out *The New Negro: An Interpretation*, a book that republished much of the material from *Survey Graphic* with additional texts and visuals, including portraits of Locke and Du Bois by Reiss. Like the Hayes portrait, these were based on exquisite pastel drawings (pl. 17 and fig. 19). In them, Reiss followed the formula that Camara Dia Holloway identified in portrait photographs by James L. Allen from the same era: his subjects are professionally dressed and situated in three-quarter view, aligning them with bourgeois propriety and rejecting the frontality of scientific and criminal photography.[54] Focusing attention on his subjects' faces, the artist rendered their clothing in outline.

Reiss also designed the Art Deco dust jacket, title page, headers, and endpieces for *The New Negro*. For these, Reiss adopted geometric and African motifs, like masks, that idealized and essentialized African culture to reflect the widespread primitivism of the period. His *Jazz Interpretations* were replaced with illustrations by Mexican-born caricaturist Miguel Covarrubias, who used streamlined forms to capture the energy of the jazz club in a modern idiom without the cubist confusion. Covarrubias had debuted similar images in *Vanity Fair* months earlier, bringing his caricatures to an urbane white audience under the headline "Enter, The New Negro, a Distinctive Type Recently Created by the Coloured Cabaret Belt in New York," alongside text by Afro-Caribbean writer Eric D. Walrond (see pl. 35). Covarrubias's caricatures, with their strongly racialized features and exaggerated gestures, unsettle us today, and some Black intellectuals, like Du Bois, objected to them in the 1920s, while Locke embraced this and other interracial collaborations.[55] The Harlem Renaissance was not a monolithic movement.

Lured from Kansas to New York by the Harlem issue of the *Survey Graphic*, Aaron Douglas took up studies with Reiss and soon created six drawings for *The New Negro*.[56] Presenting figures in silhouette with sharp angles and stylized bodies, these drawings show Douglas learning from Reiss. He quickly became one of the leading artists of the Harlem Renaissance, publishing striking illustrations and covers for *The Crisis* and *Opportunity* in 1926. Inspired by Egyptian art, Douglas stylized bodies and placed faces in profile. He experimented with complex and layered images, playing with tonal gradations, and some of his most effective covers presented iconic central elements (fig. 20). In this volume, Colette Gaiter explores Douglas's cover for *Fire!!*, one of the literary magazines assembled by younger artists in Harlem (see fig. 36). Demonstrating his ability to work in a variety of styles, Douglas also produced expressive line drawings for this issue.

On the heels of *Fire!!* came the publication of *Ebony and Topaz: A Collectanea,* which presented essays, poetry, and illustrations by young artists (pl. 18). Edited by Charles S. Johnson and featuring drawings by Charles Cullen and Richard Bruce Nugent, *Ebony and Topaz* presented some of the era's most unexpected and adventurous literature and

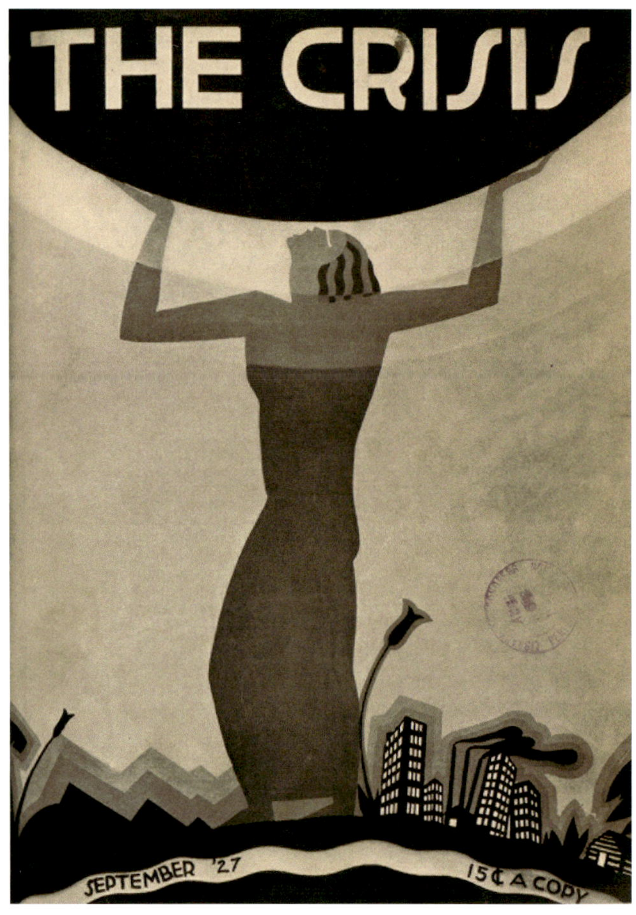

Fig. 20 Aaron Douglas (1899–1979), *The Burden of Black Womanhood*, cover from *The Crisis*, September 1927. Printed matter. Library of Congress

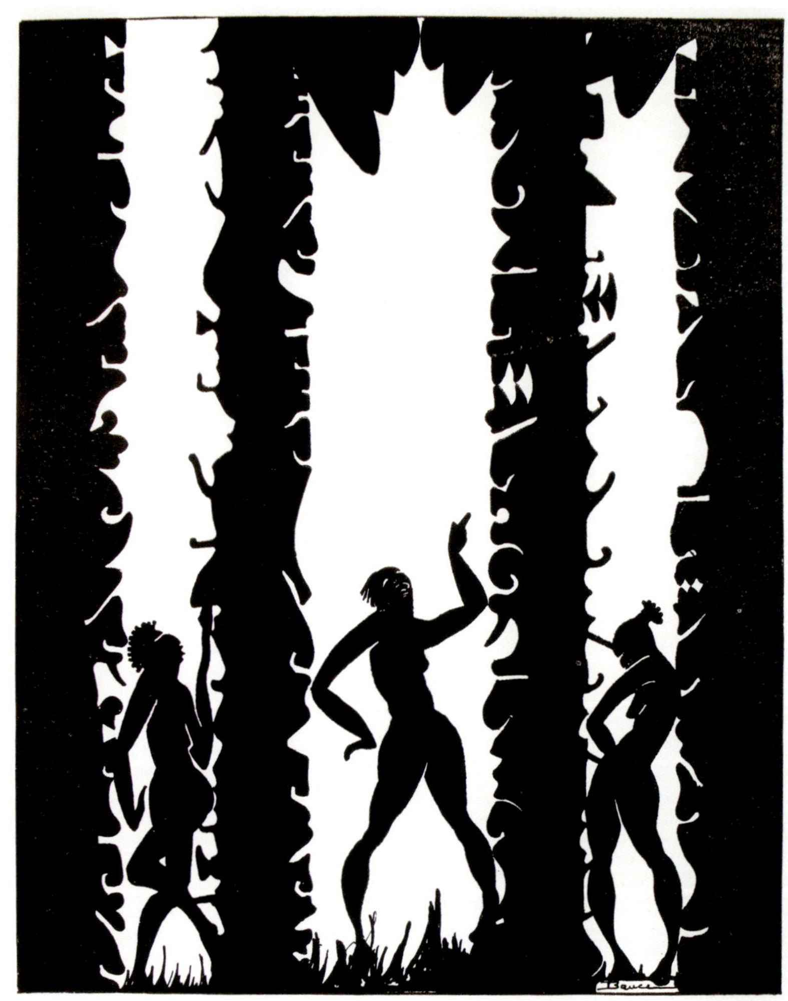

Fig. 21 Richard Bruce Nugent (1906–1987), *Four Drawings for Mulattoes*, from *Ebony and Topaz: A Collectanea*, 1927. Printed matter. Delaware Art Museum, Helen Farr Sloan Library and Archives

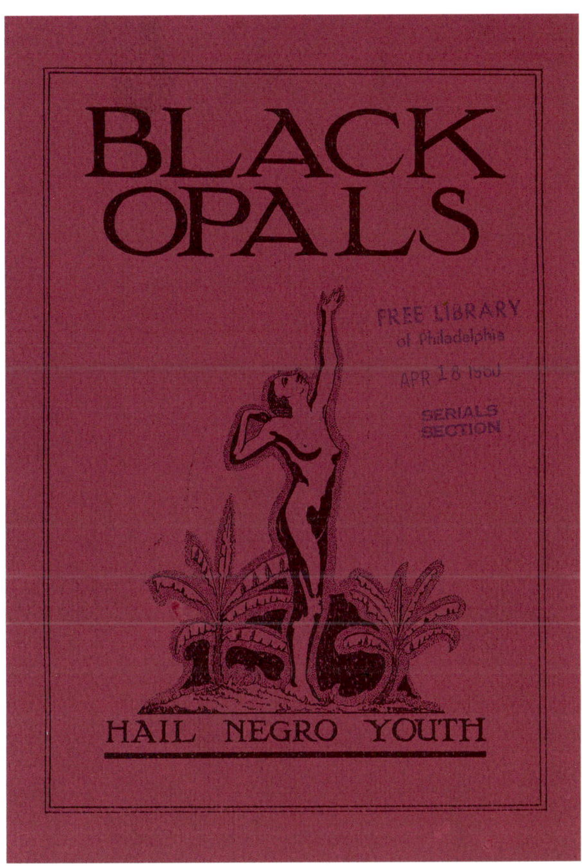

Fig. 22 Allan Freelon (1895–1960), cover from *Black Opals*, Christmas 1927. Printed matter. Courtesy of the Free Library of Philadelphia, Rare Book Department

illustration. Cullen was a white artist with close associations (but no relation) with poet Countee Cullen, who was at the center of the Harlem Renaissance. For the cover and within, Charles Cullen depicted gender-bending Black and white figures. He used delicate pen lines that recalled the scandalous work of nineteenth-century illustrator Aubrey Beardsley, especially in combination with his figures' ecstatic expressions and postures. Rejecting realism but lacking clear allegiance to Art Deco or African influences, Cullen's illustration announced the open editorial attitude of the publication, which included stories and images about interracial and homoerotic relationships. As Caroline Goeser's research has pointed out, Cullen primarily illustrated texts by gay authors and consciously included gay content, knowing that readers would interpret his images based on their perspectives. Her research also linked Nugent's *Drawings for Mulattoes* to "sites of interracial activity" and identifiable drag performers (fig. 21).[57] Decadent and decorative, the nudes in *Ebony and Topaz* were a far cry from the formalized figures delineated by Aaron Douglas and Robert Pious.

A more conservative journal, *Black Opals* hailed from Philadelphia and was the brainchild of Arthur Huff Fauset, a public-school teacher.[58] Like many little magazines, it had only a short run—in this case, four small issues.[59] The boldly colored covers featured modern designs by Allan Freelon and James Lesesne Wells. On the first three issues, Freelon's female nude reaches toward the sky, towering over the landscape behind her and demonstrating the aspiration of the subtitle "Hail Negro Youth" (fig. 22).

Perusing the Newsstand

The striking modernist magazine covers of the Harlem Renaissance would not have appeared on most newsstands in the Jazz Age. Instead, corner newsstands were awash in mass-market magazines, with cover images of beautiful white women, seasonal scenes, and humorous tableaux of family life. Their displays may have been punctuated by the stylish Art Deco imagery of the "smart magazines," like *Vogue* and *Vanity Fair,* and the comic modernity of *Life* and *Ballyhoo*.[60] Published in September 1934, illustrator J. C. Leyendecker's *End of Vacation* cover for *The Saturday Evening Post* was unusual for showing a Black man and a white woman together (pl. 19). The man's position—behind her, carrying her packages, and clearly in service to her—indicates the limited space given to African Americans in mass-market magazines during the Jazz Age. Leyendecker's scene echoed Anne Fish's cartoon with its caricatured depiction of an African American porter with large red lips—a feature reiterated in Sydney Leff's sheet music for *Ain't Misbehavin'* (see pl. 7 and fig. 18). The segregation and racial stereotyping of the era was mirrored in the popular press. For the most part, the periodicals in this section catered to white audiences and almost exclusively published the work of white authors and illustrators.[61]

On May 10, 1924, the first cover of *Liberty* introduced the publication as "The Newcomer in the Field," depicting the magazine's representative striding into a line-up that included *The Saturday Evening Post*, *The Ladies'*

Home Journal, and *Collier's*, among others. These older magazines had been founded in the nineteenth century and were reaching large national audiences by the end of the 1890s, thanks to improved paper and printing technology, inexpensive mailing costs, and the growth of commercial brands seeking national advertising platforms.[62] Photoengraving made it affordable to illustrate mass-market publications lavishly, and publishers recognized that illustrations, especially dynamic cover designs, were vital for attracting buyers.[63]

The artist placed *The Saturday Evening Post* on the *Liberty* cover at the front of the line, reflecting the publication's prominence. By 1922 the *Post*'s circulation exceeded two million—the largest in the nation. The *Post*, like *Liberty*, was a general interest magazine. Each issue featured articles on business and public affairs, as well as romantic fiction, sports, and humor.[64] The *Post* was nativist and politically conservative, and the magazine reproduced stereotypes of immigrants and African Americans. Articles and fiction extolled middle-class, small-town lifestyles and treated city life with suspicion.[65] For all its limitations, the cover of the *Post* was a high-profile assignment. Rockwell called it "the greatest show window in America for an illustrator."[66]

By the start of the Jazz Age, Leyendecker had helped establish the *Post's* dominance, illustrating dozens of eye-catching covers over the previous decade.[67] He excelled at depicting attractive men and women in stylish clothing and created memorable advertising campaigns for Arrow Collar and Kuppenheimer Suits featuring his model and partner, Charles Beach (fig. 23). Leyendecker immortalized muscled athletes and fastidious swells with aplomb, and his paintings of the young and beautiful attired in contemporary sportswear and sleek tuxedos shaped Jazz Age aspirations. Although he had a masterful grasp of modern style, Leyendecker set some of his elaborate holiday covers in the past, allowing him to explore a wider range of attire and accoutrements.[68] In 1935 his Easter cover pictured a Beau Brummell–like dandy delivering a bouquet (pl. 20). The illustrator lavished attention on his subject's fine buckskin gloves, breaches, and plum-colored jacket, as well as the voluminous linen cravat that frames his handsome face. Leyendecker set this dashing figure against a pale turquoise door to enhance the seasonal palette. Colorful and theatrical, Leyendecker's historically themed covers allowed the artist to explore versions of masculinity outside the athletic ideal of the 1920s.[69]

As the 1920s wore on, Leyendecker was overtaken by the young Norman Rockwell as the leading cover artist for *The Saturday Evening Post*. Rockwell's first cover came in 1916, and he produced almost one hundred covers in the 1920s. Influenced by Leyendecker and artists working in the tradition of Howard Pyle, Rockwell's early covers were painterly in execution, although he quickly developed his photorealistic style. His works were marked by his ability to locate and express the humor in everyday life. Rockwell's subjects were full of contemporary references, and his characters rarely had the physical appeal or chic sensibility of Leyendecker's lean beauties and chiseled athletes. Instead, he captured the awkward and ordinary, including children and older people, using models and props from his hometown in New Rochelle, New York (pl. 21).

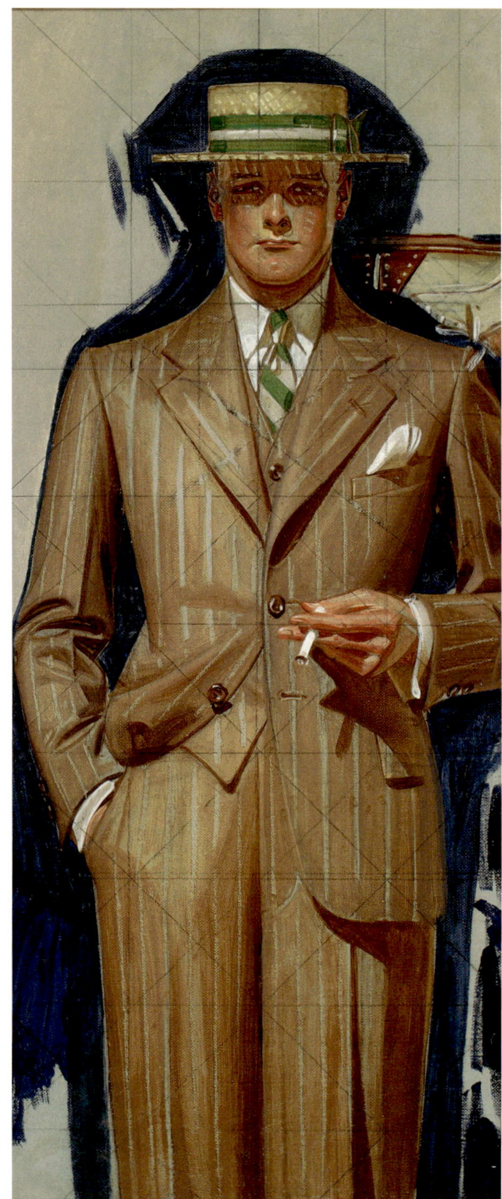

Fig. 23 J. C. Leyendecker (1874–1951), *Figure Study* for double-page advertisement for Kuppenheimer Suits, *The Saturday Evening Post*, April 20, 1929. Oil on canvas, 22 × 9¼ in. Delaware Art Museum, Acquisition Fund, 2016

A friend and neighbor to Leyendecker and Rockwell, Coles Phillips dedicated himself to depictions of modern women. For a *Post* cover from 1920, Phillips captured a young woman making a last-minute repair to her outfit before heading out (pl. 22). Working meticulously in watercolor and gouache, the artist evoked the feel of her silk stockings, kid gloves, and satin and lace dress. Phillips had perfected the depiction of the texture and translucency of fabrics, earning him a lucrative contract with Holeproof Hosiery, which advertised "hosiery of lustrous beauty and fine texture that wears so well. . . . at such reasonable prices" (see fig. 54).[70]

Years earlier, for a cover of the humor magazine *Life*, Phillips invented the "fadeaway girl"—a design in which the figure's clothing (or part of it) matches and disappears into the background—creating a clever play with negative space. Phillips continued to employ this technique on magazine covers for decades, and other artists adopted it as well. His amusing illustration *In a Position to Know* graced the cover of *Life* in 1921, catching a uniformed maid spying through a keyhole, with her improbably perfect sheer stockings on display (pl. 23). *Life*'s artists generally located humor in modern life, and their jokes often hinged on distinctions in class, gender, and age (pl. 24).[71]

Fig. 24 Charles Archibald MacLellan (1887–1961), cover for *Collier's Weekly*, May 20, 1919. Oil on canvas, 28 × 18¼ in. Delaware Art Museum, Gayle and Alene Hoskins Fund, 1987

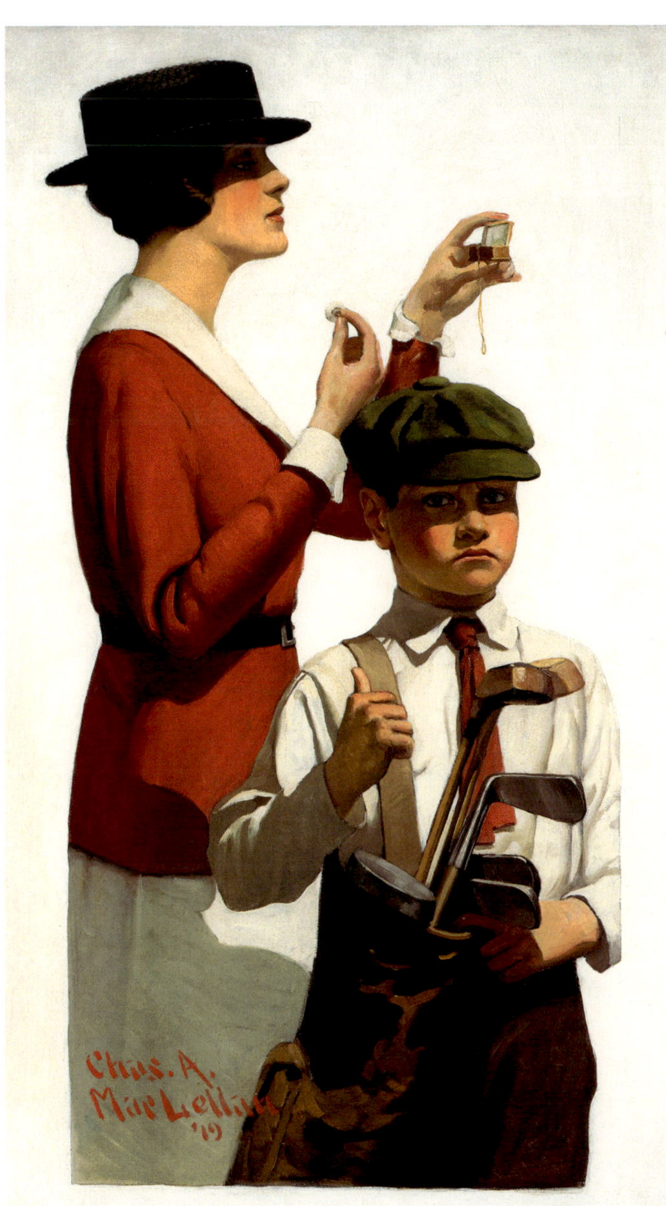

Phillips's fadeaway girl presented a fresh take on the ubiquitous "pretty girl" cover. Throughout the late nineteenth and early twentieth centuries, no subject was more widespread on the covers of mass-market magazines. Working within the bounds of this formula, Jazz Age illustrators used "pretty girl" covers to reflect contemporary culture. Revealing (and mocking) the increased participation of women in sports, Charles MacLellan painted a markedly modern woman dressed in fashionable sportswear with obvious rouge on her cheeks for the cover of *Collier's* in 1919. She has stopped her golf game to touch up her makeup, much to the annoyance of her young caddy (fig. 24).[72] Perhaps because she played in the same sphere as men, the "lady golfer" became the butt of many jokes in the 1920s.

Neysa McMein became one of the most famous illustrators of the Jazz Age with her images of beautiful women. She was producing "pretty girl" covers by 1913, but even at that early date, her women were different—self-possessed and unsmiling.[73] McMein became a celebrity, and her friends included the circle of witty writers and critics who gathered at the Algonquin Hotel and published in *The New Yorker* in the 1920s. Her celebrity was sufficient that her name featured prominently below her illustrations, even in this advertisement for Wallace Silver (see pl. 43). McMein was one of the Jazz Age illustrators perceived as arbiters of beauty and invited to judge beauty contests. A new phenomenon in the 1920s, pageants attracted the attention of comic authors and illustrators (pl. 25).[74]

Emerging in the early twentieth century and thriving in the 1920s, "smart magazines," like *Vanity Fair* and *The New Yorker*, catered to self-consciously sophisticated audiences—readers described by George H. Douglas as "well traveled, well read, well acquainted."[75] The cover art reflected their outlook by incorporating Art Deco style and motifs from modernist art. Founded in 1913, *Vanity Fair* featured a sophisticated mix of fiction, satire, criticism, and photography. Appearing in March 1923, Nicolai Remisoff's theatrical cover design resembles a stage set with striped curtains framing a central scene (pl. 26). The "backdrop" is a cityscape, with stylized clouds and off-kilter skyscrapers that seem taken from a modernist painting. With a trim waist and slender ankles, the figure in the foreground is slightly androgynous despite his tuxedo. The woman behind him looks ready for Carnival in Venice with her elaborate gown, mask, and veil, and a strange figure peeks through the curtains at the lower right. Unlike covers for *The Saturday Evening Post* or *Life,* there is no clear narrative or joke to discern. Instead, Remisoff conveyed mood and sensibility. Whatever is happening here is not for readers of *The Saturday Evening Post.*

Launched in 1925, *The New Yorker* became known for high-quality fiction, essays, reviews, and journalism. The magazine published art by an international cadre of artists whose work reflected developments in modern art and design. Their striking covers often featured urban settings and fashionable types and could be tinged with humor. Cartoons were a key feature from the start, and top illustrators like John Held Jr. and Barbara Shermund were regular contributors (fig. 25).

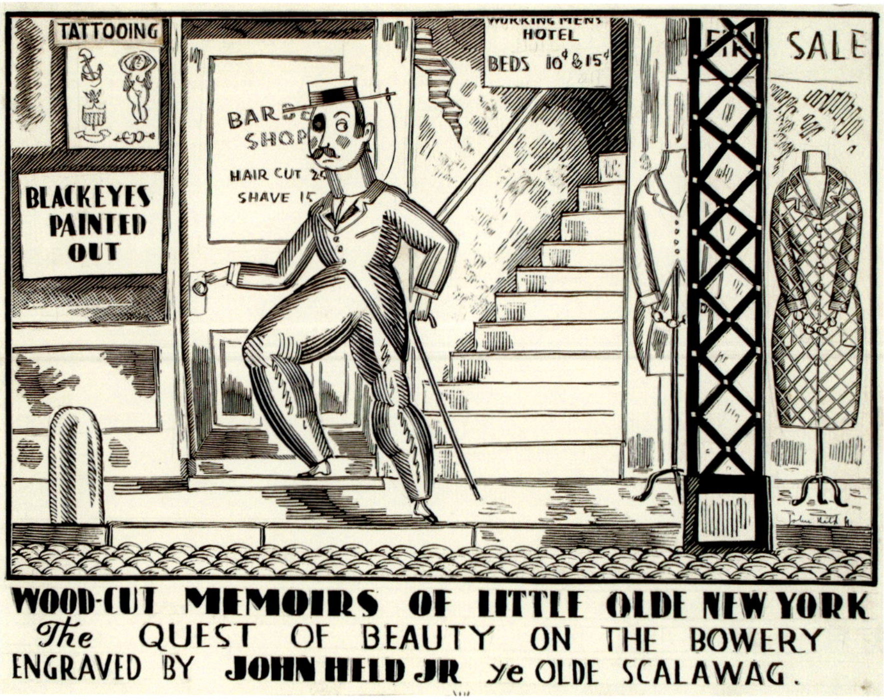

Fig. 25 John Held Jr. (1889–1958), *Olde New York*, for *The New Yorker*, February 20, 1932. Ink and graphite on illustration board, 10¾ × 13¾ in. Delaware Art Museum, Acquisition Fund, 1986

Designer and illustrator Helen Dryden pursued a similar level of Art Deco sophistication in her covers for *Vogue*. Established in 1892 to appeal to New York's upper class, by 1920, *Vogue* was published by Condé Nast (who also produced *Vanity Fair*) as a monthly fashion magazine for well-heeled women. In the '20s, Dryden absorbed the influence of Erté and imagined charming scenes of chic modern women for *Vogue's* covers. For the issue dated December 15, 1922, she used her signature clean lines and flat colors to depict a masquerade ball with costumes that harken back to the late nineteenth century: a woman wears a voluminous ball gown and flirts with an Oscar Wildean suitor bedecked in a flowing tie, pink smoking jacket, and green cape (pl. 27).

Fashion magazines were not the only publications aimed at women. As Victoria Pass explains in her essay in this volume, they were not the primary sources that interpreted and defined fashionability for middle-class readers. *Woman's World*, *Ladies' Home Journal*, *Good Housekeeping*, and *Pictorial Review* each reached millions of households and generated huge demand for illustrations to accompany their mix of contemporary fiction and domestic advice. Charming children joined attractive women on their covers, and many female illustrators found regular work illustrating women's magazines (see figs. 61 and 62). A few, like Jessie Willcox Smith, landed lucrative contracts and became household names.

A smaller number of women found success in newspapers, liberally illustrated with features, comics, editorial cartoons, and news pictures in the Jazz Age. Starting in 1907, Nell Brinkley created elaborate illustrations and clever stories that were syndicated in newspapers nationally. With fine flowing lines, her intricate ink drawings translated well to newsprint, often appearing as half-page images. Brinkley drew stylish women in fantasy narratives with handsome suitors, happy children, and cavorting cupids. *A Map of the Heart* combines many of her interests, featuring beautiful girls with perfect curls and bee-stung lips, studying with a professorial cupid (pl. 28). Her "Brinkley girls" were famous by 1908, and she enjoyed a long career as a writer, editor, and cartoonist.

Similarly high-profile were the illustrated newspaper features of artist and designer McClelland Barclay. His full-page pictures for "Girls I Adore" were captioned by Alice-Leone Moats in 1934, who had recently gained fame as the author of *No Nice Girl Swears,* "a sassy book of etiquette that immediately became a best-seller."[76] In a few amusing paragraphs, Moats described each type of woman pictured—the "worldly man-wise" woman, the "chaise-longue intellectual," the "helpless little girl"—balancing romantic advice with swipes at the pretensions of the subject and her admirers. Breaking from the others, in his final entry, Barclay depicted a woman in an evening dress enveloped by a crowd of men (pl. 29). Moats explained the type: "Every now and then a girl has the ability to give the impression that she is always surrounded by admirers and can arrange things with so much cunning that the main man in her life doesn't suspect what position he occupies."[77] Like magazine covers, full-page newspaper spreads presented high-profile spaces for artists to share their ideas with a national audience. Commissions for these large designs were generally reserved for famous illustrators like Brinkley, Barclay, and John Held Jr., whose names attracted consumers.

Although only a handful of illustrators became celebrities, many lived comfortable lives as professionals, piecing together commissions for magazines, newspapers, books, advertisements, posters, and calendars. Founded in the early twentieth century, the Society of Illustrators helped build friendships and establish professional practices for illustrators at all levels, and their annual fundraisers benefited members in need. The Society promoted its (mostly white and male) members and the field through exhibitions in New York, but their greatest fame (and windfall) in the Jazz Age came in 1923 when Society members sold the rights to the skits from their risqué annual revue. The owners of the Shubert Theater produced *Artists and Models*, a Broadway spectacle that resulted in "the public perception that illustrators were a scandalous lot."[78] The earnings from the production allowed the Society to purchase their headquarters on the Upper East Side.

In the Bookshop

Magazines and newspapers presented a variety of images by different artists, but book commissions could provide artists with opportunities to create more cohesive statements. From illustrated classics to Art Deco masterworks, extraordinary books were produced in the 1920s and '30s. Books attracted more criticism than the regular deluge of periodicals, allowing us to glimpse some discussions around illustration and book design in the Jazz Age.

Harmony of Text and Illustration

In the late 1920s, the American Institute of Graphic Arts organized exhibitions to celebrate the best illustrated books of the year. Opening in New York, these shows traveled across the country, yielding a bounty of published reviews about the current state of American illustration. In her book *Picturing the New Negro,* Caroline Goeser provides a detailed discussion of illustration's reception in print, in part by examining these exhibitions.[79] In 1927 a critic reviewing the second annual American Book Illustration show at the Art Center in New York noted the shift by publishers toward "the production of volumes in which the pictorial, typographical, and decorative elements are blended into a harmonious whole. Illustrations in an increasing number of cases have been considered not as illustrations only, but as a part of the book which must be in harmony with other parts."[80] The following year, Thomas Erwin's catalogue essay for the third annual show articulated this trend further, expressing relief in the gradual disappearance of halftone plates printed on glossy paper and inserted into novels—a practice which remained popular well into the 1930s in the illustrated classics discussed in my other essay in this volume.[81] Erwin also noted with approval the move away from "literal illustration." He wrote, "The best illustrators content themselves with complementing and decorating the author's story . . . they present the author to his audience . . . but they never attempt to tell his story."[82]

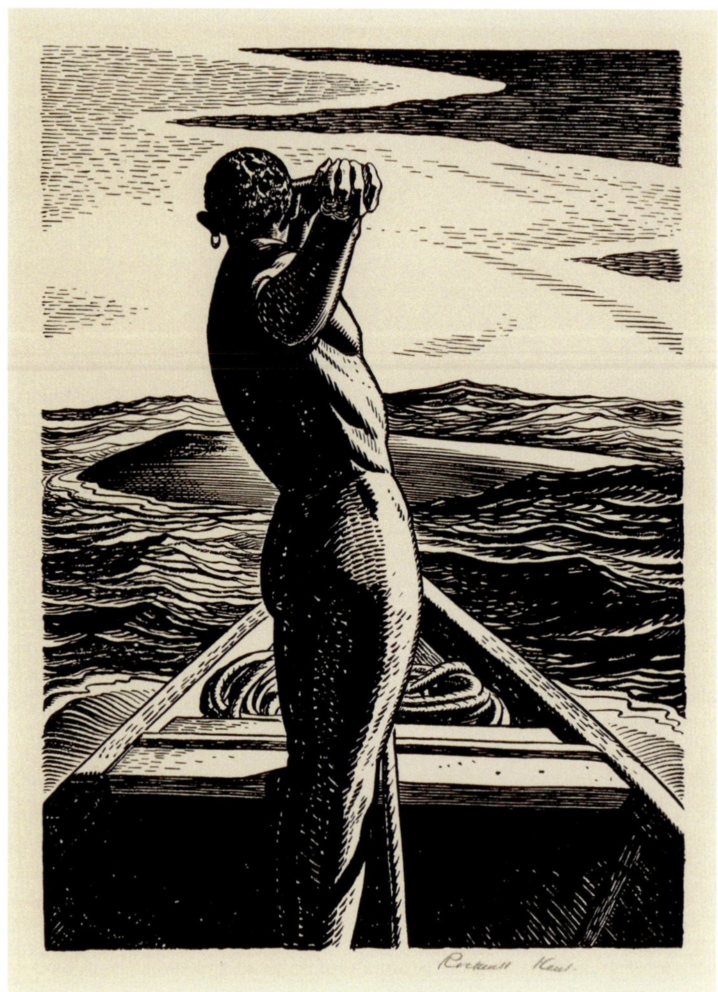

Fig. 26 Rockwell Kent (1882–1971), *The Harpooneer,* for *Moby Dick or The Whale* by Herman Melville (Chicago: The Lakeside Press, 1930). Photolithograph print, sheet: 11⅜ × 7⅞ in. Delaware Art Museum, F. V. du Pont Acquisition Fund, 1994

The 1927 exhibition included Aaron Douglas's illustrations for James Weldon Johnson's *God's Trombones,* a book of poems that sought to capture the themes and cadences of traditional African American church services. Following the author's lead, Douglas conveyed the moods and motifs of the various verses in a set of monochrome images. Douglas's illustration for *Go Down Death—A Funeral Sermon* aligns loosely with text about the Angel of Death riding his horse, "[t]hrough heaven's pearly gates, [p]ast suns and moons and stars," to bring a woman to rest "on the loving breast of Jesus" (pl. 30). A stylized horse appears, but the heavenly structures are rendered as dreamlike visions of architecture, and other elements are left out entirely. This is not, to use Erwin's words, "literal illustration." The project deeply impacted the artist. Years after the 1927 publication of *God's Trombones,* Douglas produced large color paintings revisiting these compositions.

Painter and printmaker Rockwell Kent was honored in three American Book Illustration shows, winning accolades for publications released from 1926 through 1928. Kent's most important foray into book illustration was the 1930 edition of Herman Melville's *Moby Dick* for the Lakeside Press.[83] The publication was named one of the American Institute of Graphic Art's "Fifty Books of the Year." It was very successful with critics and consumers and helped to revive the reputation of Melville's novel, transforming it into a canonical work of American literature. Kent's ink drawings evoked woodcuts (or even scrimshaw) and balanced his modernist compositions with their linear sturdiness (fig. 26). Reflecting the larger ideas about book illustration, a critic for the *Detroit Free Press* wrote, "They are full of restrained imagination, suggestive power, strong rhythmical lines, and a quality of black and white contrasts which makes them ideal illustrations for a printed book."[84]

The illustrator Edward Shenton created a sensitive pairing of text and image in his first major book commission. Working for *Scribner's Magazine,* Shenton brought a unified graphic vision to the periodical in the early 1930s. Perhaps as a cost-saving measure, his delicate pen drawings provided nearly all the images in the magazine in 1934, including the illustrations for Fitzgerald's *Tender Is the Night,* which was serialized in *Scribner's* before the book was released that April. With minute lines and delicate hatching, Shenton's pictures captured the fragile psyches and imminent dangers that propel Fitzgerald's narrative, and the first edition of the novel retained many of Shenton's drawings, which the author felt gave his book "a certain distinction"[85] (pl. 31).

Dust Jackets

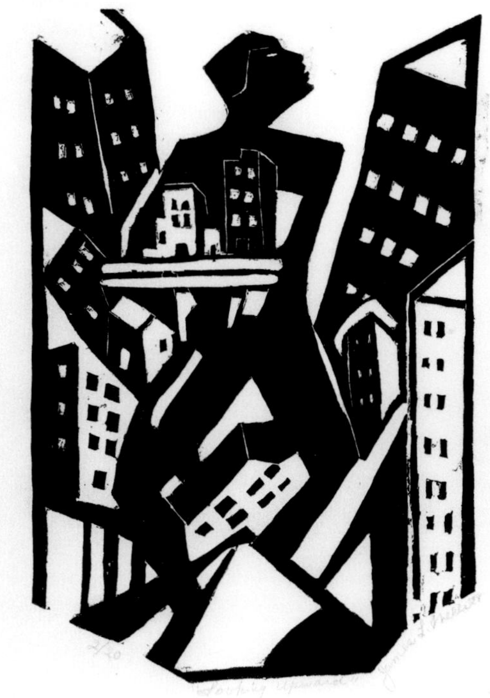

Fig. 27 James Lesesne Wells (1902–1993), *Looking Upward,* 1928. Woodcut on paper, sheet: 22 × 17 in. Smithsonian American Art Museum, Gift of Jacob and Ruth Kainen, 1993.75.2

One major shift in book design was the evolution of the dust jacket from a protective shield into an artistic envelope. In the 1920s, many decorated dust jackets reproduced the frontispiece or another appealing illustration from the book on the front cover, and artists learned to leave space for potential title treatments. In other cases—when novels were not illustrated—covers were ordered specifically. Fitzgerald was so entranced with the cover design for *The Great Gatsby*—commissioned by his publisher from artist Francis Cugat before the book was even finished—that he famously incorporated the image of *Celestial Eyes* into the story (pl. 32). The author wrote to his publisher, "For Christs sake don't give anyone that jacket you're saving for me. I've written it into the book."[86]

George W. Gage's cover for *The Door of the Double Dragon: A Romance of the China of Yesterday and To-Day* enticed readers with an intriguing image of a young woman in a bright white dress emerging from heavy doors decorated with golden dragons (pl. 33). The cover neatly encapsulates the tale of a young American woman who travels to China to paint a portrait of the emperor. Across the upper register of the painting, deep shadows convey a sense of foreboding as well as creating space for the title, printed in yellow. A slightly different version of the same subject was used as the book's frontispiece. The woman's expression is alarmed, and the caption reads: "The blood rushed to her head; her whole body was strained. The door was gradually closing."[87] The cover version is less clear, displacing the threat to the claws of the dragon. This cover and the story reflected Americans' interest in distant places and "exotic" cultures. The novel and its illustrations treated China with an orientalist combination of fascination and disdain.

Fig. 28 Loïs Mailou Jones (1905–1998), *Heritage: Illustration for Important Events and Dates in Negro History*, for *The African Background Outlined* by Carter G. Woodson (Washington, DC: Associated Publishers, 1936). Brush and ink over lithograph on paper, 7½ × 19¼ in. The Johnson Collection, Spartanburg, South Carolina

By the 1930s, designers were creating dust jackets with cohesive text and imagery that wrapped the entire book. Carter G. Woodson, who cofounded Associated Publishers to support the Association for the Study of Negro History, commissioned young artists to create bold book jackets for the press's publications. Reflecting his interest in African art and German Expressionist printmaking, James Lesesne Wells designed the jacket for *The Negro Wage Earner,* a study of African American occupations since 1890 (pl. 34). Wells reproduced the image on the back cover and spine as a stand-alone print. Depicting a man surrounded by urban towers and titled *Looking Upward*, his print echoed the language of racial uplift promoted by the New Negro movement (fig. 27).

Woodson hired Loïs Mailou Jones to design book covers and illustrations for Horace Mann Bond's *Negro Education in Alabama: A Study in Cotton and Steel* and *African Heroes and Heroines* in a similar block-printed style. Her composition *Heritage* was printed as a header for a fold-out broadsheet illustrating "Important Events and Dates in Negro History" for Woodson's *The African Background Outlined* (fig. 28). The complex frieze of figures and architectural and natural elements reveals her knowledge of African art, Art Deco, and Harlem Renaissance imagery. The commission of these striking graphics for publications in history and social science demonstrated the central importance of illustration in the Harlem Renaissance. Through images like these, the Associated Publishers created a strong visual identity at a time when critics were demanding a coherent approach to book design.

Books for Children

Children's books were an emerging field in the 1920s. Educators called for illustrated editions to engage young readers, and libraries created children's rooms and departments. In 1919 Macmillan founded the first juvenile department of a major publisher, and in 1922 Doubleday followed suit. Their publications were sold in dedicated areas of bookshops and department stores.[88] In 1932 Blanche Aller marveled at the changing and growing field: "Last year over 800 children's books were published in the United States alone."[89] Reading lists and book awards honored the best books of each year. Children's books encompassed didactic stories that taught manners and morals, illustrated alphabets, adventure stories, fantasies, science texts, and contemporary and historical fiction.

Interest in new children's books was strong enough for the publisher Little Brown to sponsor a contest in 1928. Four hundred aspiring authors submitted drafts to a jury comprised of a school librarian, an editor, and the director of Boston's Bookshop for Boys and Girls.[90] Five winning entries were published, including *The Red Cape* by Rachel M. Varble, a newspaper writer. Varble's text was printed with copious black-and-white illustrations by Henrietta Adams McClure, who specialized in delicate ink drawings of fairies, families, and flora. Illuminated letters start each chapter, and illustrated scenes mark the end of many. Her drawings were produced with crisp lines and rich patterns and met the demand for sensitivity to the page (fig. 29). One critic suggested they added "an indescribable touch of beauty to the entire book."[91] The book also featured two-color endpapers and a color frontispiece. Regardless of the critical conversations about book design, color remained a key feature in children's book publishing in the Jazz Age.

Educators were among the strongest voices for illustrated children's books. A teacher and head of college drama programs, Gertrude Parthenia McBrown published poetry for children and adults in literary journals and

Fig. 29 Henrietta Adams McClure (1876–1946), *Good Morning*, tailpiece for Chapter 3 for *The Red Cape* by Rachel M. Varble (Boston: Little, Brown, and Co., 1928). Ink on illustration board, 7 1/16 × 7 13/16 in. Delaware Art Museum, Gift of Helen Farr Sloan, 1978

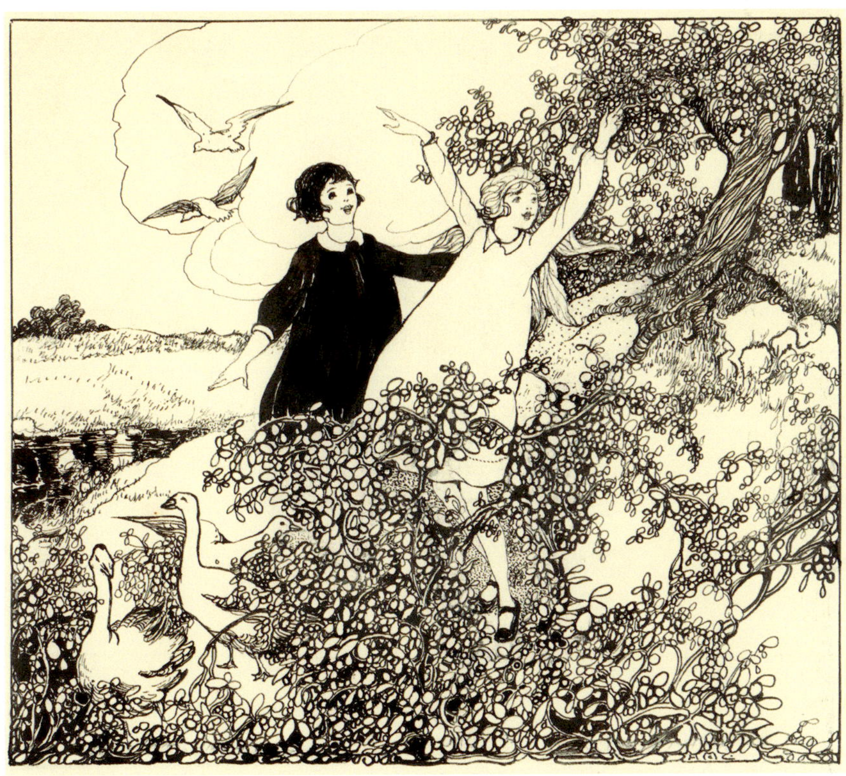

Fig. 30 Loïs Mailou Jones (1905–1998), *The Voice of Spring*, for *The Picture-Poetry Book* by Gertrude Parthenia McBrown (Washington, DC: Associated Publishers, 1935). Ink on paper, 11 3/4 × 8 3/4 in. Collection of Findlay University's Mazza Museum, Findlay, Ohio

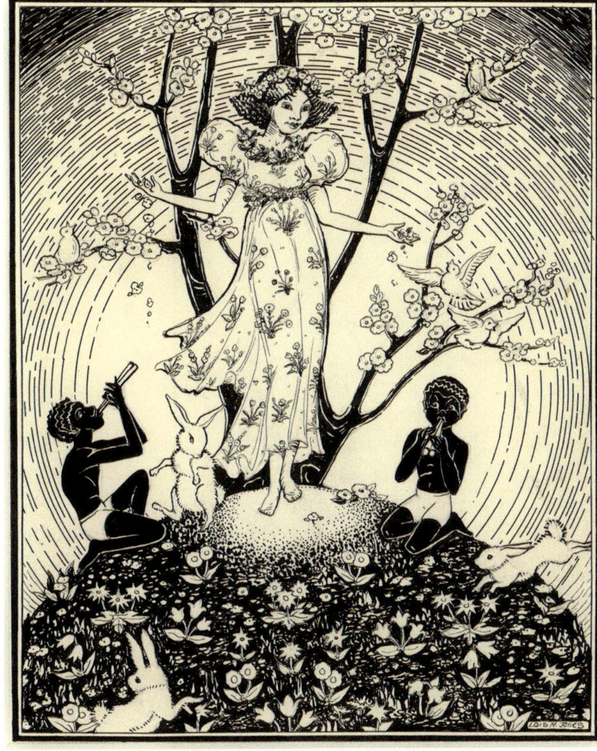

magazines.[92] An African American author, she was supported largely by the Black press. In 1935 McBrown's first book was released by Woodson's Associated Publishers. Richly illustrated with thirty-six drawings by Loïs Mailou Jones, *The Picture-Poetry Book* depicted otherworldly fairies and real-life children with curly hair and typically African American facial features. Jones rendered skin tones with linear shading, stippling, outline, and solid black ink, displaying a range of complexions to mirror those of her readers (see pls. 36, 37, and fig. 30). Her images met the modern demand for uncluttered, linear drawings that harmonized with the printed page while still providing imaginative spaces for young readers.

Arthur Huff Fauset, an African American anthropologist and elementary educator (discussed above as the force behind *Black Opals*), gathered biographies of Black leaders from Crispus Attucks and Sojourner Truth to Alain Locke for his book *For Freedom,* published in 1927. He collaborated with illustrators Aaron Douglas and Mabel Betsy Hill to enliven his book. Douglas provided a cover design with characteristic bold silhouettes, African forms, and dynamic diagonals, which was rendered in dark ink on red boards, creating an eye-catching cover (fig. 31).[93] Inside, *For Freedom* was illustrated by Hill, an accomplished children's illustrator, who reproduced the book's historical scenes in linoleum cuts (fig. 32). As Shoshana Resnikoff pointed out, "*For Freedom* made an argument to children that is only now recognized by the mainstream American public: that African-American history is American history."[94]

Jazz Age anxieties about wayward youth paralleled the investment in beautiful and educational books for the next generation. The children of flappers and jazz musicians grew up surrounded by richly illustrated publications in their homes and public libraries. In the 1930s, comic books emerged to provide youth with a new visual storytelling format, and the introduction of Superman in 1938 marked the beginning of what is often called the "golden age of comic books."[95] In the decades that followed the Jazz Age, illustrations would feature less prominently in books and magazines for adults. Today, when people think about illustration, they often think first of books for children.

Coda

As the Jazz Age came to a close in 1942, one of the most critically successful shows on Broadway was the revival of *Porgy and Bess*. Based on the 1925 novel *Porgy* by white author DuBose Heyward, the opera was composed by George Gershwin with lyrics by Heyward and Ira Gershwin. Like Heyward's novel and subsequent play, the opera presents a stereotyped view of African Americans. Gershwin required that Black actors be cast, providing opportunities for African American performers, but over time many actors and singers would refuse to take up the clichéd characterizations. The 1942 revival was produced by Cheryl Crawford and starred Todd Duncan, who had played Porgy in the original show in 1935, and the singer and actor Etta Moten, who is the subject of Jay Jackson's watercolor on the cover of this book. According to the souvenir program, the casting of Moten as Bess was "the tardy realization of George Gershwin's desire

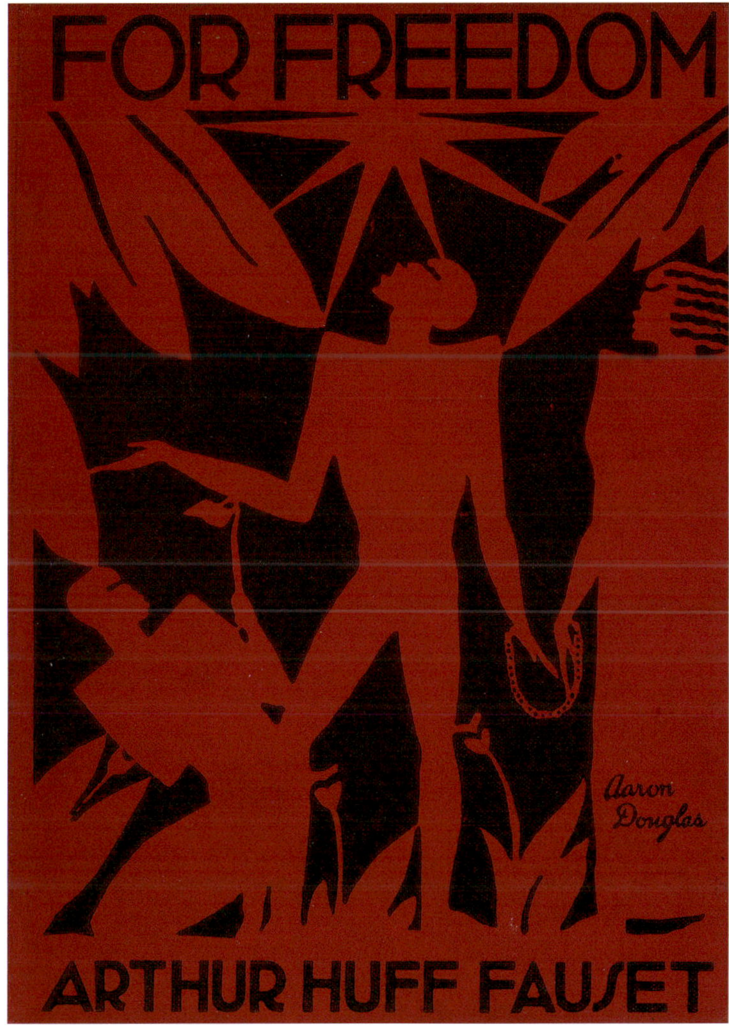

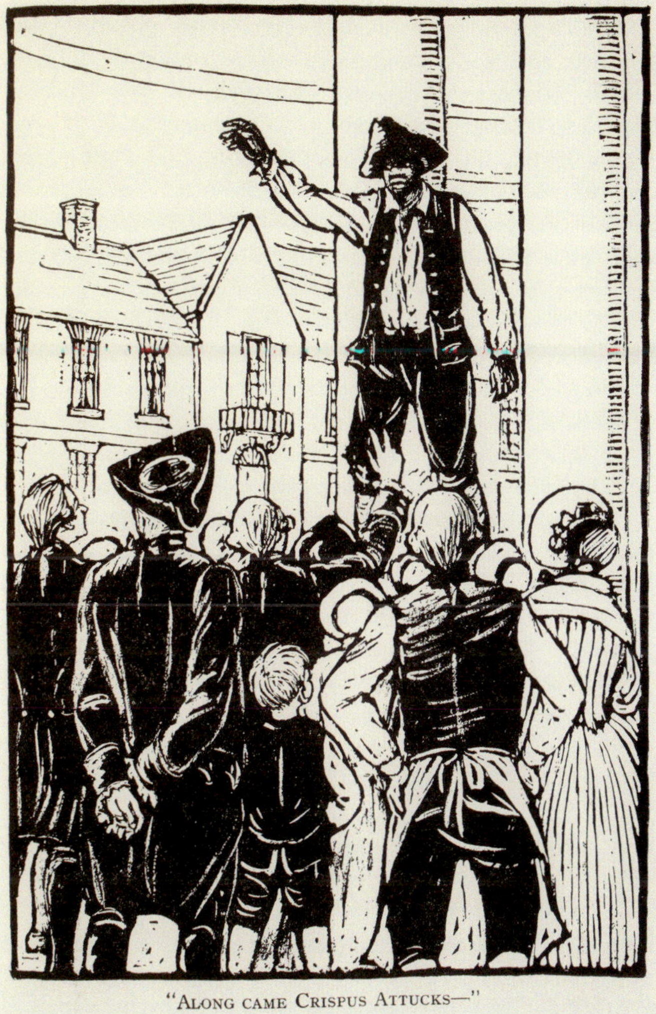

Fig. 31 Aaron Douglas (1899–1979), cover from *For Freedom: A Biographical Story of the American Negro* by Arthur Huff Fauset (Philadelphia: Franklin Pub. and Supply Co., 1934). Printed matter. Delaware Art Museum, Helen Farr Sloan Library and Archives

Fig. 32 Mabel Betsy Hill (1877–1971), *Along Came Crispus Attucks*, from *For Freedom: A Biographical Story of the American Negro* by Arthur Huff Fauset (Philadelphia: Franklin Pub. and Supply Co., 1934). Printed matter. Delaware Art Museum, Helen Farr Sloan Library and Archives

to have her create the role" in the original production.[96] These actors had achieved success on screen and stage, performing internationally, and the production itself rated a page in *Life* magazine.[97]

Although Gershwin called it a "folk opera," *Porgy and Bess* was a product of the Jazz Age. Starting in the 1920s, Gershwin pulled from jazz and blues for his compositions. With lasting hits like "Summertime" from *Porgy and Bess* and *Rhapsody in Blue*, his reputation eclipsed that of his African American sources. The story and sound of *Porgy and Bess* are rooted in the era when jazz began to drive appreciation for and appropriation of Black culture in the United States.

The Souvenir Program for the show is full of photographs of the cast, writers, producer, and composer, but its cover is an illustration by Al Hirschfeld, a white artist who gained fame for his celebrity caricatures in the Jazz Age. With its flattened forms and clear-line drawing, the image is dynamic and modern, but its depiction of the cast reflects racist stereotypes. Hirschfeld delineated the leads in his typical manner, drawn as individuals, but the surrounding figures are caricatures of African Americans

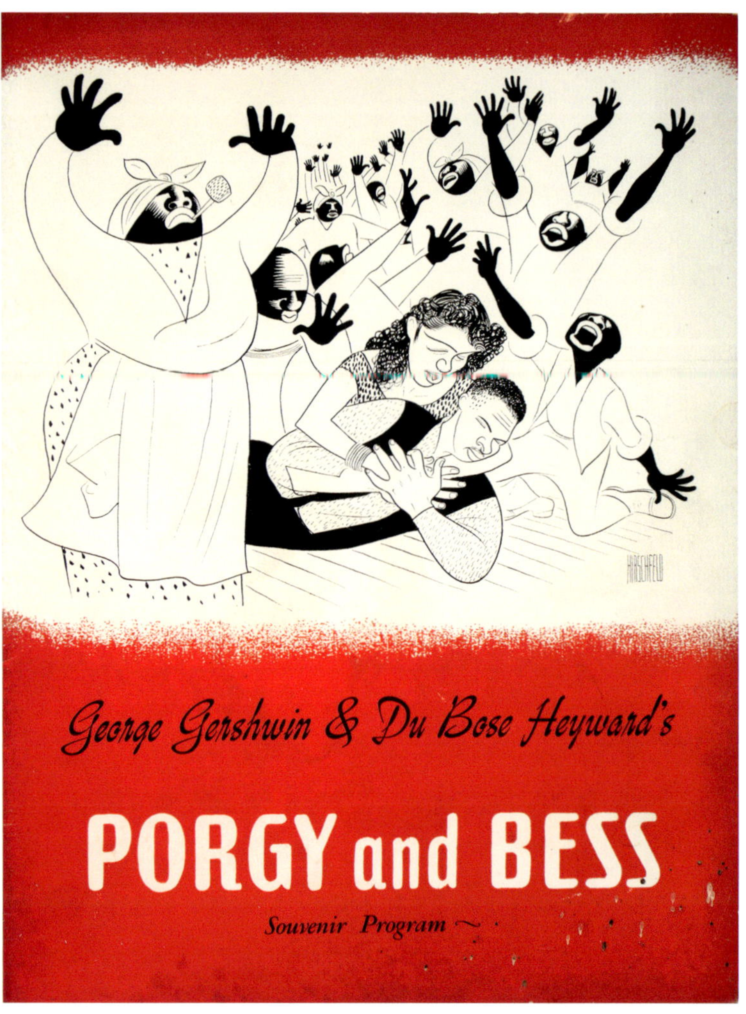

Fig. 33 Al Hirschfeld (1903–2003), cover from Souvenir Program from *George Gershwin and DuBose Heyward's Porgy and Bess*, 1942. Printed matter. Delaware Art Museum, Helen Farr Sloan Library and Archives. © The Al Hirschfeld Foundation. www.AlHirschfeldFoundation.org

Fig. 34 Fred A. Mayer (1904–?), cover from Playbill from *Porgy and Bess*, Majestic Theatre, New York, 1942. Printed matter. Delaware Art Museum, Helen Farr Sloan Library and Archives

Fig. 35 Cover from Stagebill from *Porgy and Bess*, Studebaker Theatre, Chicago, 1942. Printed matter. Delaware Art Museum, Helen Farr Sloan Library and Archives

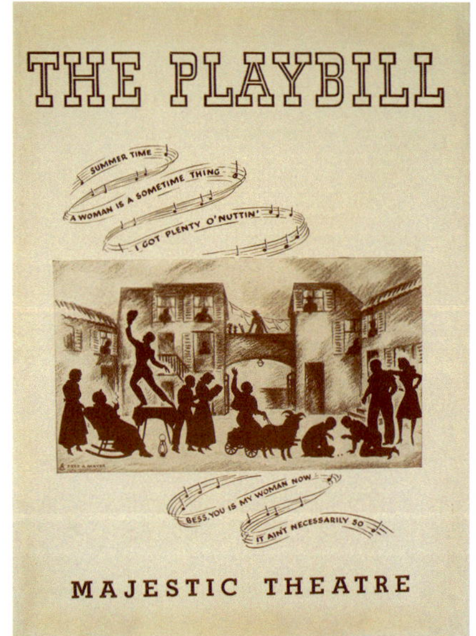

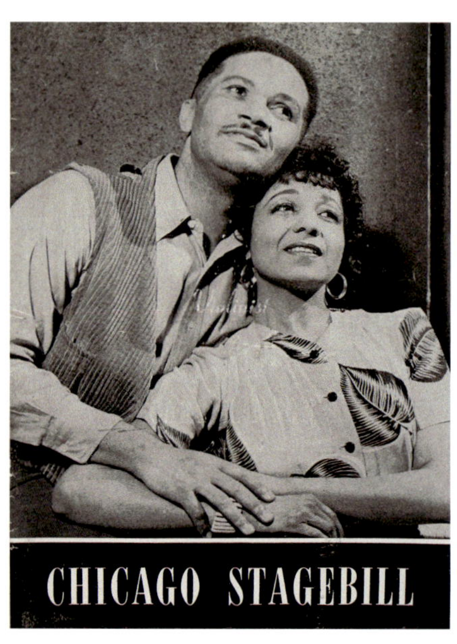

with solid black skin and large white lips that recall blackface minstrelsy (fig. 33). Hirschfeld's image appeared on the first round of playbills for the show, but it was soon replaced. The cover of the playbill from New York's Majestic Theatre from June 1942 featured a new illustration with silhouetted forms that were the specialty of white illustrator Fred A. Mayer (fig. 34). And when the production opened in November at Chicago's Studebaker Theatre, the program cover featured a publicity photograph of the leads, skirting the promises and problems of illustration altogether (fig. 35).

The Jazz Age had begun with moral panic about the behavior of American youth. Expectations around race and gender drove the fascination with and condemnation of jazz clubs, flappers, and college youths. With pretty cover girls and wholesome fiction, mainstream magazines sought to defuse these changes and reassert traditional norms, while other publications demanded change and pointed the way to alternative futures. By the early 1940s, however, magazines and newspapers were incorporating more photographs in their issues. Many of the illustrators who had recorded and shaped the previous two decades had become painters and art instructors, while others had gone to work in Hollywood. The era of flappers and speakeasies was past, and Art Deco aesthetics no longer seemed modern. But the iconic images of this vibrant era that remain, chronicled by American illustrators, fuel our understanding of the Jazz Age.

ENDNOTES

1. Coles Phillips's advertisement for Palmolive appeared in *The Ladies' Home Journal* (May 1919): 127; and *Pictorial Review* (May 1919): 88.

2. Other issues of *The Crisis* with Egyptian motifs on covers include Laura Wheeler Waring's *The Strength of Africa* cover for September 1924, Charles Dawson's *Education Number* for August 1927, Aaron Douglas's cover design for May 1928, and Joyce Carrington's cover for September 1928.

3. For a thorough analysis of Egyptian imagery in *The Crisis*, see Amy Helene Kirschke, *Art in Crisis: W. E. B. Du Bois and the Struggle for African American Identity and Memory* (Bloomington: Indiana University Press, 2007), 137–46. On page 137 she points out: "Because Europeans had appropriated ancient Egyptian civilization as part of their heritage, they already recognized it as 'high culture,' which fit into Du Bois's idea of what African American culture should strive for."

4. Historians of jazz point out that the term was also spelled "jass" and "jaz" as the music developed.

5. Mentions of jazz bands and jazz orchestras were common by 1917 in newspapers targeted to Black and white audiences.

6. "Techau Tavern," *San Francisco Chronicle*, August 28, 1916.

7. Gordon Seagrove, "Blues Is Jazz and Jazz Is Blues," *Chicago Tribune*, July 11, 1915, 54. For a deep dive into the importance of this article and the biography of its author, see Robert Loerzel, "A Tribune Reporter Discovers Jazz and Blues," https://www.robertloerzel.com/2023/07/26/a-tribune-reporter-discovers-jazz-and-blues/. Accessed October 15, 2023.

8. "The Jazz Age," *Capital Journal* (Salem, OR), October 13, 1919, 4. A more subtle take on the connection between "primitive" cultures and jazz is found in Ben Hecht, "Jazz," *Smart Set* 54 (February 1918): 117–23. For a scholarly analysis of this response, see Maureen Anderson, "White Reception of Jazz in America," *African American Revue* 36 (Spring 2004): 135–45.

9. One example of criticism of jazz dancing: "[I]t has lowered the dance to vulgarity, a source of disgust to the spectator and frequently debasement to the participant. The jazz dance is a discord in civilized society, though harmonizing well with the jungle." From "The Jazz Age," 4. Criticism of jazz dancing also came from the Black leaders. See "Sparks from the Law Enforcement Anvil," *Star of Zion*, November 1, 1922, 2. This article quotes educator Mary M. Bethune: "Jazz has done more than anything else to demoralize the womanhood of our race."

10. Notices of jazz performances constitute most mentions of jazz in the *Chicago Defender*. The phrase "jazz age" does not come up. In 1922 *Star of Zion* reported negative assessments of jazz as an immoral force but also reproduced an article from the *New Amsterdam News* that mocked these fears: "Does Jazz Dancing Craze People?," *Star of Zion,* April 27, 1922, 5.

11. "Says God Can Utilize Jazz," *Harrisburg Telegraph*, November 24, 1919, 6. Versions of this story circulated nationally. See, for example: "Jazz Age, but Pastor Hopeful," *Tacoma Daily Ledger*, November 26, 1919, 3.

12. F. Scott Fitzgerald pointed to youth as the driver of the Jazz Age, noting that plenty of elders had joined in the hedonism by 1923. "Echoes of the Jazz Age," *Scribner's Magazine* 90 (November 1931): 460–61. Phillipa Martin, "Where Is the Middle-Aged Man?," *Daily Mirror* (London, England), March 20, 1919, 7.

13. Theodore Peterson, *Magazines in the Twentieth Century* (Urbana: University of Illinois Press, 1958), 54.

14. There are many nuanced readings of the politics of wealth in the 1920s. For example, see Lynn Dumenil, *The Modern Temper: American Culture and Society in the 1920s* (New York: Hill and Wang, 1995), 3–97.

15. For a detailed discussion of *New Masses*, see Andrew Hemingway, *Artists on the Left: American Artists and the Communist Movement, 1926–1956* (New Haven, CT: Yale University Press, 2002), 7–46. On *The Masses,* see Rebecca Zurier, *Art for the Masses: A Radical Magazine and its Graphics, 1911–1917* (Philadelphia: Temple University Press, 1988).

16. More than half of the covers of *The Crisis* published in 1920, 1921, and 1922 fit the formula of "pretty girls." Others depicted works of art by Black artists, portraits of important Black men, holiday themes, or more symbolic subject matter. On the importance of beauty culture in pictures of African American women, see Deborah Willis, "Introduction," in *Posing Beauty: African American Images from the 1890s to the Present* (New York: W. W. Norton and Company, 2009), xvii–xxix.

17. Of the portraits that appeared in *The Crisis*, Deborah Willis observed: "These portraits were consciously selected for their depiction of racial progress and positive impact on perceptions of the black middle class." Willis, "The Photographic Portrait: Constructing An Ideal," in *Let Your Motto Be Resistance: African American Portraits* (Washington, DC: National Museum of African American History and Culture, 2007), 22. W. E. B. Du Bois believed in engaging art for political ends, famously writing, "I do not care a damn for any art that is not used for propaganda." Du Bois, "Criteria for Negro Art," *The Crisis* 32 (October 1926): 296.

18. W. E. B. Du Bois, "The True Brownies," in *The Crisis* 18 (October 1919): 285.

19. Caroline Goeser, *Picturing the New Negro: Harlem Renaissance Print Culture and Modern Black Identity* (Lawrence: University Press of Kansas, 2007), 75. This book is invaluable for its deep research and analysis of illustration in the Black press during the Harlem Renaissance.

20. On *Bungleton Green* and Jay Jackson, see Tim Jackson, *Pioneering Cartoonists of Color* (Jackson: University of Mississippi Press, 2016), 22–24, 61–64, 77–78.

21. On Jackie Ormes, see Nancy Goldstein, "Lost Imprints: Rediscovering the Work and Life of Cartoonist Jackie Ormes," in *Imprinted: Illustrating Race*, ed. Robyn Phillips-Pendleton and Stephanie Haboush Plunkett (Stockbridge, MA: Norman Rockwell Museum, 2022), 106–17.

22. Corey Ford, "I Wonder What Happened to Tony," *Cosmopolitan* 105 (July 1938): 39.

23. Using extensive quantitative data, Peterson points out that the advent of radio, movies, and even television did not shrink the market for magazines. Peterson, *Magazines in the Twentieth Century*, 40.

24. On caricature, see Wendy Wick Reaves, *Celebrity Caricature in America* (Washington, DC: National Portrait Gallery, 1998).

25. Quoted in Reaves, 124.

26. Marguerite Mooers Marshall, "Our 'Younger Marrieds' Outflap the 'Flappers,' a Young Author's Thought," *St. Louis Post-Dispatch*, April 21, 1922, 38.

27. N. C. Wyeth to Andrew Newell Wyeth II, March 24, 1926. Quoted in *The Wyeths: The Letters of N. C. Wyeth, 1901–1945*, ed. Betsy James Wyeth (Boston: Gambit, 1971), 719–20.

28. Alain Locke, "Harlem," *Survey Graphic* 53, no. 11 (March 1, 1925): 629.

29. The photograph is in the Carl Van Vechten Papers Relating to African American Arts and Letters, Box 86, Beinecke Rare Book and Manuscript Library, Yale University. The photographs at the Beinecke are online at https://collections.library.yale.eaccesseddu/catalog/2019632. Accessed December 10, 2023.

30. Singer's portrait is so precise that Calloway's suit and his pose can be recognized from Carl Van Vechten's photographs of the artist. As a mature illustrator, Singer would use photographic references, as he did for this portrait.

31. Donated by Calloway's daughter, several of Arthur Singer's portraits of Calloway are in the collection of the National Museum of African American History and Culture, along with posters, portraits, and caricatures by other artists. On Singer, see Paul Singer and Alan Singer, *The Wildlife Art of an American Master* (Rochester, NY: RIT Press, 2017), esp. 10–11. I am grateful to Carlos Alejandro, Executive Director of the Cab Calloway Foundation, and Alan Singer, son of Arthur Singer, for making me aware of these works and to staff at NMAAHC for confirming the date on Singer's canvas.

32. F. Scott Fitzgerald, "Echoes of the Jazz Age," *Scribner's Magazine* 90 (November 1931): 459.

33. Pulps kept costs low by hiring less successful writers and printing on cheap paper, though some hired well-known illustrators for their cover art. Confessionals, the reality television programs of magazines, relied on audience submissions, eliminating the need to pay professional authors.

34. On Steichen's time at *Vogue*, see William A. Ewing and Todd Brandow, eds., *Edward Steichen: In High Fashion, the Condé Nast Years, 1923–1937* (Minneapolis: Foundation for the Exhibition of Photography, 2008).

35. See John Henry Adams's covers for *The Crisis* from August 1921 and March 1922. See Wheeler Waring's illustrations for Jessie Fauset, "The Sleeper Wakes," *The Crisis* (October 1920): 267–74.

36. By the 1930s, Leyendecker absorbed the seamless style popularized by Rockwell and moved away from his signature patterned brushwork.

37. The use of illustration board, which is unstable from a long-term conservation perspective, may reflect the attitude of illustrators who increasingly saw their work in commercial terms.

38. "Slicks" are generally defined in contrast to "pulps"—cheap magazines that used rough wood-pulp paper.

39. Roger Reed and Jaleen Grove, "Diverse American Illustration Trends, 1915–1940," in *History of Illustration*, ed. Susan Doyle, Jaleen Grove, and Whitney Sherman (New York: Bloomsbury, 2018), 326.

40. James B. Carrington, "The Field of Art: American Illustration and the Reproductive Arts," *Scribner's Magazine* 72 (July 1922): 128. Carrington linked the revival of line drawing to the publishers' use of cheaper papers.

41. The term "Art Deco" was taken from the 1925 *Exposition internationale des arts décoratifs et industriels modernes* (International Exhibition of Modern Decorative and Industrial Arts) held in Paris. The term "Art Deco" did not come into use until the 1960s.

42. The early 1930s saw the opening of Art Deco buildings, including the Empire State Building, the Chrysler Building, and Radio City Music Hall in New York, and the Carbon and Carbide Building and Board of Trade Building in Chicago.

43. On nudes and classicism in 1920s American art, see Teresa A. Carbone, "Body Language: Liberation and Restraint in Twenties Figuration," in *Youth and Beauty: Art of the American Twenties* (New York: Brooklyn Museum, 2012), esp. 71–77.

44. Sometimes producing as many as three or four covers a day, Leff illustrated more than 2,000 songs in the 1920s and '30s. "Sydney Leff, 104, Artist with an Eye for Music, Dies" [obit.], *New York Times*, December 18, 2005, 58.

45. In 1923 brothers Connie, George, and Louie Immerman, who had immigrated from Latvia, opened Connie's Inn in Harlem.

46. The central figure in Leff's illustration for *Underneath the Harlem Moon* appears directly inspired by Al Hirschfeld's 1929 poster for the MGM film *Hallelujah*. The song was a minstrel number with racist lyrics mocking African Americans who had relocated to the city from the South.

47. Discussions with Dr. Theresa Leininger-Miller encouraged me to incorporate sheet music into this study. She pointed out its visual role in the American home.

48. Often called the *Survey Graphic,* the illustrated numbers of *The Survey* started in 1921, and by 1923, the publishers alternated between "graphic" numbers and "mid-monthly" numbers. Focused on in-depth analysis of national and international social and political topics, *The Survey* published on health issues, education reform, immigration, and child labor. The graphic numbers featured copious photographs, charts, graphs, and illustrations.

49. For a more detailed discussion of this issue of *The Survey*, see Goeser, *Picturing the New Negro*, 99–104. For the details of Reiss's commission, see Jeffrey C. Stewart, "Winold Reiss's American Studies," in *The Art of Winold Reiss: An Immigrant Modernist*, ed. Marilyn Satin Kushner (New-York Historical Society, 2021), 50–51.

50. *Survey Graphic* 53, no. 11 (March 1, 1925). The selection of the thirty-seven-year-old Hayes—an internationally renowned classical singer, not a jazz musician—may have reflected a desire for irreproachable respectability.

51. "Harlem Types, Portraits by Winold Reiss," *Survey Graphic* 53, no. 11 (March 1, 1925): 651–54.

52. Goeser, *Picturing the New Negro*, 102.

53. Joel A. Rogers, "Jazz at Home," *Survey Graphic* 53, no. 11 (March 1, 1925): 665.

54. Camara Dia Holloway, "James Latimer Allen, Artist–Photographer of the New Negro," in *Portraiture & the Harlem Renaissance: The Photographs of James L. Allen* (New Haven, CT: Yale University Art Gallery, 1999), 5–35.

55. Goeser, *Picturing the New Negro*, 159. Here, Goeser quotes Du Bois's reaction to another set of Covarrubias illustrations: "I am frank to say . . . that I think I could exist quite happily if Covarrubias had never been born."

56. On the role of the *Survey Graphic* in bringing Douglas to Harlem and his relationship with Reiss, see Amy Helene Kirschke, *Aaron Douglas: Art, Race, and the Harlem Renaissance* (Jackson: University Press of Mississippi, 1995), 13–31.

57. Caroline Goeser, "The Case of Ebony and Topaz: Racial and Sexual Hybridity in Harlem Renaissance Illustrations," *American Periodicals* 15, no. 1 (2005): esp. 95, 98–103.

58. The first issue included the statement of purpose: "*Black Opals* is the result of the desire of older new Negroes to encourage younger members of the group who demonstrate talent and ambition." For background, see Abby Ann Arthur Johns and Ronald M. Johnson, "Forgotten Pages: Black Literary Magazines in the 1920s," *Journal of American Studies* 8 (December 1974): 375–77.

59. Each issue of *Black Opals* measured only about nine by six inches and included sixteen or twenty pages.

60. Some of these magazines included work by Black artists or scenes of Harlem life—cartoons by E. Simms Campbell appeared in *Esquire* and Covarrubias caricatured African Americans in *Vanity Fair*—but these works rarely made the covers of the nation's major magazines.

61. On the policies of *The Post,* see Reed and Grove, "Diverse American Illustration Trends," 331. The cartoons of E. Simms Campbell, which appeared in *Life*, *Esquire*, and other venues, are some rare exceptions to the rule of mainstream magazines publishing only work by white artists.

62. See Dorey Schmidt, ed., *The American Magazine, 1890–1940* (Wilmington: Delaware Art Museum, 1979), and Peterson, *Magazines in the Twentieth Century*, esp. 3–17.

63. On magazine covers, see Margaret Cohen, "Telling a Magazine By Its Cover," in Schmidt, *The American Magazine*, 16–19.

64. The "Post formula" is described in Alan Nourie and Barbara Nourie, eds., *American Mass-Market Magazines* (New York: Greenwood Press, 1990), 446.

65. Peter C. Rollins, "George H. Lorimer and 'The Saturday Evening Post' (1898–1936)," in Schmidt, *The American Magazine*, 22–25, 75–78.

66. Norman Rockwell, as told to Thomas Rockwell, *Norman Rockwell, My Life as an Illustrator* (New York: Harry N. Abrams, 1960), 106.

67. Leyendecker eventually published 322 *Post* covers.

68. *Liberty's* inaugural cover includes a cartoon rendering of J. C. Leyendecker's Thanksgiving cover (December 1, 1923), which features a harsh caricature of a Native American trading a turkey to a portly pilgrim.

69. The recent exhibition, *Under Cover: J. C. Leyendecker and American Masculinity* (New-York Historical Society, May 5–August 13, 2023), highlighted the range of masculinity painted by Leyendecker. For Leyendecker's biography, see Judy Cutler and Lawrence Cutler, *J. C. Leyendecker: American Imagist* (New York: Abrams, 2007). An important critique of recent readings of Leyendecker comes from Michael J. Murphy, "Situating J. C. Leyendecker within the Conflicting Narratives of the Gay and Lesbian Past," *American Quarterly* 74 (December 2022): 1079–92. Leyendecker's holiday covers for *The Saturday Evening Post* often presented over-the-top historical subjects. See, for example, the Easter covers for April 11, 1925, and April 19, 1930.

70. Advertisement for Holeproof Hosiery, ca. 1922–24. Tearsheet, Helen Farr Sloan Library and Archives, Delaware Art Museum.

71. On *Life,* see Rowland Elzea, "That Was 'Life,'" in Schmidt, *The American Magazine*, 10–15, 78.

72. The lady golfer would be a running joke in the popular press through the 1920s.

73. On McMein, see https://www.illustrationhistory.org/artists/neysa-mcmein. Accessed October 21, 2023. Brian Gallagher, *Anything Goes: The Jazz Age Adventures of Neysa McMein and Her Extravagant Circle of Friends* (New York: Times Books, 1987). The Delaware Art Museum owns the original drawing for one of her earliest cover girl designs: Cover illustration for the *Sunday Magazine of the Chicago Record-Herald,* September 28, 1913. Pastel on laid paper, $19\frac{11}{16} \times 13\frac{11}{16}$ in. Gift of Helen Farr Sloan, 1988.

74. The Miss America pageant originated in 1921. Beauty contests were a fad worthy of note in the 1920s, becoming the subject of fiction and illustration.

75. George H. Douglas, *The Smart Magazines: 50 Years of Vanity Fair, The New Yorker, Life, Esquire, and The Smart Set* (Hamden, CT: Archon Books, 1991), 9.

76. "Alice-Leone Moats, 81, Journalist, Is Dead," *New York Times*, May 16, 1989, B6.

77. Alice-Leone Moats, "McClelland Barclay's Girls I Adore," *Philadelphia Inquirer*, March 18, 1934, 93.

78. Reed and Grove, "Diverse American Illustration Trends," 324.

79. Goeser, *Picturing the New Negro*, 145–70.

80. "American Book Illustrations at the Art Center," *Brooklyn Daily Eagle*, December 11, 1927, 64.

81. Quoted in Goeser, *Picturing the New Negro*, 164–65.

82. Thomas Erwin, quoted in "Best of American Illustration," *Cincinnati Enquirer*, December 8, 1928, 11.

83. Kent's illustrated *Moby Dick* was issued as a limited edition in three volumes and a trade edition.

84. "Weyhe Galleries," *Detroit Free Press,* March 23, 1930, 55.

85. Quoted in Edward H. Shenton, "Edward Shenton: Illustrator, Author, Teacher," *Illustration* 9, no. 33 (Spring 2011): 68: https://issuu.com/illomag/docs/shenton. Accessed December 1, 2023.

86. Quoted in Charles Scribner III, "Celestial Eyes: From Metamorphosis to Masterpiece," *Princeton University Library Chronicle* 53, no. 2 (Winter 1992): 144: https://doi.org/10.2307/26410056.

87. Hector Blanding, *The Door of the Double Dragon: A Romance of the China of Yesterday and To-Day* (New York: W. J. Watt and Co., 1920), frontispiece.

88. Barbara Bader, *American Picturebooks from Noah's Ark to the Beast Within* (New York: Macmillan, 1976), 23.

89. Blanche C. Aller, "Choosing Children's Books," *The Elementary English Review* 9 (October 1932): 202. According to Aller, by 1932, academics had begun to produce studies of children's reading habits and preferences.

90. "Rachel M. Varble Wins Recognition," *Courier-Journal* (Lexington, KY), September 2, 1928, 21.

91. S. H D. "The Red Cape," *Cincinnati Enquirer*, September 14, 1928, 8.

92. On McBrown's *The Picture-Poetry Book,* see also Goeser, *Picturing the New Negro*, 117–19, 200–1.

93. Inspired by African masks, the figures' eyes are rendered as slits, and the influence of Egyptian art is apparent in the way his angular figures are pictured with frontal torsos and profile faces and in the stylized papyrus flowers that bloom from the lower edge. On Douglas and Egyptian forms, see Kirschke, *Art in Crisis*, 141–43.

94. Shoshana Resnikoff, "For Freedom, by Arthur Huff Fauset," for The Wolfsonian—FIU Blog, February 11, 2021: https://wolfsonian.org/blog/2021/05/. Accessed October 19, 2023. In this period focused on racial uplift, similar projects were undertaken by other Black artists and authors, including Charles Dawson's *ABCs of Great Negroes*.

95. Jesse Kowalski, "Comics: Comic Books," in *Illustration History*: https://www.illustrationhistory.org/genres/comics-comic-books. Accessed December 1, 2023.

96. "The Players," *George Gershwin & DuBose Heyward's Porgy and Bess: Souvenir Program* (New York: Al Greenstone, 1942), 13. The opera opened with Anne Brown in the role of Bess, with Moten taking over several weeks into the production. The Hirschfeld cover likely depicts Brown rather than Moten, and that may be why it was replaced with Mayer's more generic imagery while the show was still on view in New York.

97. "Porgy & Bess: Brilliant Revival Is a Hit," *Life* 12 (February 23, 1942): 65.

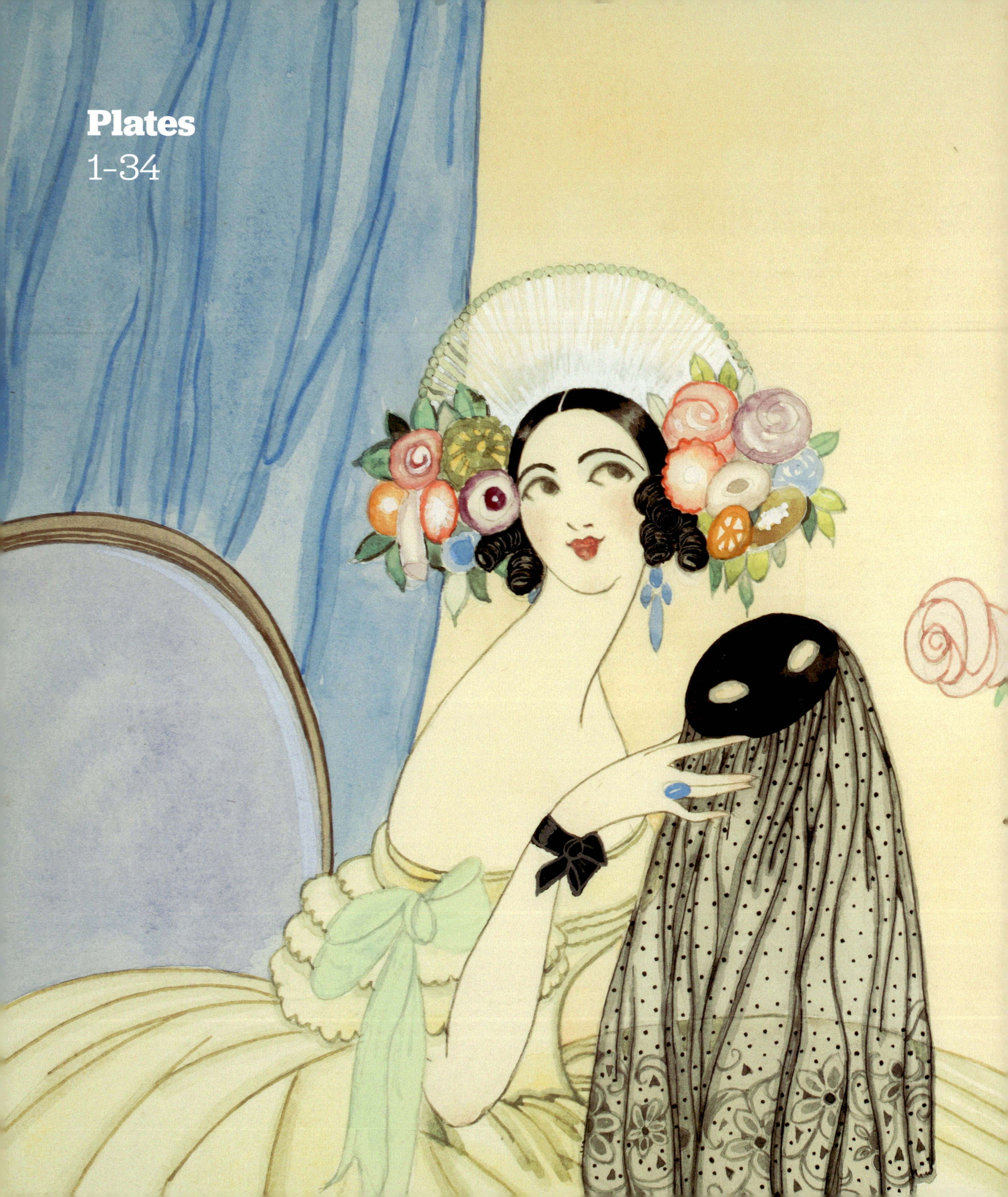

Plates

1–34

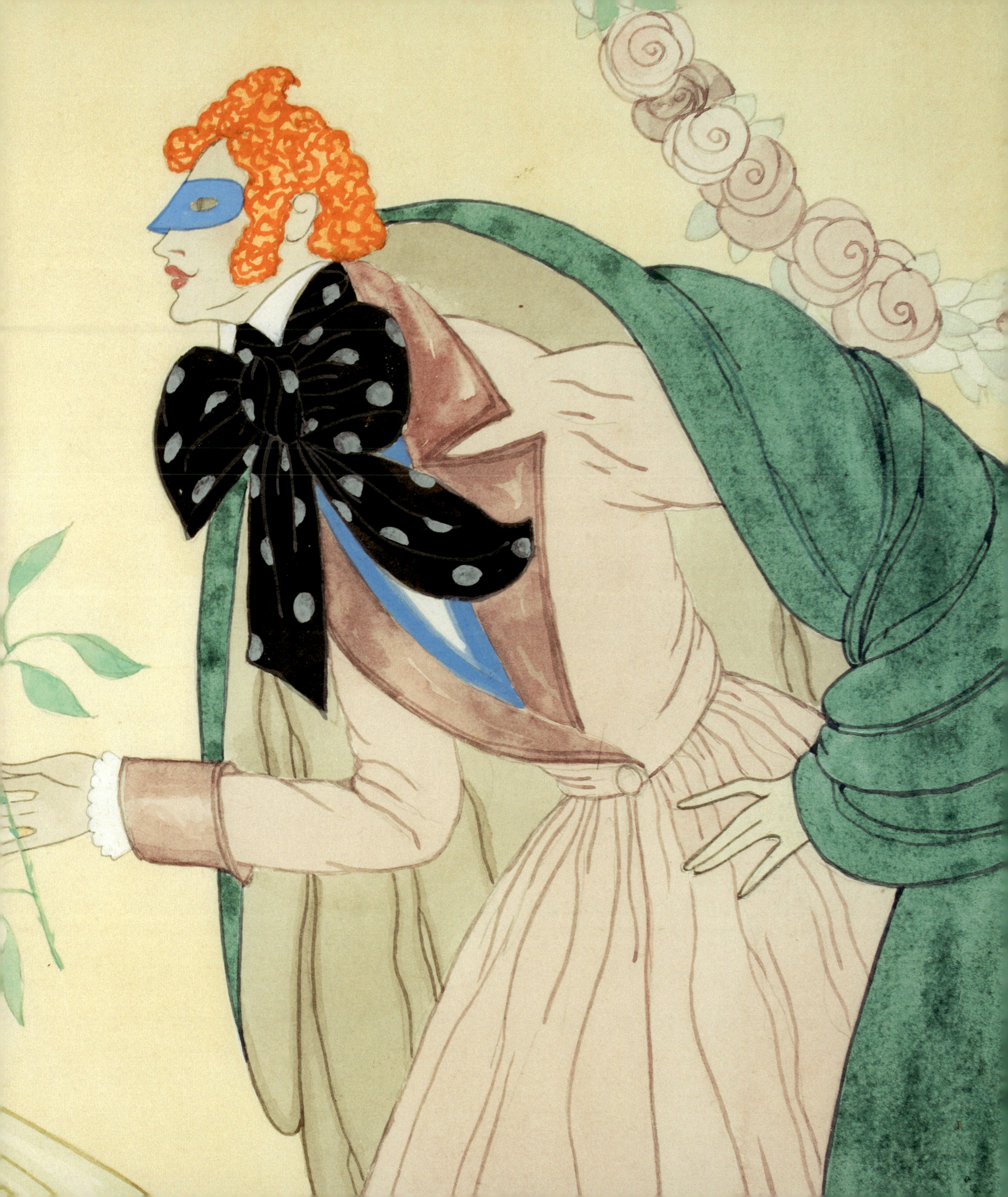

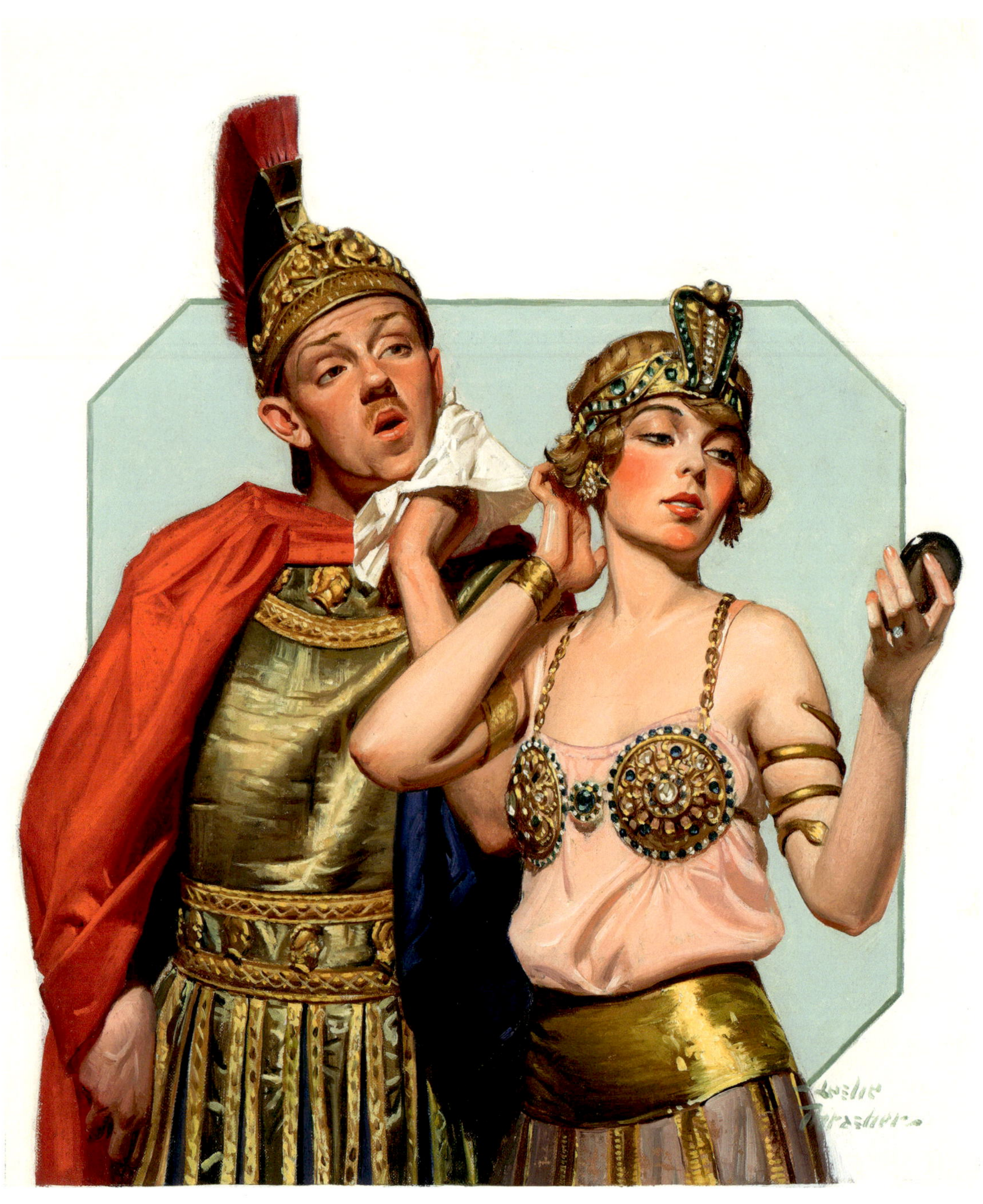

1

Leslie Thrasher (1889–1936)
I'm Dyin', Egypt, Dyin', cover for *Liberty*, April 23, 1927
Oil on canvas, 20 × 16⅛ in.
Delaware Art Museum, Gift of Mrs. Audrey Thrasher de Russow, 1973

2

J. C. Leyendecker (1874–1951)
Income Tax 1926, cover for *The Saturday Evening Post*, January 2, 1926
Oil on canvas, 33 × 25¼ in.
From the Collection of Lura J. Dolas and Theodore M. Dolas

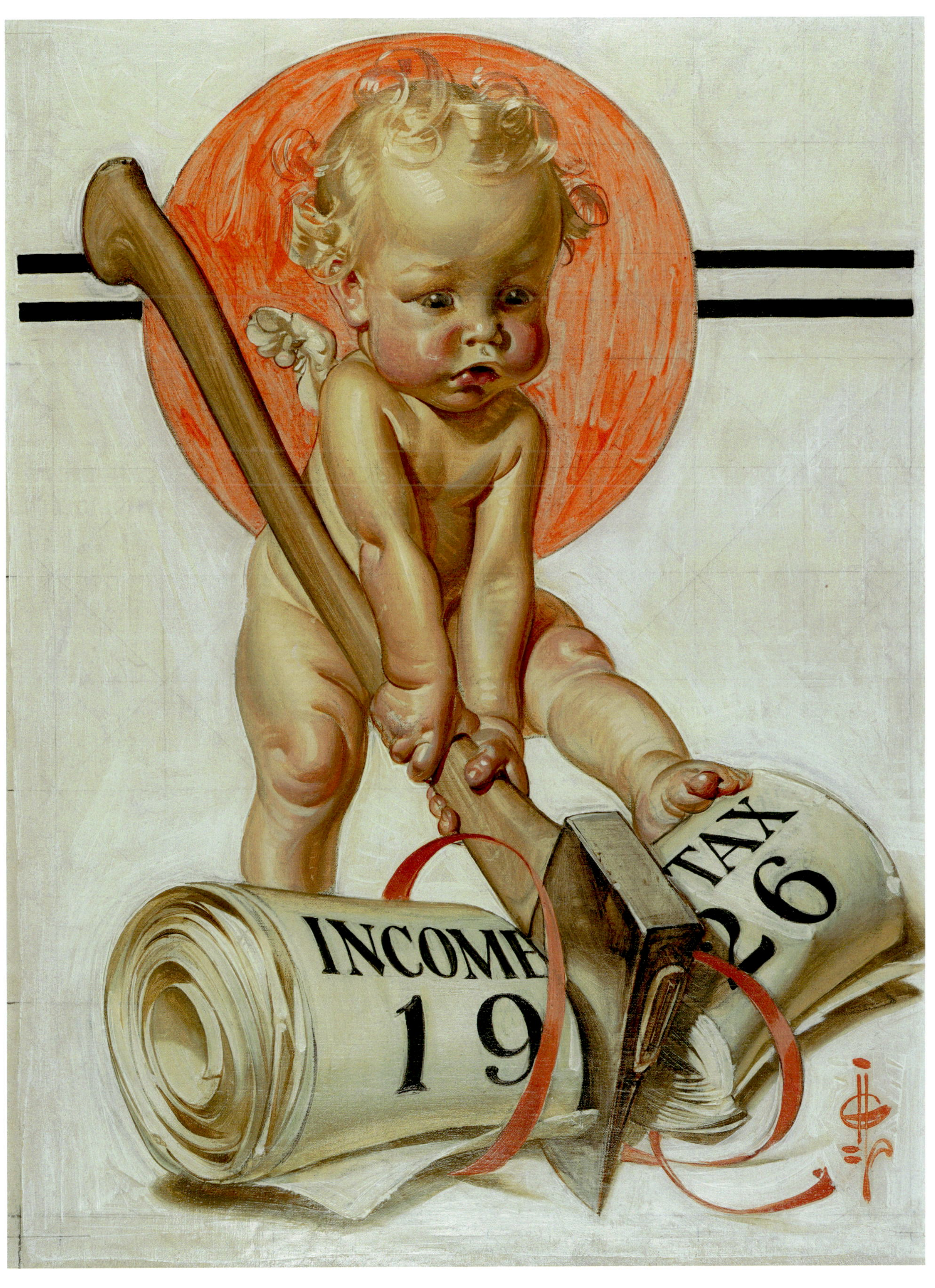
INCOME
TAX
19
26

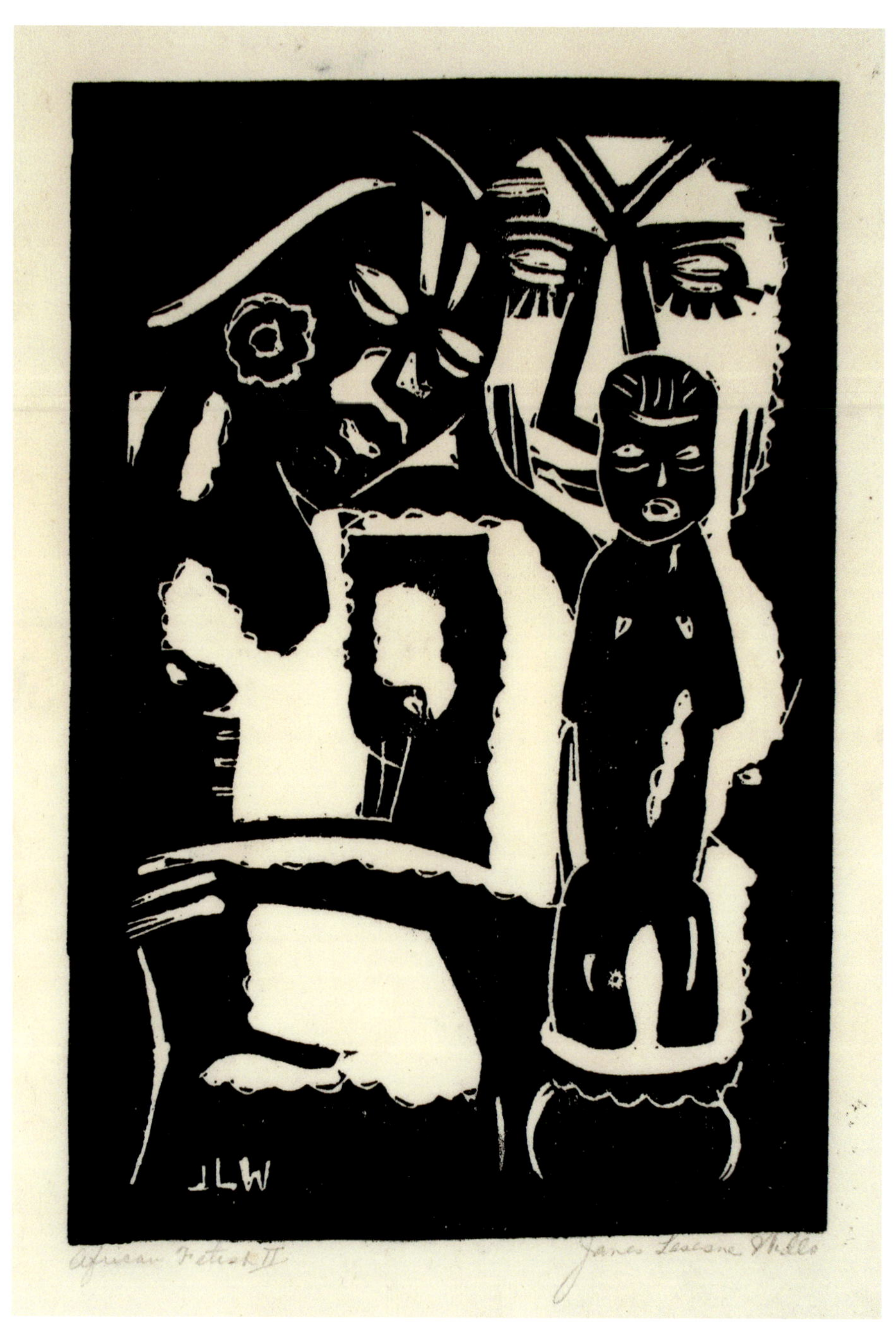

3

James Lesesne Wells (1902–1993)
African Fetish II (African Family), ca. 1929, for *New Masses*, August 1929

Linoleum cut, $8\frac{13}{16} \times 5\frac{13}{16}$ in.
Delaware Art Museum, Acquisition Fund, 2020

4

Frederick C. Alston (1895–1987)
Light of the World, 1929

Gouache on board, 25 × 17 in.
Delaware Art Museum, Acquisition Fund, 2021

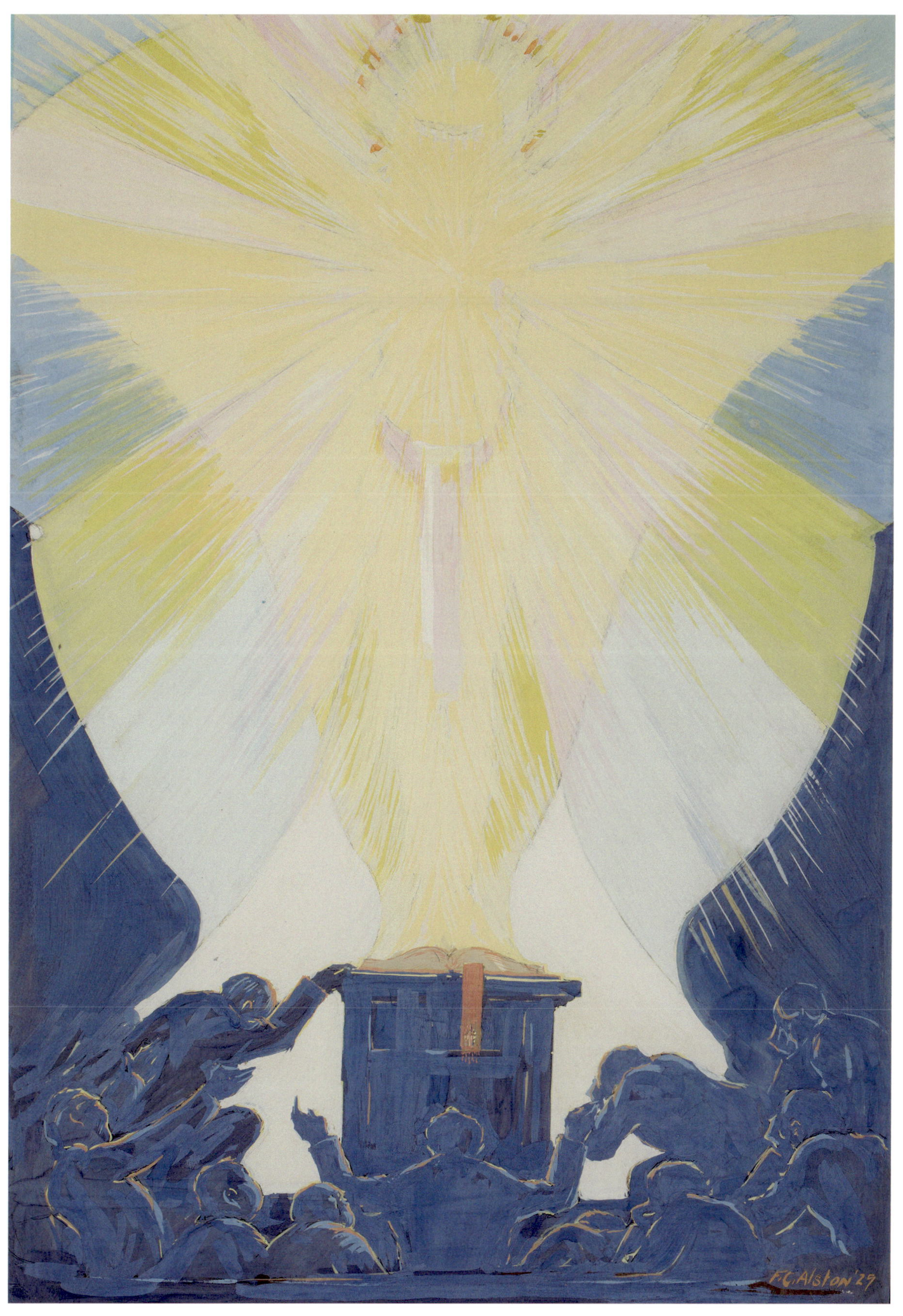
F.C. Alston '29

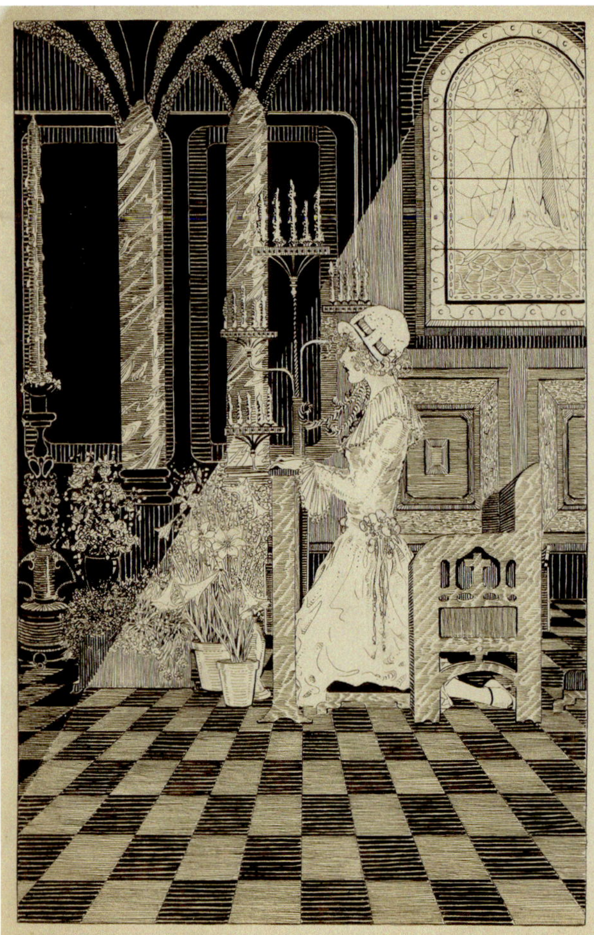
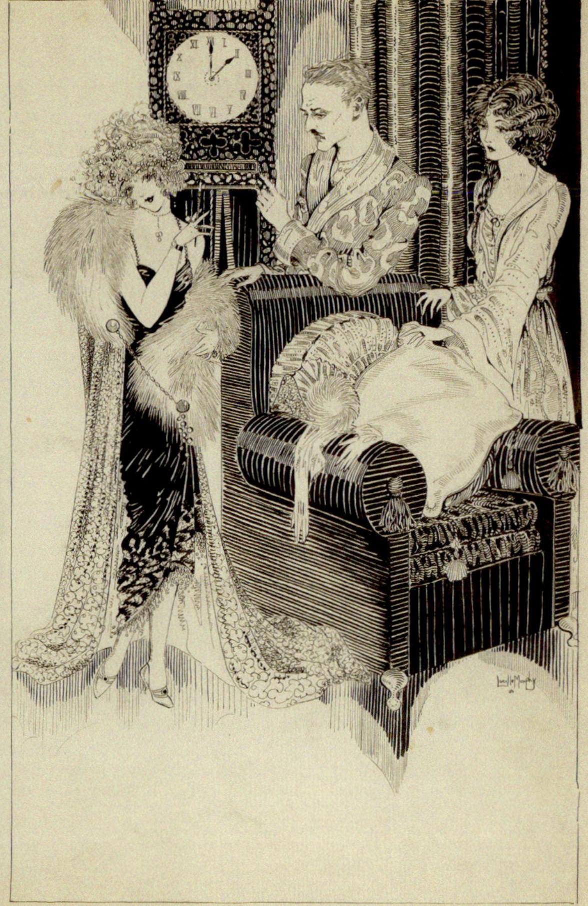

5

Lucile Murphy (1873–1956)
The Flapper—When She Is Good She Is Very Good—but—When She Is Bad She Is Horrid, 1924
Ink on illustration board, 10 3/8 × 13 5/16 in.
Delaware Art Museum, Gift of John Sloan Memorial Foundation, 1982

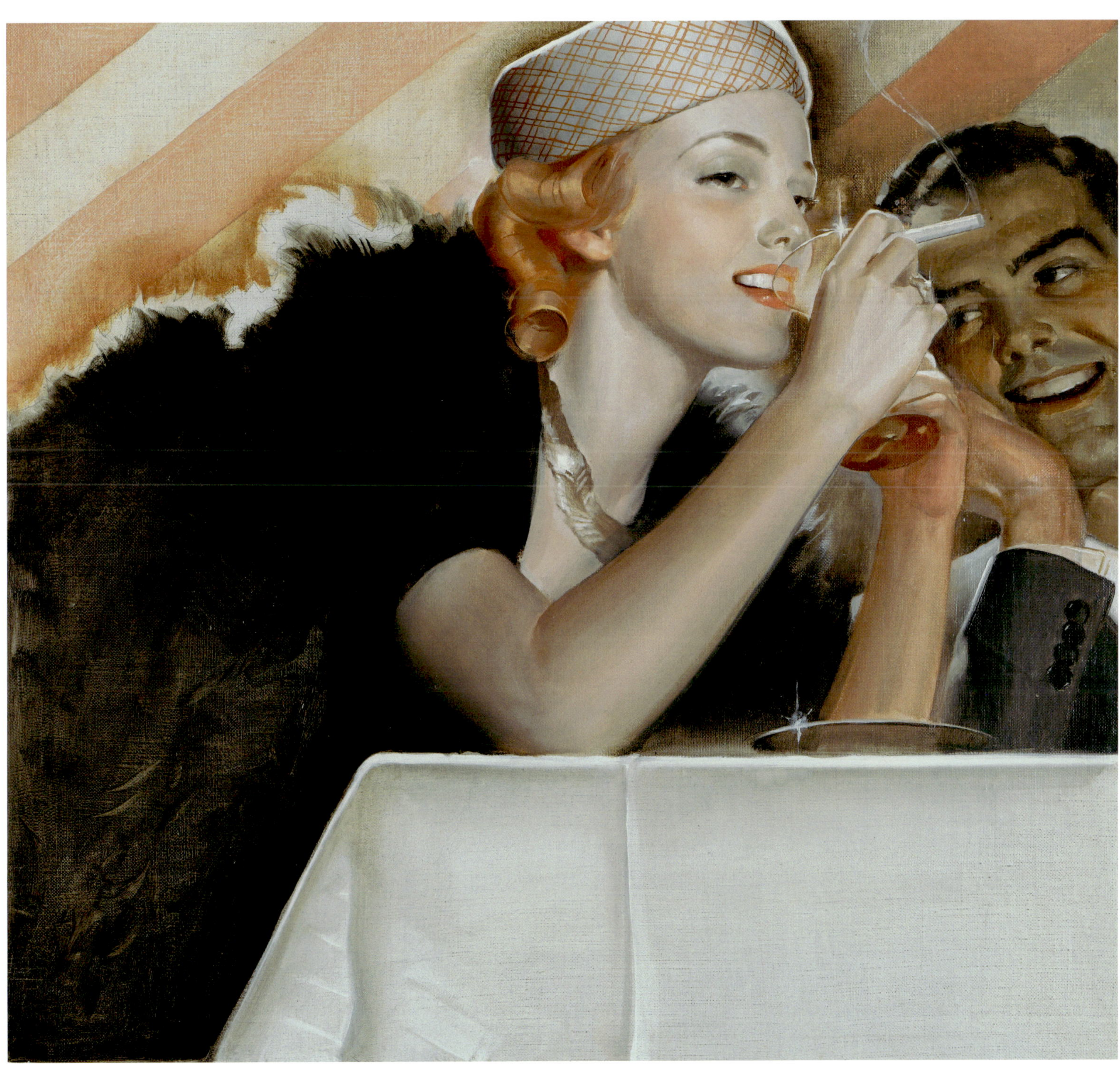

6

Michael Dolas (1912–2010)

Edie's love life was a revolving door, for "I Wonder What Happened to Tony" by Corey Ford, *Hearst's International Combined with Cosmopolitan*, July 1938

Oil on canvas, 27 × 27¼ in.
From the Collection of Lura J. Dolas and Theodore M. Dolas

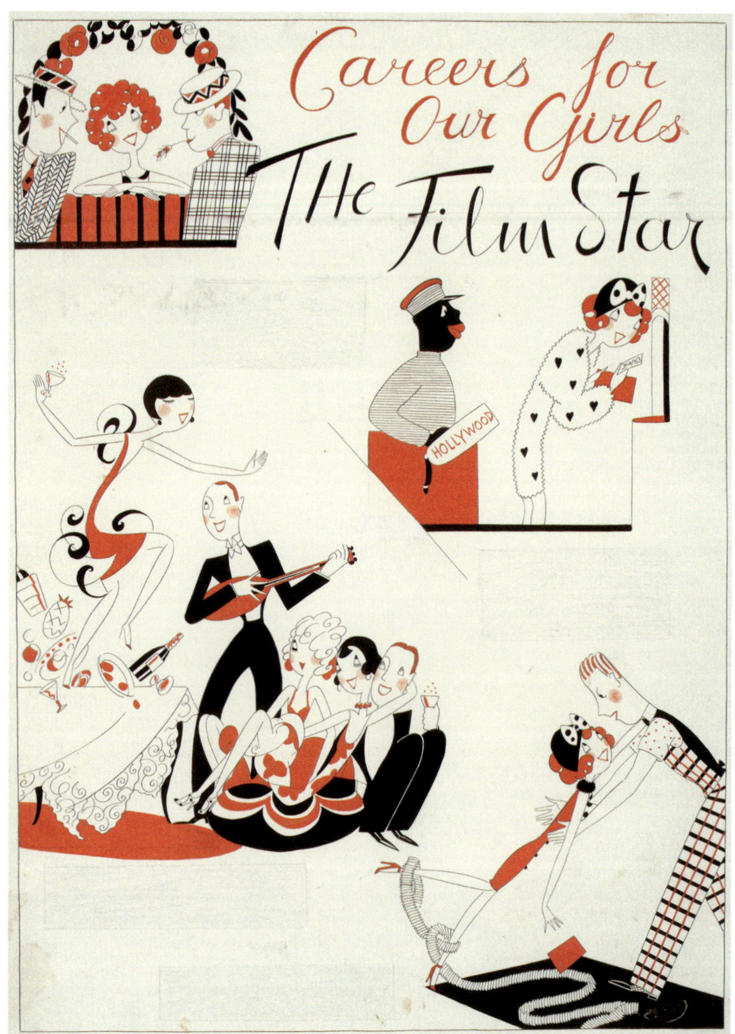

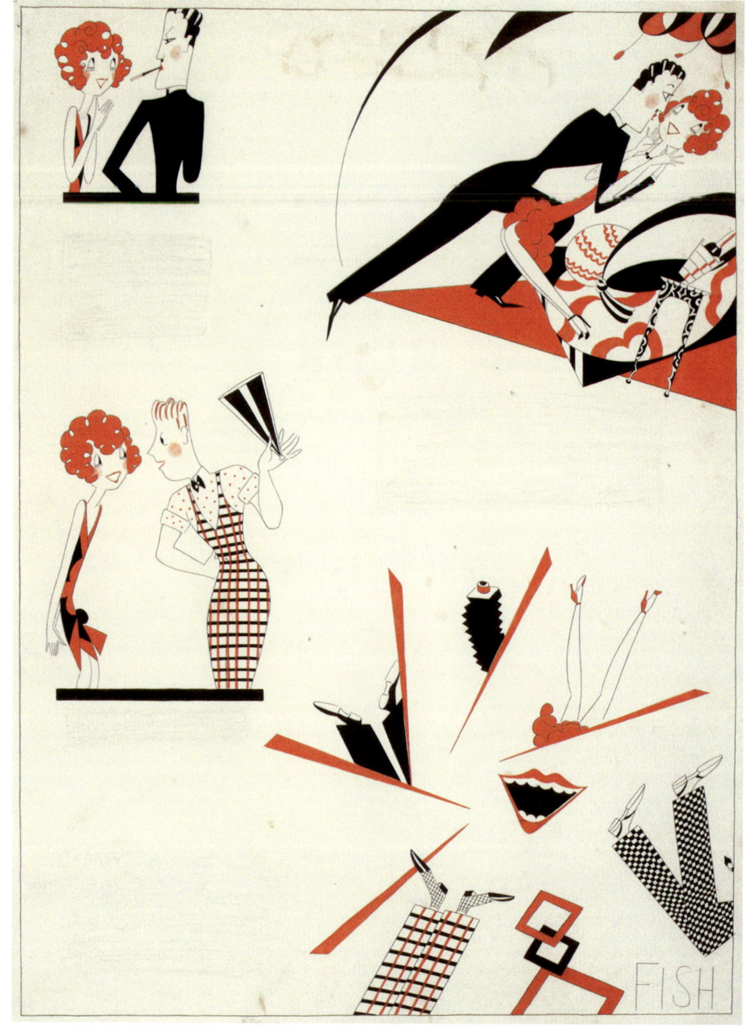

7

Anne Harriet Fish (1890–1964)
Careers for Our Girls: The Film Star, unpublished illustration for *Hearst's International Combined with Cosmopolitan*, December 1928

Gouache, ink, and graphite on paper, each: 19 × 13½ in.
Delaware Art Museum, Acquisition Fund, 2023

8

Russell Patterson (1893–1977)
Cover for *Ballyhoo*, July 1933

Watercolor, graphite, and gouache on illustration board, 11¾ × 8½ in.
Delaware Art Museum, Gift of Mr. and Mrs. William Radebaugh, 1978

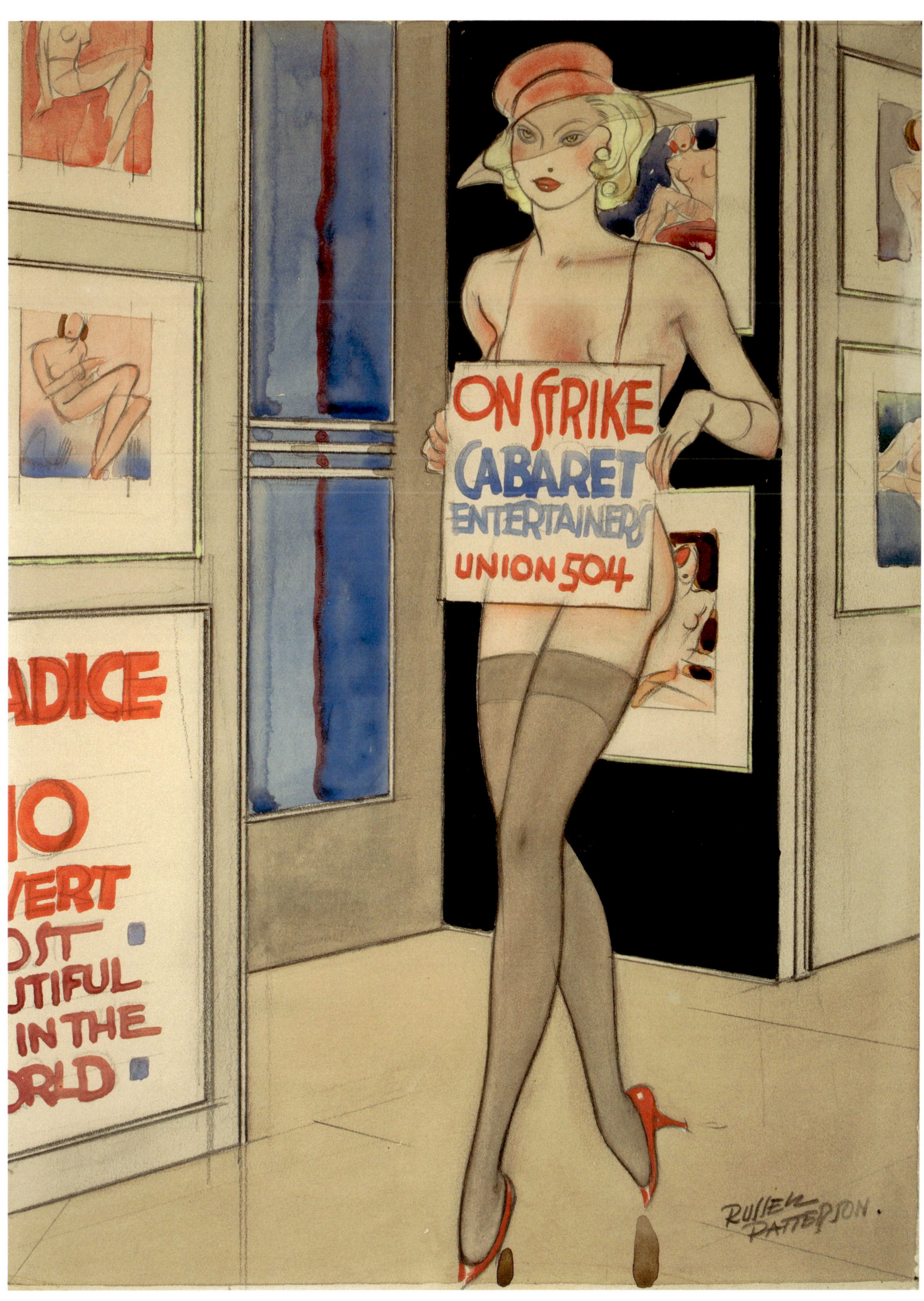
ON STRIKE
CABARET
ENTERTAINERS
UNION 504
RUSSELL PATTERSON.

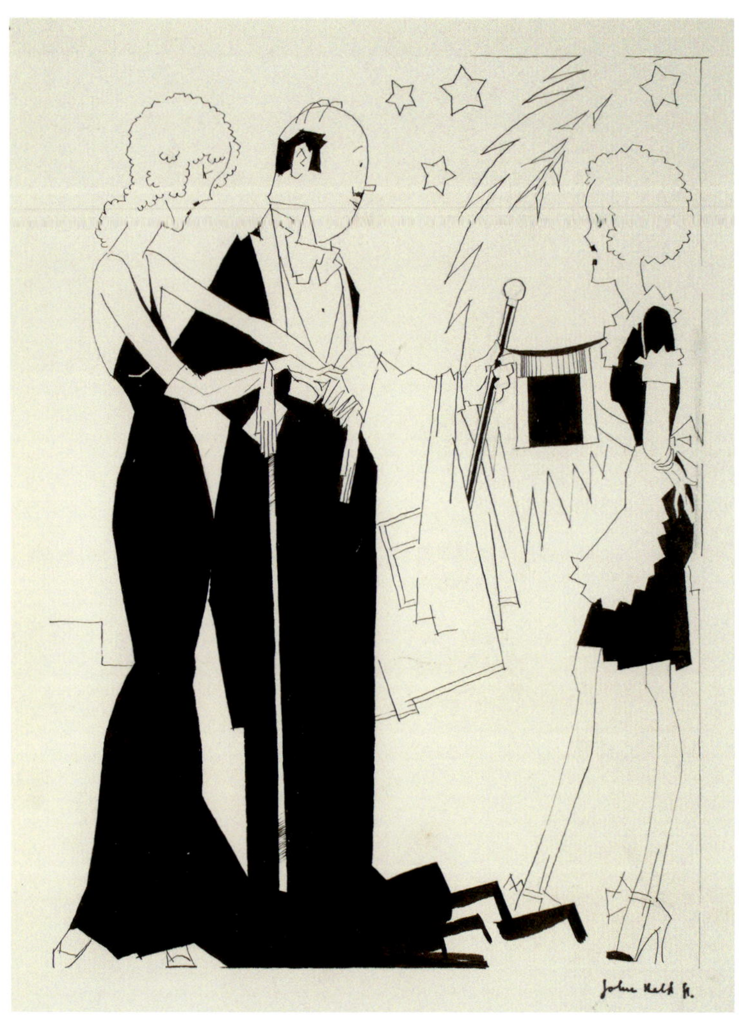

9

John Held Jr. (1889–1958)
Then we went to the Silver Slipper, for *The Flesh is Weak* (New York: Vanguard Press, 1931)
Ink on illustration board, sheet: 15 × 10¾ in.
Delaware Art Museum, Acquisition Fund, 1986

10

Erté (Romain de Tirtoff, 1892–1990)
Californie, costume design for *Milliardaires Americaines* at Théatre Fémina, Paris, 1917
Gouache with ground-powdered bronze on thin board, 8½ × 6½ in.
Delaware Art Museum, Acquisition Fund, 2018

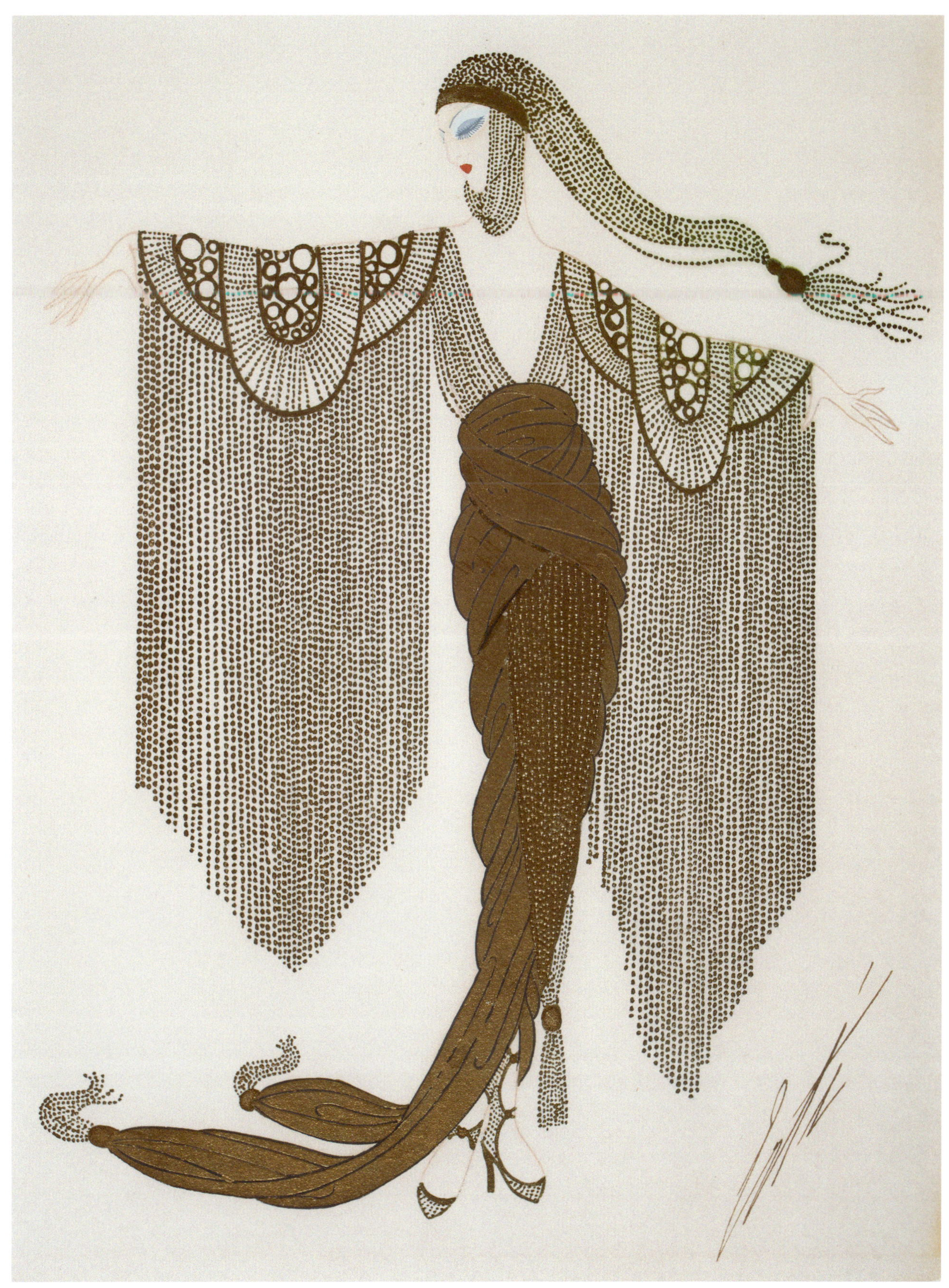

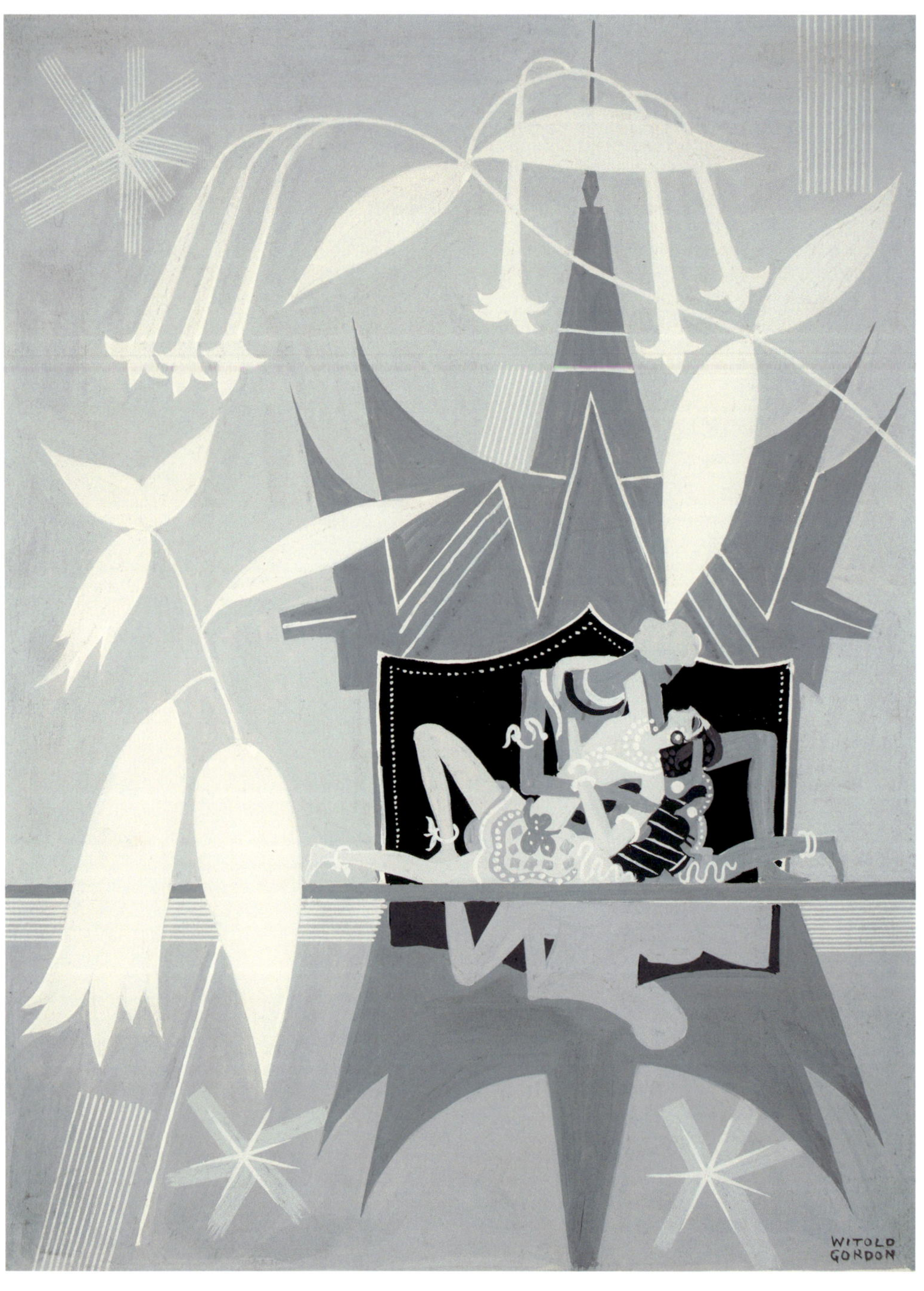

11

Witold Gordon (1885–1968)
Amoré, for *The Travels of Sindbad*, unpublished, 1932

Gouache on board, 12½ × 9¼ in.
Delaware Art Museum, Acquisition Fund, 2022

12

Beatrice Anderson (1910–?)
Design for an advertisement for Parfums Luyna, ca. 1925

Watercolor and gouache on illustration board, 13¹³⁄₁₆ × 10⁷⁄₁₆ in.
Delaware Art Museum, Louisa du Pont Copeland Memorial Fund, 2007

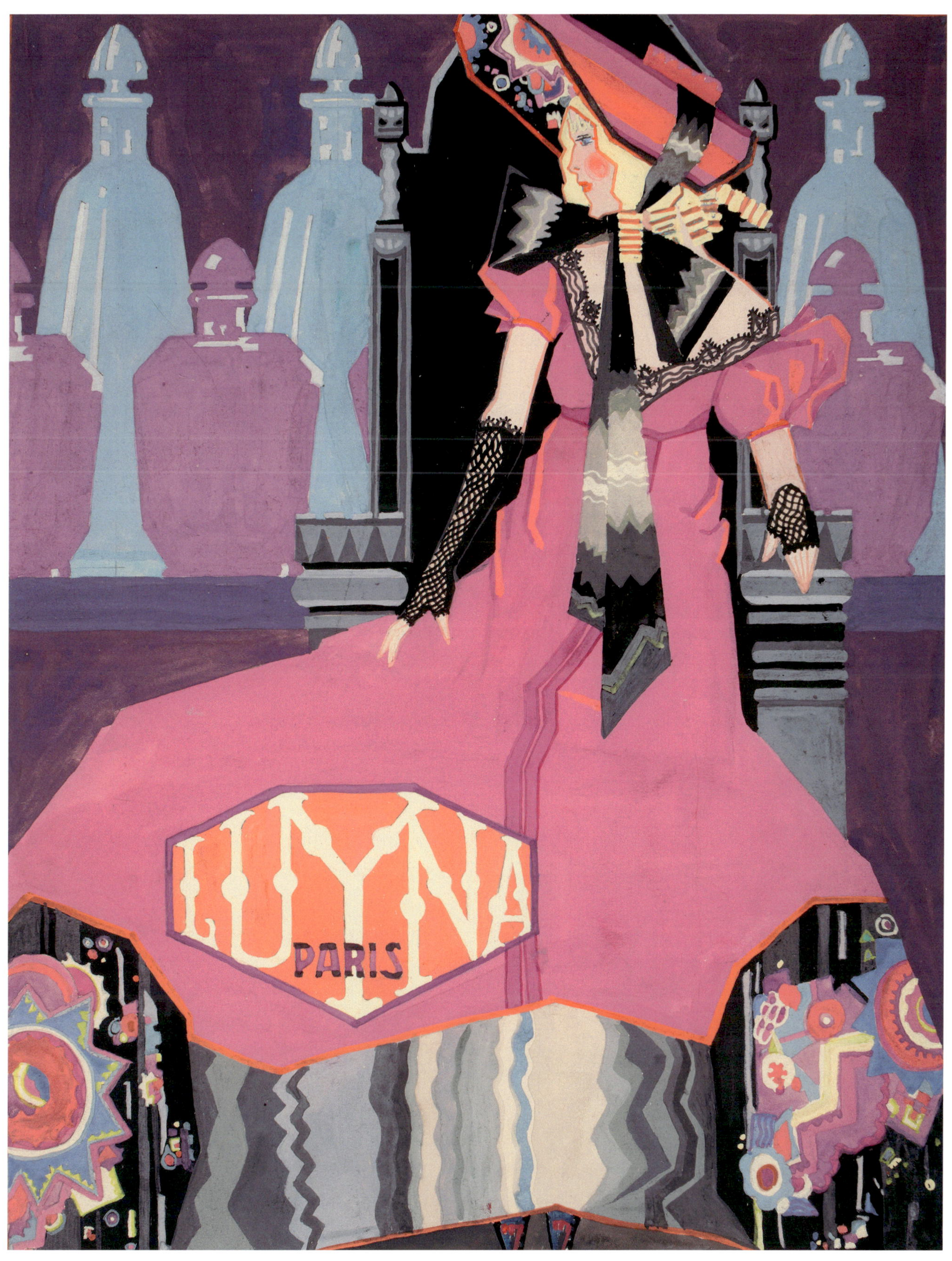
LUYNA
PARIS

13

Weimer Pursell (1906–1974)

Chicago World's Fair, A Century of Progress, 1833–1933, 1933

Offset color lithograph, sheet: 41½ × 27⅝ in.
Delaware Art Museum, Gift of Helen Farr Sloan, 1978

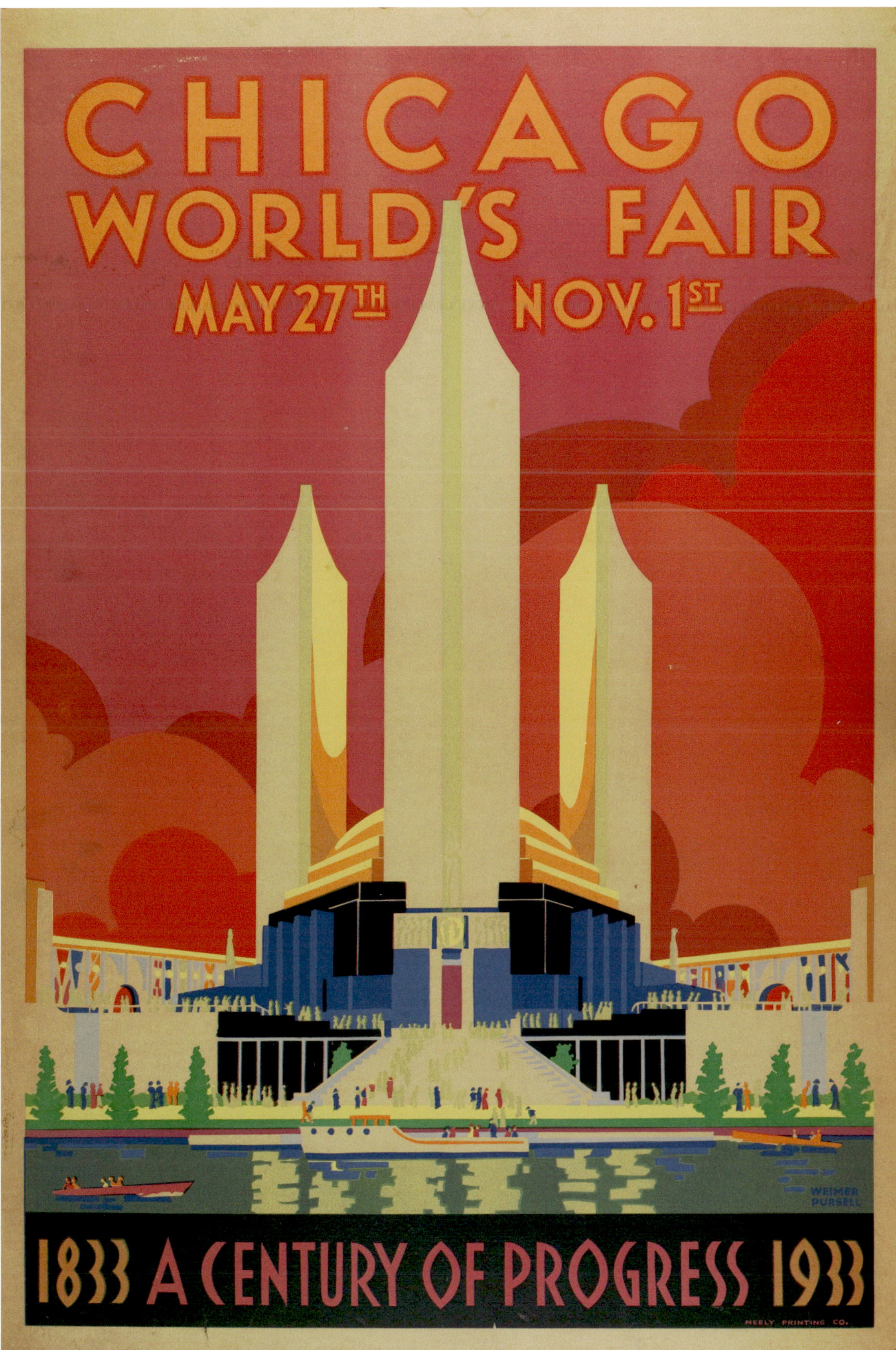
CHICAGO
WORLD'S FAIR
MAY 27TH NOV. 1ST
WEIMER PURSELL
1833 A CENTURY OF PROGRESS 1933
NEELY PRINTING CO.

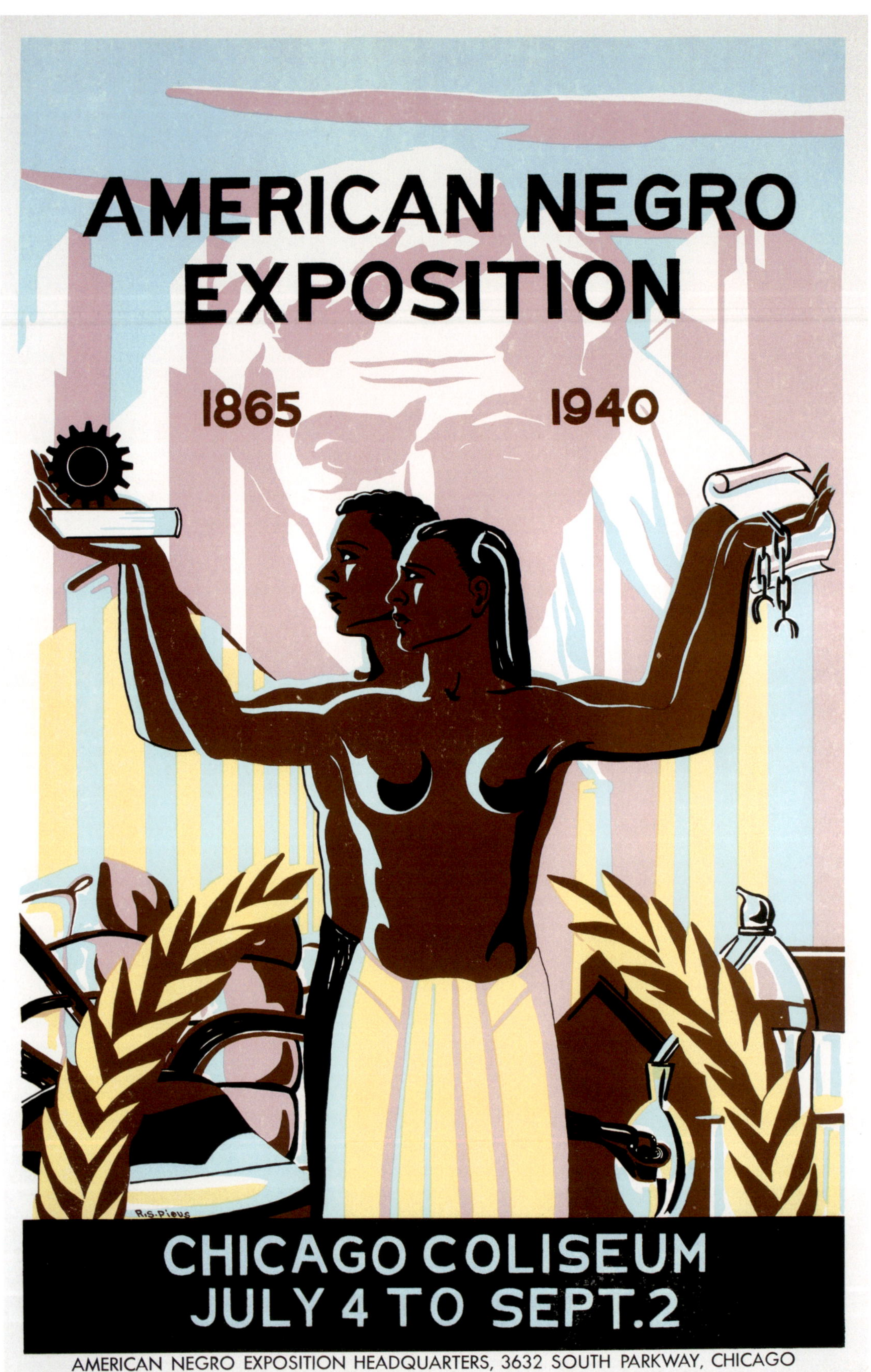
AMERICAN NEGRO
EXPOSITION
1865 1940
CHICAGO COLISEUM
JULY 4 TO SEPT. 2
AMERICAN NEGRO EXPOSITION HEADQUARTERS, 3632 SOUTH PARKWAY, CHICAGO

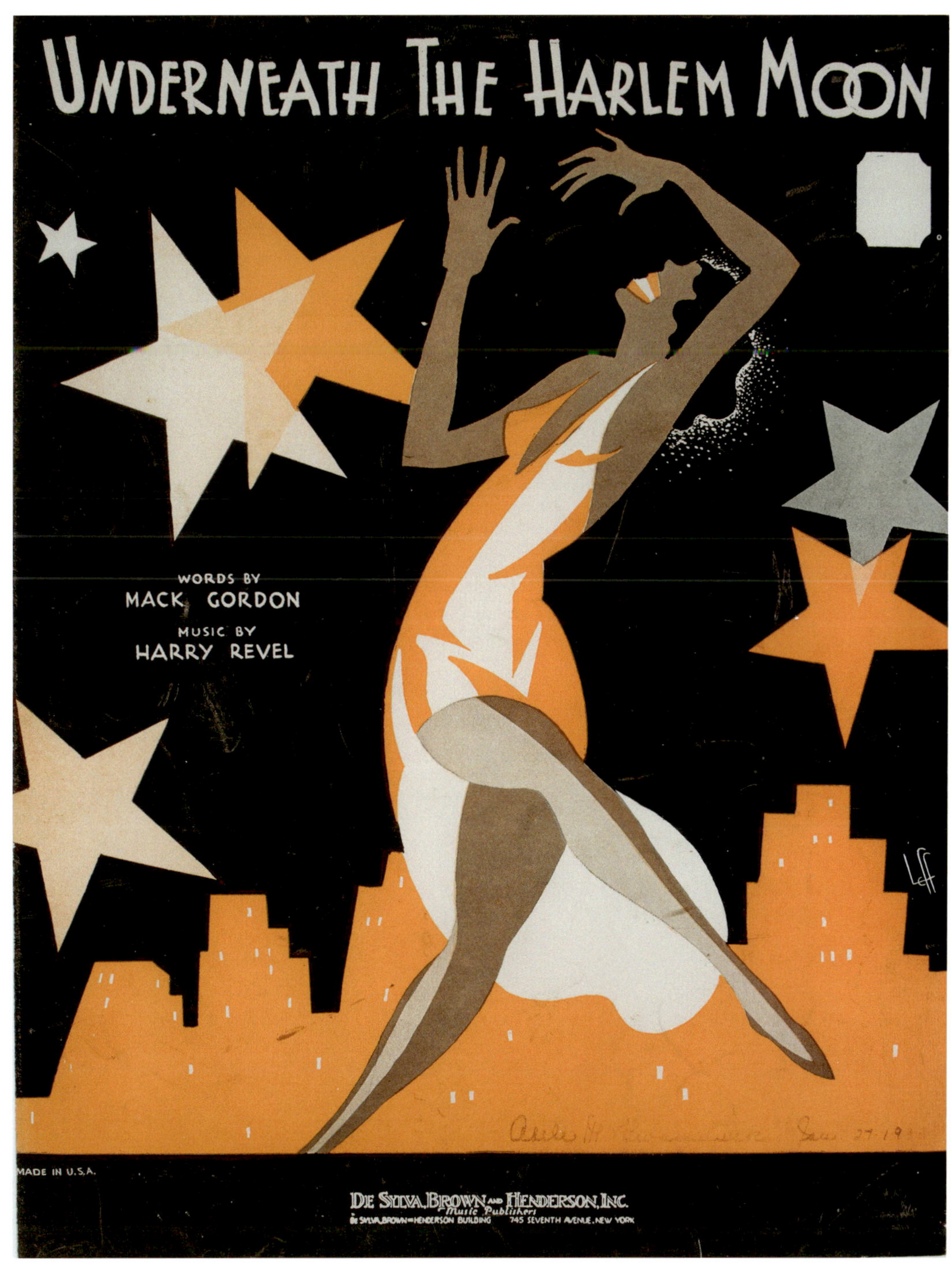

14

Robert Pious (1908–1983)
American Negro Exposition Poster, 1940

Screen print, sheet: 21⁵⁄₁₆ × 13½ in.
Delaware Art Museum, Acquired through the Gift of Norman P. Rood, 2019

15

Sydney Leff (1901–2005)
Cover from *Underneath the Harlem Moon*, 1932
(New York: De Sylva, Brown and Henderson)

Printed matter
Delaware Art Museum, Helen Farr Sloan Library and Archives

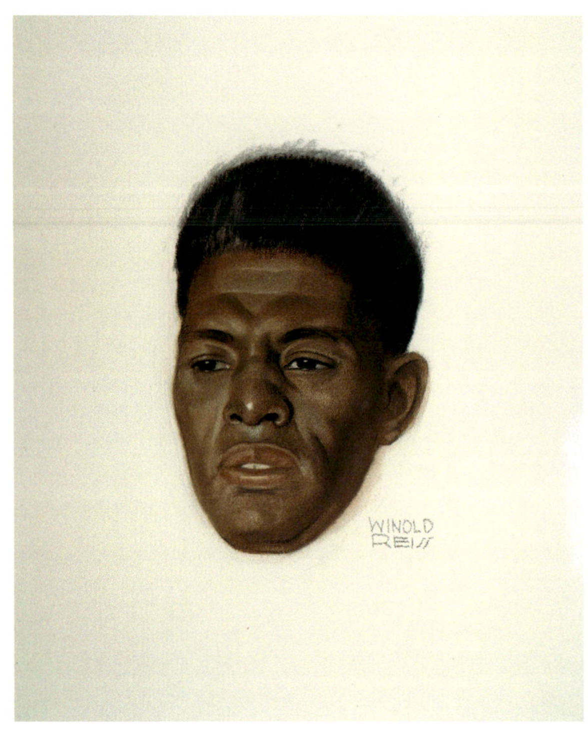

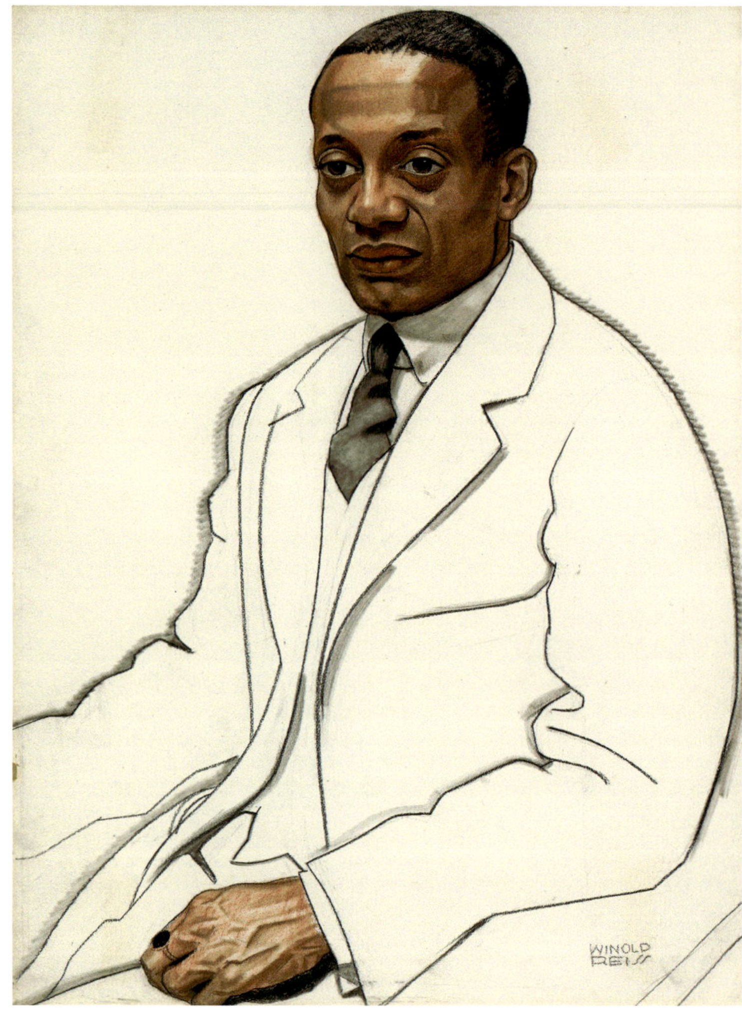

16

Winold Reiss (1886–1953)

Roland Hayes, 1924, study for *Survey Graphic*, March 1, 1925

Pastel on illustration board, 19 7/16 × 16 in.
National Portrait Gallery, Smithsonian Institution; purchase funded by Lawrence A. Fleischman and Howard Garfinkle with a matching grant from the National Endowment for the Arts

17

Winold Reiss (1886–1953)

Alain Leroy Locke, ca. 1925, study for *The New Negro: An Interpretation* (New York: Albert & Charles Boni, 1925)

Pastel on illustration board, sheet: 29 7/8 × 21 5/8 in.
National Portrait Gallery, Smithsonian Institution; purchase funded by Lawrence A. Fleischman and Howard Garfinkle with a matching grant from the National Endowment for the Arts

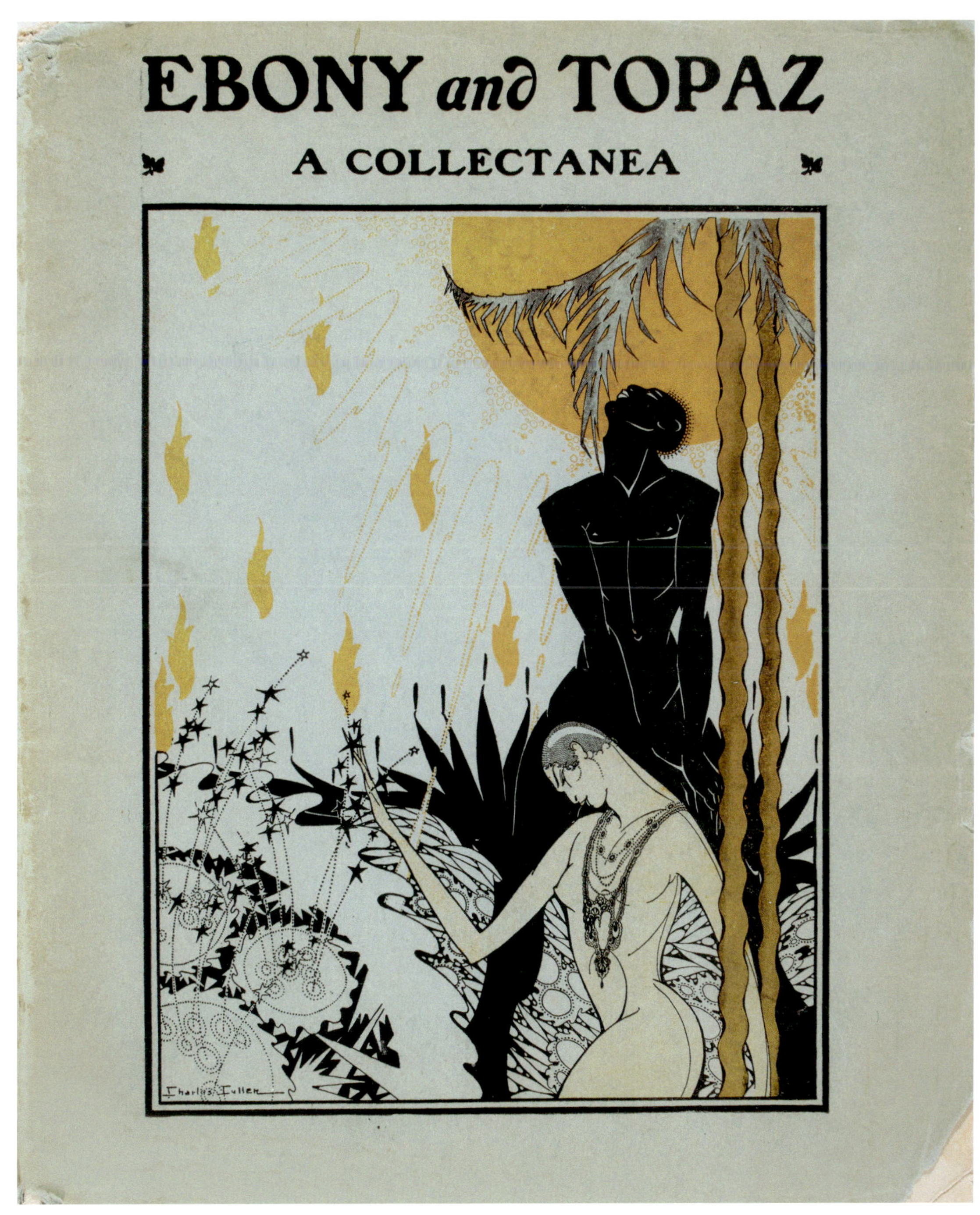

18
Charles Cullen (1887–?)
Cover from *Ebony and Topaz: A Collectanea*, 1927
Printed matter
Delaware Art Museum, Helen Farr Sloan Library and Archives, Gift of Christine Oaklander, 2019

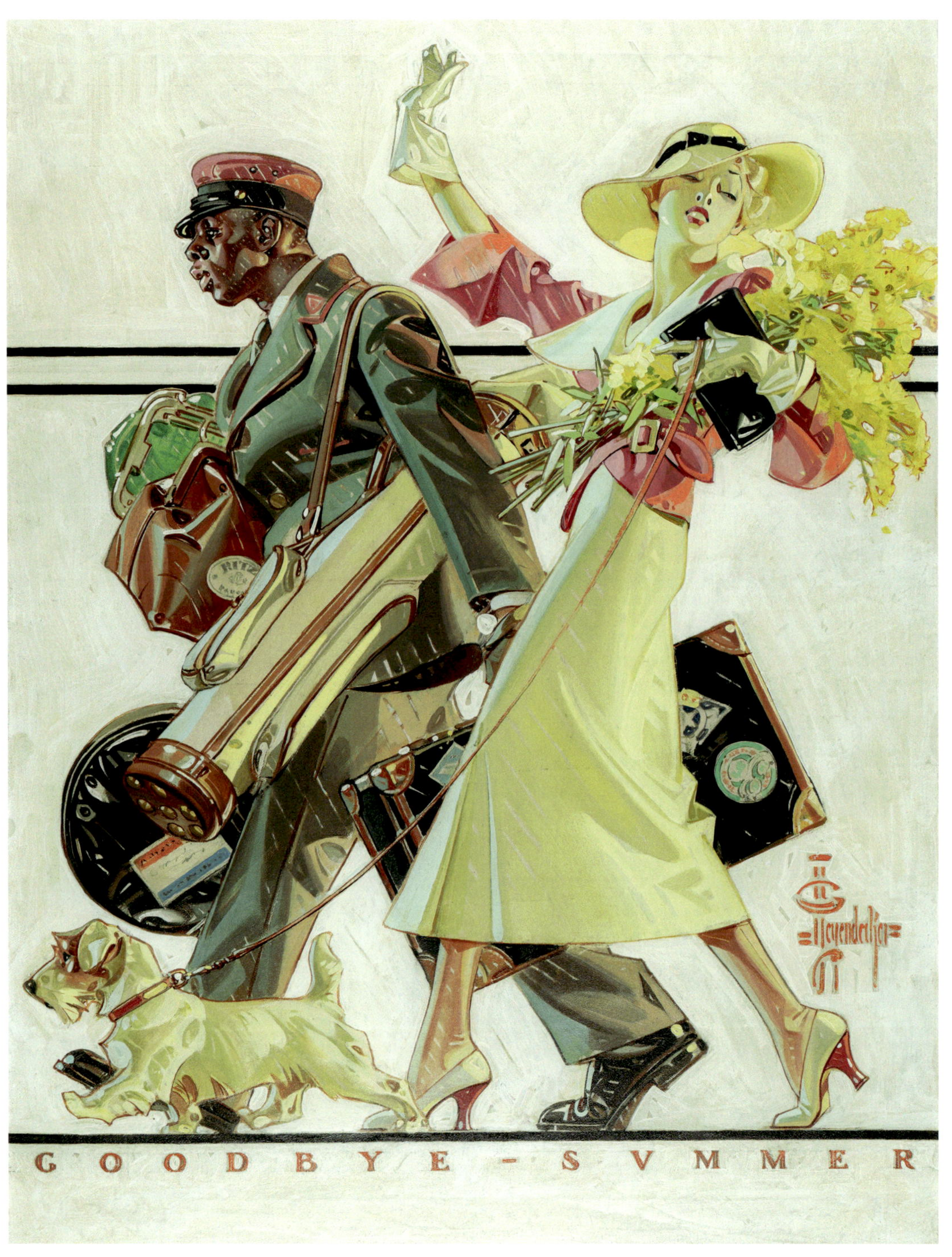

19

J. C. Leyendecker (1874–1951)

End of Vacation, cover for *The Saturday Evening Post*, September 15, 1934

Oil on canvas, 36¼ × 29 in.
From the Collection of Lura J. Dolas and Theodore M. Dolas
Illustration © SEPS licensed by Curtis Licensing Indianapolis, IN. All rights reserved

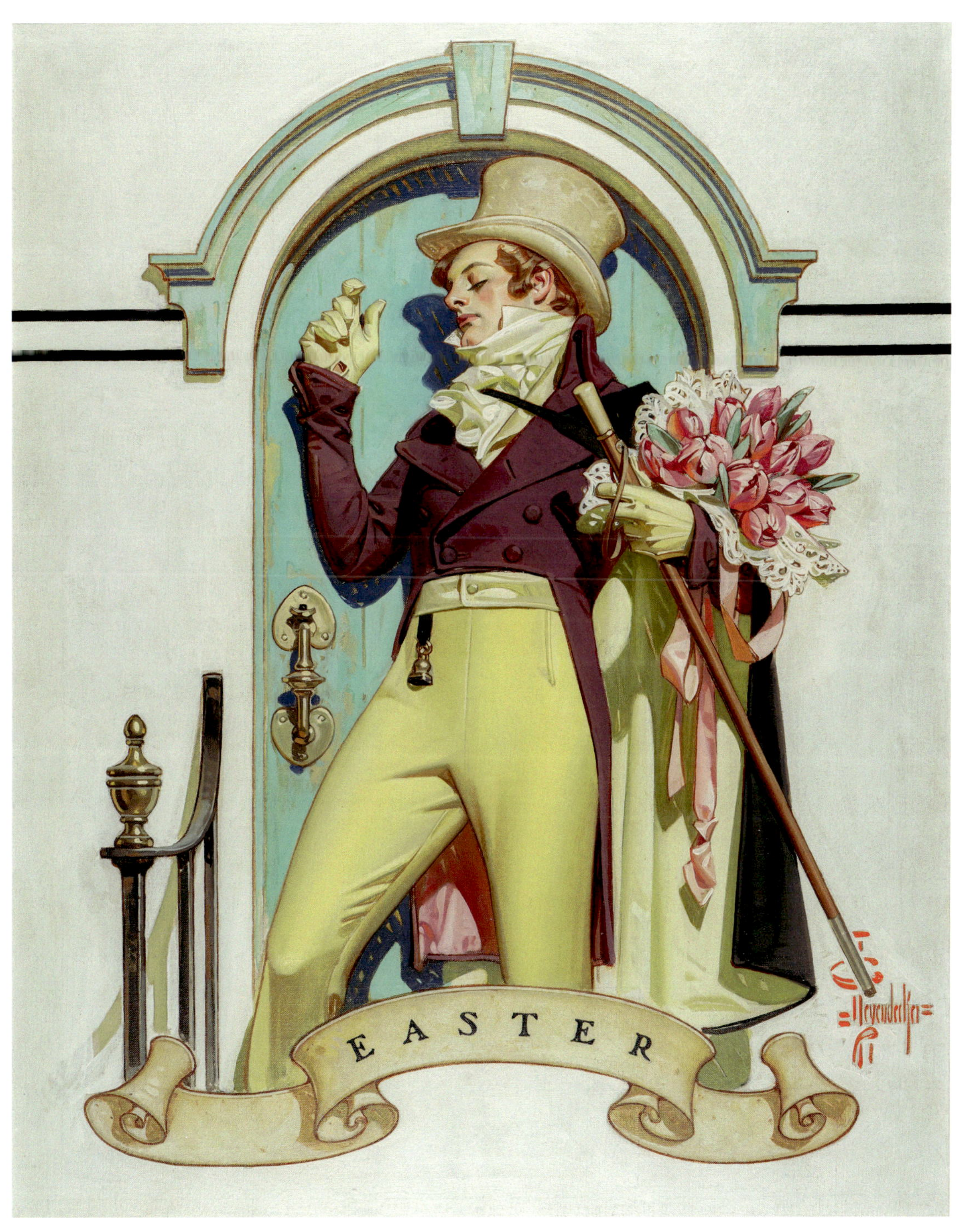

20

J. C. Leyendecker (1874–1951)

Easter Bouquet, cover for *The Saturday Evening Post*, April 20, 1935

Oil on canvas, 36¼ × 29 in.
From the Collection of Lura J. Dolas and Theodore M. Dolas
Illustration © SEPS licensed by Curtis Licensing Indianapolis, IN. All rights reserved

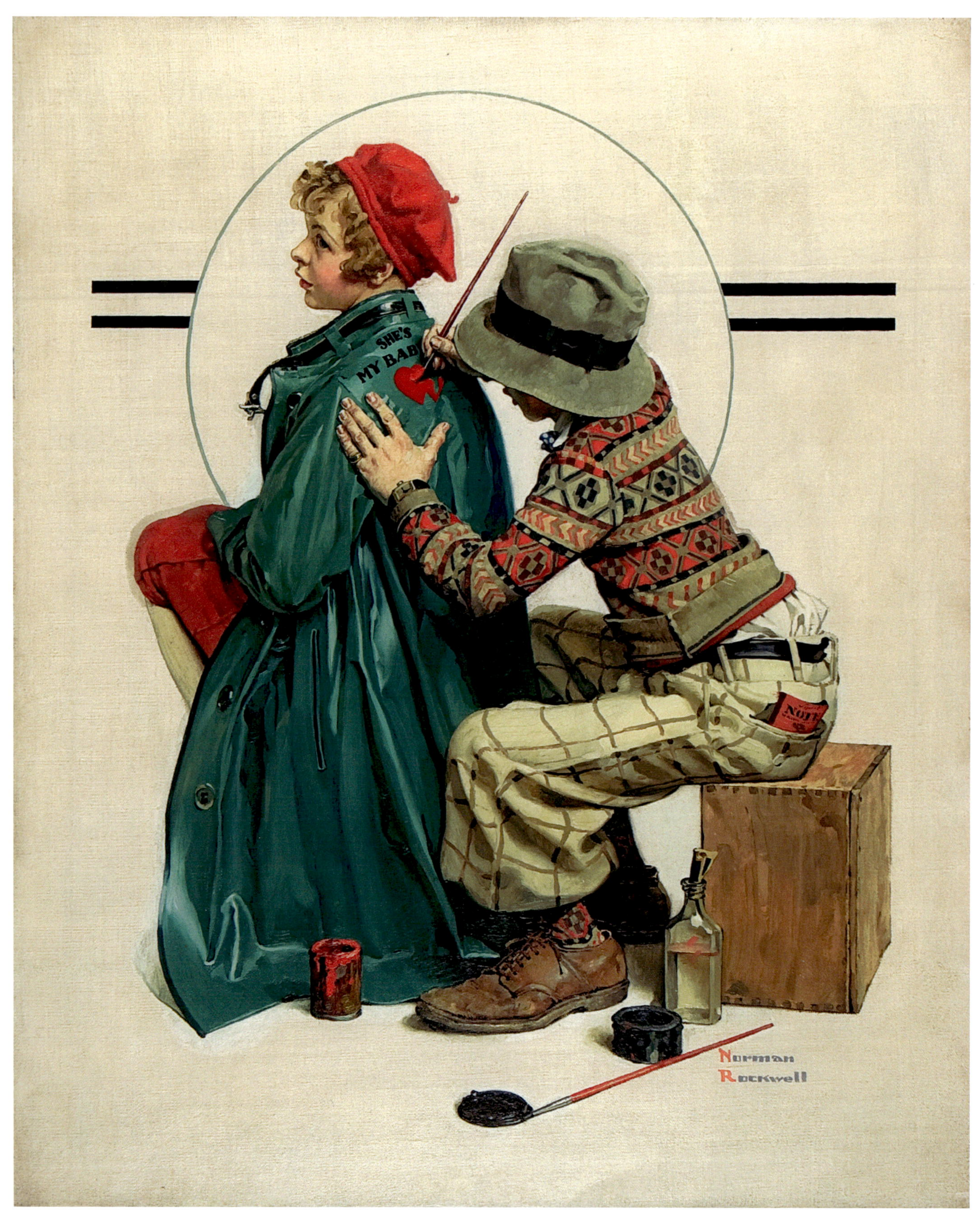
SHE'S
MY BAB
Norman
Rockwell

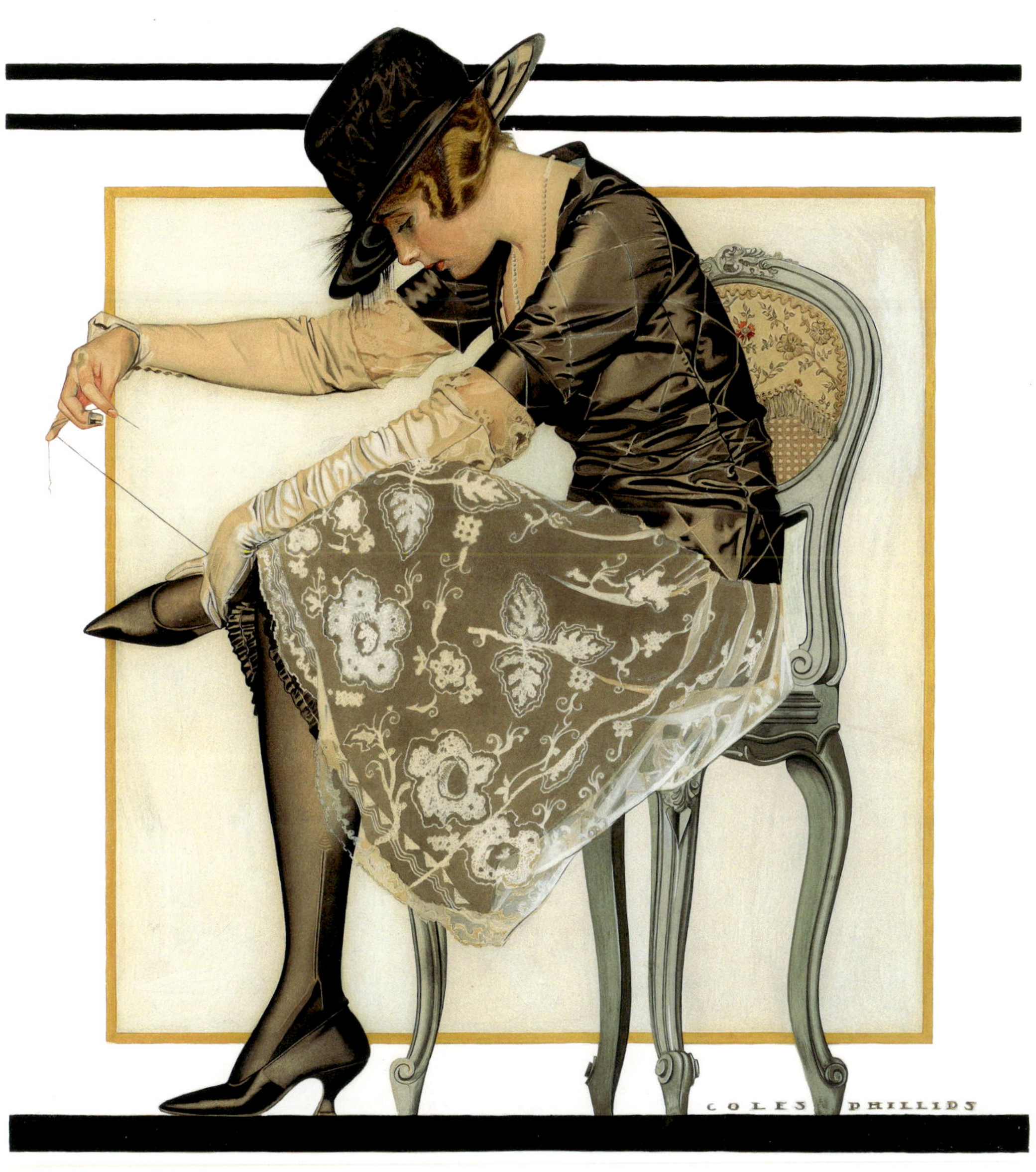

21

Norman Rockwell (1894–1978)

Boy Painting Girl's Slicker (She's My Baby), cover for *The Saturday Evening Post*, June 4, 1927

Oil on canvas, 32 × 26 in.
Norman Rockwell Museum Collection, Gift of Mr. and Mrs. William M. Young Jr., NRM.2007.06

22

C. Coles Phillips (1880–1927)

Cover for *The Saturday Evening Post*, October 2, 1920

Watercolor, gouache, and graphite on illustration board, 20 × 16 in.
Delaware Art Museum, Acquisition Fund, 1988

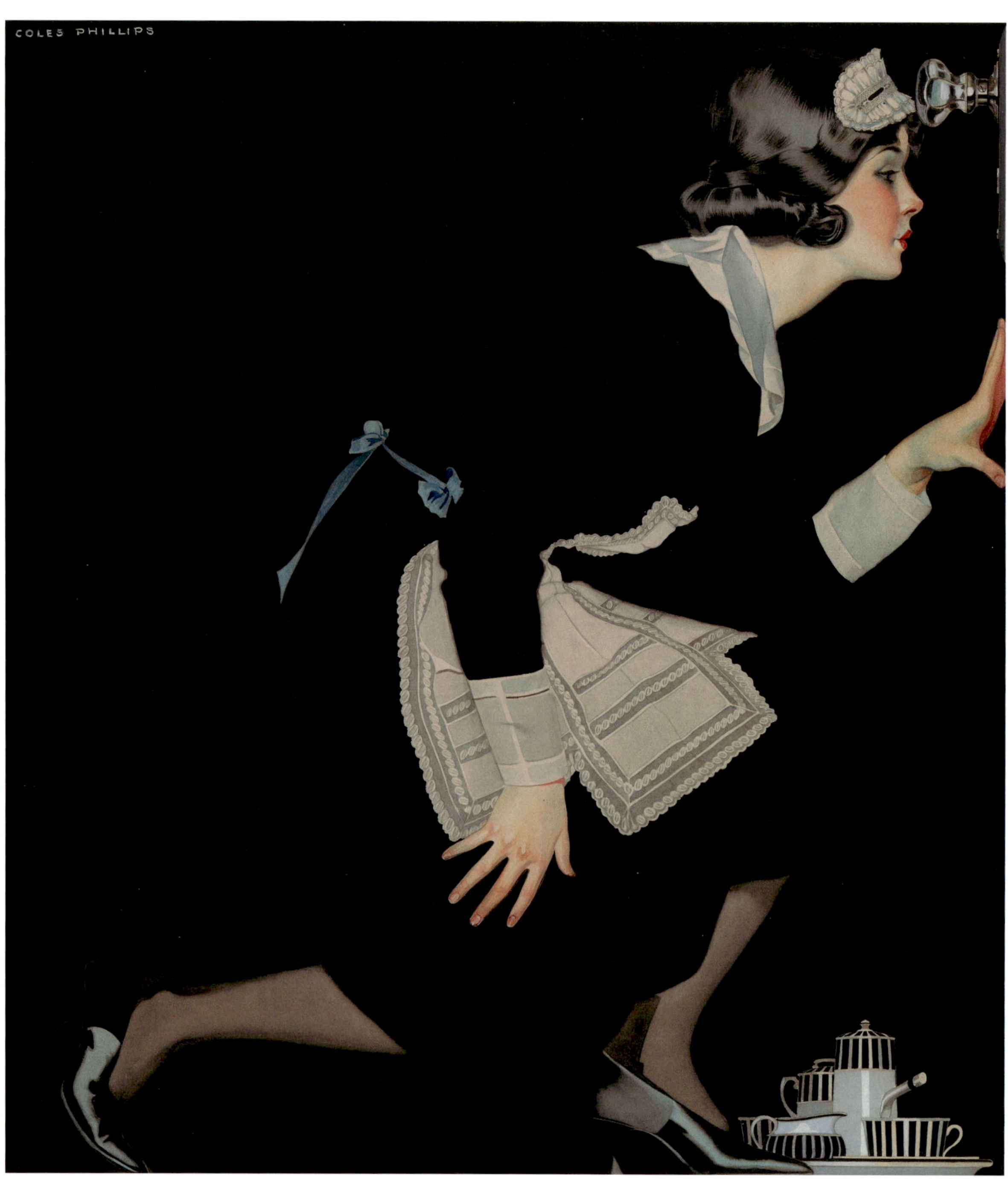

23

C. Coles Phillips (1880–1927)

In a Position to Know, cover for *Life*, April 7, 1921

Gouache, sheet: 19 7/16 × 16 15/16 in.

Metropolitan Museum of Art, New York, Gift of Jacqueline Loewe Fowler, 2020

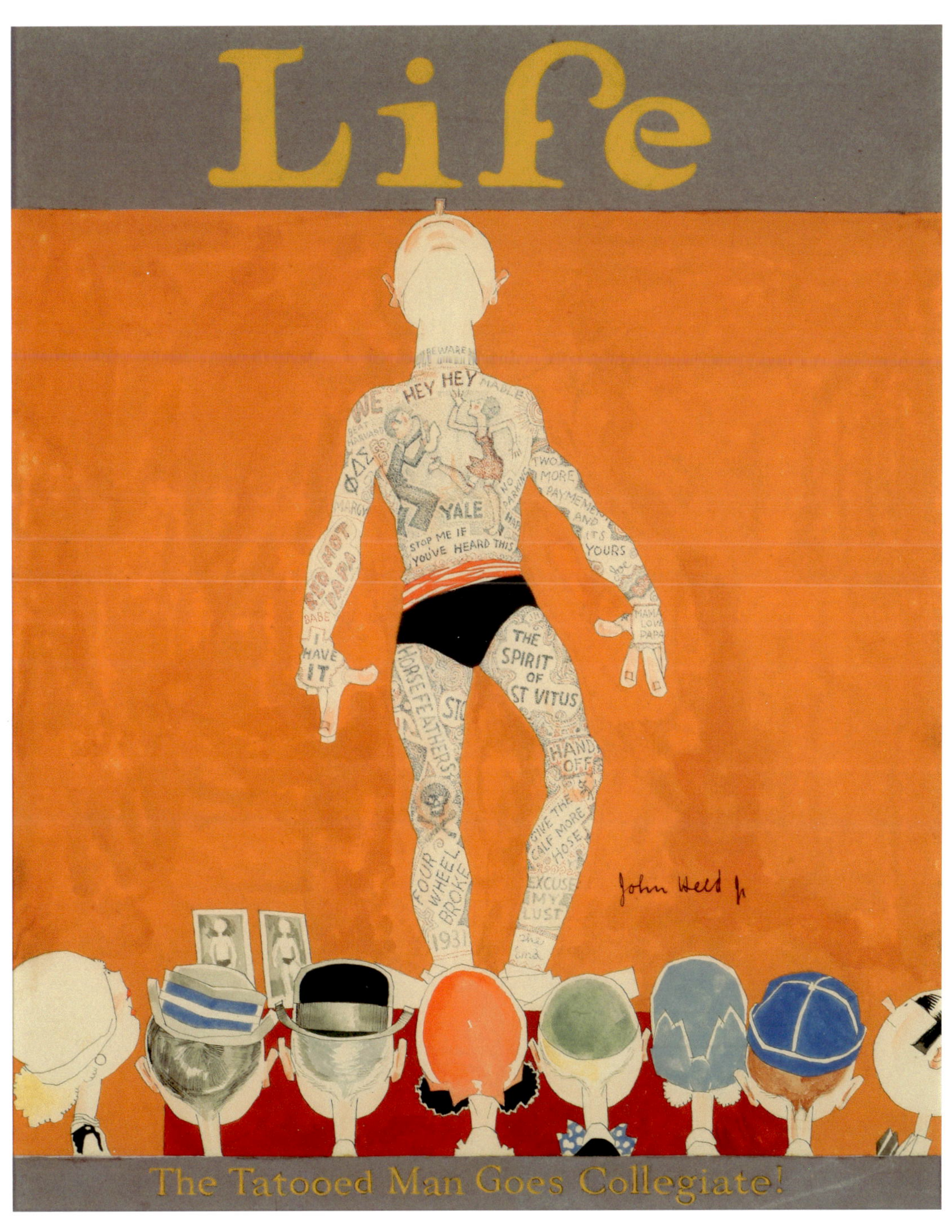

24

John Held Jr. (1889–1958)

The Tattooed Man Goes Collegiate!, cover for *Life*, March 1, 1928

Gouache, watercolor, ink, and graphite on illustration board, 16 1/16 × 12 5/8 in.
Delaware Art Museum, Acquisition Fund, 1986

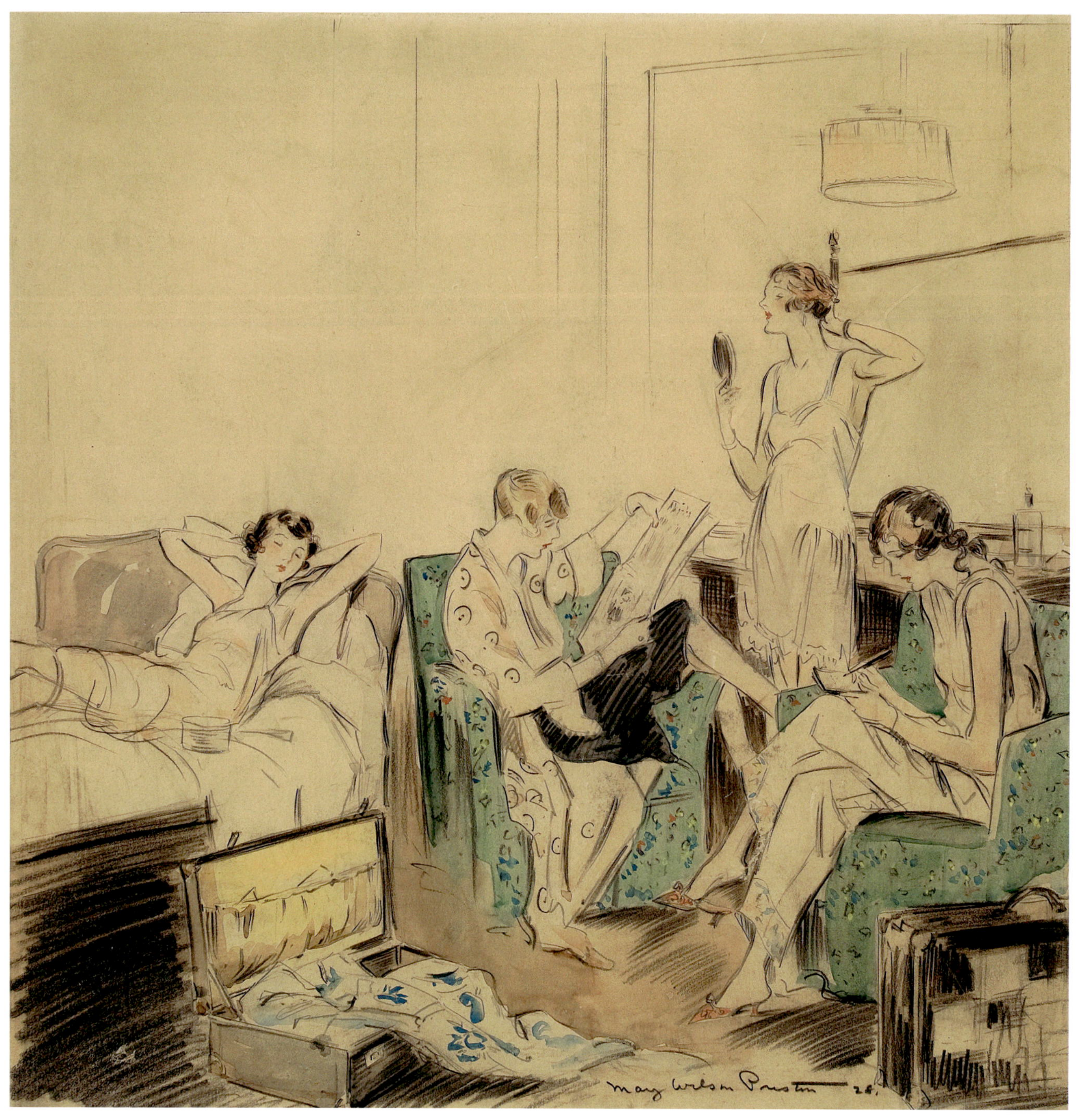

25

May Wilson Watkins Preston (1873–1949)
I am in a room with three other girls—Miss Philadelphia, Miss Cincinnati and Miss Beaumont. It is a little crowded, for "Miss Brooklyn and Queens" by Edith Fitzgerald, *The Saturday Evening Post*, June 15, 1929

Charcoal and watercolor on illustration board, 16½ × 17¼ in.
Delaware Art Museum, Gift of Helen Farr Sloan, 1987
Illustration © SEPS licensed by Curtis Licensing Indianapolis, IN. All rights reserved

26

Nicolai Remisoff (1887–1975)
Cover for *Vanity Fair*, March 1923

Gouache and black paper on illustration board, sheet: 14½ × 10⅞ in.
Delaware Art Museum, Acquisition Fund, 1991

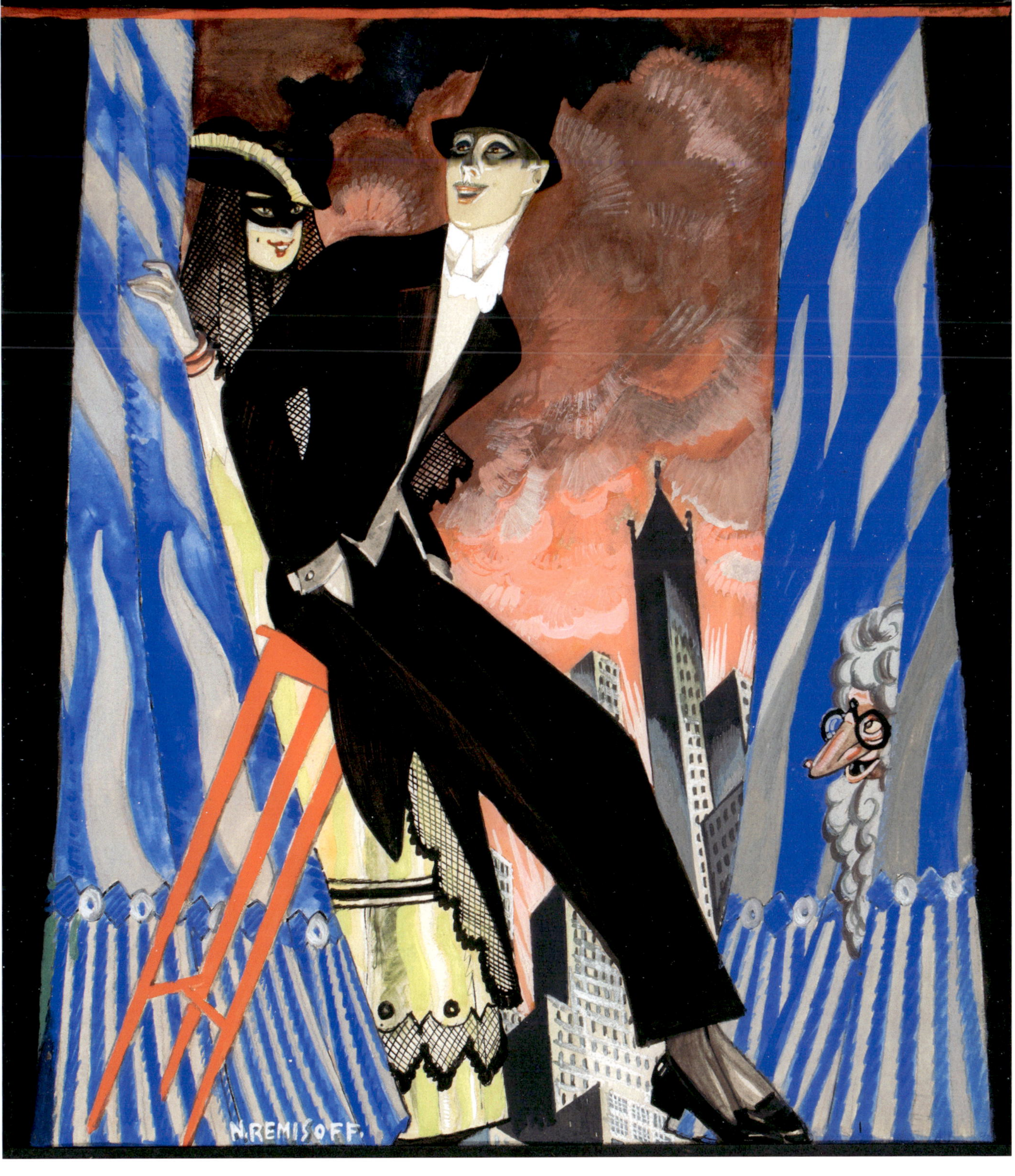
VANITY FAIR
N. REMISOFF.

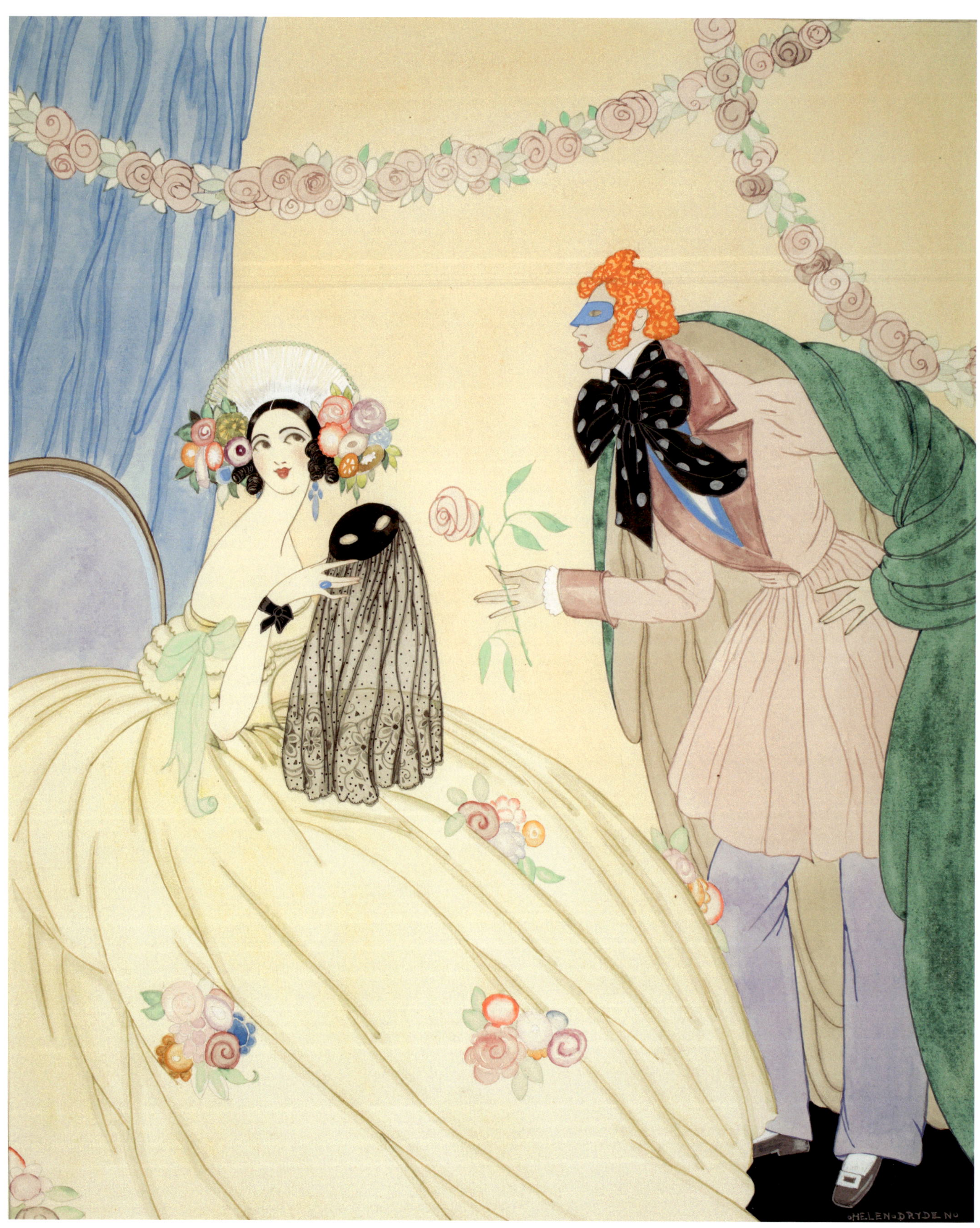
HELEN DRYDEN

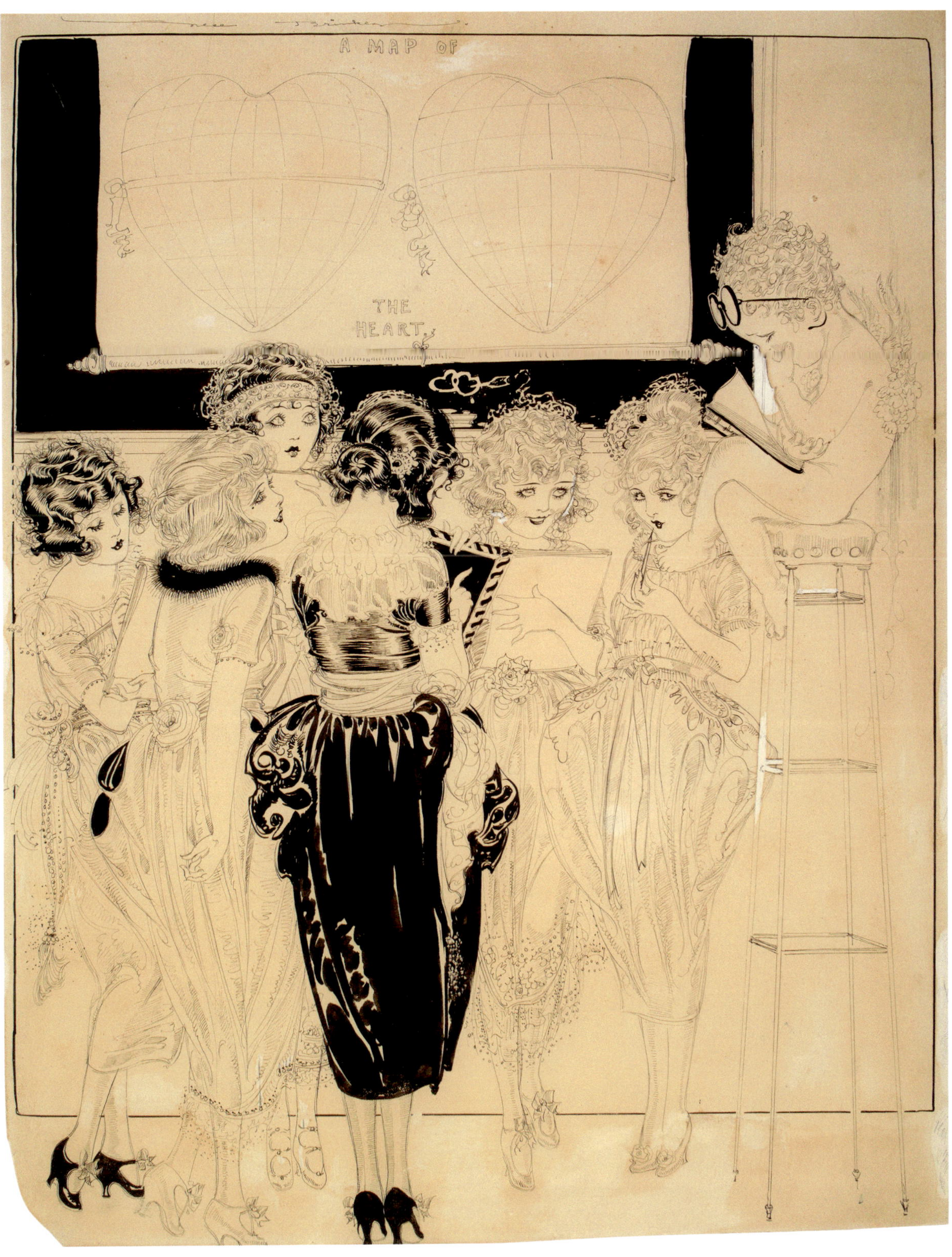

27

Helen Dryden (1882–1981)

Cover for *Vogue*, December 15, 1922

Gouache, ink, and watercolor on paper, sheet: 19 × 15½ in.
Delaware Art Museum, Acquisition Fund, 1991

28

Nell Brinkley (1886–1944)

A Map of the Heart, ca. 1917–1920

Ink on illustration board, 14¼ × 11 in.
Delaware Art Museum, Acquisition Fund, 2014

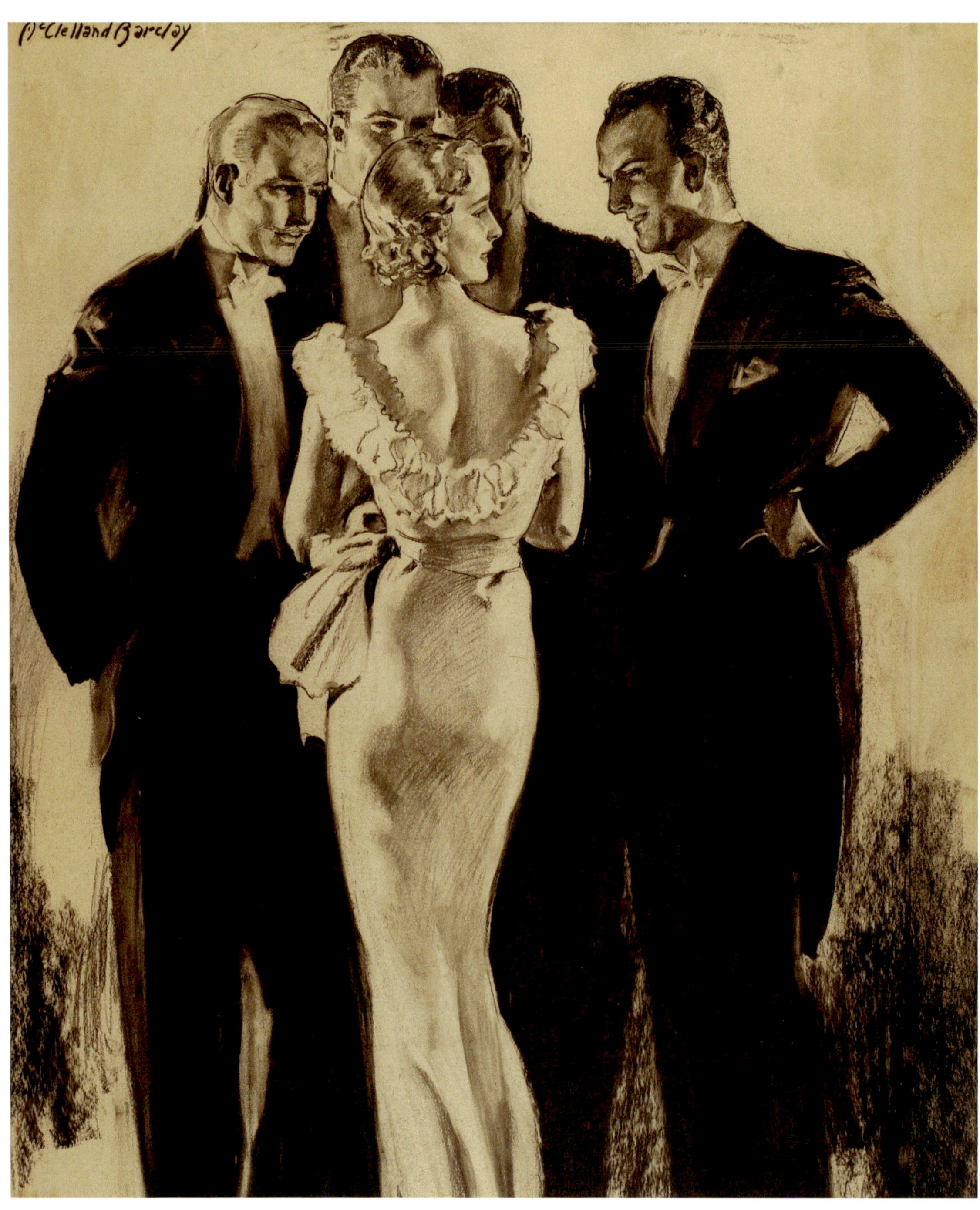

29

McClelland Barclay (1891–1943)

Girls I Adore, for "Girls I Adore" by McClelland Barclay with text by Alice-Leone Moats, King Features Syndicate, *Philadelphia Inquirer*, March 18, 1934

Charcoal on illustration board, 31 9/16 × 25 7/8 in.
Delaware Art Museum, F. V. du Pont Acquisition Fund, 1992

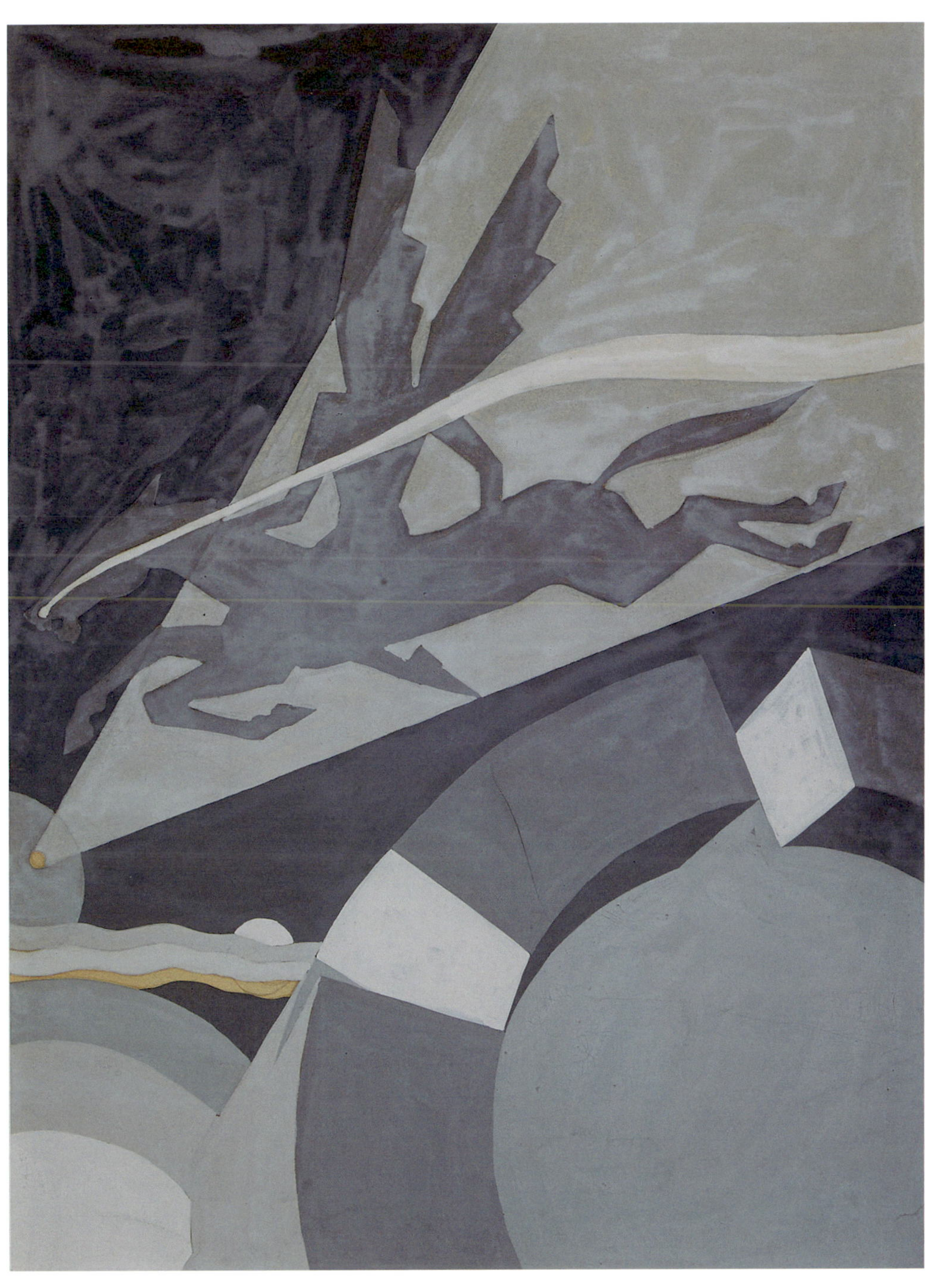

30

Aaron Douglas (1899–1979)

Go Down Death—A Funeral Sermon, for *God's Trombones* by James Weldon Johnson (New York: The Viking Press, 1927)

Gouache with graphite underdrawing on paper, 13⅜ × 9³⁄₁₆ in.
SCAD Museum of Art, courtesy of the Walter and Linda Evans Collection of African American Art

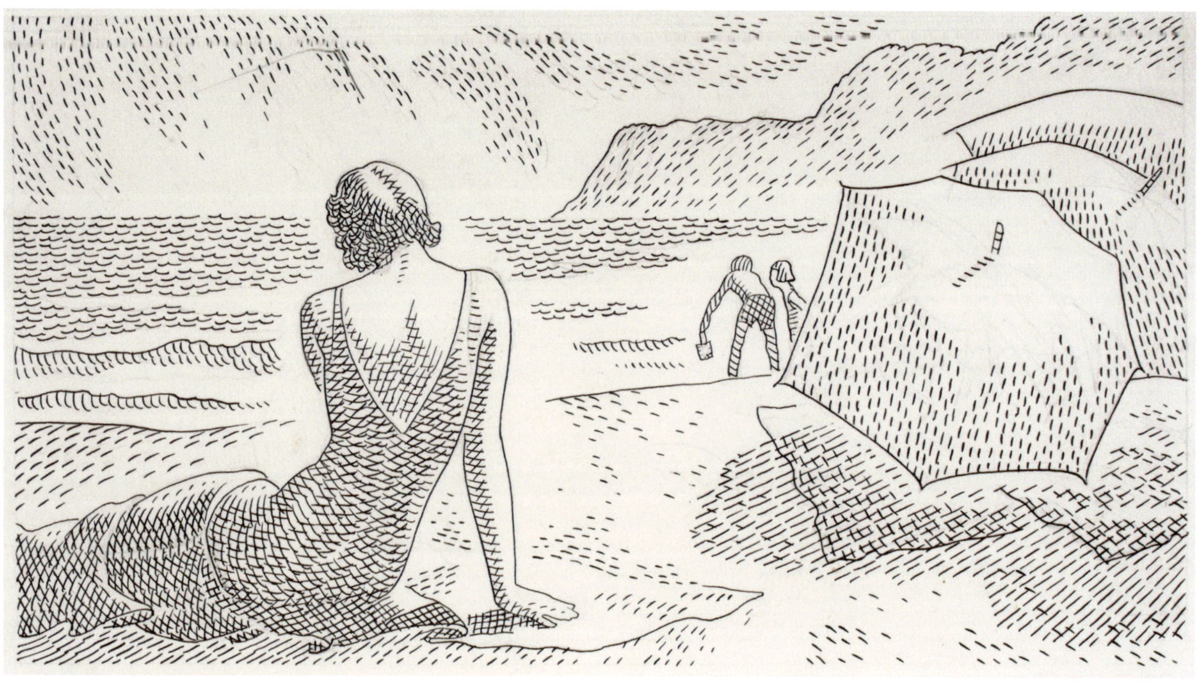

31

Edward Shenton (1895–1977)
Rosemary Hoyt on the Beach, for *Tender Is the Night* by F. Scott Fitzgerald (New York: Charles Scribner's Sons, 1934)

Ink and graphite on paper, 3¼ × 5⅞ in.
Delaware Art Museum, Acquisition Fund, 2022

32

Francis Cugat (1896–1981)
Celestial Eyes, cover for *The Great Gatsby* by F. Scott Fitzgerald (New York: Charles Scribner's Sons, 1925)

Gouache on paper, 25⅝ × 17¾ in.
The Graphic Arts Collection, Princeton University Library

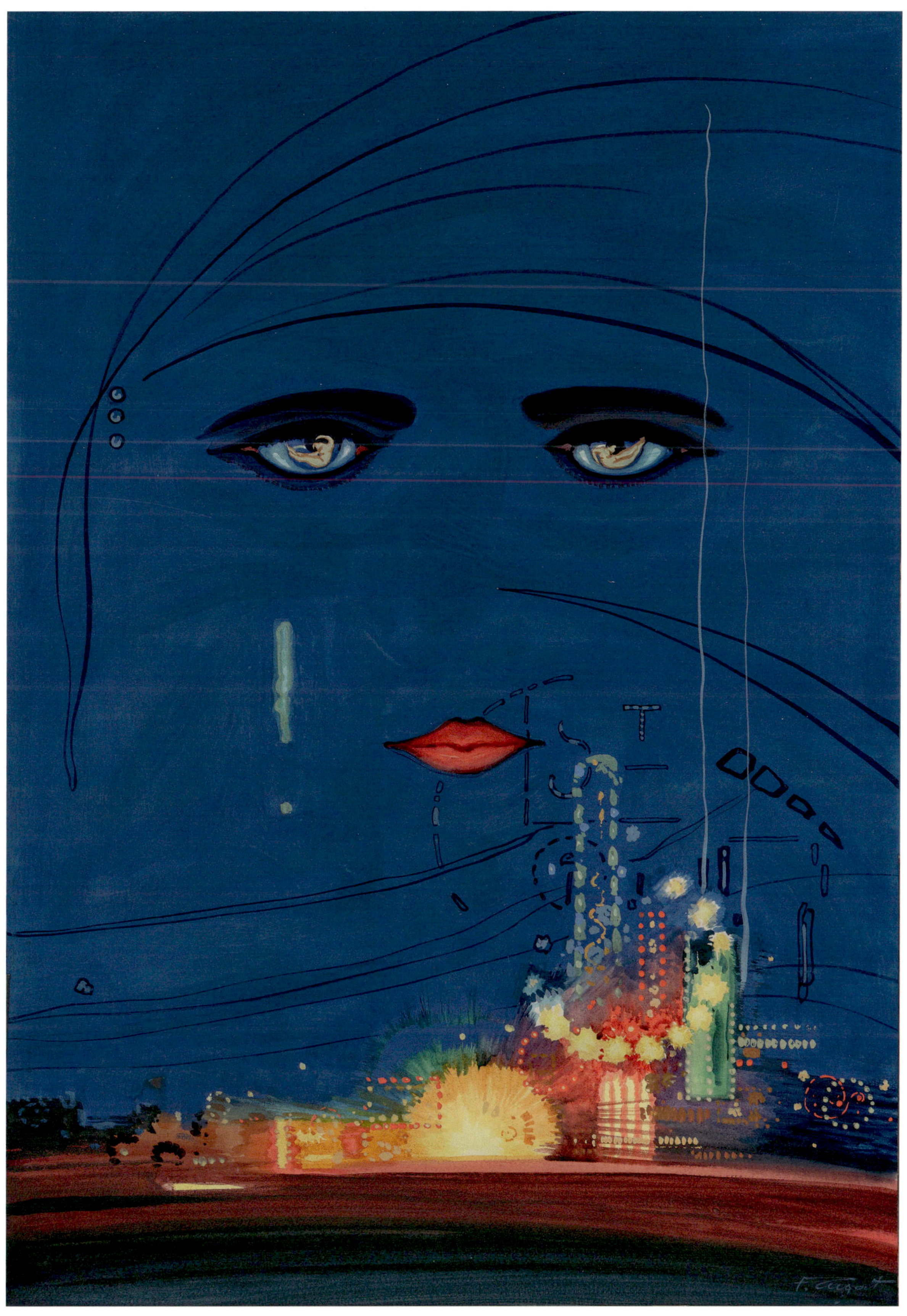

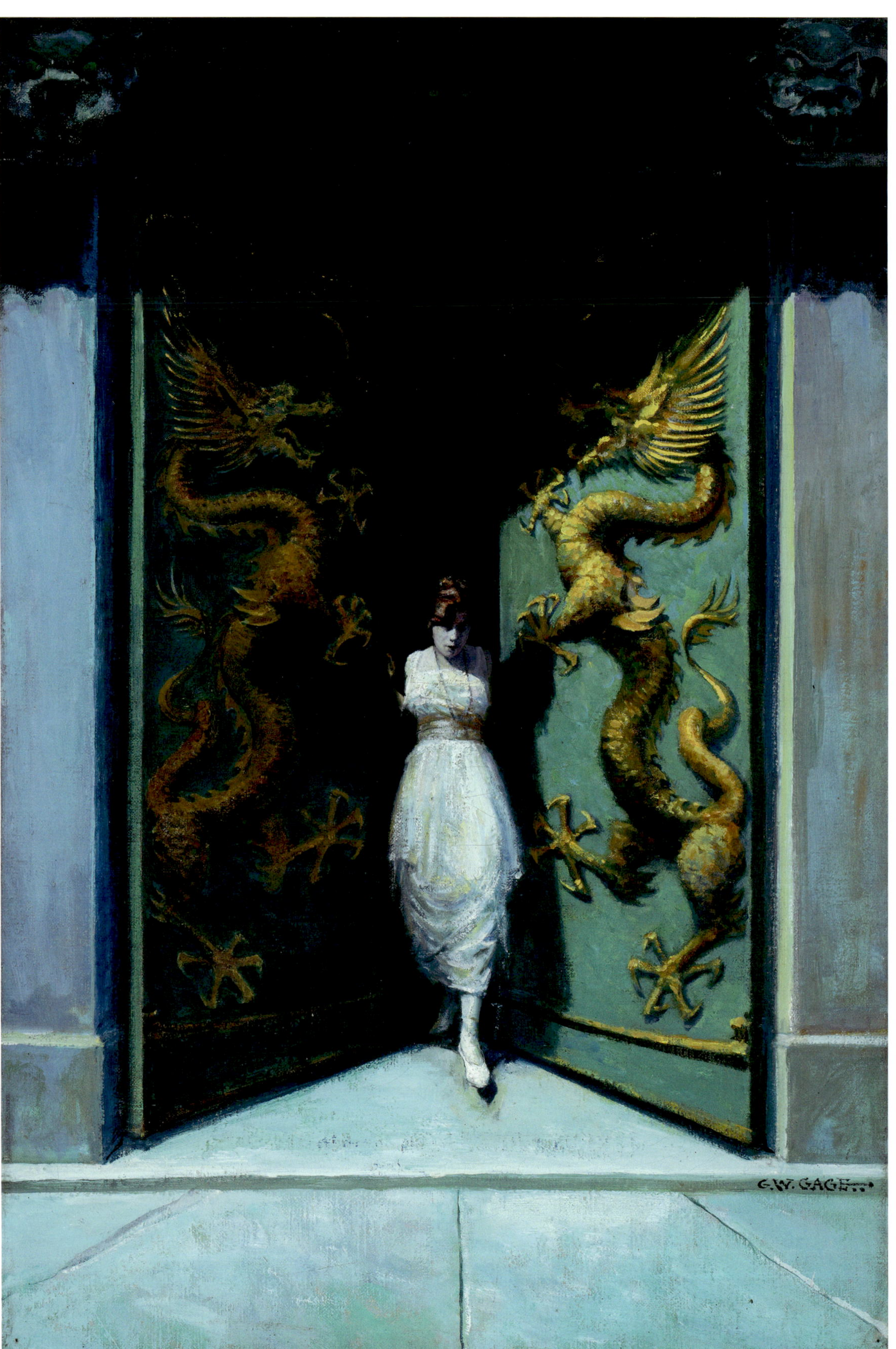
G.W. GAGE

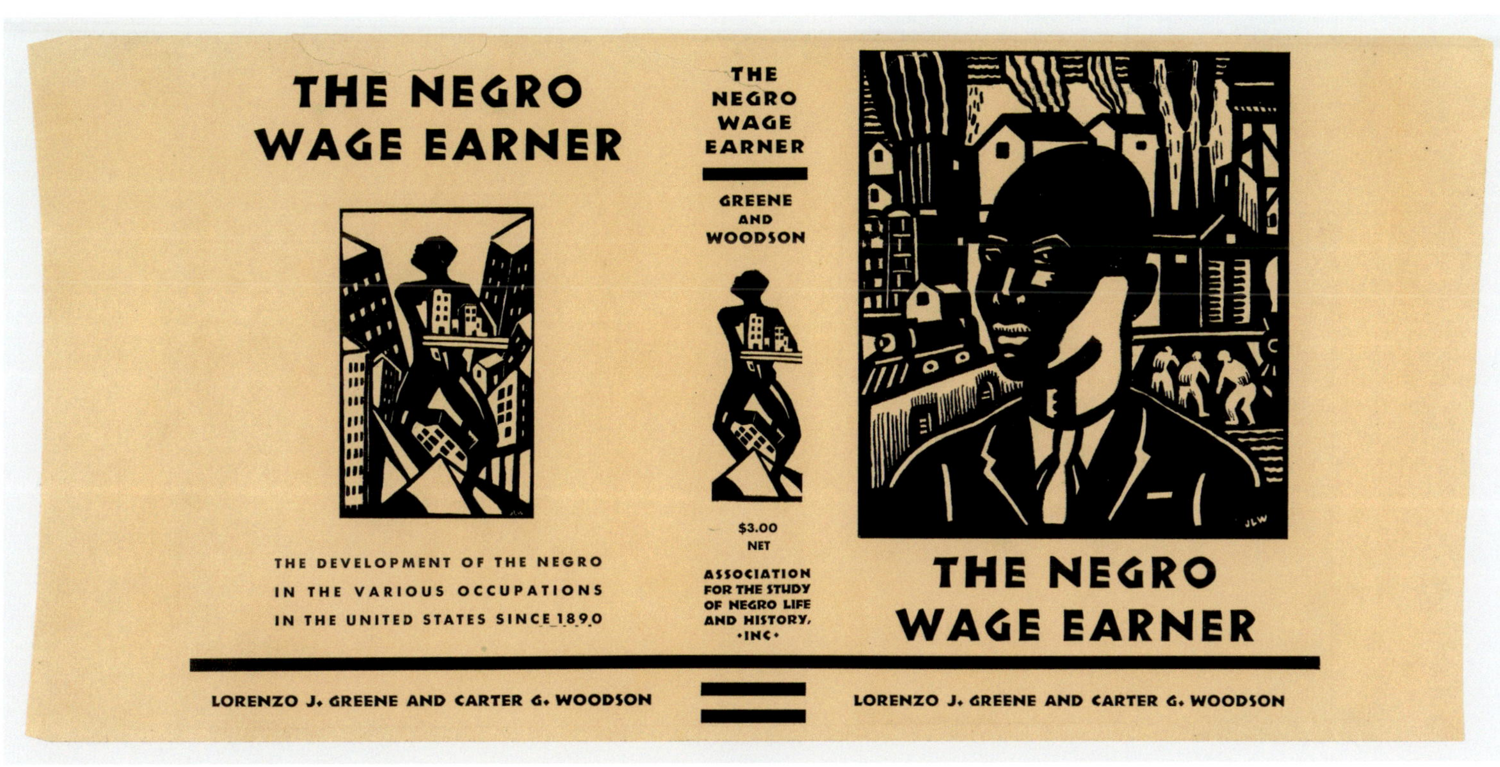

33

George W. Gage (1887–1957)
Dust jacket for *The Door of the Double Dragon: A Romance of the China of Yesterday and To-Day* by Hector Blanding (New York: W. J. Watt and Co., 1920)
Oil on canvas, 29¼ × 19⅝ in.
Delaware Art Museum, Louisa du Pont Copeland Memorial Fund, 1977

34

James Lesesne Wells (1902–1993)
Dust jacket for *The Negro Wage Earner* by Lorenzo J. Greene and Carter G. Woodson (Washington, DC: The Association for the Study of Negro Life and History, 1930)
Offset print of linoleum cut, 9 × 14¼ in.
Addison Gallery of American Art, Phillips Academy, Andover, MA, Gift of James Lesesne Wells, 1990.46

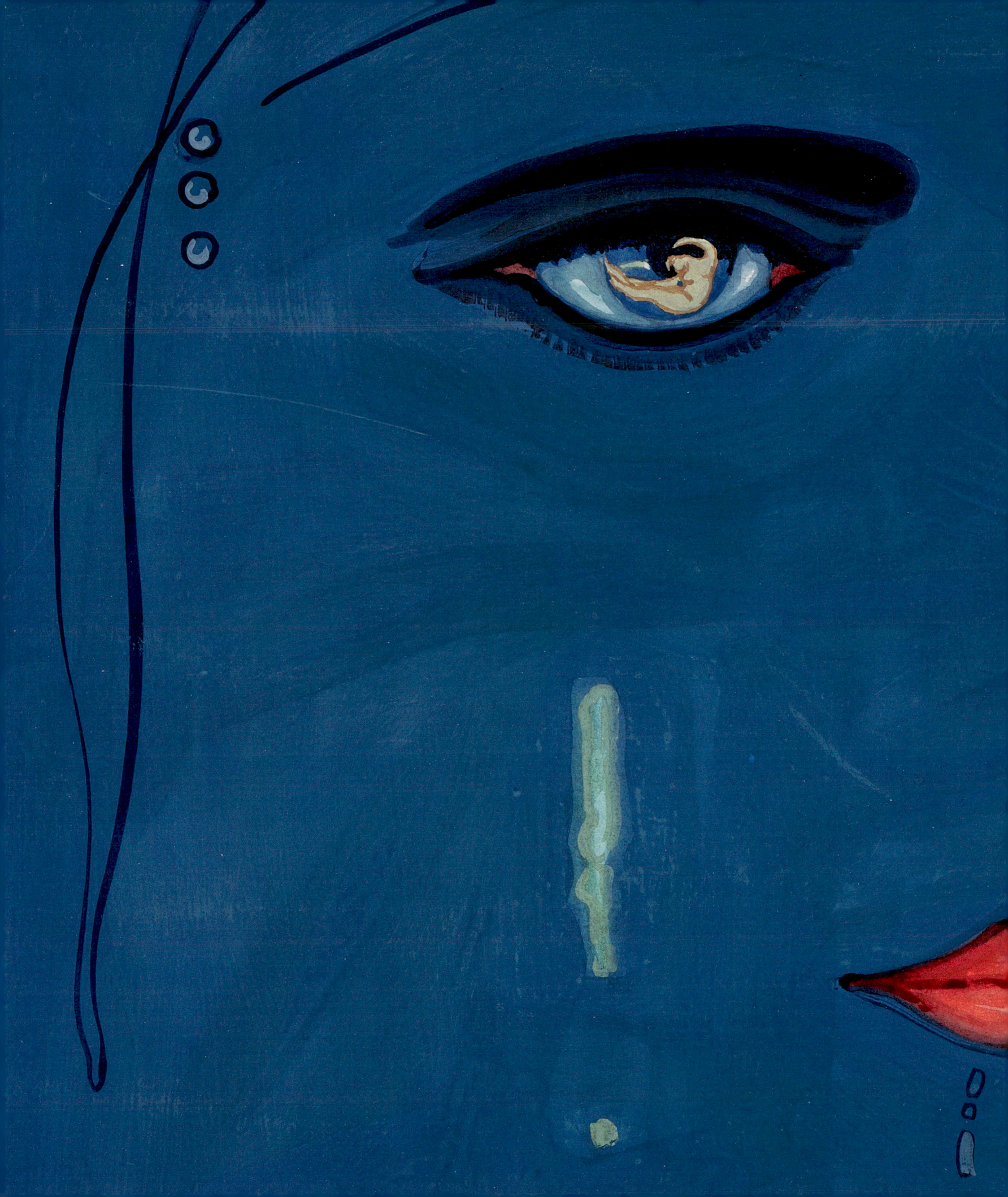

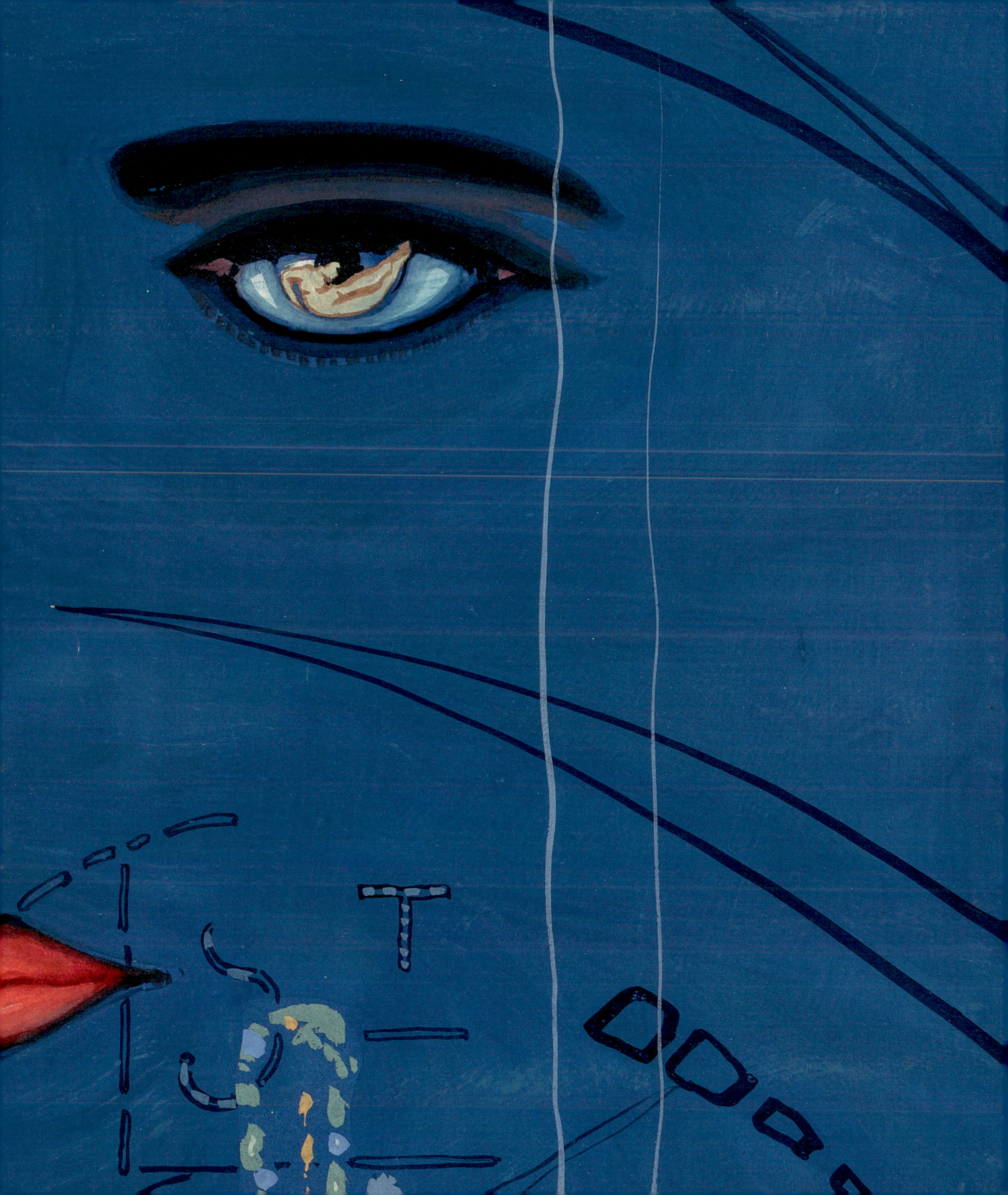

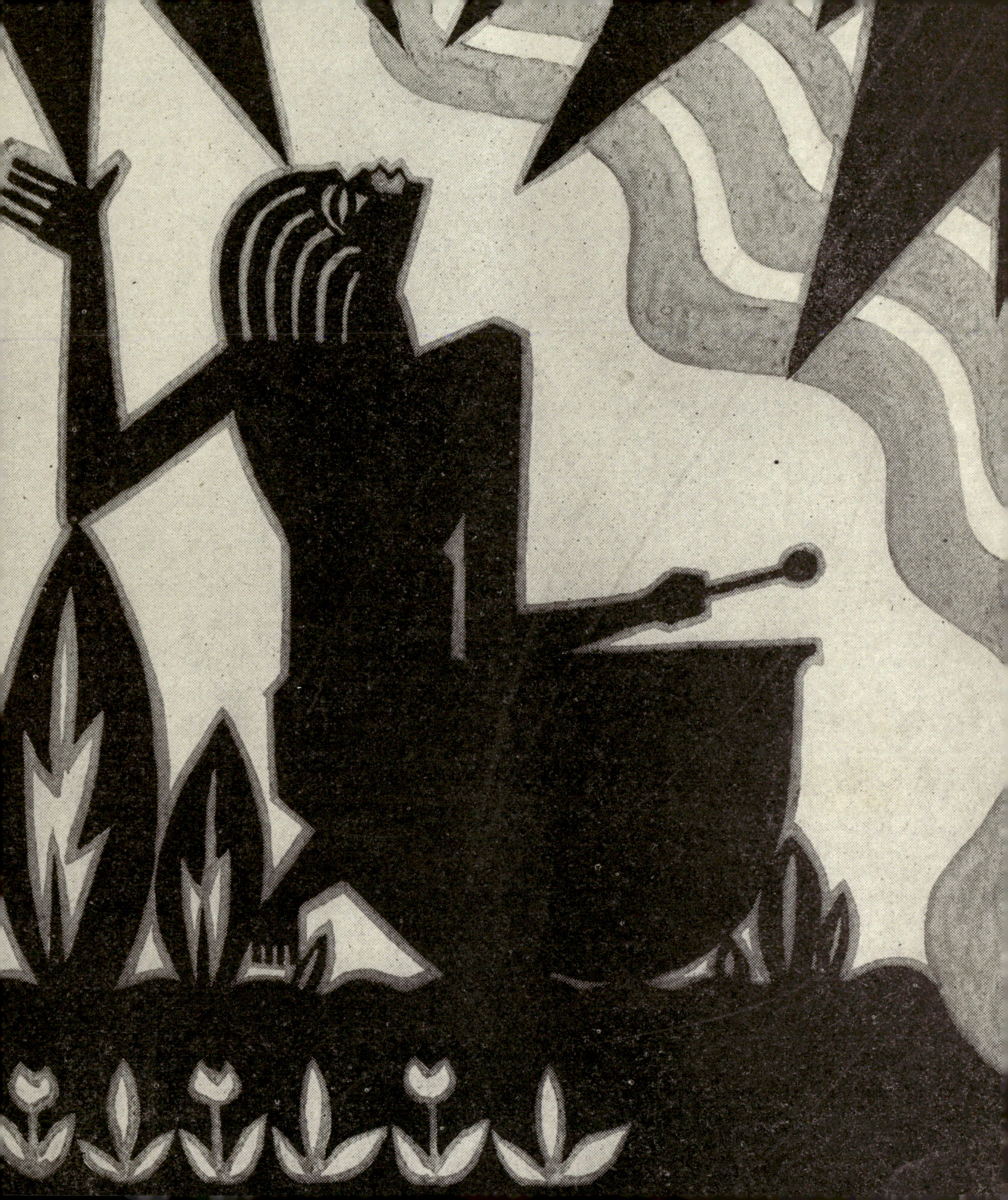

Colette Gaiter

Authenticity/ Assimilation/ Appropriation
Cultural Mashup and Race Reckoning

Detail of fig. 38

Authenticity

> Your problem, Langston, my problem, no our problem is to conceive, develop, establish an art era. Not white art painted black. . . . Let's bare our arms and plunge them deep through laughter, through pain, through sorrow, through hope, through disappointment, into the very depths of the souls of our people and drag forth material crude, rough, neglected. Then let's sing it, dance it, write it, paint it. Let's do the impossible. Let's create something transcendentally material, mystically objective. Earthy, Spiritually earthy. Dynamic.[1]
>
> —Aaron Douglas to Langston Hughes, December 21, 1925

Imagine two different 1920s drawings of Black men's heads in which each man has dark skin and prominent thick lips accentuated in profile. Each image occupies most of the space on a publication cover. One portrait is by the African American artist, designer, and illustrator Aaron Douglas (fig. 36). The other is by the Mexican artist, illustrator, and later anthropologist Miguel Covarrubias (fig. 37). Both artists' works were celebrated in the Jazz Age, but by different audiences. In the 1920s and '30s, Aaron Douglas's print work was made for publications by and for Black people in the Harlem Renaissance, while Covarrubias mostly created illustrations for mainstream (white) publications like *Vanity Fair*. Each artist's work was perceived differently depending on the context and audience.

Aaron Douglas's work embodied the "profound racial consciousness," promoted by the foundational scholar of Black American studies, W. E. B. Du Bois, as early as 1903.[2] These emerging ideas would later be incorporated into the artistic, social, and political movements of "The New Negro" and Negritude, which encouraged Black diasporan people who were colonized or previously enslaved to look to Africa for inspiration.[3] Douglas's work transformed ancient Egyptian and traditional African visual conventions that abstracted figures into silhouettes, often showing bodies and heads in profile (fig. 38). According to Frank Mehring, "Douglas wanted to portray African American lives, dreams, and realities to provide a new sense of racial uplift, self-recognition, and general appreciation of the contributions of African Americans to modern American culture. Silhouettes played a key role in his artistic vision."[4]

Douglas's cover illustration for the publication *Fire!!* combined his signature African-inspired geometric shapes into a human head, creating

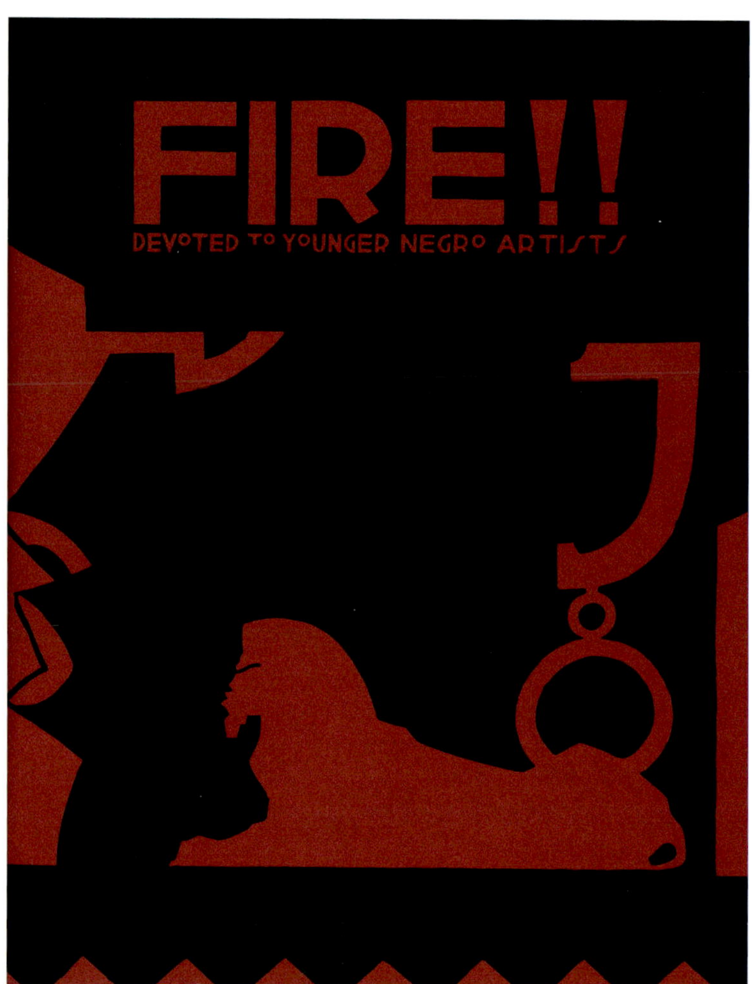

Fig. 36 Aaron Douglas (1899–1979), cover from *Fire!!: Devoted to Younger Negro Artists*, 1926 (facsimile edition, Elizabeth, NJ: The Fire!! Press, n.d.). Printed matter. Delaware Art Museum, Helen Farr Sloan Library and Archives

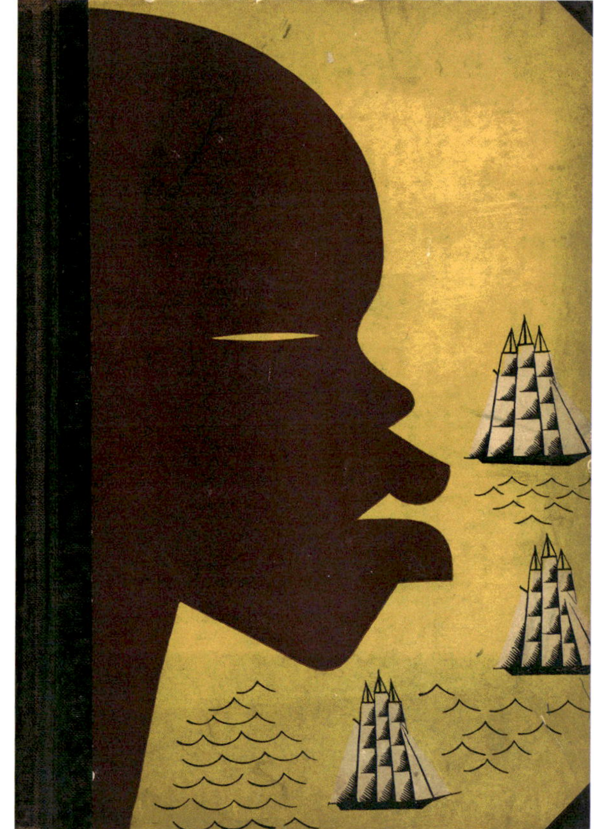

Fig. 37 Miguel Covarrubias (1904–1957), cover from *Adventures of An African Slaver* (New York: Albert & Charles Boni, 1928). Printed matter. Delaware Art Museum, Helen Farr Sloan Library and Archives

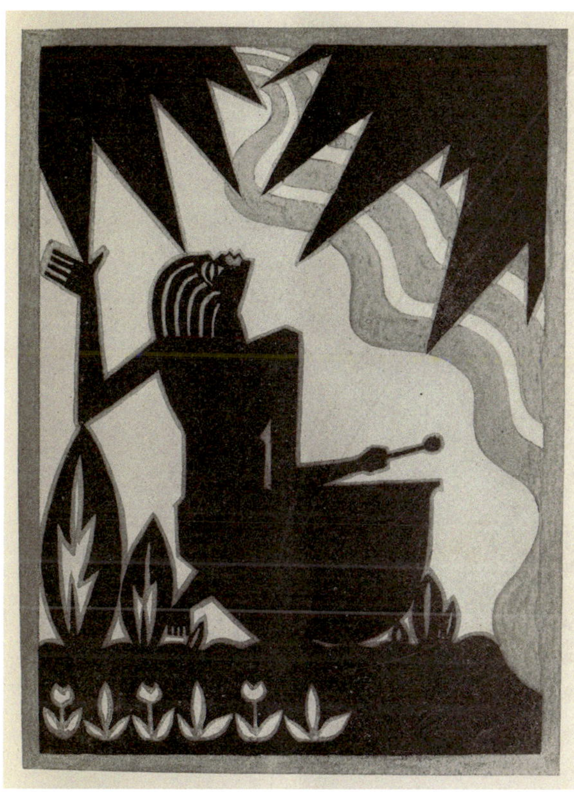

Fig. 38 Aaron Douglas (1899–1979), *Invincible Music: The Spirit of Africa*, from *The Crisis*, February 1926. Printed matter. New York Public Library, Schomburg Center for Research in Black Culture, Jean Blackwell Hutson Research and Reference Division

an optical illusion of shifting foreground and background elements. The letterforms in the title text and triangles across the bottom of the page exemplify Art Deco-style typography and graphics inspired by non-Western artifacts "discovered" by white designers in the early 1900s. *Fire!!*'s cover stated that it was "Devoted to Younger Negro Artists." Writer Wallace Thurman edited this first and only issue of the publication, which included work by writer Langston Hughes, graphic artist Richard Bruce Nugent, and other emerging Harlem Renaissance luminaries. Douglas's bold, modern design and celebration of African sources expressed the radical artistic agenda of the contributors, many of whom were still in their twenties.[5] In overdue recognition of his groundbreaking work in graphic design and illustration, Aaron Douglas was posthumously awarded a 2018 AIGA Medal, "the most distinguished honor in the profession of communication design."[6]

Miguel Covarrubias's cover illustration for the 1928 edition of *Adventures of An African Slaver* showed a less geometric silhouette of a Black man's head. His horizontal sliver of an eye and slightly open lips are directed toward tall ships in the distance, representing those that brought enslaved Africans across the world to live in brutal captivity. The book presented the narrative of Captain Théodore Canot, a slave trader for three decades, who described the economic structure and violent practices of the slave trade in the early nineteenth century. Despite the book's intentions, some Black leaders deemed this depiction problematic. Similar images that showed exaggerated facial features denigrated Black people by cultivating a negative visual stereotype from natural (and different from white norms) features and constructing associations with "savagery."[7]

W. E. B. Du Bois, whose seminal work *The Souls of Black Folk* illuminated the idea of racial "double consciousness," was among those who believed Covarrubias's work perpetuated negative stereotypes. Du Bois first defined double consciousness in 1897 as a "two-ness" of being "an American, a Negro; two souls, two thoughts, two unreconciled strivings; two warring ideals in one dark body, whose dogged strength alone keeps it from being torn asunder."[8] Du Bois's understanding of African American experiences enhanced his sensitivity to negative representations of Black figures. This acuity easily became hypervigilance in the face of omnipresent and violent racism in the early twentieth century when the Ku Klux Klan resurged and expanded beyond the South. As author David W. Horowitz explained, in the 1920s, "the second Ku Klux Klan" emerged and "sought organizational respectability and political power by fashioning a massive fraternal and patronage machine behind a public agenda of law enforcement, civic improvement, and social reform."[9] In other words, they embedded their racism inside social and political concerns that normalized an extreme right-wing agenda. In this type of political climate, images of Black faces and figures could easily be contentious.

The problem, of course, was not the images but their perception. Miguel Covarrubias was Mexican, and although he was close with many Black writers and artists of the Harlem Renaissance, his ability to move in and out of white society and the success of his illustrations with white publishers made his work suspect.[10] By repeating negative images and omitting positive ones in popular media, most white Americans were insidiously and relentlessly taught, primarily through illustrations, to believe damaging stereotypes at the time of the Jazz Age. Du Bois pointed out that African Americans (Negroes then) were required to move through life proud of their identities as Black people while being perceived as inferior by white people.

With their comically exaggerated wide grins, thick lips, and oversized white teeth, Covarrubias's caricatures of "The New Negro" for *Vanity Fair* in 1924 echoed racist imagery even as they ostensibly celebrated new urban lifestyles (see pl. 35). His work incorporated the same visual stereotypes used by white companies like Currier and Ives in the previous century.[11] The paradox of Covarrubias's work was that even though he was a friend of Harlem Renaissance writers and artists and participated in jazz culture, by default, his drawings became part of the societal database of biased perceptions. The "New Negro" illustrations in *Vanity Fair* attempted to visualize a range of archetypes of Black people in the Harlem Renaissance. Only after decades of celebrating Blackness and seeing authentic and diverse representations of Black people is it possible to look at Covarrubias's provocative illustrations with a nuanced evaluation.

As Wendy Wick Reaves wrote in her book *Celebrity Caricature in America* about Covarrubias's work, "His drawings were therefore emphatically racial. Rather than individual portraits, his figures were more often types—the dancing waiter, the gambling man. . . . The emphasis on racial features and characteristics in his comic drawings offended some black leaders for their stereotypical exaggerations."[12] For *Vanity Fair*, Covarrubias also made unflattering caricatures of high-society white people like the socialite and etiquette authority Emily Post, who was reportedly amused by his portrayal.[13] The difference between these drawings and the controversial ones of people of color was that the portraits did not hurt the society members' social and economic standings because they had so much privilege and capital in their worlds. For Black people, every negatively perceived media portrayal fueled racist fires and further embedded stereotypes into white racial consciousness. Covarrubias's drawings might have hurt celebrities' feelings, but their livelihoods and social standing stayed intact.

In his jazz drawings, Covarrubias seemed most interested in body movement and inserted faces as generic representations. In books like *Negro Drawings* and *Blues*, he sought to capture the energy of African American musicians and dancers by simplifying the forms of his figures and emphasizing their movements (figs. 39 and 40). Frank Crowninshield championed Covarrubias's works in *Vanity Fair* and praised his drawings for their "'aliveness,' a feeling of actuality, plus a rhythmic, almost sensuous movement."[14]

Covarrubias's drawings of "New Negroes" answered the call for authenticity made by Aaron Douglas in his 1925 letter to Langston Hughes, quoted in the epigraph. Responses to the images aligned along a spectrum from disgust to fascination, parallel to white reactions to jazz. The music's Black authenticity and musical novelty elicited those reactions. Encouraging people to dance naturally in response to music, rather than following steps to specific dances, challenged prevailing ideas of propriety and personal control. Raymond Cogniat, a French art critic interested in

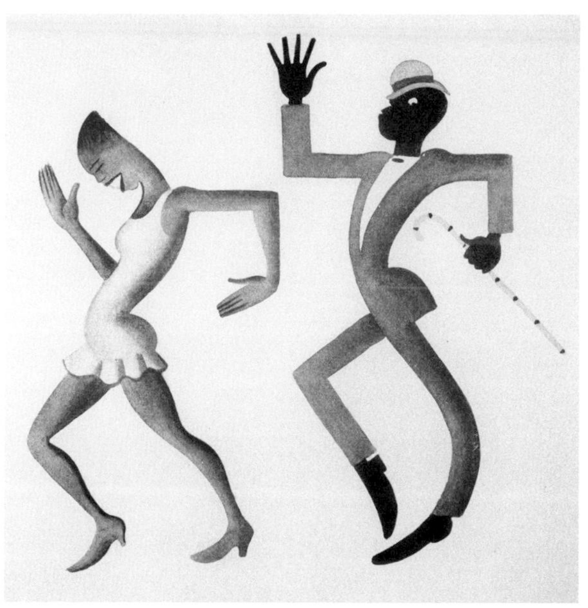

Fig. 39 Miguel Covarrubias (1904–1957), *The Stomp*, from *Negro Drawings by Miguel Covarrubias* (New York: Alfred A. Knopf, 1927). Printed matter. Delaware Art Museum, Helen Farr Sloan Library and Archives

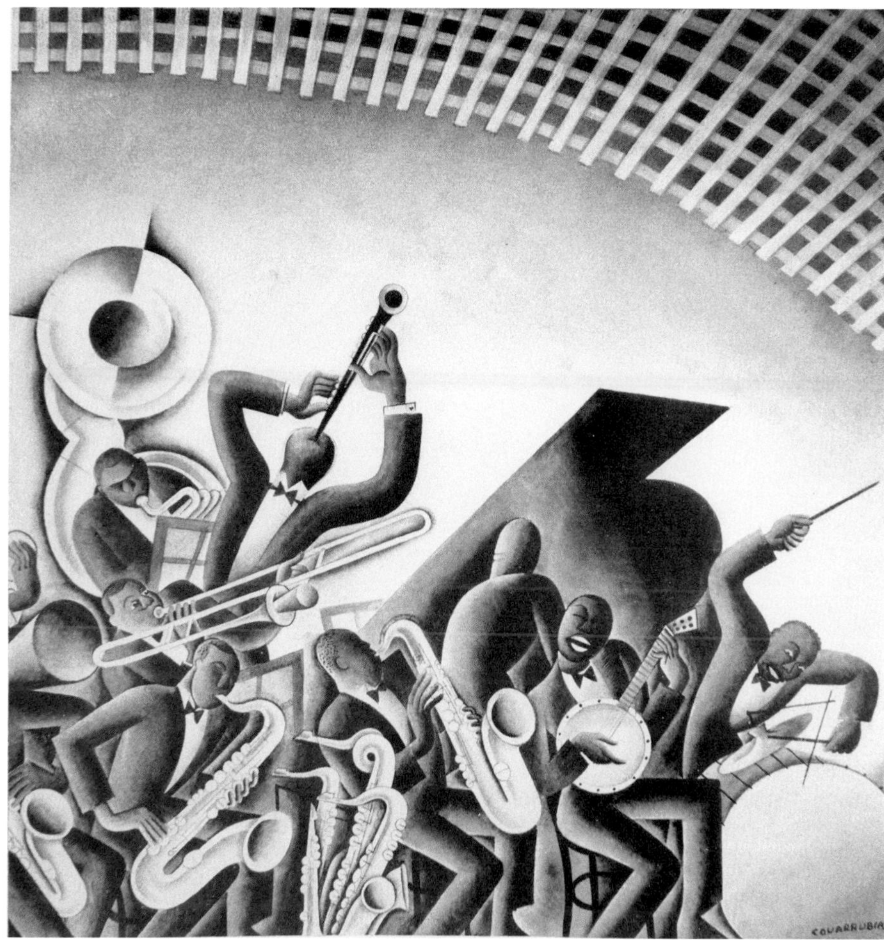

Fig. 40 Miguel Covarrubias (1904–1957), frontispiece from *Blues: An Anthology*, ed. W. C. Handy (New York: Albert & Charles Boni, 1926). Printed matter. Delaware Art Museum, Helen Farr Sloan Library and Archives

both African art and American jazz, maintained that the Black American dancer Josephine Baker "gave cohesion" to the sense of "savage frenzy and passionate rhythms" seeping into France during the Jazz Age.[15] This observation, although meant as praise, normalized prevailing negative stereotypes of the time. Tribal dances showing Black people responding to drumbeats became pervasive through popular Tarzan movies in the 1930s, further promoting the idea that responsive dancing was another sign of "savagery."

In the same way Black dance was maligned, African tribal art, which stylized figures and did not practice realism, was labeled as "primitive" by white Western artists and historians. Even though African art was appreciated aesthetically, it was considered crude and based on convention and craft rather than ideas. In reality, African tribal art was highly symbolic and functional in communicating societal ideas. Art historians misinterpreted abstract representation as a lack of skill. Starting in the late nineteenth century, Western artists embraced the art of "primitive" cultures and appropriated it to reshape modern art profoundly. In the early 1900s, for example, Picasso famously employed lessons learned from the study of African art to create Cubism. It was ironic that the same culture that labeled art by Indigenous people of color as "primitive" expansively idealized, emulated, and appropriated its forms and concepts in the 1920s. The Jazz Age elevated African-inspired music, design, and art as white scientists and academics worked to prove definitively that Black people were the inferior race. Like artists emulating African art, white people who went to jazz clubs and listened to Black music in the 1920s and '30s wanted what mainstream authoritative culture deemed unacceptable, but they found to be seductively authentic.

Recent research draws parallels between the enthusiasm for jazz in the '20s and hip-hop music today, suggesting that the perception of authenticity drives attraction to a culture that thrives outside of mainstream approval. In their article titled "Why Elites Love Authentic Lowbrow Culture: Overcoming High-Status Denigration with Outsider Art," researchers from Carnegie Mellon argue that 1920s flappers, jazz aficionados spanning decades, and contemporary middle-class hip-hop fans of all races are attracted to cultural expression that is rejected by standard gatekeepers like formal educational canons, critics, or people with status-bestowing job titles.[16] Some elites seek alternative experiences that originate from within people rather than being traditionally cultivated and externally approved. The very act of "discovering" cultural expression that does not look for mainstream approval gives the participant a sense of autonomy and authenticity.

In the 2020s, hip-hop is the most listened-to genre of popular music not because so many people relate directly to lyrics that speak to specific socio-economic experiences but because audiences identify with the impulses driving the expression. The fascination may look like voyeurism or a contemporary version of primitivism, but it is not entirely. People are drawn to authentic cultural expressions created outside of authoritative requirements and restrictions.

The idea of "high-lowbrow" experiences embodies the notion that "elites" elevate seemingly "lowbrow" cultural production and aesthetics through their participation and de facto seal of approval. This elevation is often true economically but not experientially. Cultural products like the hip-hop musical *Hamilton* took advantage of the high-lowbrow societal construction, allowing people from outside the demographic group that created it to experience hip-hop the same way segregated clubs catering to white elites allowed them to experience Black people playing jazz. These same people most likely would never have gone to an authentic jazz venue with a primarily Black clientele. By publishing Covarrubias's illustrations alongside captions written by Black poet Eric D. Walrond, *Vanity Fair* allowed its urbane readers to appreciate the latest in entertainment whether or not they visited Harlem's jazz clubs. The price of a ticket to *Hamilton* made this musical constructed around rapping, a component of hip-hop, an essentially elitist experience. Any New York subway rider in the late 1970s and 1980s could experience a spontaneously created rap battle as a call-and-response performance. Those events would not be recorded, sold, or exploited. They were one-of-a-kind, real-time, authentic experiences. The same could be said for early performances of jazz, described by Joel A. Rogers in 1925 as "a joyous revolt from convention, custom, authority, boredom, even sorrow—from everything that would confine the soul of man and hinder its riding free on the air."[17]

Differences in authenticity also existed in visual art. The female body was often the subject in Jazz Age art, illustration, and design. In stark contrast to boundaries imposed by Victorian and Gilded Age requirements for women's dress and behavior, the female form was freed and objectified in popular illustrations of the 1920s and '30s. Intention and reception were again dependent on the artist and context. Comparing a Cotton Club program cover showing a naked Black woman (except for high heels) in a performance pose to Black artist Robert Pious's cover for the American Negro Exposition program in 1940, the Black woman's bare breasts are perceived differently (see pl. 14 and fig. 41). In this era, photographs of bare-breasted Black and Indigenous women regularly appeared on tourist postcards and in the pages of the *National Geographic* magazine, presented as "primitive." These seemingly innocuous images promoted ideas

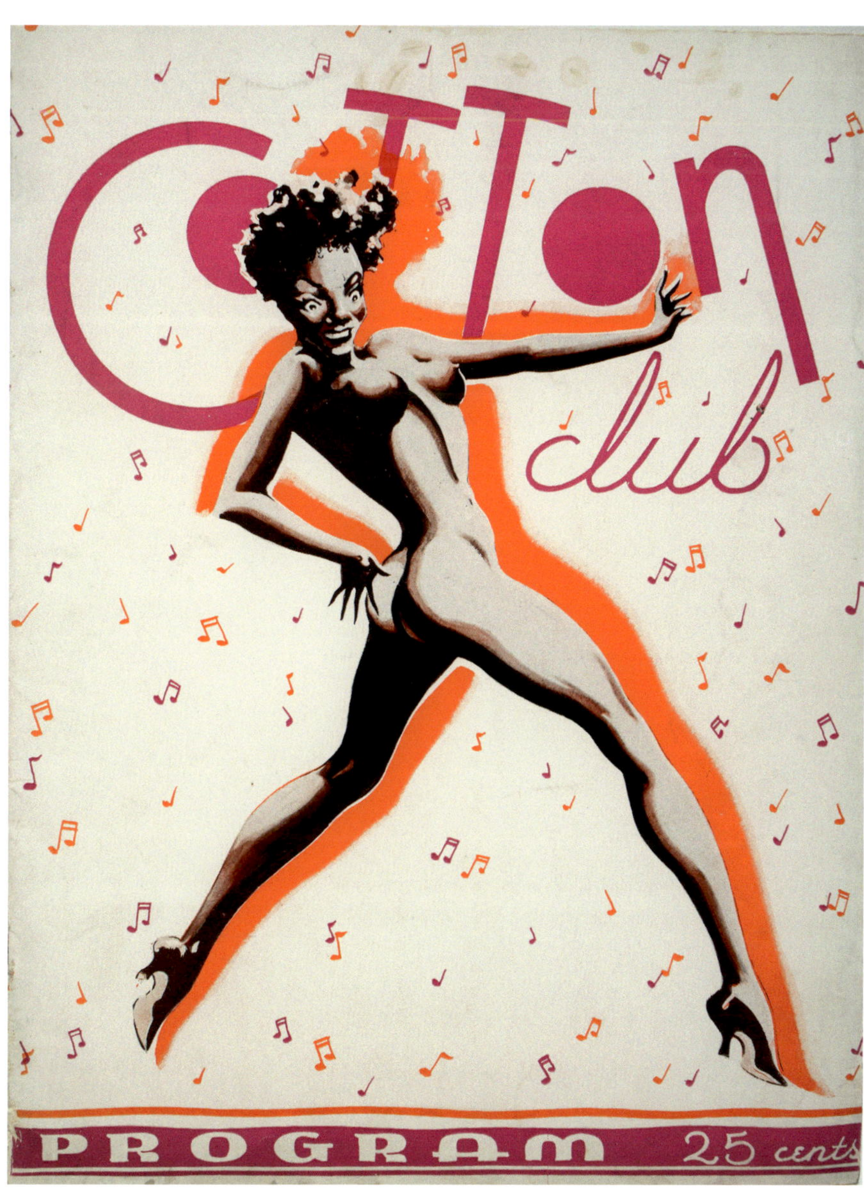

Fig. 41 Artist unknown, cover from *Cotton Club Program*, ca. 1939. Printed matter. Delaware Art Museum, Helen Farr Sloan Library and Archives

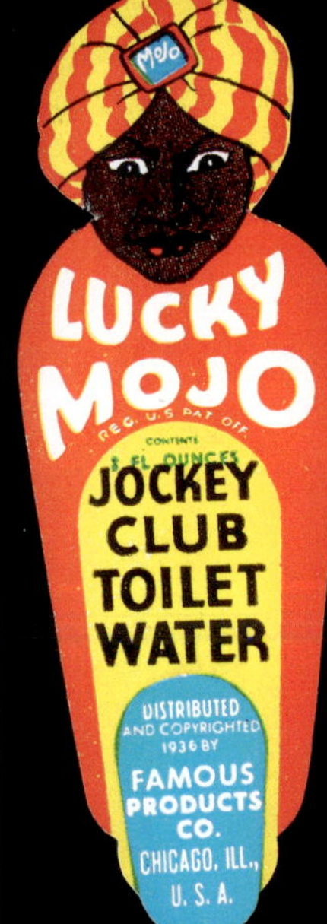

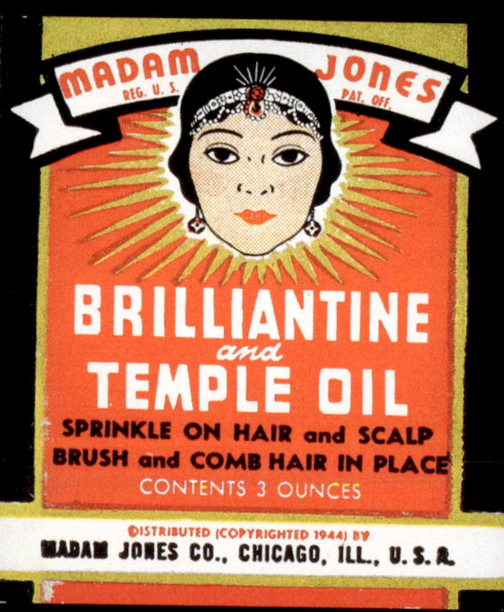

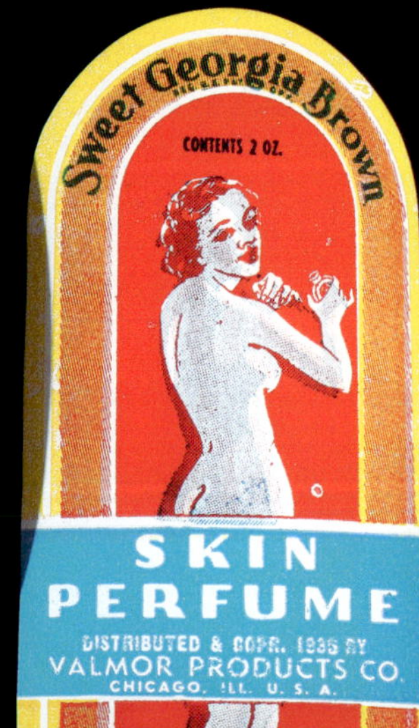

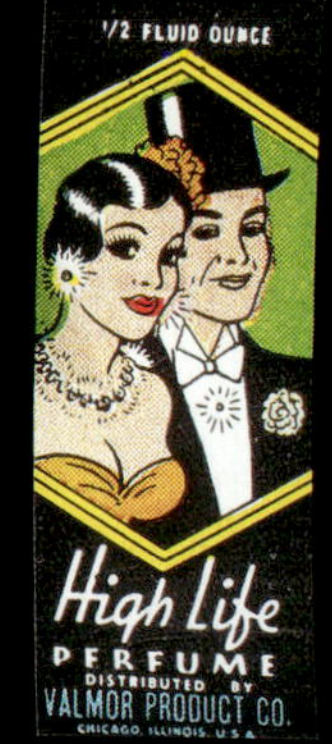

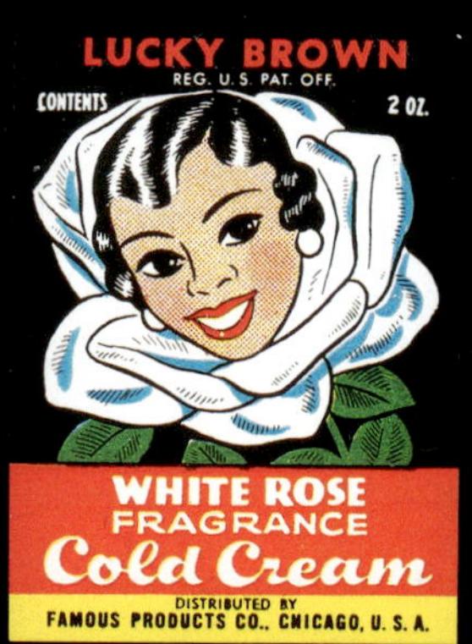

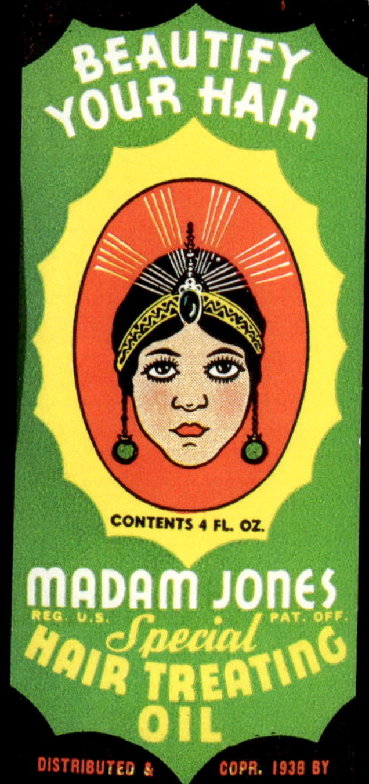

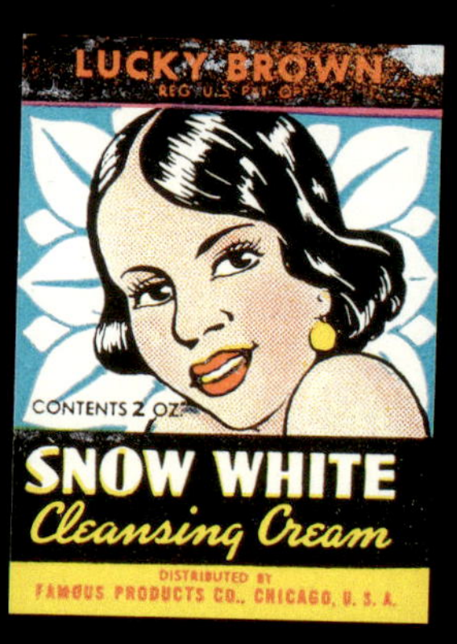

Fig. 42 Valmor Labels. Printed matter. Collection of Colette Gaiter

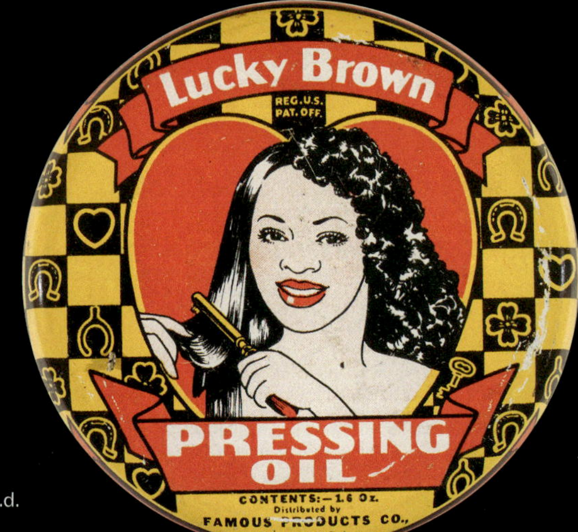

Fig. 43 Tin for Lucky Brown Pressing Oil, n.d. Painted tin, 2¾ (dia.) in. Private collection

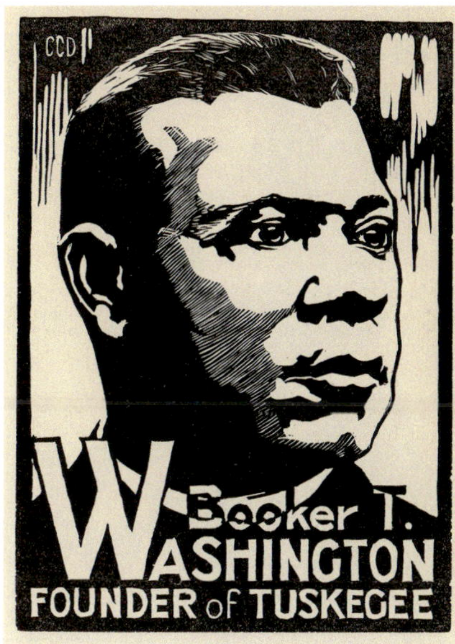

Fig. 44 Charles C. Dawson (1889–1981), from *The ABCs of Great Negroes* (Chicago: Dawson Publishers, 1933). Printed matter. Courtesy of the Free Library of Philadelphia, Social Science and History Department

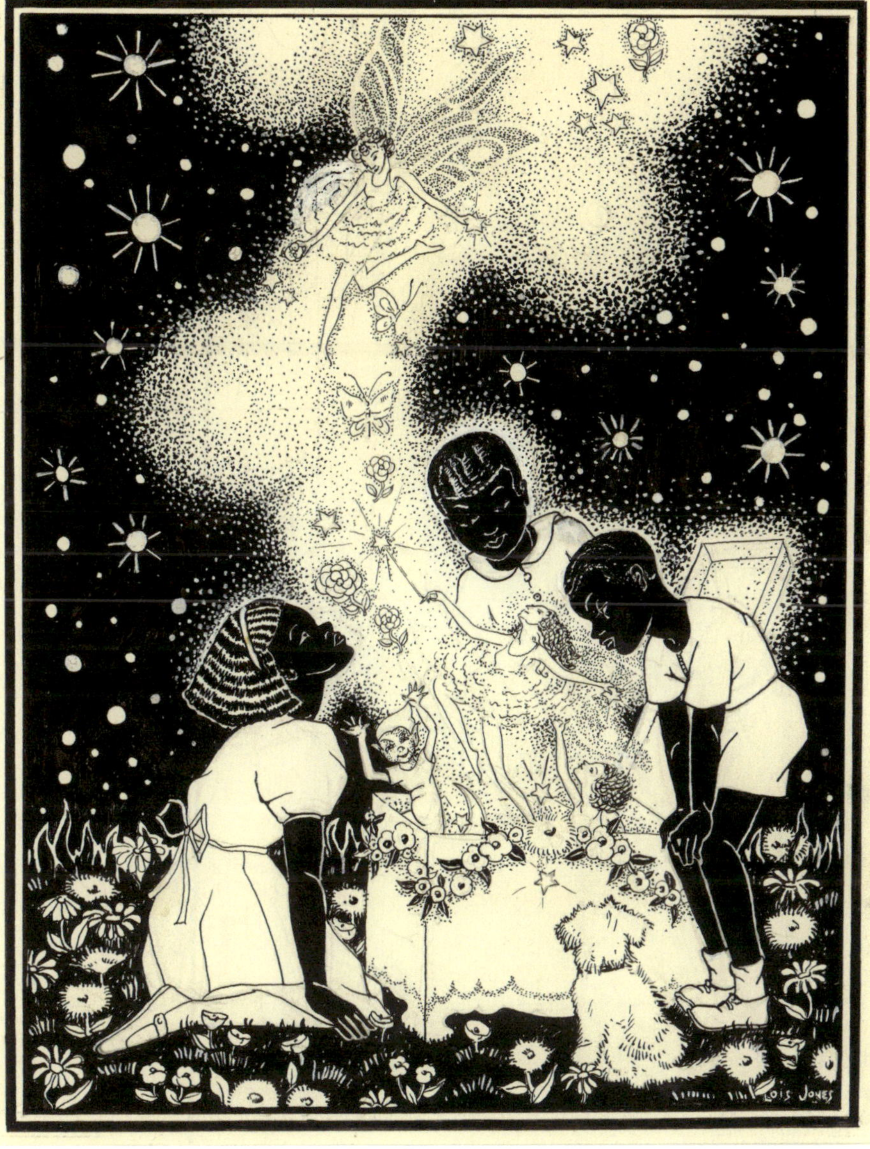

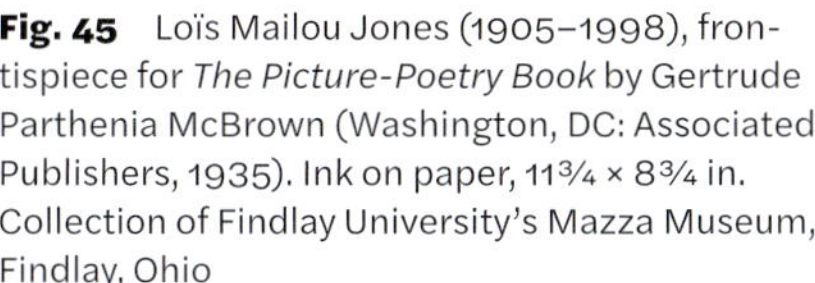

Fig. 45 Loïs Mailou Jones (1905–1998), frontispiece for *The Picture-Poetry Book* by Gertrude Parthenia McBrown (Washington, DC: Associated Publishers, 1935). Ink on paper, 11¾ × 8¾ in. Collection of Findlay University's Mazza Museum, Findlay, Ohio

of cultural "backwardness" in native people of color worldwide, insidiously and effectively supporting white supremacy. The supposed intention was anthropological and educational, but in a repressed, white-dominated society, these photographs offered a voyeuristic and titillating glimpse of body parts that could only otherwise be acceptably viewed in art museums in paintings of nudes presented as culturally elevated works of art. Pious's depiction was of an authentic Black woman, dressed as she would be in her native environment, holding broken chains and a book, which could represent using knowledge to resist assimilation. For Black people in the Jazz Age, celebrating connections to Africa contradicted pressure to assimilate to white standards of appearance, behavior, or creative expression. As Aaron Douglas expressed in his letter to Langston Hughes, Black people needed to reach into "the very depths of the souls of our people."[18]

Assimilation

At the same time that some Harlem Renaissance Black visual artists like Aaron Douglas depicted African-inspired scenes, those working for white businesses promoted the assimilationist aesthetics required of their employment. Illustrations created for the Valmor Products Company in Chicago visualized racial assimilation as the products facilitated those goals. Creams, pomades, lotions, and oils for skin lightening and hair "taming" and straightening had labels featuring light-skinned, wavy-haired women and men of color that illustrated the products' transformative claims (figs. 42 and 43). Charles C. Dawson and Jay Jackson's prolific illustration work helped make the Valmor company profitable and enduring. Covers and illustrations for *The Crisis* and *Opportunity* consistently showed women dressed according to conventions of respectability and molded by the Black beauty culture of that time.[19]

Working at their day jobs, Dawson and Jackson helped Valmor sell assimilation. In other projects, they illuminated Black History and elevated Black aesthetics. These seemingly oppositional pursuits demonstrate Du Bois's identified conundrum of "double consciousness." These artists promoted assimilation and the opposite of Black authenticity to make a living. Through their creative pursuits, they were "race men," doing the work of "elevating the race" however they could.[20] Jay Jackson worked as a cartoonist for the nationally distributed Black newspaper the *Chicago Defender* and made illustrations of people like Etta Moten, while Dawson created and self-published the book *The ABCs of Great Negroes* (fig. 44).

These three children's book drawings by Loïs Mailou Jones illustrate what we now call "code-switching" in a visual form. Two illustrations show Black children, identified as such by darker skin and textured hair, who otherwise could be white children in their respective contexts (see pls. 36 and 37). In the third illustration, the children have Negro features and unmistakably Black skin (fig. 45). The first two illustrations show assimilationist aesthetics elevated by companies like Valmor. In contrast, the third illustration shows Black children drawn in the spirit of the Harlem Renaissance, showcasing Black aesthetics. Jones, who also worked as a textile designer in her early career, turned to Afrocentric painting during the later Black Arts movement.

Appropriation

> Quiet as it's kept, the music we call jazz began life as an experimental remix of dance grooves from Africa and Europe that got chopped and screwed by high-stepping bluesicians of New Orleans over a century ago. From the git-go, the jazz thing has been as much about alchemy as flashy chops.
>
> Everything we love about modern song, noise, and dance sprang from swing and bebop roots: r&b, rock, Motown, funk, disco, hip-hop, Detroit techno, Chicago house, drum & bass, et al. are all extensions of a movement-inciting continuum that started in antebellum New Orleans' Congo Square—breakbeat culture's ground zero.[21]
>
> —Greg Tate

The era known as the Jazz Age was a racial cultural mashup across disciplines—music, literature, theater, and art. Cultural artifacts and practices of this time foreshadowed the effect of late twentieth-century hip-hop on music and the larger creative world. Jazz images provided "empirical evidence," supposedly proving claims of inherent racial inferiority. Similarly, hip-hop encouraged perceptions of young Black urban males as dangerous criminals. Despite these negative connotations, jazz and hip-hop are firmly embedded in American culture and influence culture far beyond music.

Maureen Anderson's 2008 article "The White Reception of Jazz in America" called out white critics' hostile critical reception of jazz in the 1910s and '20s:

> By asserting in 1925 that jazz 'is a release of all suppressed emotions at once' (Rogers, 30), J. A. Rogers created a description that whites would expand on in order to label jazz in Harlem culture as primitive and evil. Jazz served in several ways as a precursor to fifties' be-bop and rock-'n'-roll, eighties' pop, and nineties' rap. Principal among them is that jazz critics, like critics of these later musical forms, were often diabolical in their attacks on the music. Motivated by political and racial concerns, many jazz critics during the Harlem Renaissance publicized their dislike of jazz music in order to express their dislike of African Americans.[22]

Jazz is currently regarded as a sophisticated music genre, revered worldwide and celebrated for its African American roots. An October 2022 article from *Billboard* maintained that hip-hop was still the most popular genre of music after overtaking rock in 2018.[23] Blues, jazz, R&B, gospel, soul, and hip-hop created the "Afro-Americanization of popular music."[24] 2023 marks the fiftieth anniversary of hip-hop, which spawned exhibitions like the Baltimore Museum of Art's *The Culture: Hip Hop and Contemporary Art in the 21st Century,* among many others across the country.

Jazz and hip-hop are two original African American forms of music that are internationally celebrated, re-interpreted, and disseminated. Neither of these musical forms would exist without the infusion of African traditions. Work created by African American visual artists is only recently being researched and exhibited from as far back as the time of enslavement. Looking closely at the work of Black artists, illustrators, and designers from the concurrent Harlem Renaissance and Jazz Age through publications and commercial art sources expands understanding of all American visual and material culture. African American artists, designers, and illustrators of the Jazz Age and Harlem Renaissance changed representations of Black people and helped move visual communication toward modernism. Instead of relying on white depictions of Black Americans, which most often communicated bias and contributed to racism and stereotyping, African American visual artists crafted an accurate and proud identity. The style of Art Deco, an integral part of Jazz Age visualization, was appropriated from African visual abstraction.[25] Black artists reclaimed their heritage as part of an interdisciplinary movement, while white artists assumed a style that looked new, modern, and simple after a period of Western ornamental aesthetics inspired by nature.[26] Harlem Renaissance and Jazz Age Black artists participated in African-inspired Art Deco and saw modernism as a symbol of progress for Black people in the United States.

In addition to appreciating these Black visual artists' work on its own merits, it is essential to acknowledge the double consciousness required to produce work simultaneously for themselves and their people—and for a predominately white society determined to diminish them and separate them from their heritage. Contemplating intersections between art, music, and race in the Jazz Age offers a way to look at cultural suppression and unacknowledged appropriation. Early white critics of jazz described the music and dancing it inspired with phrases like "jungle gifts of the American negro [*sic*]," as if that was a bad thing.[27] African Americans have, to date, had the most profound cultural influence on music in the context of all the arts. Perhaps it is because the music was clearly so different from existing popular music. Black music and art from the early 1900s contributed indelible cultural experiences that embody pride and pure joy—and reveal pain—to American collective consciousness. Early Jazz Age music and images became part of culture's evolutionary flow, moving the "exotic" or "deviant" into creative products that are authentically attributed, assimilated into contemporary culture, and continue to be appropriated, remixed, and mashed up to create the next new thing.

ENDNOTES

1. Aaron Douglas to Langston Hughes, December 21, 1925, James Weldon Johnson Memorial Collection of Negro Arts and Letters, Beinecke Rare Book and Manuscript Library, Yale University; quoted in Amy Helene Kirschke, *Aaron Douglas: Art, Race, and the Harlem Renaissance* (Jackson: University Press of Mississippi, 1995), 78–79.

2. Mamadou Badiane, "Negritude and Negrismo," in *Encyclopedia of Race and Racism*, ed. Patrick L. Mason, 2nd ed., (Detroit, MI: Gale, Cengage Learning, 2013).

3. Badiane, "Negritude and Negrismo."

4. Frank Mehring, "How Silhouettes Became 'Black': Winold Reiss and the Visual Rhetoric of the Harlem Renaissance," in *Circulation*, ed. François Brunet (Chicago: Terra Foundation for American Art, 2017), 192.

5. For a detailed discussion of *Fire!!*, see Caroline Goeser, *Picturing the New Negro: Harlem Renaissance Print Culture and Modern Black Identity* (Lawrence: University Press of Kansas, 2007), 30–31, 89–93.

6. https://www.aiga.org/inspiration/talks/aaron-douglas-2018-aiga-medalist-aaron-douglas. Accessed October 23, 2023. The award was first given in 1920. In 2007 Georg Olden posthumously became the first African American to receive an AIGA medal. In 2015 Emory Douglas became the first living Black person to be recognized as a medalist by the AIGA.

7. Examples include Paul Colin's pictures of Josephine Baker, published in the portfolio *Le Tumulte Noir par Paul Colin* (Paris: Éditions d'art, Succès, 1929) as lithographs with pochoir coloring on paper (Merrill C. Berman Collection, New York).

8. W. E. B. Du Bois, "Strivings of the Negro People," *Atlantic* 80 (August 1897): 194; Du Bois, *The Souls of Black Folk* (1903; repr., New York: Penguin, 1989), 5.

9. David A. Horowitz, "The Normality of Extremism: The Ku Klux Klan Revisited," *Society* 35 (September/October 1998): 71. This tactic mirrors aspects of 2023 US right-wing politics that minimize escalating racial extremism while espousing conservative values.

10. Goeser points out how white publishers selected Covarrubias's work over that of Black artists. Goeser, *Aaron Douglas: Art, Race, and the Harlem Renaissance*, 104.

11. Colette Gaiter, "The New Visual Abnormal," in *The Black Experience in Design: Identity, Expression & Reflection*, ed. Anne H. Berry (New York: Allworth Press, 2022), 132.

12. Wendy Wick Reaves, *Celebrity Caricature in America* (Washington, DC: National Portrait Gallery, 1998), 178.

13. Reaves, 3.

14. Frank Crowninshield, "Introduction," *Negro Drawings by Miguel Covarrubias* (New York: Alfred A. Knopf, 1927), n.p. [9].

15. Anna Kisselgoff, "Josephine Baker; Dancing through the Jazz Age," *New York Times*, March 29, 1987: https://www.nytimes.com/1987/03/29/arts/dance-view-joesphine-baker-dancing-through-the-jazz-age.html.

16. Oliver Hahl, Ezra W. Zuckerman, and Minjae Kim, "Why Elites Love Authentic Lowbrow Culture: Overcoming High-Status Denigration with Outsider Art," *American Sociological Review* 82 (August 2017): 828–56: http://www.jstor.org/stable/26426358. Accessed October 9, 2023.

17. Joel A. Rogers, "Jazz at Home," *Survey Graphic* 53, no. 11 (March 1, 1925): 665.

18. Quoted in Kirschke, *Aaron Douglas: Art, Race, and the Harlem Renaissance*, 79.

19. The company employed many Black workers in its Chicago South Side facilities and paid both Dawson and Jackson as employees, but they did not receive credit for their work until much later. In 2015 the Chicago Cultural Center presented an exhibition of Valmor art called "Love for Sale," which was the first comprehensive exhibition of the artwork produced for the brand between the 1920s and 1980s: https://www.chicago.gov/city/en/depts/dca/supp_info/valmor.html.

20. Eric S. Charry, *A New and Concise History of Rock and R&B through the Early 1990s* (Middletown, CT: Wesleyan University Press, 2020), 14; citing Zora Neale Hurston, *Dust Tracks on the Road: An Autobiography* (New York: Lippincott, 1942): "A 'Race Man' was somebody who always kept the glory and honor of his race before him. . . . It was a mark of shame if somebody accused: 'Why, you are not a Race Man (or woman).' People made whole careers of being 'Race' men and women. They were champions of the race."

21. Greg Tate, "Why Jazz Will Always Be Relevant," in *Ain't But a Few of Us: Black Music Writers Tell Their Story*, ed. Willard Jenkins (Durham, NC: Duke University Press, 2022), 264.

22. Maureen Anderson, "The White Reception of Jazz in America," *African American Review* 38 (Spring 2004): 135.

23. Isanul Ahmed, "Is Hip-Hop's Dominance Slipping? 'My Concern Is the Magic Is Gone,'" Billboard.com, posted October 18, 2022: https://www.billboard.com/pro/hip-hop-music-most-popular-genre-dominance-slipping/. Accessed October 23, 2023.

24. Mehring, "How Silhouettes Became 'Black,'"183.

25. Jane Goldberg, "Celebrating a Little-Known Influence on Art Deco," *New York Times,* January 11, 1996: https://www.nytimes.com/1996/01/11/garden/celebrating-a-littleknown-influence-on-art-deco.html.

26. Art Nouveau, William Morris, and the Arts and Crafts movement resisted the Industrial Revolution but were overpowered by simplicity (which was not new), technology, and modernity.

27. "The Jazz Age," *Capital Journal* (Salem, OR), October 13, 1919.

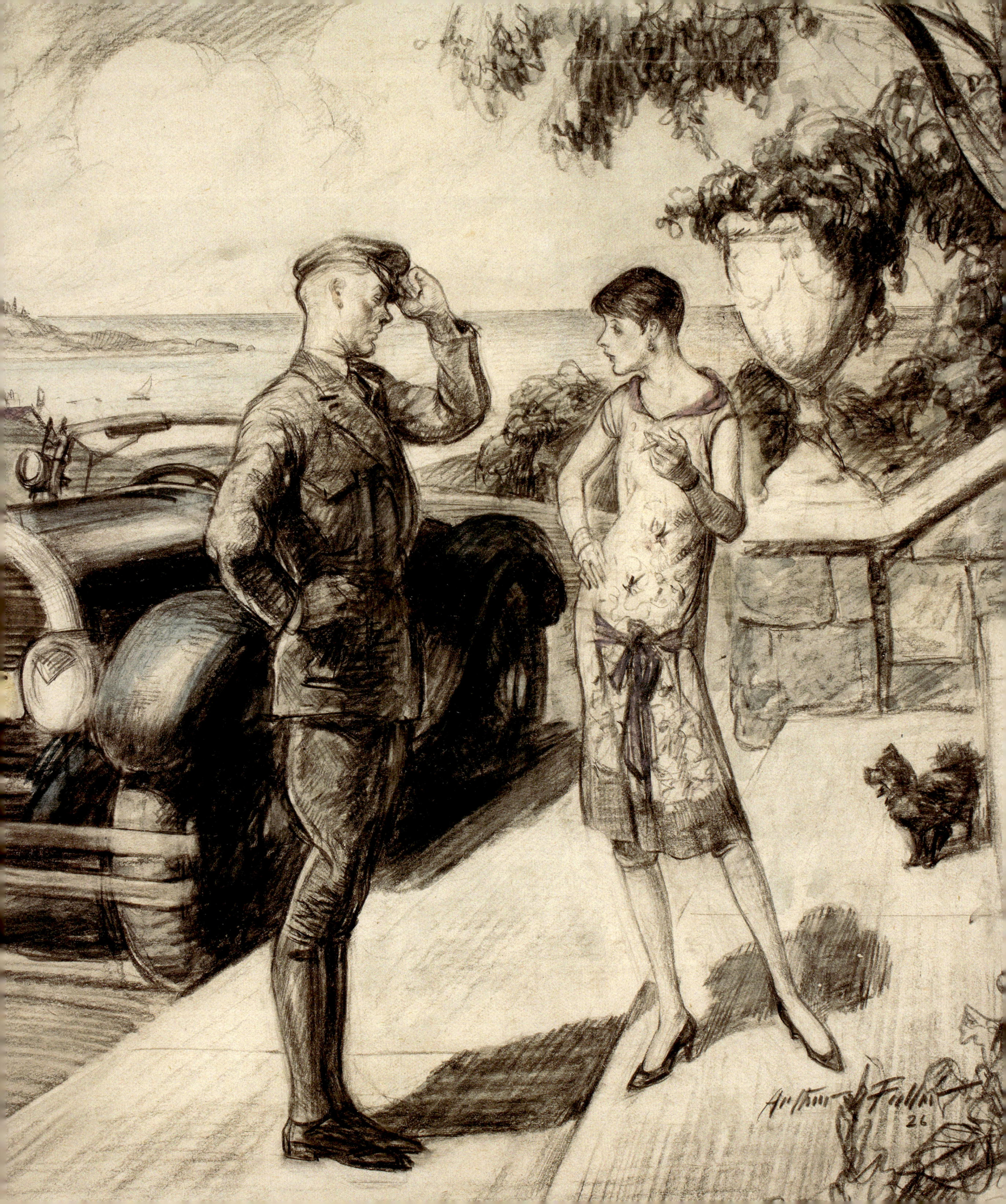

Victoria Rose Pass

Fashioning Jazz Age Illustration

A slim figure in a bathing suit stands on a beach framed with palm trees (fig. 46). In a boat on the water, a man in similar attire stares intently through large binoculars. The tagline below seems to render his thoughts: "It's a GIRL!" The gawker's confusion is the crux of the joke. At first glance, the main figure reads as masculine. The swimsuit, with its green and white striped sleeveless top and yellow and black shorts, clings close to a figure with only the barest hint of breasts. Her gender is revealed by her actions: the woman is powdering her cheeks, gazing into an open compact. She is emphatically modern, publicly applying makeup and wearing a short hairstyle and a very brief androgynous swimsuit. Conceived by Russell Patterson, this illustration appeared on the cover of the satirical magazine *Life*, where the gag was one of many that poked fun at the new fashions favored by youth in the 1920s.[1]

In an illustration from John Held Jr.'s 1929 story "A Man of the World," a young man lounges on a chair, a candlestick phone carefully balanced in one hand and a cigarette dangling from the other (fig. 47). His oversized trousers complement his slim-fitting shirt. He wears a bold polka-dotted necktie, and his other ties are tossed nonchalantly on the arm of a lamp. A college student, he is the epitome of casual cool in his wide-legged Oxford bags. His body is arranged in diagonals that contrast sharply to the right angles of his surroundings, enhancing the impression of youthful insouciance—an attitude that endures even when he discovers that his onetime girlfriend is pregnant and is far more interested in returning to his card game.[2]

Arthur Davenport Fuller depicts Miss Fifi Printon in an illustration for the 1926 story "The Bad Little Egg," by Sophie Kerr (pl. 38). She wears a short bob haircut and a drop-waisted dress that reveals the tops of her rolled stockings. With one hand on her hip and a cigarette in the other, she stands talking to the chauffeur, John, who narrates the story. Fifi is described by John in disapproving terms as "one of these slippy little bean-pole babies with her hair slicked like a cat had licked it, and her stockings rolled down, and her skirts shortened up, and enough red and yellow and black paint slopped on her face to cover a motor truck, and a cigarette dangling off her lip continual, and all over she was strung on wires."[3] Fifi, the "Bad Little Egg" of the title, smokes, drinks, stays out late, drives recklessly, and flirts with her driver. And she has all the visual hallmarks of a flapper: the slim boyish figure, scantily clad, with clanging bracelets and obvious makeup.

These three illustrations reflect the excitement and anxiety many Americans felt in response to the enormous cultural shifts after World

Detail of pl. 38

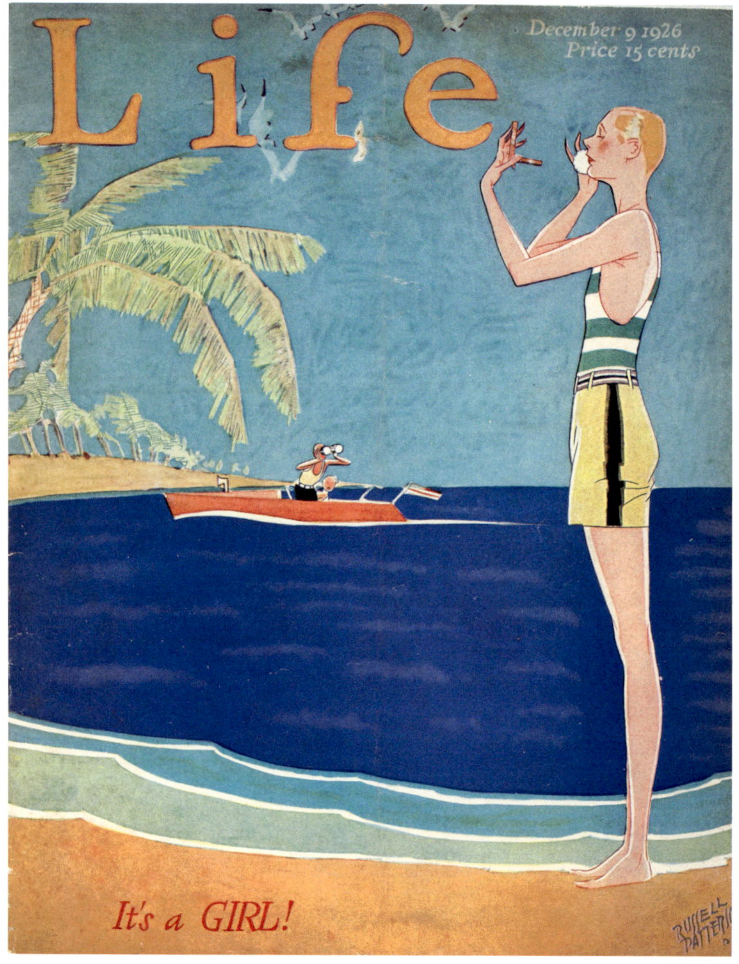

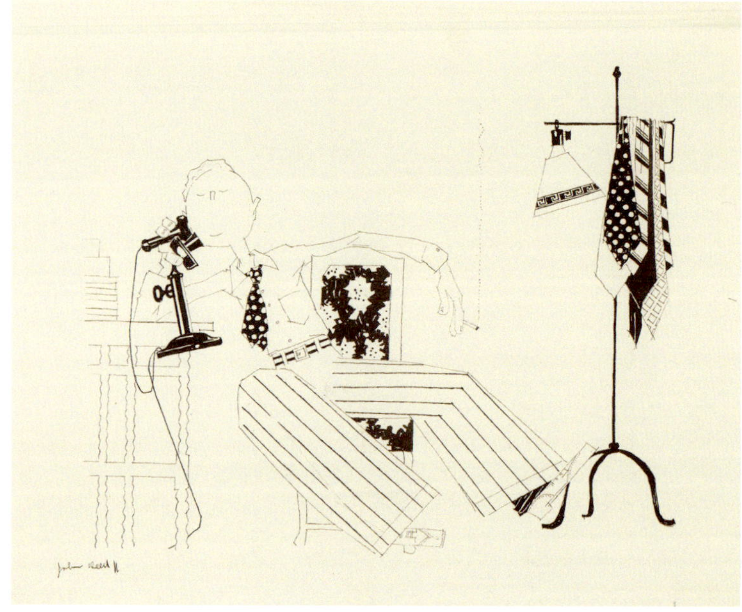

Fig. 46 Russell Patterson (1893–1977), *It's a Girl!*, cover from *Life*, December 9, 1926. Printed matter. Delaware Art Museum, Helen Farr Sloan Library and Archives

Fig. 47 John Held Jr. (1889–1958), *Mr. Harkness Talking*, for "A Man of the World," *Grim Youth* (New York: Vanguard Press, 1930). Ink on illustration board, 11 × $14\frac{15}{16}$ in. Delaware Art Museum, Special Purchase Fund, 1969

War I. The growth of youth culture and the expansion of the popular press resulted in a proliferation of images representing young people and the fashions that expressed their new attitudes. Illustrators had a significant role in helping to construct and promote what sartorial modernity looked like in the postwar years.

Youth in Print

The 1920s saw an explosion of an increasingly nationalized popular culture through movies, radio, and magazines. The circulation of magazines in the US nearly doubled from 1900 to 1923.[4] Magazines were crucial to the dissemination of new fashions. Articles, stories, and illustrations reflected and shaped the popular understanding of modern styles. Fashion magazines such as *Vogue* and *Harper's Bazaar* were only part of that landscape. In the 1920s and '30s, ideas about fashionability and modernity for both men and women came from a wider variety of sources, including men's and women's magazines, movie magazines, and general interest publications like *Collier's* and *The Saturday Evening Post*, as well as syndicated cartoons and comic strips in newspapers.

The stories in these periodicals, both fiction and nonfiction, reflected the changing lives of Americans during this time. More women were seeking higher education and entering the job market, and if they were white, they were newly eligible to vote. Young people were moving away from their families, driving automobiles, and playing sports. The Great Migration of African Americans from the rural South to northern cities led to the growth of neighborhoods like Harlem in New York and Bronzeville in Chicago. The jazz music played in these neighborhoods was soon heard in nightclubs catering to white audiences. Jazz ushered in a new sound for popular music and, with it, athletic dances like the Charleston and the Black Bottom. A sexual revolution was fueled by the privacy offered by cars, as well as more open discussion of sexuality and the increasing availability of birth control. These changes were mapped onto clothing by American authors and illustrators. The Bad Little Egg's badness is represented in how she dresses.

Keeping It Casual

While men's fashions changed more slowly than women's, there were many subtle ways that writers and illustrators could use clothing to convey modernity and personal character. By the 1920s, the sack suit was firmly established as the standard man's uniform. The stylish cut, with a distinctive slim fit and a tapered waist, is evident on the men attending a college dance in May Wilson Watkins Preston's illustrations for "Honor" in *The Saturday Evening Post* (fig. 48). The shoulders have a natural drape, and the trousers are slim fitting. Among the tuxedos, one man stands out for his blue sports coat and gray slacks, clothing typical of the university setting where the story unfolds.

Fig. 48 May Wilson Watkins Preston (1873–1949), *Without thinking, without caring, he walked two steps out on the floor,* for "Honor" by Charles Wertenbaker, *The Saturday Evening Post*, August 3, 1929. Charcoal and watercolor on illustration board, sheet: 20 3/16 × 16 7/16 in. Delaware Art Museum, Gift of Helen Farr Sloan, 1987. Illustration © SEPS licensed by Curtis Licensing Indianapolis, IN. All rights reserved

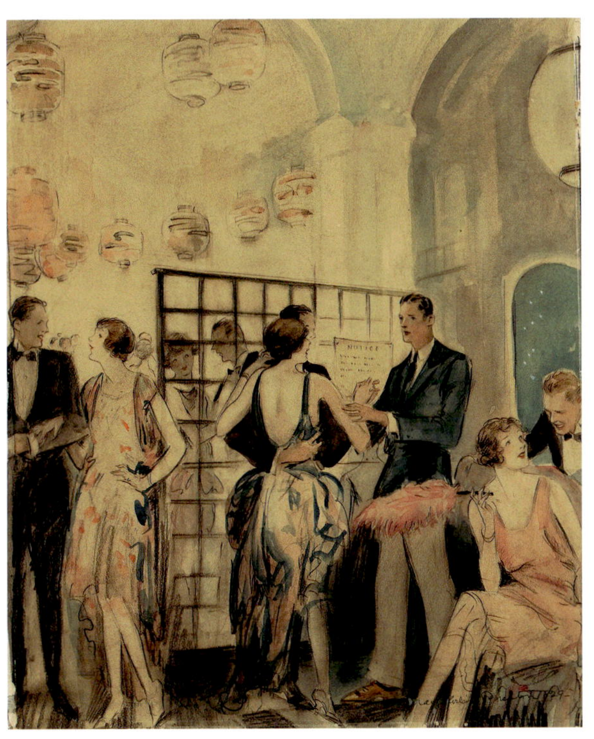

Casual styles drawn from sportswear, such as sweaters and baggy knickers known as plus-fours (because four inches of fabric hung over the knee band), began to appear in cities and on college campuses. Softer sport coats worn with flannel trousers became a popular replacement for full suits for many collegiate activities. Rolled collars began to replace stiff ones, though neckties remained an essential accessory. The style is seen in the ensembles worn in Henrietta McCaig Starrett's illustration of young men at boarding school (pl. 39).

In his drawings and stories, John Held Jr. captured the new and casual style of his characters, including the occupant of Kappa House named Spug Harkness, who is the protagonist in "A Man of the World" (see fig. 47). Spug's attire, like his faddish raccoon coat worn in another illustration, expresses his modern sensibility as much as the telephone he comfortably holds. Spug wears Oxford bags, a type of very baggy trouser supposedly adopted by Oxford students to wear over knickers, saving them a trip back to the dormitories to change into the more relaxed style after class.[5] These were significantly different than the slim-cut trousers and sack suits worn by most men at the time, and they signaled his youth and associated him with his privileged university setting.

In John P. Marquand's 1926 story "The Blame of Youth," even forty-three-year-old Armitage Gleason looked to collegiate styles when he outfitted himself for a return to an old haunt from his youth, the Pentecost Harbor Club (fig. 49). He describes buying "the white flannels, the buckskin shoes, and the socks and neckties from the collegian counter at Poole's," especially for the trip.[6] In Arthur William Brown's illustration, Armitage relaxes in the club with a distinctly upper-class group in casual sportswear.

Many histories note how men's fashion was democratized beginning in the second half of the nineteenth century with the increasing availability of ready-to-wear clothing. Even so, the cachet of fashionable styles in the 1920s and '30s relied on their associations with wealth and class. Tailors and designers looked to Princeton and other Ivy League campuses for the newest trends in menswear. It was the seal of approval provided by the white upper classes who occupied those spaces that could make sportswear (and even eventually workwear such as jeans) fashionable for the masses. With only about eight percent of Americans attending college in 1920, illustrations were an important way these styles spread. Stories such as F. Scott Fitzgerald's "Basil and Cleopatra," which appeared in *The Saturday Evening Post* with watercolors by Henrietta McCaig Starrett, showed college men in sportswear on and off the football field (fig. 50).[7] Fashion historian Deidre Clemente has charted the ways that college students pioneered the casual styles that would eventually permeate the American wardrobe.[8] She notes significantly, "Dressing down became democratic in its accessibility, but rich, white men got to do it first. Race, class, and gender determined who wore casual clothing, how early in the century they wore it, and often, what form it took."[9]

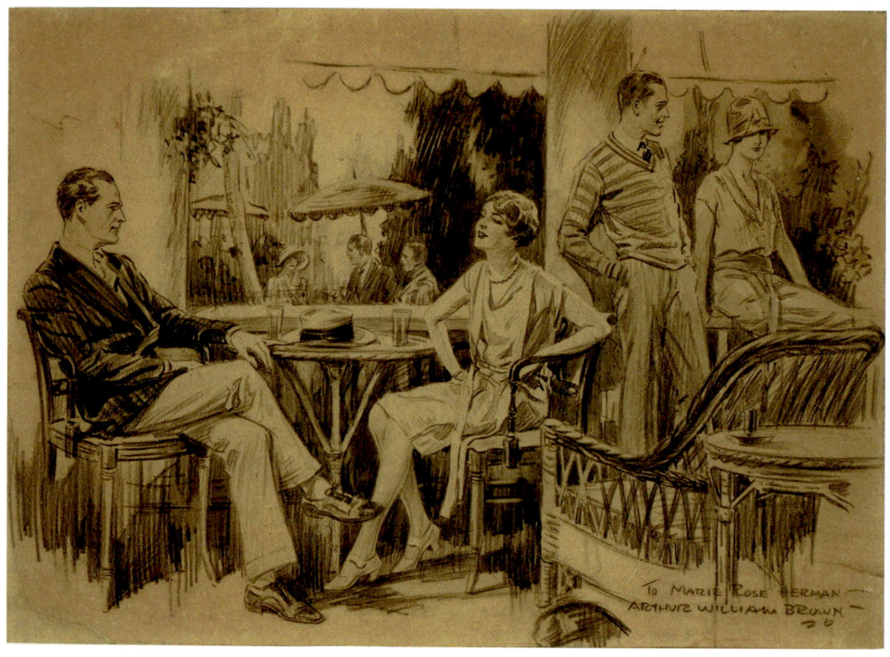

Fig. 49 Arthur William Brown (1881–1966), *"Yes," she said, "we're here." And suddenly she smiled. "I think it's awfully crowded here, don't you?,"* for "The Blame of Youth" by John P. Marquand, *The Saturday Evening Post*, May 29, 1926. Graphite on illustration board, sheet: 14½ × 19⅞ in. Delaware Art Museum, Gift of Mr. and Mrs. William Radebaugh, 1976

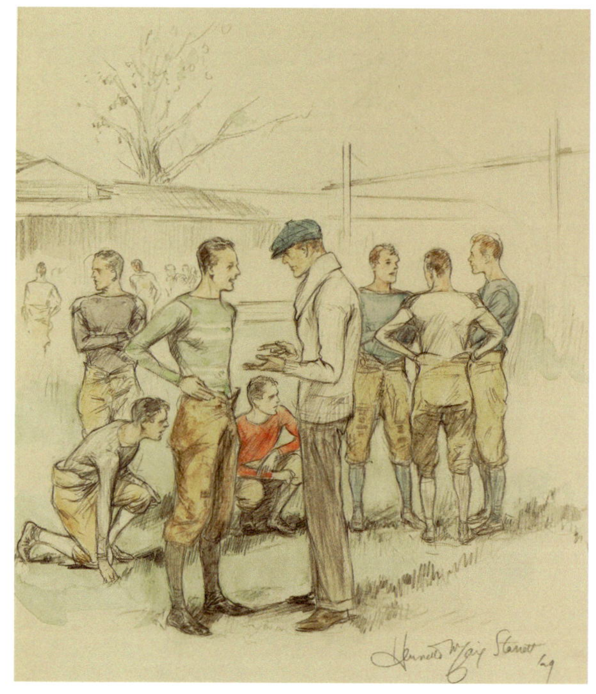

Fig. 50 Henrietta McCaig Starrett (1893–1963), *At the end of four days he was reconciling himself to obscurity for the rest of the season when the voice of Carson, assistant coach, singled him suddenly out of a crowd of scrub backs,* for "Basil and Cleopatra" by F. Scott Fitzgerald, *The Saturday Evening Post*, April 27, 1929. Charcoal, graphite, and watercolor on illustration board, sheet: 13 15/16 × 10⅞ in. Delaware Art Museum, John Sloan Purchase Fund, 1981. Illustration © SEPS licensed by Curtis Licensing Indianapolis, IN. All rights reserved

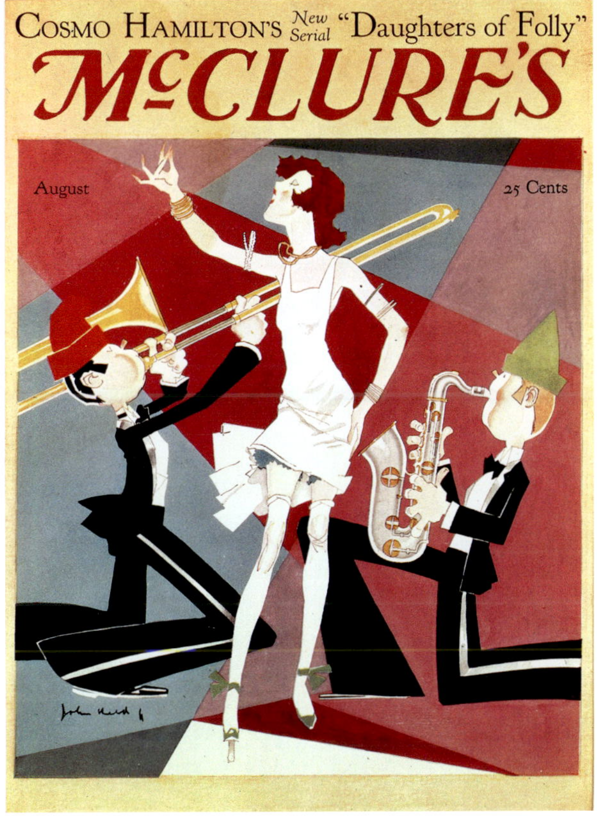

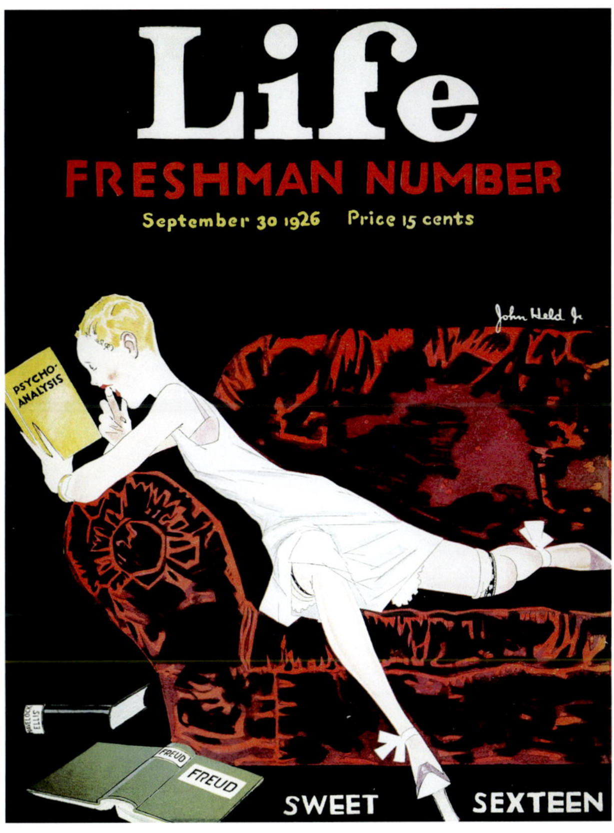

Fig. 51 John Held Jr. (1889–1958), cover from *McClure's*, August 1927. Printed matter. Granger Historical Picture Archive, Brooklyn, New York

Fig. 52 John Held Jr. (1889–1958), cover from *Life*, September 30, 1926. Printed matter. Granger Historical Picture Archive, Brooklyn, New York

Flapper Philosophy

If the college man was the icon of youthful men's apparel in the 1920s, then the flapper was his feminine equivalent and a favorite among illustrators at the time. These flappers, with their embrace of modern styles, modern music, and modern morals, troubled many Americans. Jazz was so critical to the image of the flapper that "The Bad Little Egg" is illustrated dancing the Charleston, although that is never mentioned in the story. Fifi's style and her bad habits repel her chauffeur, who prefers her maid Ella, who dresses simply in handmade clothing. The narrator disparages the flapper, but for the illustrator and presumably the readers, Fifi is far more exciting than Ella, who appears in only one drawing. Fifi represents all that is wrong with young women in the 1920s, but she dominates the story and its illustrations, as flappers dominated the pages of American magazines.

John Held Jr. produced iconic images of flappers, who dance across the covers of *Life* magazine, embodying the syncopated rhythms of jazz with their limbs boldly akimbo. They smoke, dance the Charleston, shout at football games, drive, drink, and read Freud (figs. 51 and 52). They are clearly understandable as flappers through their clothing: short skirts (sometimes above the knee) that often reveal the tops of rolled stockings; stacks of bracelets and armlets; swinging strands of pearls; cloche hats; short, bobbed haircuts; and high heels.

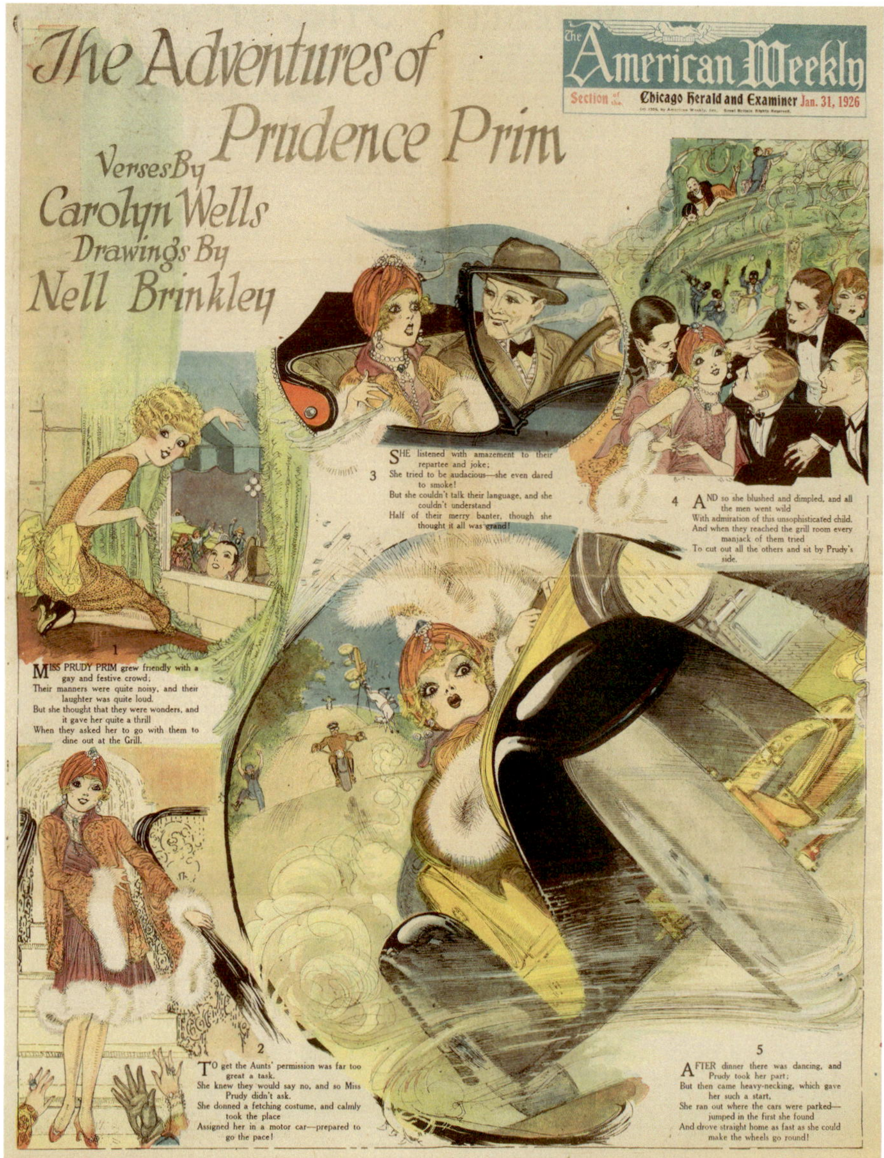

Fig. 53 Nell Brinkley (1886–1944), *The Adventures of Prudence Prim*, from *American Weekly, Chicago Herald and Examiner*, January 31, 1926. Printed matter. Delaware Art Museum, Helen Farr Sloan Library and Archives

Clothing was a critical means of expressing and representing freedom.[10] Flapper style offered a visual language women could use to assert control over their own bodies and sexuality, as well as providing new comfort and mobility that allowed them to participate in public life in ways that challenged old orthodoxies. This shift is revealed in the sheer number of representations of the flapper that put her directly at odds with her more conservative elders. In Charles Dana Gibson's amusing cartoon, *Have you a book innocent enough for grandma and grandpa to read?*, the contrast of skirt lengths and hat styles tells a significant part of this story of the generational divide (pl. 40).

Women also began to cut their hair short in larger numbers, sparking a moral panic in the US about the social implications of bobbed hair—well represented in the anxiety around the androgyny of Russell Patterson's *Life* cover girl. Newspaper headlines screamed: "Bobs Hair, Kills Herself: Disappointed School Girl Throws Herself into River," "Resents Wife's Hair Bob: Reading Husband Protests So Loudly the Neighbors Call Police," "Employers' Views Vary on Girl Who Bobs her Hair: 'We Don't Want Baby Dolls,'" Says One—'Let Girls Show Their Ears,' Says Another—Opinions Differ," and "Youth Shoots Fiancee [*sic*], Jumps off Tower When She Bobs Hair."[11]

Visible makeup, which had been viewed as disreputable in the preceding decades, was not only becoming acceptable, but women were increasingly taking up space by applying cosmetics in public.[12] The woman gazing into her compact was ubiquitous on magazine covers (see pls. 1, 41, and fig. 24). Lipstick and other cosmetics became potent signifiers of modernity. In 1932 a writer for *Vogue* explained, "If we were perpetuating the gestures of the twentieth century for posterity, certainly putting on lipstick would head the list."[13] Women were becoming more visible in public spaces, and so were their bodies.

Nell Brinkley's flapper Prudence Prim was the epitome of such a modern woman (fig. 53). With her bobbed yellow curls, short skirts, rolled stockings, and bee-stung lips, Prudence climbed mountains, went to the beach in revealing swimsuits, and cavorted with men, all to her aunts' horror.[14] Faith Burrows's daily single-panel comic *Flapper Filosofy* featured fashionably attired women with a joking tagline, sometimes at the flapper's own expense (pl. 42). In a 1927 interview, F. Scott Fitzgerald, whose fiction had helped to codify the image of the flapper, explained: "The girls I wrote about were not a type—they were a generation. Free spirits—evolved through the war chaos and a final inevitable escape from restraint and inhibitions."[15]

The flapper was such an exciting and confounding figure in popular culture because she represented ideas of freedom for women, as well as freedom from the past—a strong desire on the heels of the horrors of World War I and the 1918 influenza pandemic. While the lived realities of these freedoms were contingent and depended on the privilege women already had based on race and class, they did carry a significant symbolic weight.

Fig. 54 C. Coles Phillips (1880–1927), advertisement for Holeproof Hosiery, 1922. Printed matter. Delaware Art Museum, Helen Farr Sloan Library and Archives

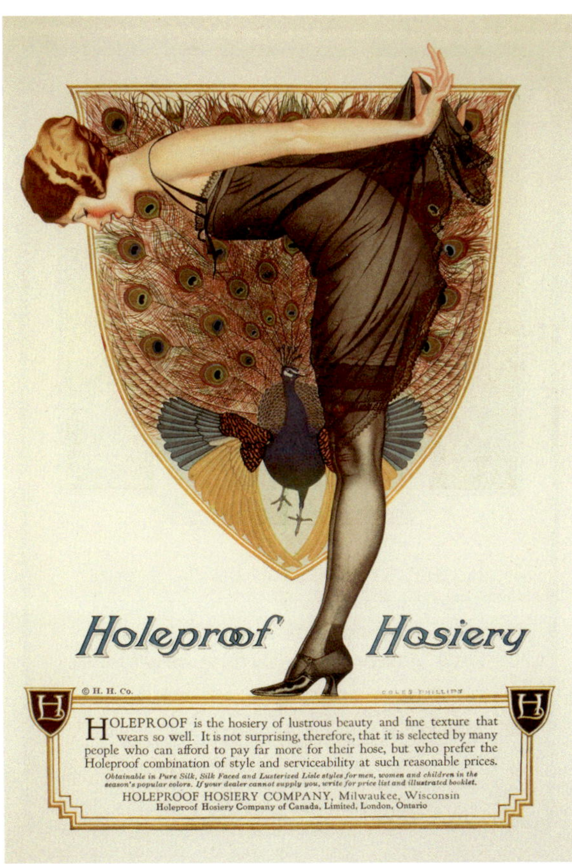

Underneath It All

For women and the illustrators who depicted them, revealing clothing was another significant way of signaling modernity. This extended beyond skirt length, with dresses that featured bare shoulders and open backs, providing a challenge to traditional lingerie. Neysa McMein's *The Admirable Hostess* focuses on the very open back of a fashionable evening gown (pl. 43). Illustrated by Coles Phillips, a 1922 advertisement for Holeproof Hosiery shows the filmy light undergarments worn by a modern young woman (fig. 54). Under her black slip, the model's camiknickers (or step-ins) are just visible, as are her elastic band garters. The sheer silk stockings she wears were a key part of a fashionable ensemble of the period because hemlines rose to show so much more of the leg than in previous decades.[16] Rolling stockings over an elastic garter under her knee to secure them revealed the wearer's bare knees when she sat down and even perhaps her bare thigh while dancing or moving.[17] They also allowed a woman to show that she was not wearing a corset or girdle—traditionally, stockings would have been secured with clips that hung from them. Unlike Phillips's demure model, a woman who rolled her stockings was signaling freedom from structuring undergarments and from confining sexual mores.

Generally, going without foundation garments was the prerogative only of young, thin women. Other women chose lighter-weight girdles made more flexible through the use of elastic and sometimes without the steel boning common in earlier generations. In 1931 Lastex was introduced, a fine thread of rubber produced by extruding raw latex. This thread could be machine knit, yielding textiles that could stretch in all directions.[18] Lastex girdles allowed for more movement, especially bending at the waist. Even with these technical developments, "girdle" was just as often merely a name applied to a garment that had much in common with old-fashioned corsets, including steel boning, "employed to shake off passé connotations."[19]

Becoming a Flapper

The idealized flapper was always slender. Showing the lack of a corset or girdle was not only about freedom but also reflected a new ideal of a modern "natural" body emerging after World War I—a body tamed by diet and exercise.[20] The rising popularity of ready-to-wear clothing and the standardized sizing system that went along with it were other ways that fashion reinforced the slender body as the modern ideal.[21] A new category in ready-to-wear emerged by 1915, "stoutwear." Companies like Lane Bryant catered to fat women catalogue shopping for fashionable clothes in the 1920s and '30s, though with a distinct emphasis on styles that were "slimming" or camouflaged the wearer's size.[22]

The clothing catalogue was a significant force in American fashion and relied on illustrations to show off the latest styles for sale. Catalogues allowed women all over the country, including in rural areas, to participate in the modern trends if they had the money. They also provided women of color the comfort of shopping from home rather than facing the indignities found at white-owned establishments. The wide variety of women's magazines in the period offered a range of ways for consumers to buy or make the newest styles. While *Vogue* and *Harper's Bazaar* catered to the higher end of the market, *Ladies' Home Journal*, *Woman's Home Companion*, *McCall's*, *Pictorial Review*, *The Delineator*, and *Redbook* offered fashions for women with midrange budgets, particularly those who made their own clothes or had access to a dressmaker.[23] Manuel de Lambarri's 1929 illustration for *Vogue* shows how illustrators relied on simple stock poses and meticulous drawing to ensure that the most important details of a garment were visible to the reader (pl. 44). These magazines used glamorous illustrations to sell dressmaking patterns, and *Modern Priscilla* and *Woman's World* even offered "Semi-Made Frock" kits consisting of partially sewn pieces of fashionable dresses that could be finished at home.

Most of the bodies represented in these illustrations were not only thin but also white. There were, however, some spaces where Black women could be seen in modern dress, primarily in African American newspapers

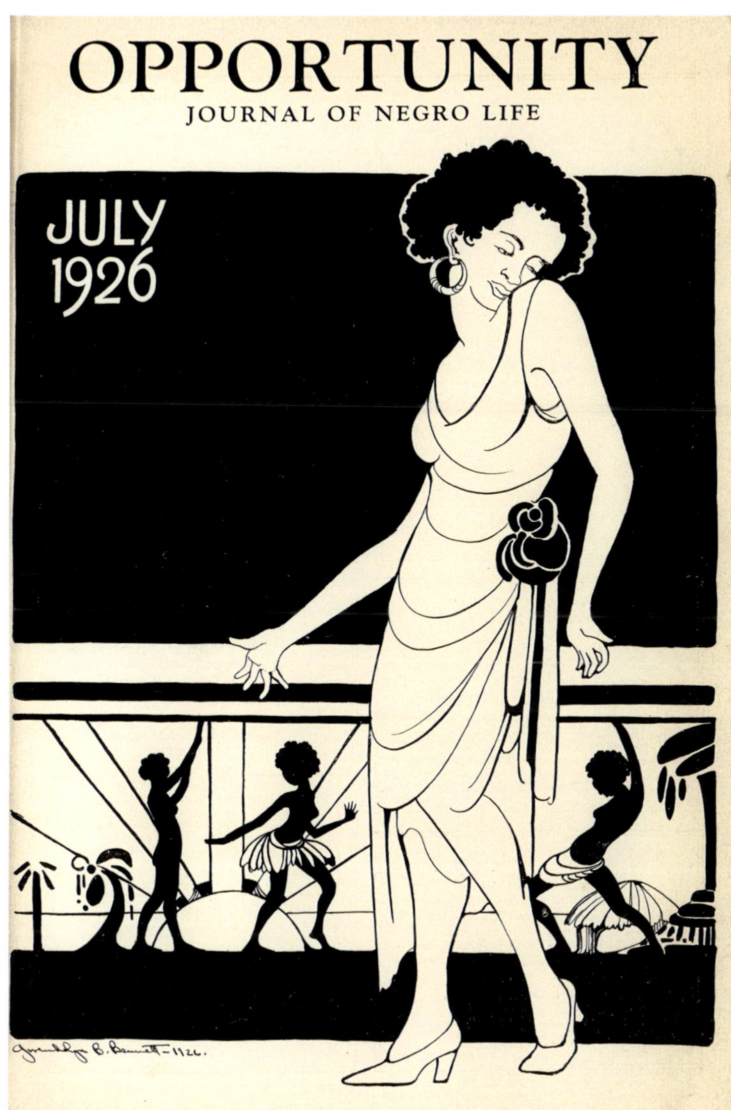

Fig. 55 Gwendolyn Bennett (1902–1981), cover from *Opportunity*, July 1926. Printed matter. New York Public Library, Schomburg Center for Research in Black Culture, Jean Blackwell Hutson Research and Reference Division

and magazines. For instance, the July 1926 cover of *Opportunity* illustrated by Gwendolyn Bennett features a Black woman in a fashionable short haircut and short, sleeveless evening gown (fig. 55). The images behind her suggest the sorts of caricatures of Africans often found as decoration in jazz clubs, showing the ways that jazz music and culture was frequently tied to Africa as much as to African Americans.[24] This cover may have been created when Bennett was living in Paris and studying art. In her regular culture column "The Ebony Flute," in December 1926, Bennett mentions the great success of Josephine Baker and other African American performers in Paris.[25] The central dancing figure in the background of her July cover is a reference to the banana skirt that Baker made famous in her performances at the Folies Bergère.[26] This cover is exceptional for *Opportunity*—a publication focused on racial advancement. In these spaces, the figure of the flapper was often viewed with suspicion, if not outright contempt, by leaders concerned with Black women projecting an image of respectability to combat racism and over-sexualized depictions in the mainstream media.[27] A 1922 article in the *Chicago Defender* explained, "true, we have a few rattle-brained 'flappers,' but the great majority dress and act in a manner convincing to any fair-minded person that virtue and good breeding are not confined solely to the Caucasian race."[28] Brooks embraces the image of the modern woman, creating an alluring and glamorous cover girl swaying to the rhythms of jazz.

Advertisements for beauty products marketed to Black women, from both Black and white-owned brands, included images of Black women. *Half-Century Magazine*, whose tagline read: "a colored magazine for the home and home maker," advertised itself as helping readers to "dress smartly at the lowest cost," and "to see our own beautiful women depicted in the latest and smartest costumes of Dame Fashion."[29] As Noliwe M. Rooks has documented, the magazine was trailblazing in using photographs of African American models who "represent a variety of heights, skin colors, and weights" on its fashion pages starting in 1916. "[A]s a result, the fashion pages in *Half-Century Magazine* became one of the first spaces in print media where dark-skinned African American women could find role models they might wish to emulate."[30] The magazine also included fashion illustrations representing Black women, which tended to emphasize the same slender and light-skinned ideal as seen in the pages of white women's magazines, along with ads for skin bleaching creams and hair straightening products; nonetheless, the broad range of women featured in photographs undercut the power of these narrow, white beauty ideals.

The increasing availability of ready-to-wear clothing is often understood as "reflect[ing] the continuous democratization of fashion and the erosion of cultural and class distinctions."[31] However, as is clear from the rhetoric about Black flappers, access to clothing did not change the pressures on women of color to act as representatives for their whole race or ethnicity. Celebrities such as Anna May Wong and Josephine Baker might be recognized as emphatically modern women by parts of the press and even the public, but this was always contingent. The choices made by women of color, famous or not, were far more heavily policed than those of white women, often by families, churches, workplaces, or other communities.[32]

Conclusion

Illustrators played a critical role, not just in representing the styles people wore in the Jazz Age, but in helping to attach meanings to these styles. For readers who would never set foot on a college campus, let alone Princeton, dance in a club in Harlem, or walk down the street in Paris, Manhattan, or even Chicago, illustrations—particularly in magazines—provided strong visual representations of these spaces. These images helped to construct ideas of femininity, masculinity, class, and race. While readers could creatively project themselves into these scenes or the clothing, they were also shown how they perhaps did not fit into the fashionable ideals of the Jazz Age. By the same token, more than ever before, images of stylish modernity were available to people of all classes and races in the US, as was clothing that spoke to the fads and fashions of the time, whether it was a dime store accessory or a gown from an exclusive boutique. These illustrations, along with movies and popular music, helped youth culture to become a powerful influence on the lifestyle and aesthetics of the 1920s.

ENDNOTES

1. *Life*, December 9, 1926, cover.

2. John Held Jr., "A Man of the World," *Scribner's Magazine*, December 1929, 641–48.

3. Sophie Kerr, "The Bad Little Egg," *Liberty*, November 6, 1926, 8.

4. Theodore Peterson, *Magazines in the Twentieth Century* (Urbana: University of Illinois Press, 1956), 54.

5. Daniel Delis Hill, "Fashion Fads and Fancies of the 1920s," in *Berg Encyclopedia of World Dress and Fashion, Vol. 3: The United States and Canada*, ed. Phyllis G. Tortora (Oxford, UK: Bloomsbury Academic, 2010): http://dx.doi.org/10.2752/9781847888525.EDch031511. Accessed July 26, 2023.

6. John P. Marquand, "The Blame of Youth," *Saturday Evening Post*, May 29, 1926.

7. F. Scott Fitzgerald, "Basil and Cleopatra," *Saturday Evening Post*, April 27, 1929.

8. Deirdre Clemente, *Dress Casual: How College Students Redefined American Style* (Chapel Hill: The University of North Carolina Press, 2014), 4.

9. Clemente, *Dress Casual,* 5–6.

10. See Einav Rabinovitch-Fox, "Dressing the Modern Girl: Flapper Styles and the Politics of Women's Freedom," in *Dressed for Freedom: The Fashionable Politics of American Feminism* (Urbana: University of Illinois Press, 2021), 81–116. For the French context, see also Mary Louise Roberts, "Sampson and Delilah Revisited: The Politics of Fashion in 1920s France," in *The Modern Woman Revisited: Paris between the Wars*, ed. Whitney Chadwick and Tirza True Latimer (New Brunswick, NJ: Rutgers University Press, 2003), 65–94.

11. "Bobs Hair, Kills Herself," *New York Times*, June 1, 1924, 22; "Resents Wife's Hair Bob," *New York Times*, May 3, 1926, 26; "Employers' Views Vary on Girl Who Bobs her Hair," *Boston Post*, August 14, 1921, 33; "Youth Shoots Fiancee, Jumps off Tower When She Bobs Hair," *Miami Tribune*, May 5, 1926, 8.

12. Historian Kathy Peiss argues that "as they put on a feminine face, these women briefly claimed public space, stopping the action, in a sense, by making a spectacle of themselves." Peiss, *Hope in a Jar: The Making of America's Beauty Culture* (New York: Metropolitan Book, Henry Holt and Company, 1998), 186.

13. "The Gospels of Beauty," *Vogue*, February 15, 1932, 88; cited in Peiss, *Hope in a Jar: The Making of America's Beauty Culture*, 155.

14. "The Adventures of Prudence Prim" ran on the covers of Hearst's *American Weekly* Sunday magazine sections from October 18, 1925, to February 21, 1926.

15. F. Scott Fitzgerald quoted in Margaret Reid, "Has the Flapper Changed?," *Motion Picture Magazine*, July 1927, 104.

16. Shortening skirts was a style championed by wearers rather than designers. Hill, "Fashion Fads and Fancies of the 1920s."

17. Daniel Delis Hill, "Fashion Fads and Fancies of the 1920s."

18. Elastic was available much earlier, but because it was woven with thicker strips of rubber, it only stretched in one direction. Percy Adamson, Elastic Yarn, US patent 1822847, filed June 11, 1931, and issued September 8, 1931: https://patents.google.com/patent/US1822847?oq=percy+adamson.

19. Jill Fields, "'Fighting the Corsetless Evil': Shaping Corsets and Culture 1900–1930," in *Beauty and Business Commerce, Gender, and Culture in Modern America*, ed. Philip Scranton (New York: Routledge, 2001), 119.

20. Lauren Downing Peters, "On Fat Clothes: Unraveling Plus-Size Design Discourse," *Design Issues* 38, no. 1 (Winter 2022): 20–21.

21. Cookie Woolner, "American Excess: Cultural Representations of Lillian Russell in Turn-of-the Century America," in *Historicizing Fat in Anglo-American Culture*, ed. Elena Levy-Navarro (Columbus: The Ohio State University Press, 2010), 132.

22. See Lauren Downing Peters, "Flattering the Figure, Fitting in: The Design Discourses of Stoutwear, 1915–1930," *Fashion Theory* 23, no. 2 (2019): 167–94.

23. By the mid-1920s, sewing machines were virtually ubiquitous in American homes, and many women made their own fashionable clothes: "Some 98 percent of farm families and 92 percent of city folk owned a sewing machine by 1925." Linda Przybyszewski, *The Lost Art of Dress: The Women Who Once Made America Stylish* (New York: Basic Books, 2014), 7.

24. See Susan L. Hannel, "The Influence of American Jazz on Fashion," in *Twentieth-Century American Fashion*, ed. Linda Welters and Patricia A. Cunningham (New York: Berg, 2005), 64–70.

25. Gwendolyn Bennett, "The Ebony Flute," *Opportunity*, December 1926, 391.

26. Cherene Sherrard-Johnson, "Illustration, Publishing, and the Female Artists of the Harlem Renaissance," in *Imprinted: Illustrating Race*, ed. Robyn Phillips-Pendleton and Stephanie Haboush Plunkett (Stockbridge, MA: Norman Rockwell Museum, 2022), 100.

27. Sherrard-Johnson, 100. See also Caroline Goeser, *Picturing the New Negro: Harlem Renaissance Print Culture and Modern Black Identity* (Lawrence: University Press of Kansas, 2007), 190–95.

28. "The 'Flapper' Age," *Chicago Defender*, July 29, 1922, 12.

29. Noliwe M. Rooks, *Ladies' Pages: African American Women's Magazines and the Culture That Made Them* (New Brunswick, NJ: Rutgers University Press, 2004), 71.

30. Rooks, 87.

31. Rabinovitch-Fox, *Dressed for Freedom*, 88.

32. For instance, in Nella Larsen's book *Quicksand*, protagonist Helga Crane bristles at the sartorial restrictions placed on the Black women who work at Naxos, a school for African American children in the rural South. The more senior female leadership at Naxos police fashions formally and informally, insisting on modest and conventional styles in muted and neutral colors. Larsen, *Quicksand* (New York: Alfred A. Knopf, 1928), 37–40: https://www.google.com/books/edition/Quicksand/dPdaAAAAMAAJ?hl=en&gbpv=0. See also Rooks, *Ladies' Pages*, 65–88.

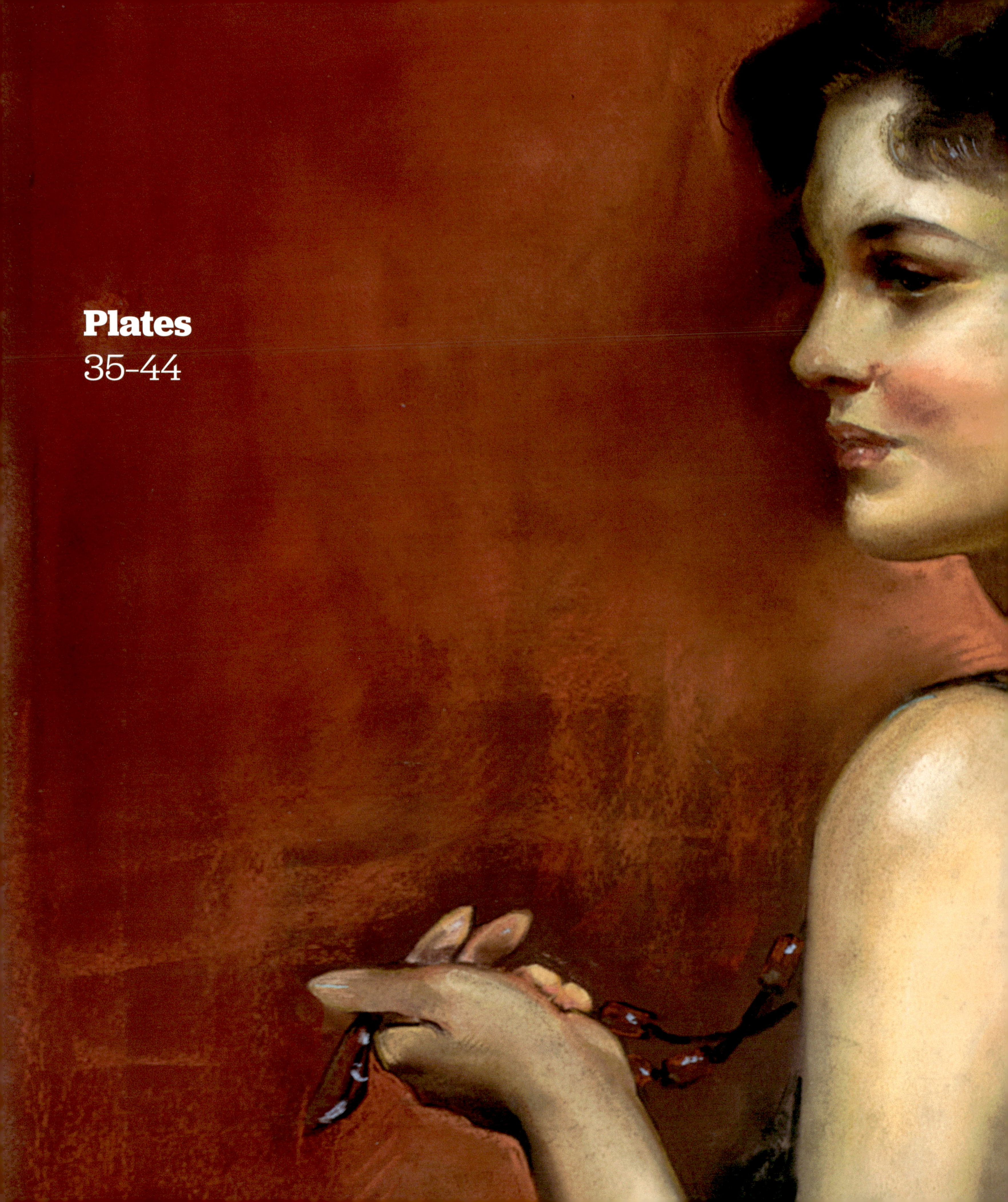

Plates
35–44

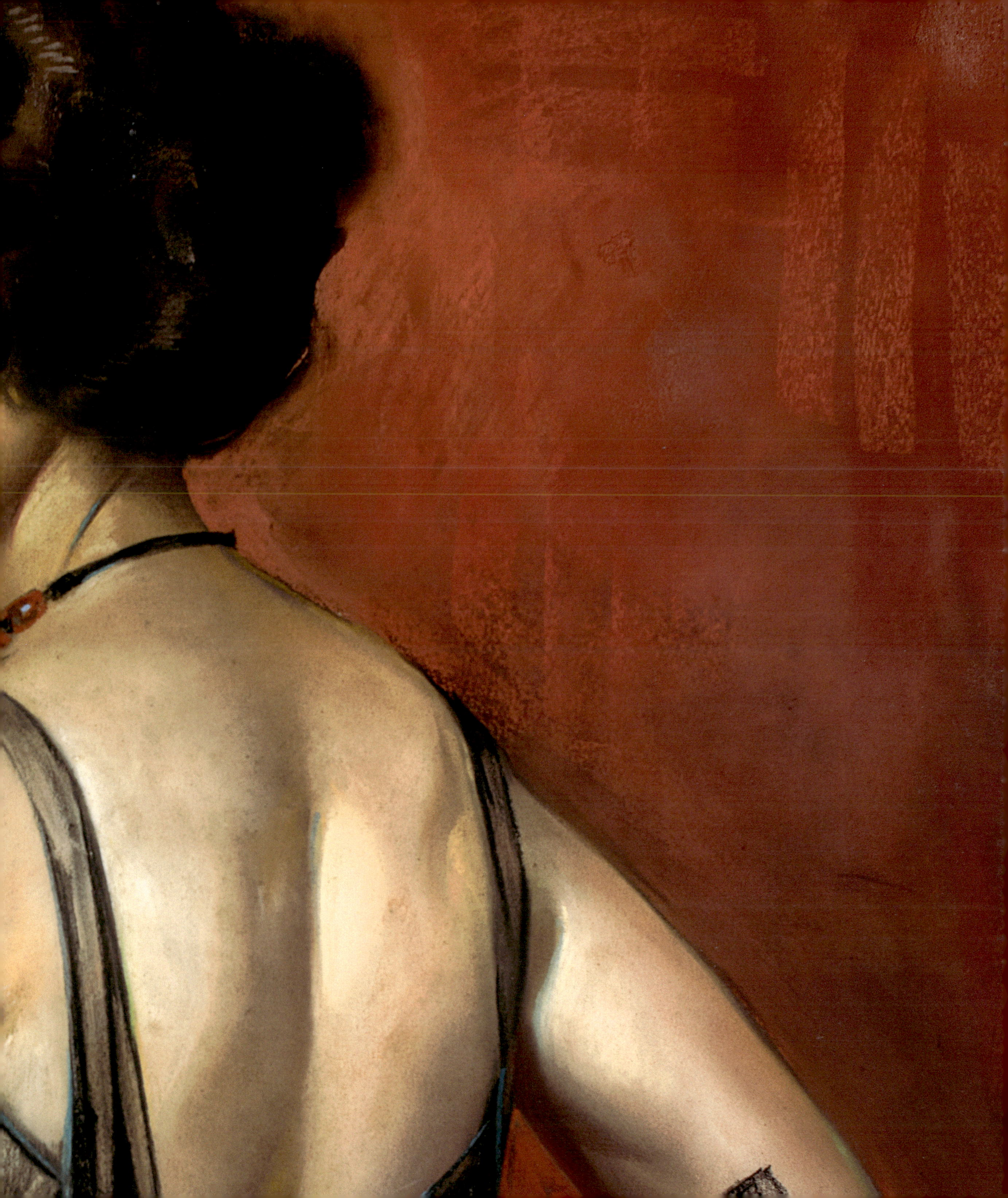

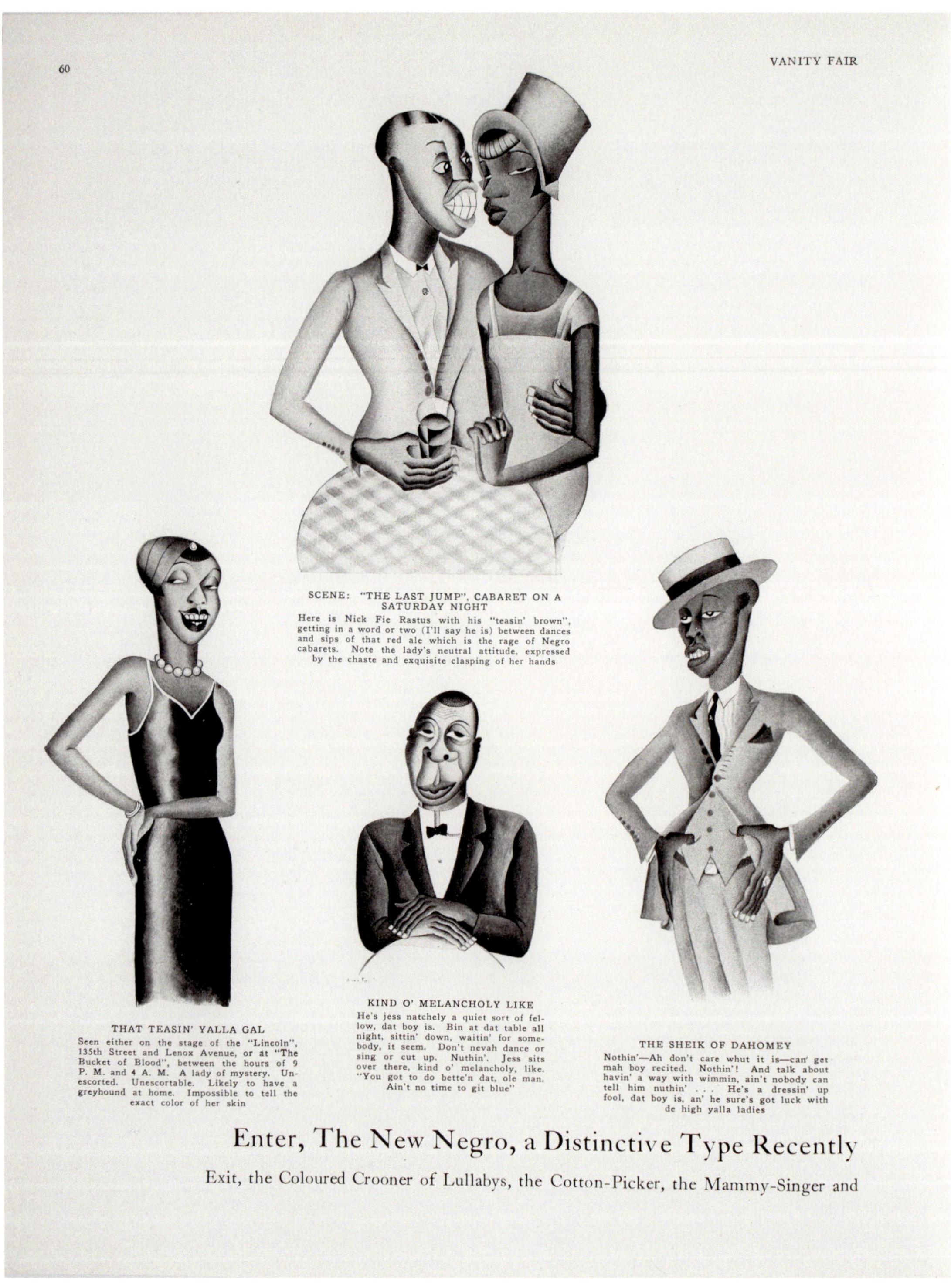

60 VANITY FAIR

SCENE: "THE LAST JUMP", CABARET ON A SATURDAY NIGHT

Here is Nick Fie Rastus with his "teasin' brown", getting in a word or two (I'll say he is) between dances and sips of that red ale which is the rage of Negro cabarets. Note the lady's neutral attitude, expressed by the chaste and exquisite clasping of her hands

THAT TEASIN' YALLA GAL

Seen either on the stage of the "Lincoln", 135th Street and Lenox Avenue, or at "The Bucket of Blood", between the hours of 9 P. M. and 4 A. M. A lady of mystery. Unescorted. Unescortable. Likely to have a greyhound at home. Impossible to tell the exact color of her skin

KIND O' MELANCHOLY LIKE

He's jess natchely a quiet sort of fellow, dat boy is. Bin at dat table all night, sittin' down, waitin' for somebody, it seem. Don't nevah dance or sing or cut up. Nuthin'. Jess sits over there, kind o' melancholy, like. "You got to do bette'n dat, ole man. Ain't no time to git blue"

THE SHEIK OF DAHOMEY

Nothin'—Ah don't care whut it is—can' get mah boy recited. Nothin'! And talk about havin' a way with wimmin, ain't nobody can tell him nuthin' . . . He's a dressin' up fool, dat boy is, an' he sure's got luck with de high yalla ladies

Enter, The New Negro, a Distinctive Type Recently

Exit, the Coloured Crooner of Lullabys, the Cotton-Picker, the Mammy-Singer and

35

Miguel Covarrubias (1904–1957)

Enter, the New Negro, a Distinctive Type Recently Created by the Coloured Cabaret Belt in New York, from *Vanity Fair*, December 1924

Printed matter

Delaware Art Museum, Helen Farr Sloan Library and Archives

The Sketches on these two pages
by MIGUEL COVARRUBIAS

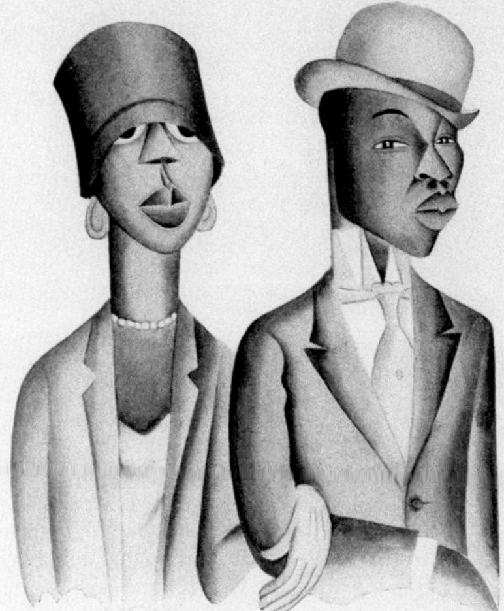

ON A SPREE

Scene: Stage Door at the "Chocolate Dandies"

Looks as if dese folks is got the blues, don't it? Well, that ain't it, prezactly. Ah wants to tell you that dey's gwine "out" to a party, dat's what. That boy swings a mean wheel-barrow; and de gal, she ain't so bad, neither. She sure can shake a wicked soap sud

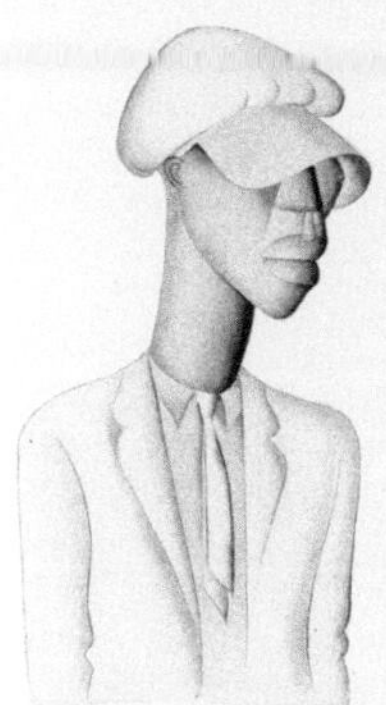

8 A. M. ON LENOX AVENUE

"Got a job fo' you, Coolie." "Nigger, keep still! I bin in New York gwine on to twenty years now and I ain't nevah had no job. Go on 'bout yo' bizness. . . . . Az Ah was tellin' yo', Lovey, Ah had five to win and two for a place. . ."

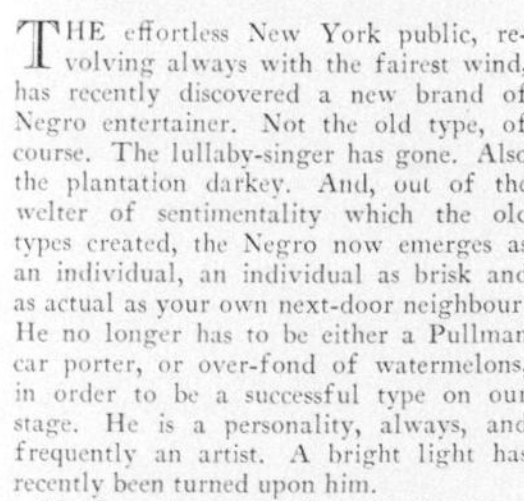

2 A. M. AT "THE CAT AND THE SAXOPHONE"

"Boy, do that thing! Tell 'em about me! You tell 'em, sister. Be yourself, now! 'S pretty, too, Ah mean she ain't ugly. Oh! Kiss me, papa! You're pretty from the ground up"

THE effortless New York public, revolving always with the fairest wind, has recently discovered a new brand of Negro entertainer. Not the old type, of course. The lullaby-singer has gone. Also the plantation darkey. And, out of the welter of sentimentality which the old types created, the Negro now emerges as an individual, an individual as brisk and as actual as your own next-door neighbour. He no longer has to be either a Pullman car porter, or over-fond of watermelons, in order to be a successful type on our stage. He is a personality, always, and frequently an artist. A bright light has recently been turned upon him.

The first all-coloured show, *Shuffle Along*, written, produced and acted by Negroes, was presented the season before last on Broadway, and immediately became a sensation. Since then we have seen its successors, *Runnin' Wild*, *Chocolate Dandies*, *Honey*, and *Dixie to Broadway*. We have also seen a great number of Negro cabarets which have flared up in every part of New York, from the fashionable districts to the Harlem black belt—all flourishing under white, or partial white, patronage.

In the accompanying sketches, Miguel Covarrubias, the young Mexican artist, has miraculously caught the somewhat exotic spirit of the new Negro, as he is seen to be, both on the stage and in the more characteristic moments of his life around the cabarets. The captions for these eight drawings were written by Eric D. Walrond, a talented Negro poet.

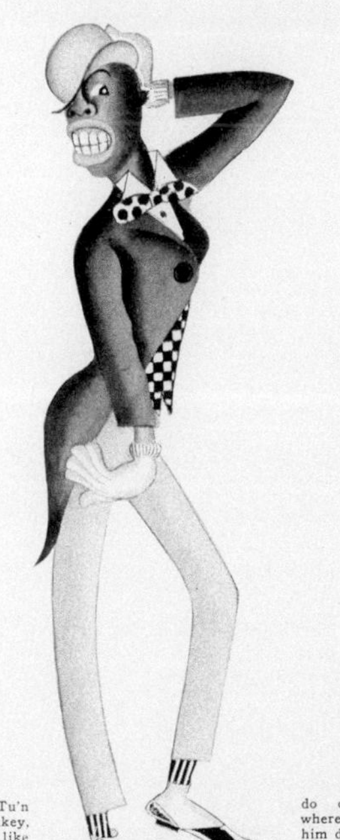

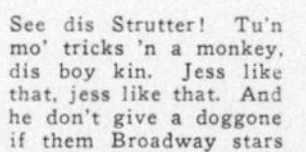

See dis Strutter! Tu'n mo' tricks 'n a monkey, dis boy kin. Jess like that, jess like that. And he don't give a doggone if them Broadway stars do come on uptown where he is at, and see him do he stuff, and den go on back downtown and strut his stuff as if they jess got it natchely

Created by the Coloured Cabaret Belt in New York

the Darky Banjo-Player, for so Long Over-Exploited Figures on the American Stage

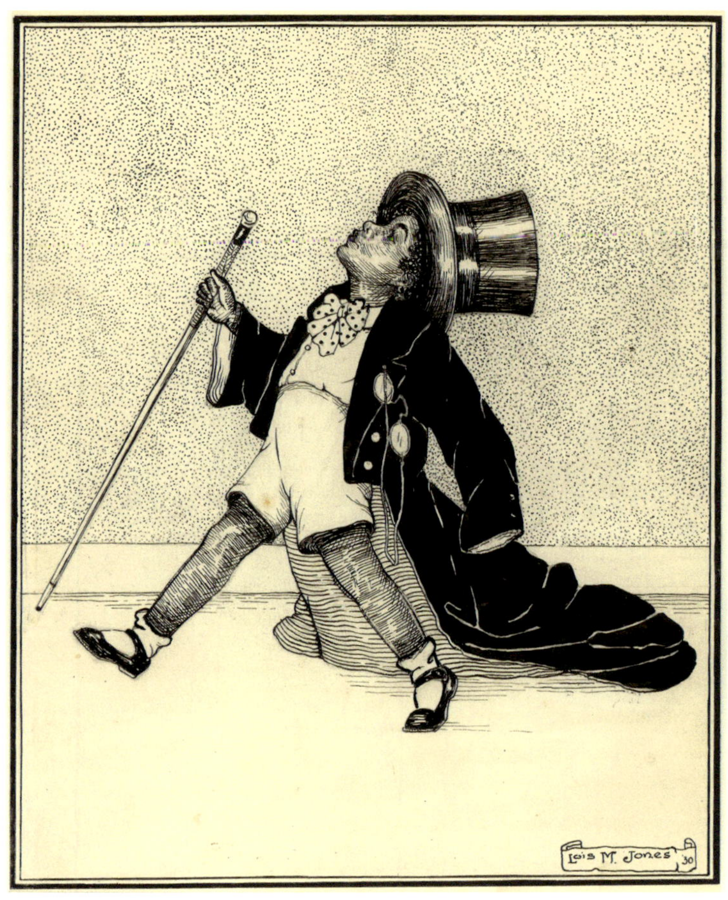

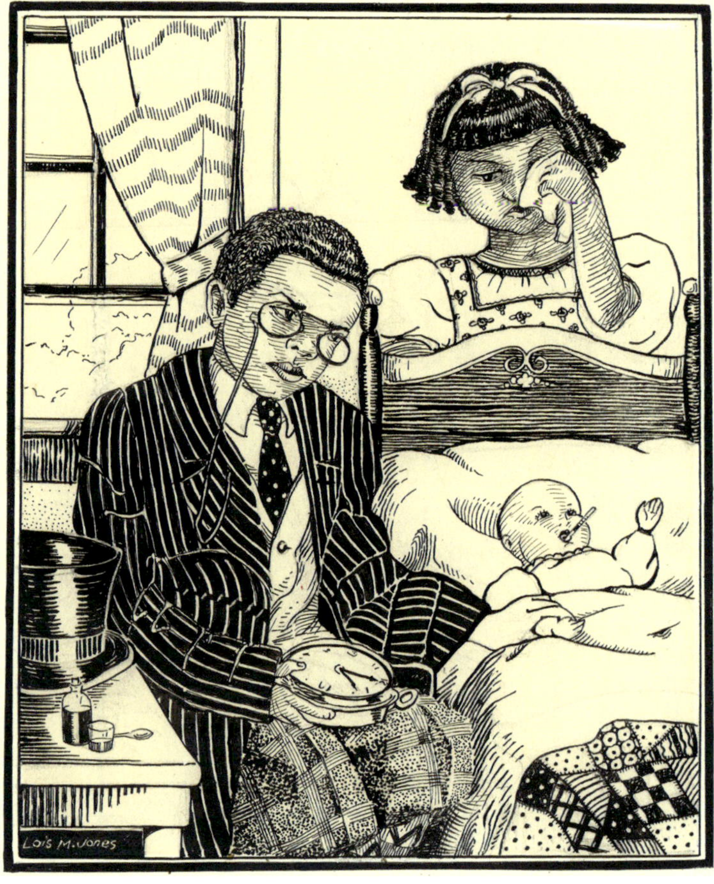

36

Loïs Mailou Jones (1905–1998)

A Lawyer, for *The Picture-Poetry Book* by Gertrude Parthenia McBrown (Washington, DC: Associated Publishers, 1935)

Ink on paper, 11¾ × 8¾ in.
Collection of Findlay University's Mazza Museum, Findlay, Ohio

37

Loïs Mailou Jones (1905–1998)

She's Sick, for *The Picture-Poetry Book* by Gertrude Parthenia McBrown (Washington, DC: Associated Publishers, 1935)

Ink on paper, 11¾ × 8¾ in.
Collection of Findlay University's Mazza Museum, Findlay, Ohio

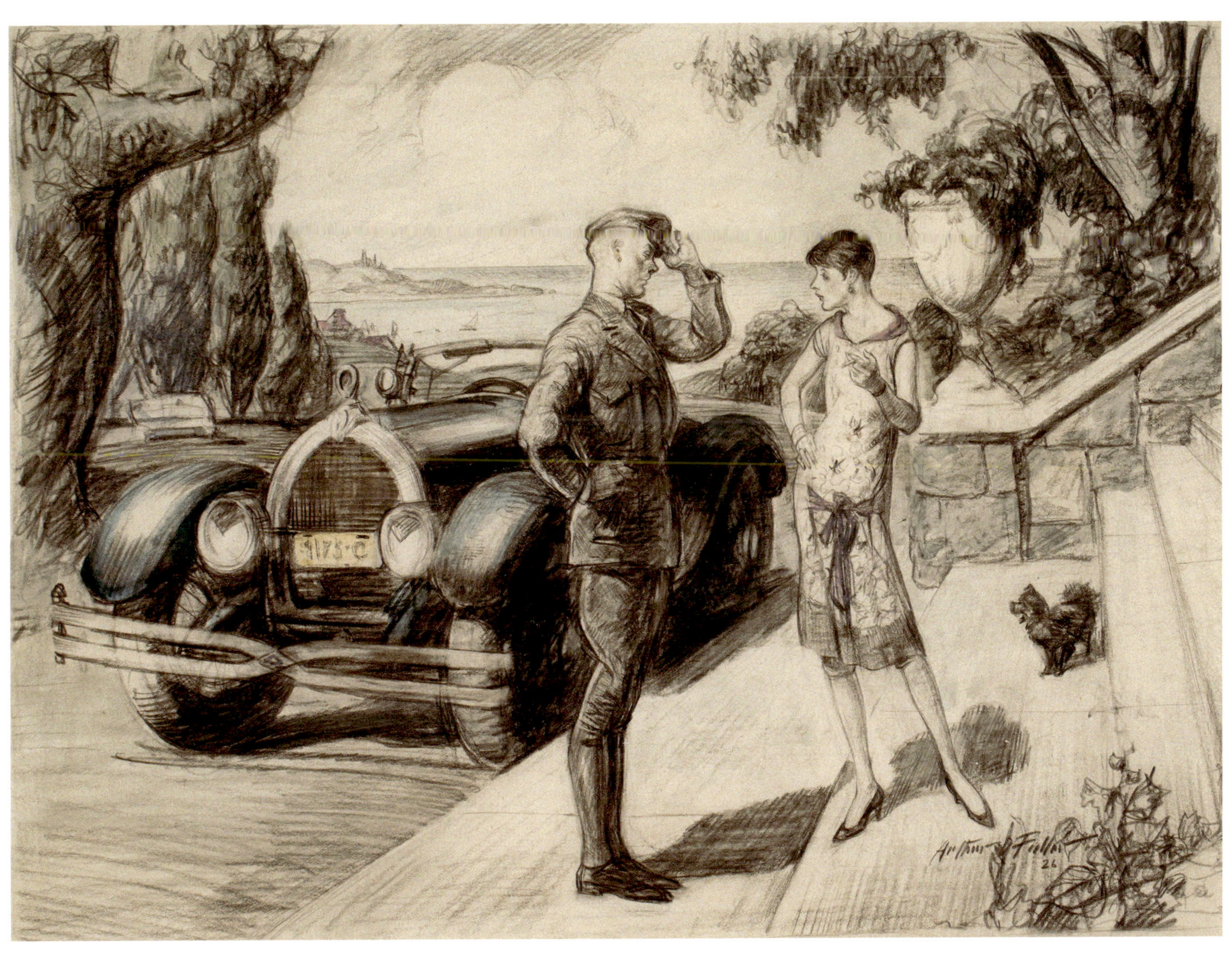

38

Arthur Davenport Fuller (1889–1966)

I was scared her ma might hear her, so I looks blank and touches me cap, for "The Bad Little Egg" by Sophie Kerr, *Liberty*, November 6, 1926

Graphite and watercolor on board, 11½ × 15$\frac{1}{16}$ in.
Delaware Art Museum, Gift of Helen Farr Sloan, 1987

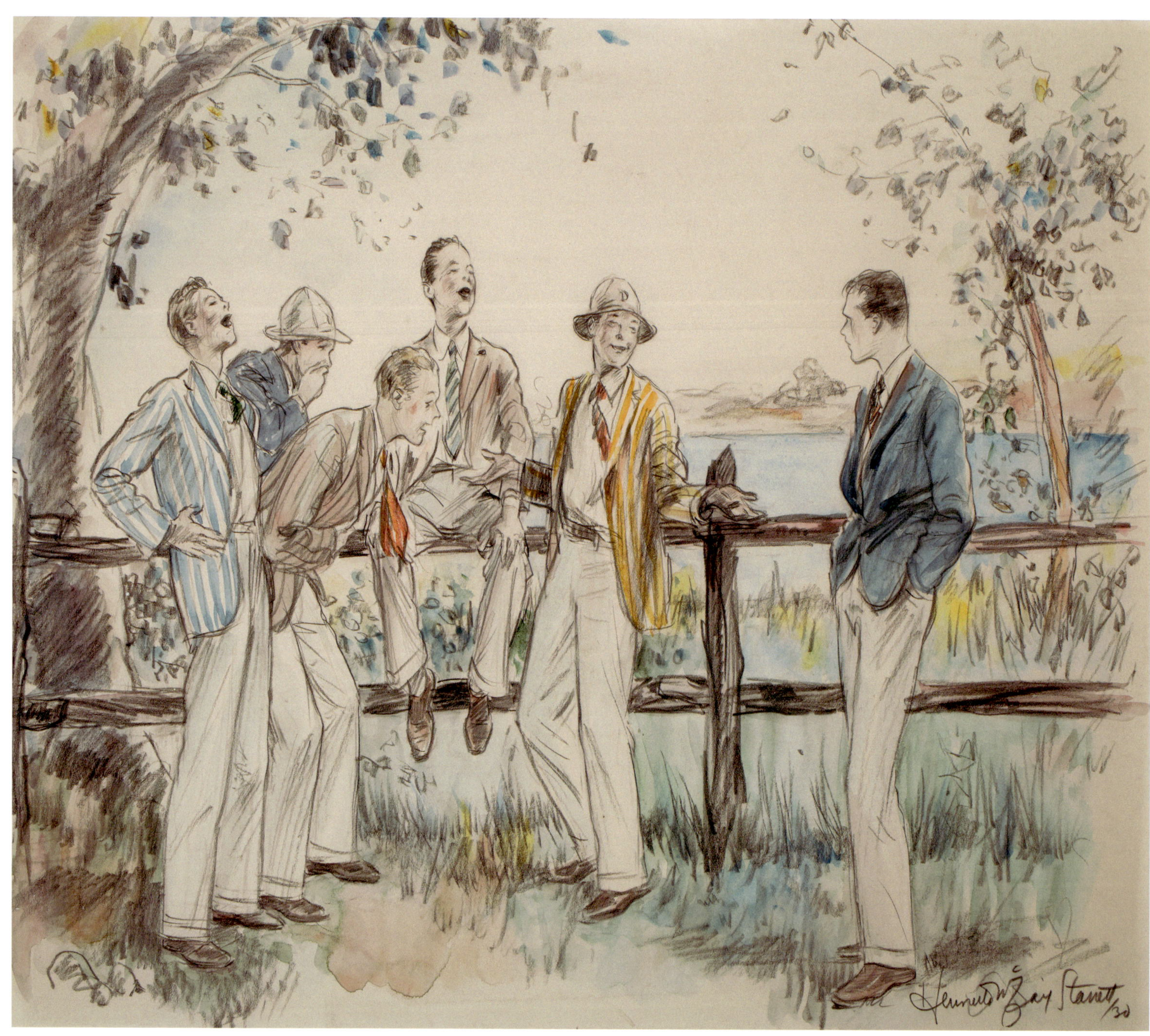

39

Henrietta McCaig Starrett (1893–1963)

"Mr. Smith"—they were all instructed now by a boy called Fraser—"is a sensation with women," for "Some Day You'll be Sorry" by James Gould Cozzens, *The Saturday Evening Post*, June 21, 1930

Crayon and watercolor on illustration board, 15 15/16 × 19 15/16 in.
Delaware Art Museum, John Sloan Memorial Foundation, 1981
Illustration © SEPS licensed by Curtis Licensing Indianapolis, IN. All rights reserved

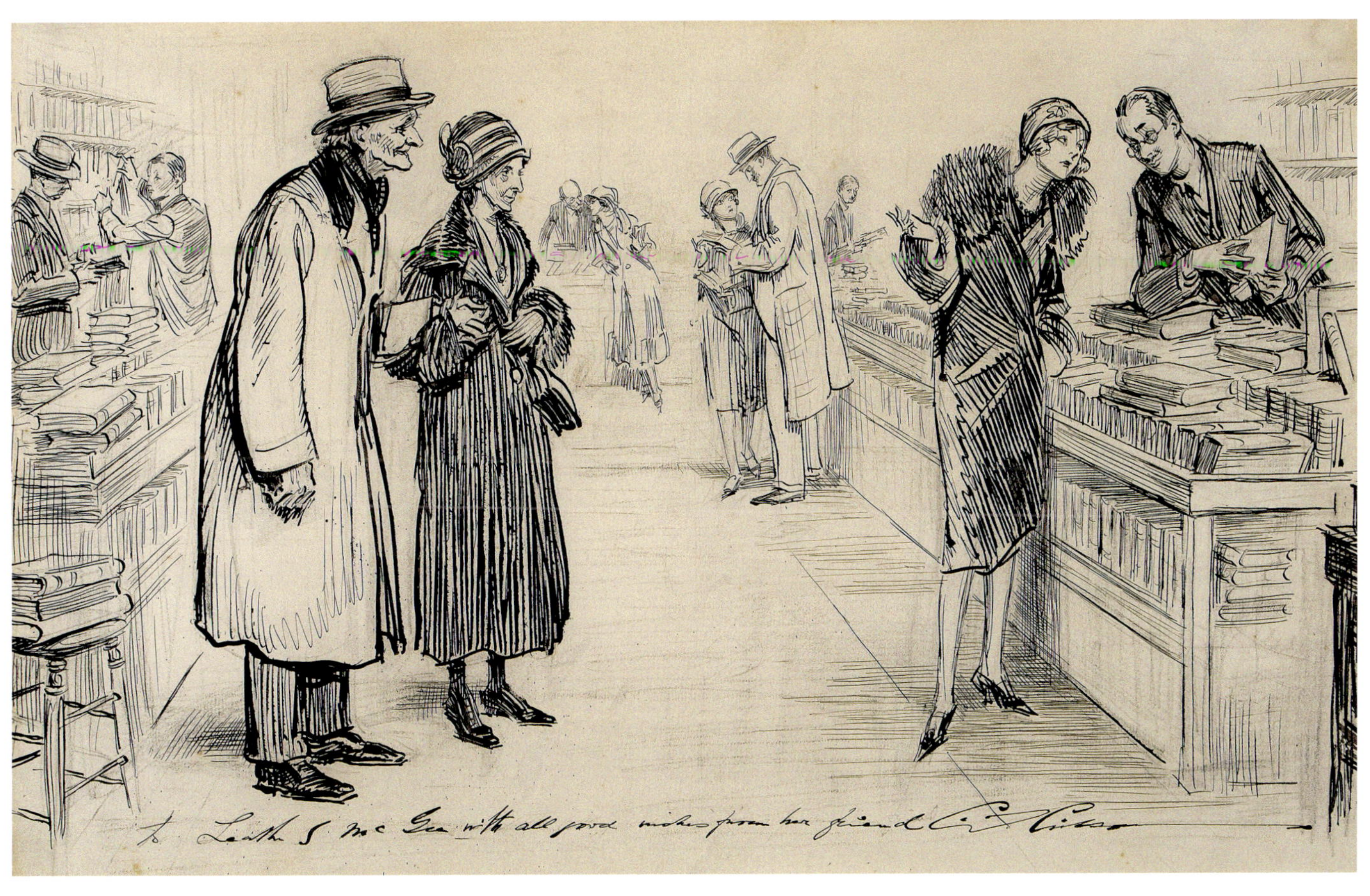

40

Charles Dana Gibson (1867–1944)
Have you a book innocent enough for grandma and grandpa to read?, for *Hearst's International combined with Cosmopolitan*, March 1926

Ink and graphite on illustration board, sheet: 15 × 21¼ in.
Delaware Art Museum, Gift of Helen Farr Sloan, 1983

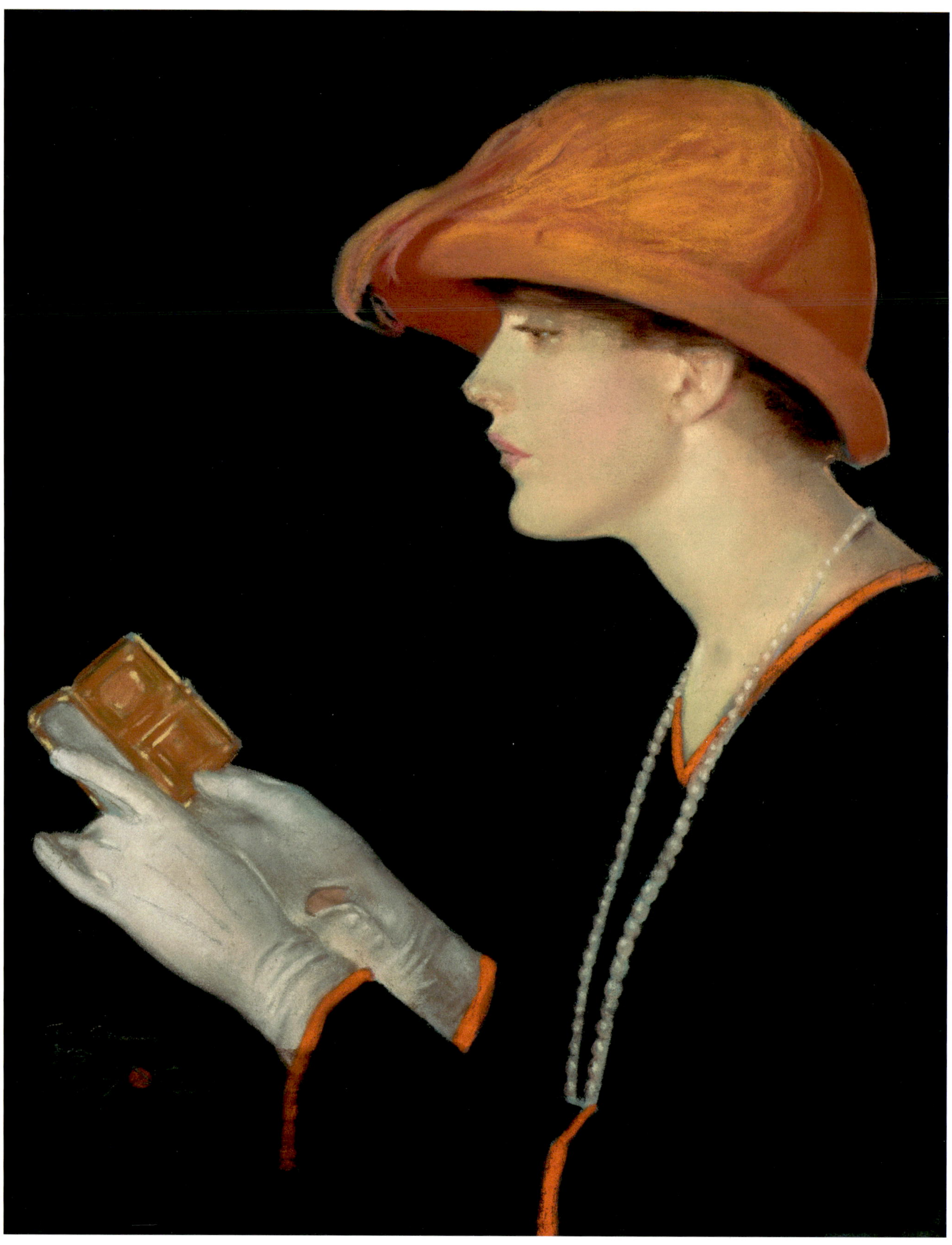

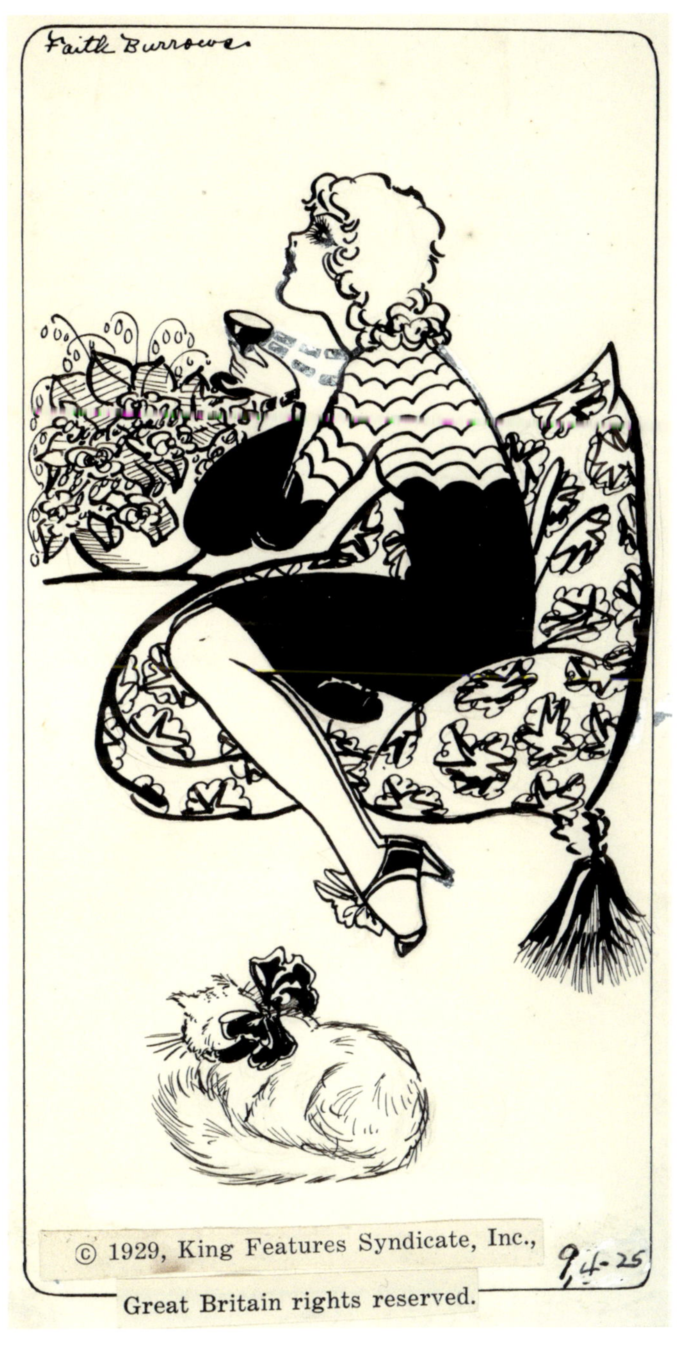

41

Penrhyn Stanlaws (1877–1957)

Cover for *Collier's Weekly*, October 4, 1924

Pastel on painted canvas, 22 × 17 in.
Delaware Art Museum, Acquisition Fund, 2015

42

Faith Burrows (1904–1997)

While her old grandmother is becoming spiritually prepared the modern daughter is becoming spiritually preserved, for *Flapper Filosofy*, King Features Syndicate, *Cincinnati Enquirer*, September 25, 1929

Pen, ink, and wash on stiff paper, 6⅜ × 3⅜ in.
Delaware Art Museum, Acquisition Fund, 2019

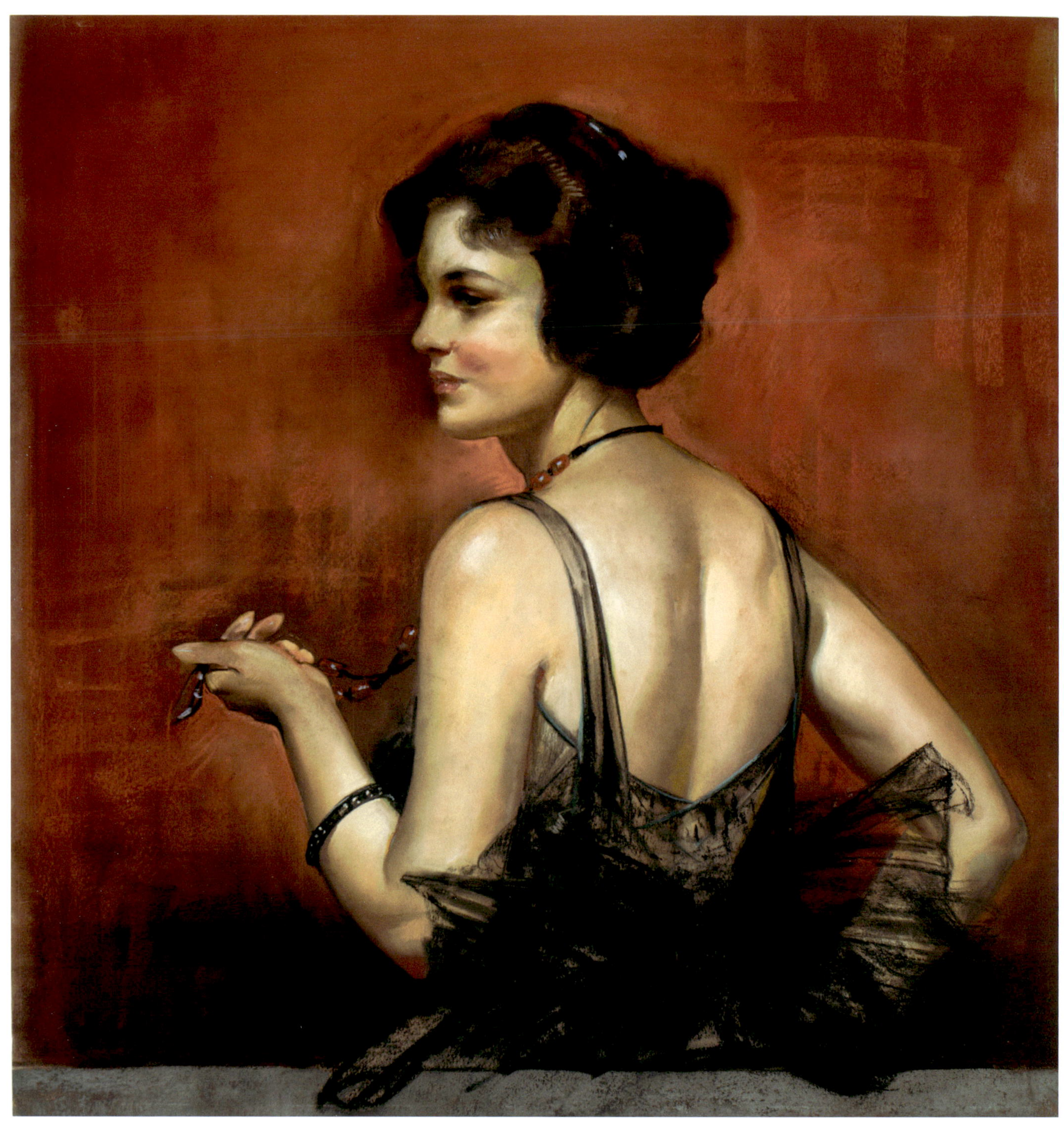

43

Neysa McMein (1888–1949)

The Admirable Hostess, advertisement for Wallace Silver, *The Saturday Evening Post*, January 8, 1921

Pastel on board, 30⅛ × 28⅝ in.
Delaware Art Museum, Acquisition Fund, 2022

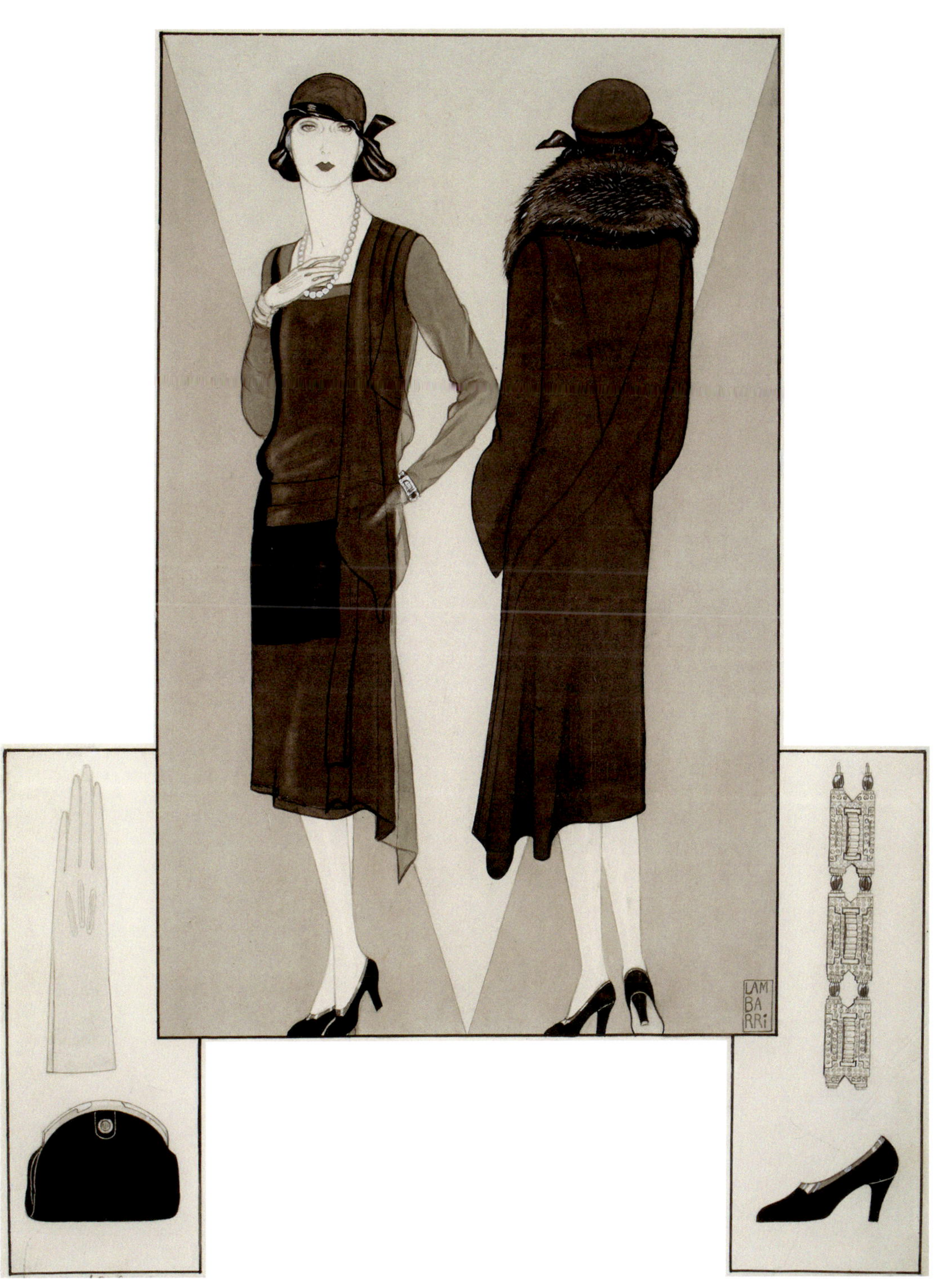

44

Manuel de Lambarri (1891–1973)

Fashion illustration, for *Vogue*, November 10, 1929

Ink and wash and gouache on illustration board, 16¼ × 11¾ in.
Delaware Art Museum, John Sloan Memorial Foundation, 1981

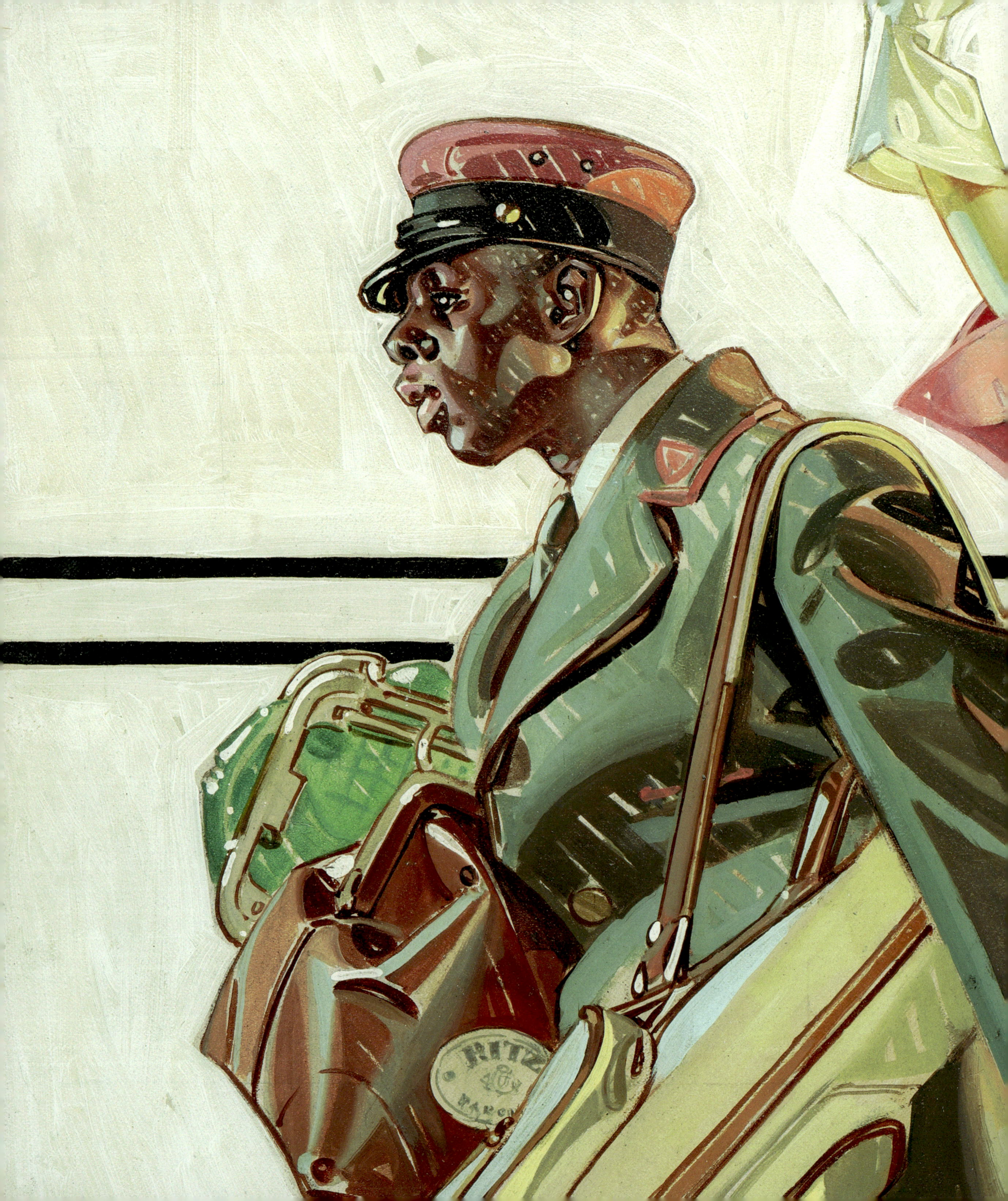
RITZ

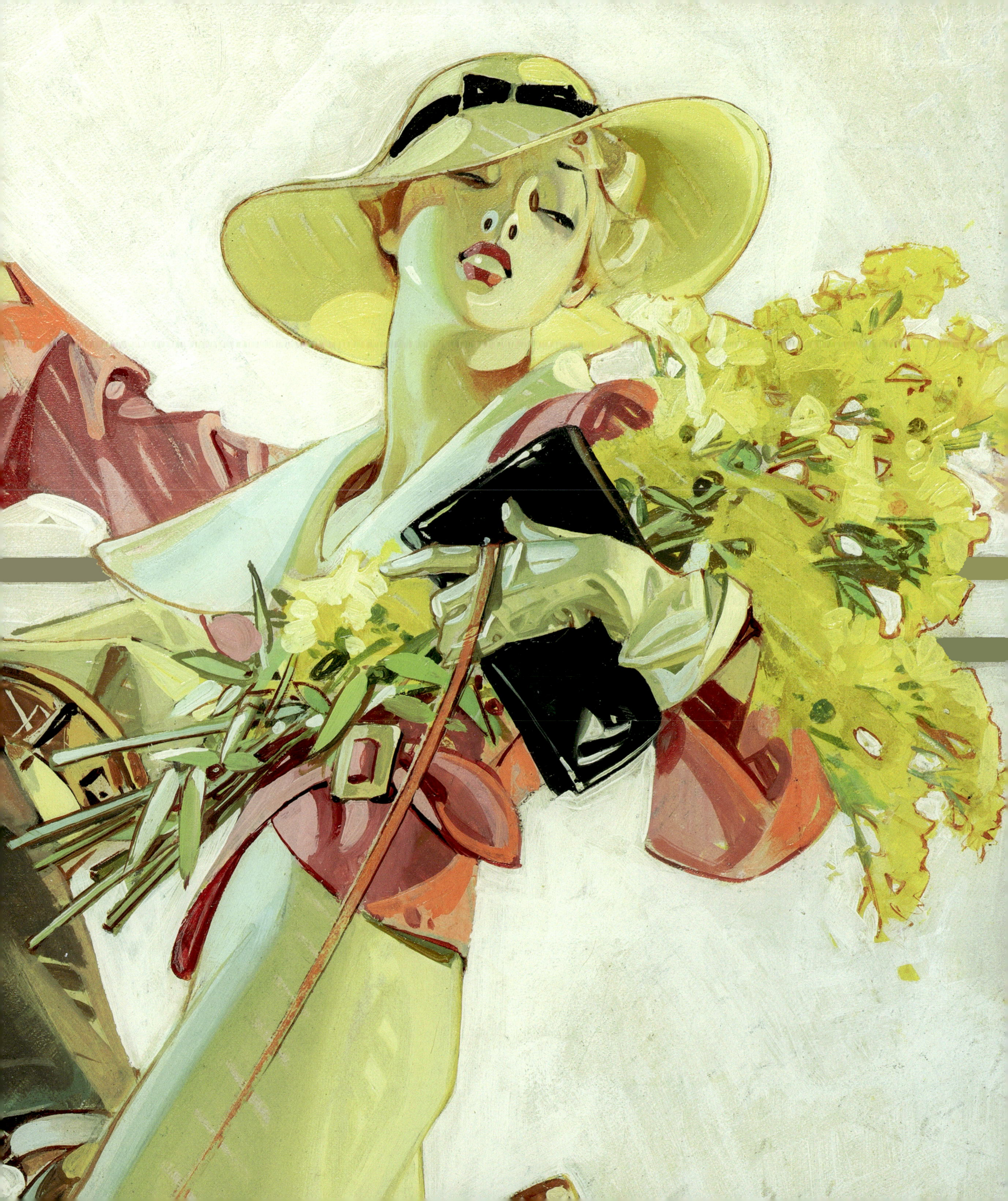

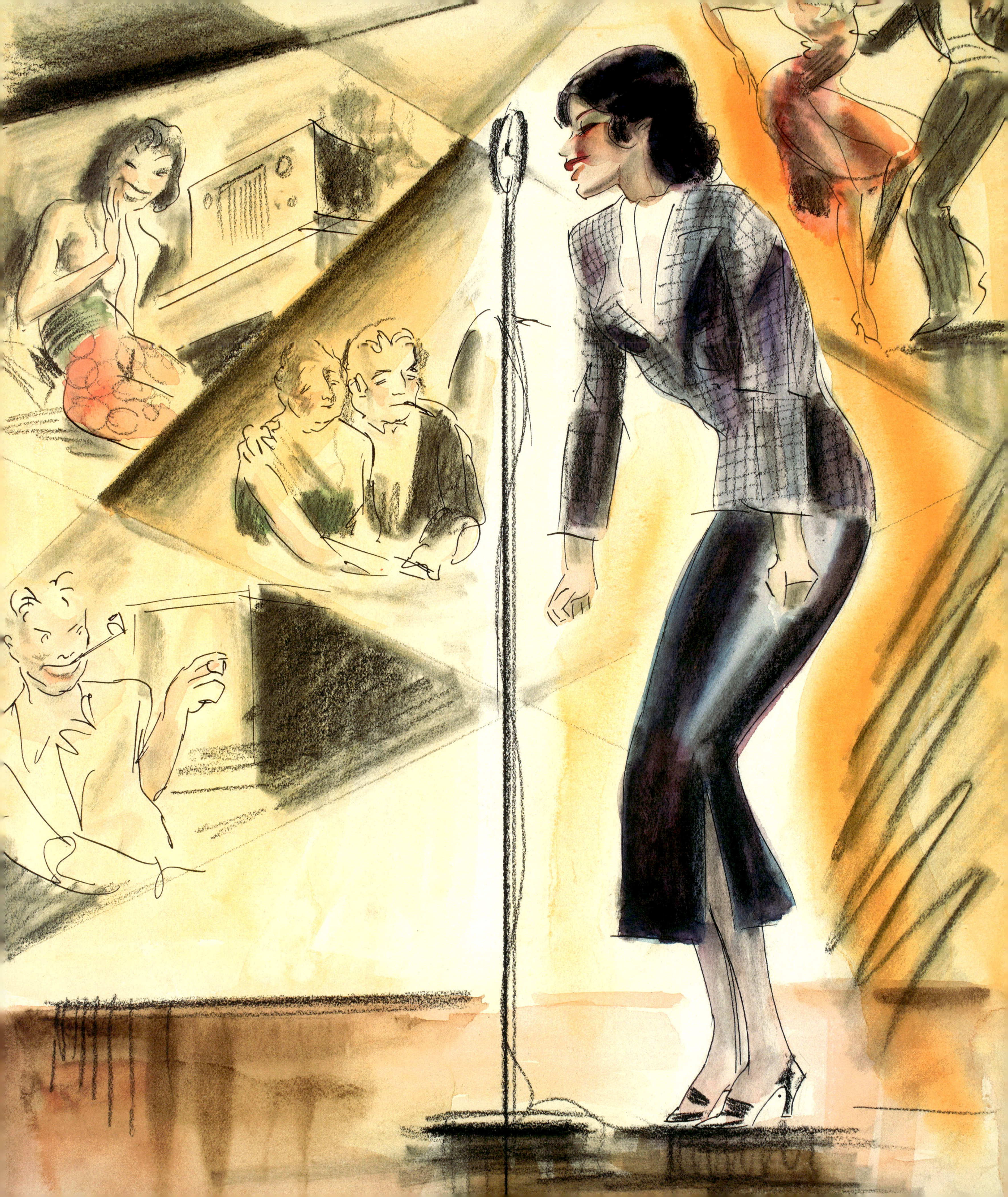

Chris Dingwall

Machine Age Watercolors

Jay Jackson's three watercolor sketches of Etta Moten feature the performer in full-figure portraits mid-performance: poised before a microphone, twirling on stage, basking in applause (pls. 45–47). Each also has Moten in a skintight dress, with Jackson's fine line and bold brushstrokes accentuating the curves of her long legs and slender waist. But in Jackson's vision, the sheer dresses do not simply highlight the lines of her body; they express the vitality and colors of her live performance. As they convey Moten's command over her physique and voice, Jackson's brush and pen become an extension of Moten's own creative will—at least as Jackson imagined it. For as Moten the actor overtakes the devices recording her, so does Jackson the artist overlay his dreamy watercolors on the technological scene of mass cultural production, blurring the leering white cameramen and sound engineer into the background.

The watercolors were an almost perfect meeting of artist and model. Jackson was a prolific cartoonist and featured illustrator for the *Chicago Defender*, among the most widely circulated and widely read African American newspapers in the nation. Moten was one of the most famous African Americans in the world, her tours and concerts receiving extensive coverage in the Black press and in the *Defender* in particular. Produced on the occasion of the American Negro Exposition, a massive exhibition of African American progress and arts held in the Chicago Coliseum over the summer of 1940, the drawings were assured an audience in the tens of thousands. But although Jackson signed them, it is unclear why he painted them. It is unlikely Moten modeled for Jackson; the scenes seem to be drawn from Jackson's own memories, fantasies, or publicity photographs of the famous actor. Perhaps media mogul Claude A. Barnett, Moten's second husband, commissioned the drawings to celebrate his wife's star turn at the exposition in *Jubilee! Cavalcade of Negro Theater*, a musical revue penned by Arna Bontemps and Langston Hughes that was performed live and broadcast over WBBM radio.[1] Perhaps Jackson meant to enter the drawings in the exposition's juried watercolor competition—and catch the eye of the powerful Barnett, the exposition's chief organizer and coordinator of the art exhibits. (He would have been outshone by Eldzier Cortor and Jacob Lawrence.)[2] What we know is that the paintings found their way to the Moten/Barnett estate and then were purchased by the Delaware Art Museum in 2022.

The watercolors are extraordinary works nonetheless: at once a product and an interpretation of the history of Jazz Age illustration. They mark pivotal moments in the careers of Moten and Jackson, who were each

Detail of pl. 45

testing the limits of visual reproduction technologies to represent African Americans in American mass culture.

Born in rural Texas in 1901, Moten was the daughter of a schoolteacher and a pastor in the African Methodist Episcopalian church. Although she was a talented member of the church choir, Moten's stellar career was not preordained. The family followed the father's pastorship to Los Angeles and Kansas City, where a seventeen-year-old Etta married a grocer named Curtis Brooks, with whom she moved to Oklahoma, had three daughters, and divorced. She was already a seasoned performer with the Jackson Jubilee Singers and in Topeka radio when she moved her children back to Kansas to enroll in a BA program in voice and drama at the University of Kansas, graduating in 1931 and moving to New York.[3] From there her rise from Broadway to Hollywood was meteoric. After several showstopping yet uncredited turns in madcap musical comedies throughout the 1930s and a highly publicized performance of "The Forgotten Man" for Franklin Delano Roosevelt at the White House in 1934, Moten eschewed the limited and often degrading roles for Black women in Hollywood by pursuing a relentless touring schedule of theatrical performances, musical recitals, and radio broadcasts in the United States and around the world. Her "marvelous success both in her work in the theater and in broadcasting" was everywhere apparent, Barnett wrote from Buenos Aires during Moten's three-month tour of Brazil and Argentina in 1936. "[T]he papers have been full of her pictures and she is on billboards everywhere."[4]

As the founder of the Associated Negro Press, Barnett had built a media empire out of his wire service for African American newspapers at the same time Moten was launching her career. When they met in Chicago in 1931, just as Moten was on her way to Hollywood, the attraction between the two strivers was immediate. When they married in 1934, theirs became a "partnership in power," as historian Gerald Horne puts it, and they worked together to achieve their "global ambitions" as publisher and performer.[5] But while her husband created his power by leveraging his connection to the Black public sphere to gain access to government and industry leaders, Moten drew her power by cultivating a hypnotic sonic and visual presence. In a review of a concert in 1934, a *Defender* correspondent offered a nuanced analysis, describing the tension between the "control" Moten exercised over her mellow "mezzo-contralto voice" and the "thrills" she produced for her "large mixed audience" at the St. Louis University auditorium: "She was not only mistress of tone delivery and control but she added facial pictures that were tremendously effective."[6] The folklorist and writer Zora Neale Hurston put a finer point on the mass appeal of the "seductive Etta." A close friend who had cast Moten in her all-Black musical revue *Fast and Furious* (1931), Hurston perhaps confided something of her own attraction when she asked Barnett about the origins of the "famous love affair": "What part of you responded first? Your eye, your ear or, shall we say your libido?"[7]

While Moten was making her public persona into a widely reproduced image, Jackson was becoming a prolific maker of mass-produced images. Indeed, his circuitous route to the top of his profession paralleled Moten's in more than one respect. Born in Oberlin, Ohio, in 1905, Jackson dropped out of high school when he was thirteen to take up a series of grueling jobs—railroad worker in Columbus, steel worker in Pittsburgh, boxer in Delaware, Ohio—before a professor at Ohio Wesleyan University encouraged his interest in commercial art. At the age of nineteen, Jackson dropped out of college, married, had two daughters, and started a sign painting shop. Overexposure to lead-based paints compelled him to close his shop and move his family to Chicago, where he found work designing posters at the Warner Brothers theater chain, eventually rising to the level of First Poster Artist and shop foreman.

Jackson's life was upended again when his wife and eldest daughter died in 1924. A twenty-two-year-old single father, Jackson remade himself as a freelance cartoonist and illustrator for the *Pittsburgh Courier* and the *Chicago Defender*—cornerstones of the national African American press—making a name for himself as a versatile and popular illustrator and cartoonist. By the end of the decade, he was the *Defender*'s star staff artist who illustrated featured essays and helmed dozens of comic strips from long-running mainstays such as *Bungleton Green* to single-panel gags. His prodigious output depended upon the work of Eleanor K. Poston, an office worker at the *Defender* whom he married in 1935. Theirs was a "working partnership," according to Jackson's obituary in the *Defender*, "with Eleanor writing gags and verses for many of Jay's cartoons." "She became so much a part of his work," the tribute continued, that she "developed into a cartoonist in her own right."[8]

Jackson's partnership with Poston coincided with a turn in his interests as an illustrator and satirist toward the politics of Black female beauty. Women's fashion, behavior, and style were frequent subjects of his *Defender* cartoons, particularly *As Others See Us*, which poked fun at the pretensions of working-class Southern migrants who spent lavishly on clothes and cosmetics without learning the rules of bourgeois comportment. In the "moving theater" of the South Side of Chicago, as Davarian Baldwin writes, "where black people were staging new visions of blackness in the particular ways they looked and were looked at," women were seen at once as bearers of respectability and refinement and as "objects of acquisition, among a wide variety of other commodities."[9] Jackson did his part to contribute to the commodification of women's beauty in African American visual culture. He illustrated catalogues and product labels for the tonics, potions, love charms, and beauty products sold by the Valmor Products Company to African American consumers—even as he satirized the use of skin bleacheners and hair-straighteners in *As Others See Us*.

In different ways Jackson and Moten had built careers navigating and capitalizing upon the politics of race and gender that defined the work of African American cultural workers across fields of American culture from popular music to the fine arts. But in Jackson's watercolors, Moten was an object of neither ridicule nor acquisition; she was someone who knew how to be seen. Jackson asks the viewer to think twice about fetishizing the performer. In the background, he shows cartoonish figures leering at Moten: a stage director, a cameraman, a smitten husband in an opera box earning the scorn of his date (see pls. 45–47). Notably, Jackson draws these figures as indistinct white men in contrast to the more fully rendered views of Moten's Black auditors listening in on the radio or dancing at home. A fourth watercolor signed by Jackson but which does not appear to feature Moten may nevertheless complete the series: a scene of Black couples slow dancing in full suits and gowns while listening to Moten sing (fig. 56). Moten was not a passive body merely to be consumed by the eye and ear; in the words of the *Defender* reviewer, she was an artist fully in command of the processes of making thrilling "pictures" and in intimate communion with her distant audience.[10]

For Jackson, painting Moten opened new possibilities to demonstrate his range as an artist and social commentator. Unlike his cartoons, reproduced in flat monochrome on cheap newsprint, the watercolors allowed Jackson to illustrate the process of his and Moten's art as something in tune with but distinct from the technologies that brought them to mass audiences. By stressing the play between poise and motion, Jackson illustrated the conditions of cultural work that Walter Benjamin had theorized four years earlier in a different social context. Drawing from his own formative experiences in media-saturated interwar Berlin and Paris, Benjamin proposed that the human artistry of the actor could redeem the alienating effects of mass reproduction. No longer imbued with the authentic aura of a live performance, film actors continually "tested" their humanity against the apparatus of the film set: they "must operate with [their] whole living person" in front of cameras and editing equipment that "split [up] the actor's performance." Benjamin's image almost perfectly anticipated Jackson's portraits of Moten: "To perform in the glare of the arc lamps while simultaneously meeting the demands of the microphone is a test performance of the highest order. To accomplish it is to preserve one's humanity in the face of the apparatus."[11]

While surrounding her with cameras, microphones, and glaring stage lights, Jackson shows Moten as the commanding figure: a triumph of humanity—and Black womanhood—over the machine. But by conveying Moten's performance in watercolor, rather than print illustration, Jackson at once recuperated Moten's image from the circuits of mechanical reproduction and commodification while marking the limitations that defined both of their careers as African American cultural workers: Jackson among the most prolific cartoonists of his generation largely unknown outside the Black press; Moten among the most talented actors who would never lead a motion picture, despite Barnett's intensive lobbying of Hollywood moguls on his wife's behalf. Although audiences may have heard Moten's voice severed from Moten's image—she dubbed Barbara Stanwyck in *Ladies of the House* (1932) and Ginger Rogers in *Professional Sweetheart* (1933)—Jackson presented Moten as an image of a fully embodied and autonomous performer, his kaleidoscopic sweep of colors at once evoking and compensating for the voice that his paints could not reproduce.[12]

Jackson's watercolors would have been easily overlooked among the thousands of images that were exhibited, produced, and circulated within the American Negro Exposition—a deluge Jackson contributed to with his single-panel *Exposition Follies* comic series that lampooned attendees in the *Defender*. But if Jackson's watercolors represented a rare aesthetic form where African American humanity could be envisioned in

Fig. 56 Jay Jackson (1905–1954), *Couples Dancing*, ca. 1940. Watercolor, ink, and charcoal on paper, $12\frac{9}{16} \times 9\frac{11}{16}$ in. Delaware Art Museum, Acquisition Fund, 2022

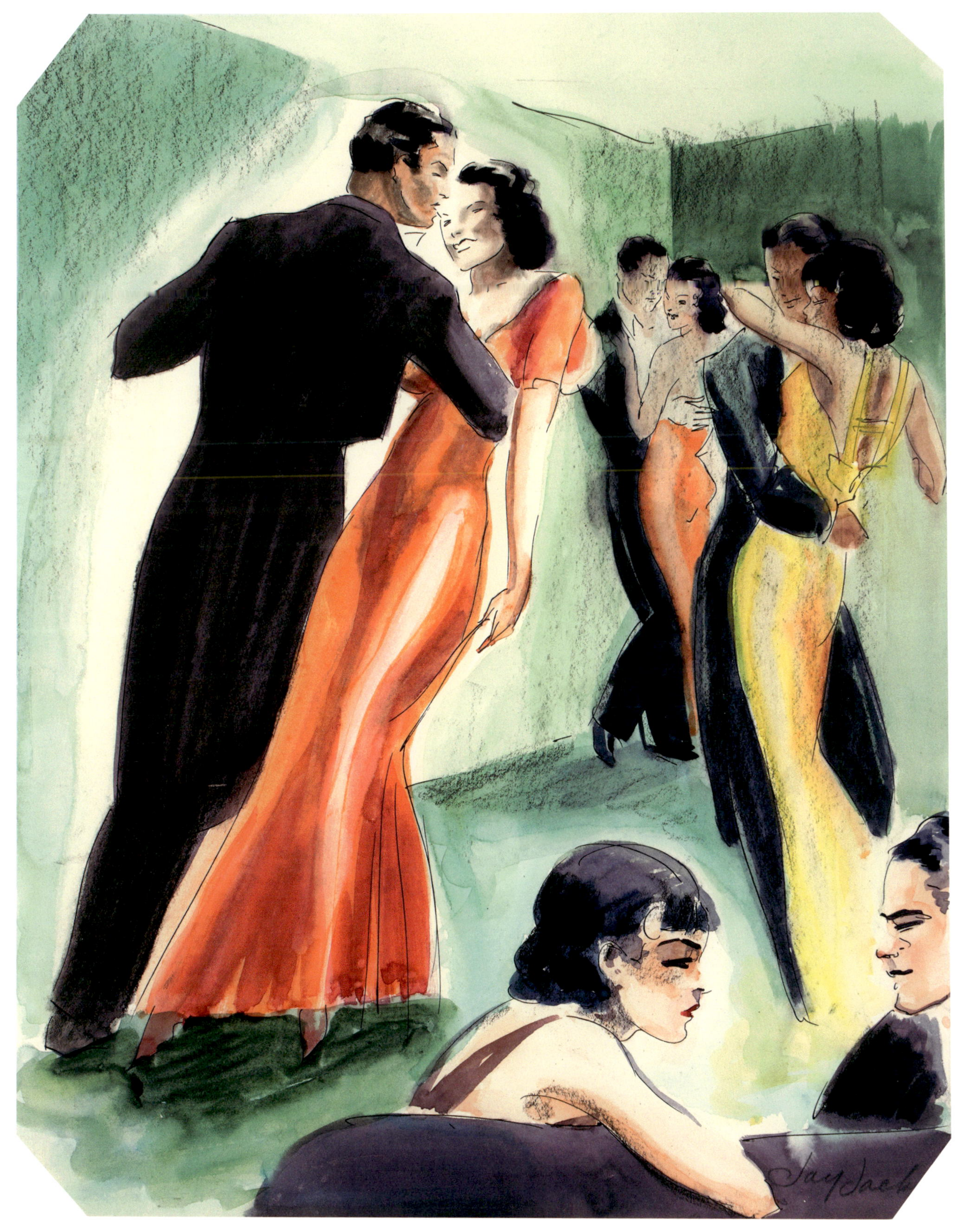

full Technicolor, they also presaged new horizons for Black cultural enterprise and experiment. After the war, Jackson and Poston would move to Los Angeles, where he would dabble in early television, making inroads into the burgeoning television industry as a feature artist in *Telecomics* before his untimely death in 1954.[13] After a cyst in her vocal cords caused Moten to retire from singing, she kept up her role as a socialite, activist, and maven of African American media. In a 1957 radio interview in Ghana with Martin Luther King Jr., who had just led the Montgomery Bus Boycott, Barnett contemplated the revolutionary prospects of the "birth of a new nation" free of imperial control. "Rather than pattern after the West, they can certainly profit by the mistakes of the West. And one of the newspapers from Britain I noticed said they are walking a tightrope without the springboard underneath, the net of the Colonial Office there to catch them if they should fall. But when you ask an African if he is ready, does he think that they're ready, they'll say, 'Well, was your country ready?' And of course, that shuts you up, doesn't it?"[14]

Moten apprehended the nations of postcolonial Africa as Jackson had once apprehended Moten: a power remaking herself in her own image.

ENDNOTES

1. "Etta Moten Stars as a Radio Emcee," *Chicago Defender*, August 3, 1940, 21.

2. "Name Winners in Exposition Art Exhibit," *Chicago Defender*, August 10, 1940, 9.

3. Biographical information about Etta Moten Barnett is drawn from Moten's interview with Timuel D. Black Jr., in Black, ed., *Bridges of Memory: Chicago's First Wave of Black Migration* (Evanston, IL: Northwestern University Press, 2003), 99–105; Gerald Horne, *The Rise and Fall of the Associated Negro Press: Claude Barnett's Pan-African News and the Jim Crow Paradox* (Urbana: University of Illinois Press, 2017), 51–54; Bob McCann, "Moten, Etta," in *Encyclopedia of African American Actresses in Film and Television* (Jefferson, NC: McFarland & Company, 2010), 242–43.

4. Claude A. Barnett to Herbert Hoey, April 29, 1936, in Claude A. Barnett Papers; quoted in Horne, *The Rise and Fall of the Associated Negro Press*, 53.

5. Horne, *The Rise and Fall of the Associated Negro Press*, 52; Adam Green, *Selling the Race: Culture, Community, and Black Chicago, 1940–1955* (Chicago: University of Chicago Press, 2007), chap. 3.

6. "Etta Moten, Screen Star, Thrills Large Audience," *Chicago Defender*, November 24, 1934, 6.

7. Zora Neale Hurston to "Dear Claude" (n.d.), in Claude A. Barnett Papers; quoted in Horne, *The Rise and Fall of the Associated Negro Press*, 52.

8. "Jay Jackson's Art Work Was Seasoning for Life," *Chicago Defender*, June 5, 1954, 7; Tim Jackson, "Jay Jackson," in *African American National Biography*, ed. Henry Louis Gates Jr. (Oxford, UK: Oxford University Press, 2008).

9. Amy M. Mooney, "Seeing 'As Others See Us': The *Chicago Defender* Cartoonist Jay Jackson as Cultural Critic," *MELUS* 39, no. 2 (June 2014): 115–20; Davarian Baldwin, *Chicago's New Negroes: Modernity, the Great Migration, and Black Urban Life* (Chapel Hill: University of North Carolina Press, 2007), 45.

10. "Etta Moten, Screen Star, Thrills Large Audience," 6.

11. Walter Benjamin, "The Work of Art in the Age of Its Technological Reproducibility: Second Version," [1935–36], trans. Edmund Jephcott and Harry Zohn, in Benjamin, *The Work of Art in the Age of Its Technological Reproducibility, and Other Writings on Media*, ed. Michael W. Jennings et al. (Cambridge, MA: Harvard University Press, 2008), 29, 30, 31. See also Joel Dinerstein, *Swinging the Machine: Modernity, Technology, and African American Culture between the World Wars* (Amherst: University of Massachusetts Press, 2003).

12. Horne, *The Rise and Fall of the Associated Negro Press*, 8, 52–53; McCann, "Moten," 242.

13. "Jay Jackson's Art Work Was Seasoning for Life," 7.

14. Etta Moten Barnett, interview with Martin Luther King Jr. (March 6, 1957). Martin Luther King Jr., Papers, Stanford University: https://kinginstitute.stanford.edu/king-papers/documents/interview-etta-moten-barnett.

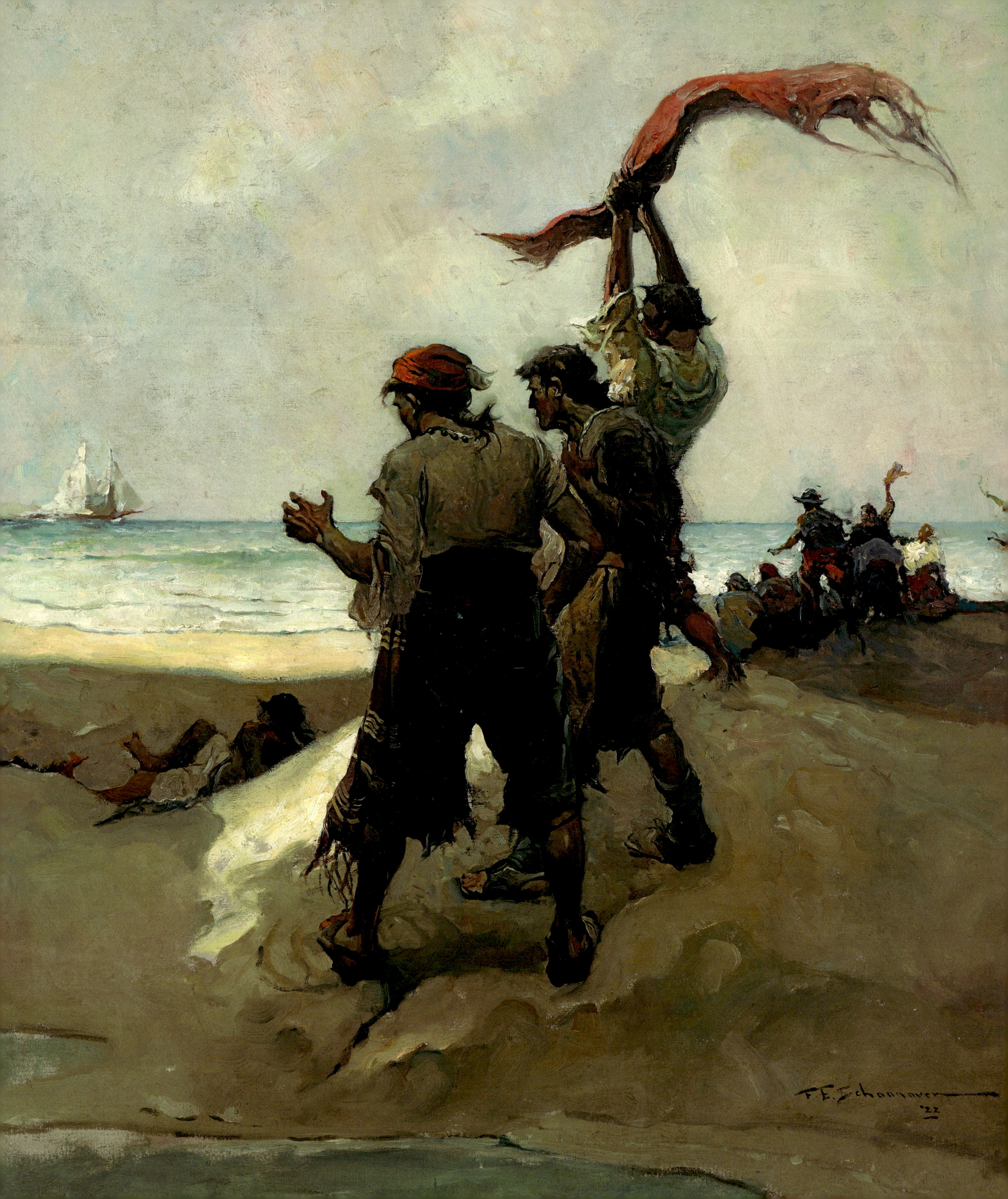
F. E. Schoonover
'22

Heather Campbell Coyle

Pyle's Legacy in Jazz Age Illustration

A trio of ragged pirates cluster on a white sand beach, wearing filthy shirts and tattered breeches. One waves a red cloth, signaling a ship in the background. His back is turned, but the tension of the moment is captured in the muscles of the brawny sailors (pl. 48). The illustration, by Frank E. Schoonover, does not indicate whether the ship—so small and pale in color that it could be a mirage—has spotted them. The artist leaves the author to tell the tale, perhaps recalling a lesson from his teacher Howard Pyle: "[P]icture the supreme moment leaving to the imagination what precedes and follows."[1] Imbued with suspense and painted with gusto, Schoonover's picture is a perfect homage to Pyle.

Strolling through a bookshop or flipping through magazines at a newsstand in the 1920s, Pyle's visual legacy would have been everywhere. Adventure stories were illustrated with painterly pictures of swashbuckling pirates and dueling cavaliers. Detailed images of colonial America appeared in popular histories, as well as advertisements for modern products from cars to chemicals. And dynamic compositions lured readers deep into romantic tales. Some of the finest of these were made by Pyle's former pupils and their students, who were at the height of their careers during the Jazz Age.

For over thirty years before his death in 1911, Pyle found success by producing illustrations that connected with readers. Nearly all pirate pictures owe a debt to Pyle, who practically invented the modern vision of buccaneers, galleons, and treasure chests in paintings like *Which Shall Be Captain?* (fig. 57). In addition, his paintings illustrated national history, and his drawings delineated the members of King Arthur's Round Table. Pyle's illustrations appeared in the leading literary magazines of his day, and he published elegant books beloved by children and adults.

In 1894 Pyle turned to teaching, first at the Drexel Institute in Philadelphia and then at his own school in Wilmington, Delaware. As Joyce K. Schiller has described, Pyle didn't dwell on the practicalities of painting. Instead, he pushed his pupils to become storytellers, to create illustrations that served as "prods to the imagination."[2] His students quickly found assignments—Pyle's connections with publishers were part of the appeal of studying with him—and built significant careers during their teacher's lifetime.[3] When Pyle died, an obituary described him as "almost the father of American magazine illustration as it is known to-day."[4] A decade after his death, Pyle's students were illustrating the books, magazines, calendars, posters, and prints found in millions of American homes.

Detail of pl. 48

Illustrating Adventure

Pyle trained his students to mentally connect with their subject matter, telling them, "[P]roject your mind into the subject until you actually live in it. Throw your heart into the picture and jump in after it."[5] This approach led to stirring images like Schoonover's desperate pirates. Schoonover, who excelled at producing the dramatic, historically driven pictures that had been his teacher's specialty, created this memorable illustration for Ralph D. Paine's "Blackbeard the Buccaneer." One of many pirate stories published in the 1920s, Paine's tale was serialized in 1922 in *The American Boy*, the most popular magazine for young people in that decade.[6]

In 1920 Pyle's student Thornton Oakley illustrated an edition of Charles Kingsley's *Westward Ho!*, a fictional tale of Francis Drake and other privateers in the Caribbean.[7] Early in the story, Oakley's *Amyas upon the Quay at Bideford* provides a panoramic view of a busy harbor village (fig. 58). Amyas Leigh, the young protagonist of the story, pauses to take in the scenery while a man descends the stairs behind him. His hand rests on the hilt of his sword, foreshadowing the kidnapping, battles, and adventures to come. Oakley draws attention to the armed man and links him to the protagonist by picturing him with a red cape that matches the cap Amyas wears. Pyle and Schoonover used red strategically to guide the viewer through a picture.

Produced for the same youth audience, Wyeth's painting *Johnny's Fight with Cherry* illustrated *Drums* by James Boyd, a novel about a boy growing up during the American Revolution (pl. 49). Wyeth's approach to the commission recalled his teacher's dedication to researching the historical places and people he illustrated.[8] Wyeth traveled to Edenton, North Carolina, to observe and photograph the colonial-era waterfront where this scene was set, and he prominently included extant eighteenth-century buildings in the background.[9] Wyeth's attention to the scenery, with its dazzling sky and sun-dappled buildings, demonstrates his deep interest in landscape painting.[10] Finishing the picture, he wrote to his father that the project "gave me a good chance to show an interesting view of Edenton as well as a lively scrap."[11]

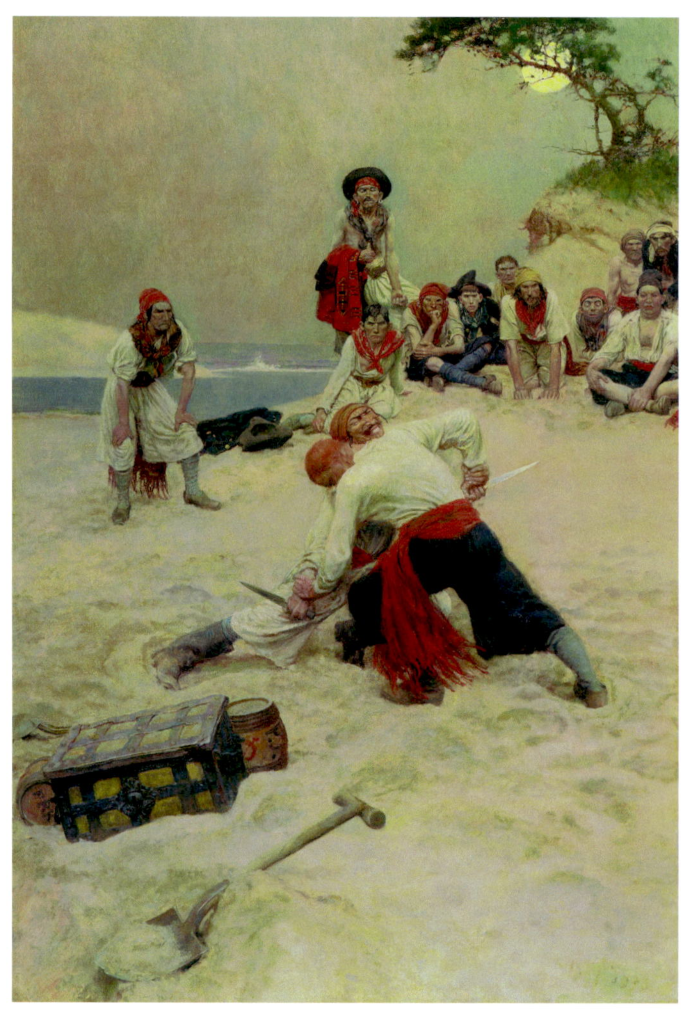

Fig. 57 Howard Pyle (1853–1911), *Which Shall Be Captain?*, for "The Buccaneers" by Don C. Seitz, *Harper's Monthly Magazine*, January 1911. Oil on canvas, 48 × 31¾ in. Delaware Art Museum, Gift of Dr. James Stillman, 1994

New Venues for Old Stories

Historical subjects by Wyeth, Stanley Arthurs, and Harvey Dunn reflected the continued allure of the Colonial Revival. Fostered by the centennial celebrations of 1876, Americans looked to the nation's past to understand themselves and their world. In the late nineteenth century, authors and illustrators celebrated George Washington, Ben Franklin, and Thomas Jefferson in popular histories and historical fiction for children and adults. Later, with the tumult of World War I, the Bolshevik Revolution, the Red Scare, and continued immigration in the 1920s, the nation entered a period marked by isolationism and nativism, and Colonial Revival soared

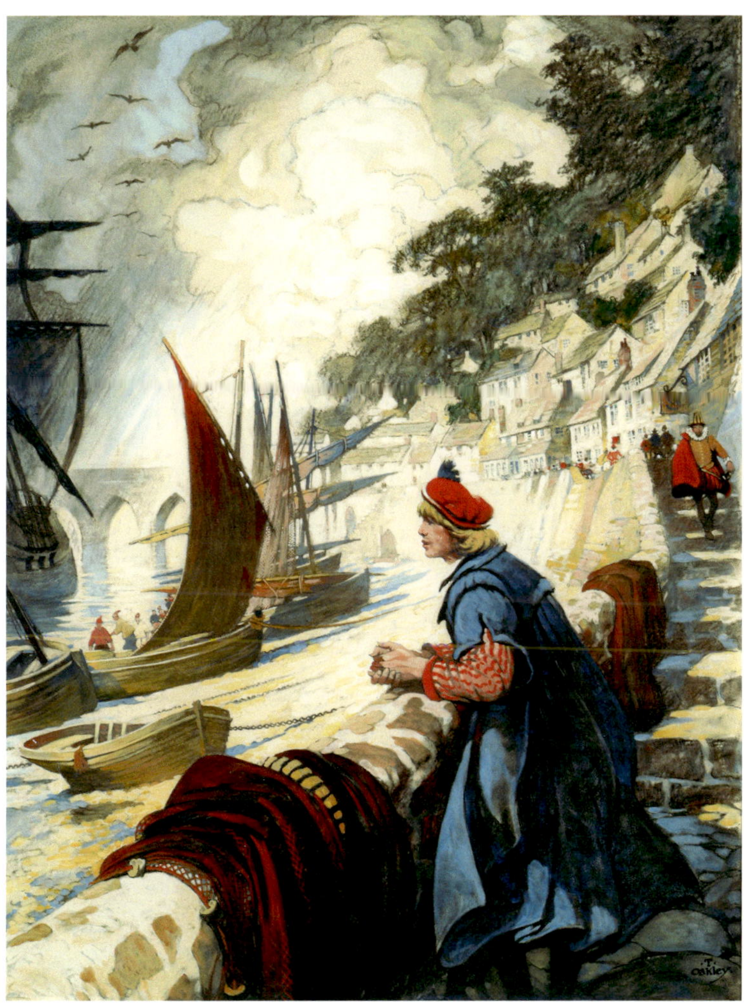

Fig. 58 Thornton Oakley (1881–1953), *Amyas upon the Quay at Bideford*, for *Westward Ho! Or the Voyages and Adventures of Sir Amyas Leigh, Knight, of Burrough, in the County of Devon, in the Reign of Her Most Glorious Majesty Queen Elizabeth* by Charles Kingsley (Philadelphia: George W. Jacobs, 1920). Gouache and charcoal on illustration board, 31¾ × 23⅝ in. Delaware Art Museum, Gayle and Alene Hoskins Endowment Fund, 1981

again. Domestic architecture looked to the past, young women took up needlework, and historic preservation efforts escalated.[12] Henry Ford started Greenwood Village in Michigan; the du Ponts began transforming Winterthur; and John D. Rockefeller Jr. launched the preservation and restoration of Colonial Williamsburg.[13] While some Americans were hanging out in jazz clubs, many more were reading stories set in colonial America.

Trained to create convincing historical scenes, Pyle's students benefitted from this enthusiasm for the past, but the details of their commissions speak to new avenues in the publishing industry. Ambitious historical paintings by Arthurs and Dunn were produced for advertising rather than as story illustrations. In the early twentieth century, advertising expanded beyond the back pages and inside covers of magazines, transforming the popular press. Mass-market magazines like *The Saturday Evening Post* (and even *The American Boy*) published illustrated advertisements, including full-page designs, for companies eager to reach their readers. The infusion of advertising money allowed publishers to lower magazine prices, leading to massive increases in circulation by the mid-1920s. Companies also distributed illustrated calendars, posters, and other paper ephemera to keep their brand names in sight of their clients. Starting in 1921, Maxfield Parrish famously designed calendars for Edison Mazda, and throughout the Jazz Age, many illustrators found themselves working for advertising companies or directly for corporations rather than publishers and art editors.

From 1922 through 1927, Arthurs produced historical scenes for monthly calendars printed by Ketterlinus Lithographic Manufacturing Company. His 1924 image of Commodore John Barry is typical of this work (pl. 50). Arthurs primarily painted historical subjects, including murals, and, like Pyle and Wyeth, he incorporated accurate details into his romantic visions of the past. The illustration depicts a specific historical subject, described on the reverse of the calendar page, in a moment of dramatic activity. His loose brushwork and bright colors create a lively image in reproduction. Years later, Arthurs would reuse this image of adventure on the high seas to illustrate two books.[14] Painted for a similar commission, Arthurs's *New Year's Eve* depicts a night watchman calling at a picturesque village inn in colonial New England. This large canvas was made for a calendar produced by Brown and Bigelow, a company that issued cards, calendars, and prints for individual sale and distribution by corporate clients (fig. 59). Arthurs's vibrant images suited the aims of printers eager to communicate their ability to capture a full spectrum of color.

In 1928 Dunn painted a series of elaborate pictures to promote Duco automobile lacquer for the DuPont Company (pl. 51). His detailed paintings appeared in full-page, full-color advertisements in the nation's most

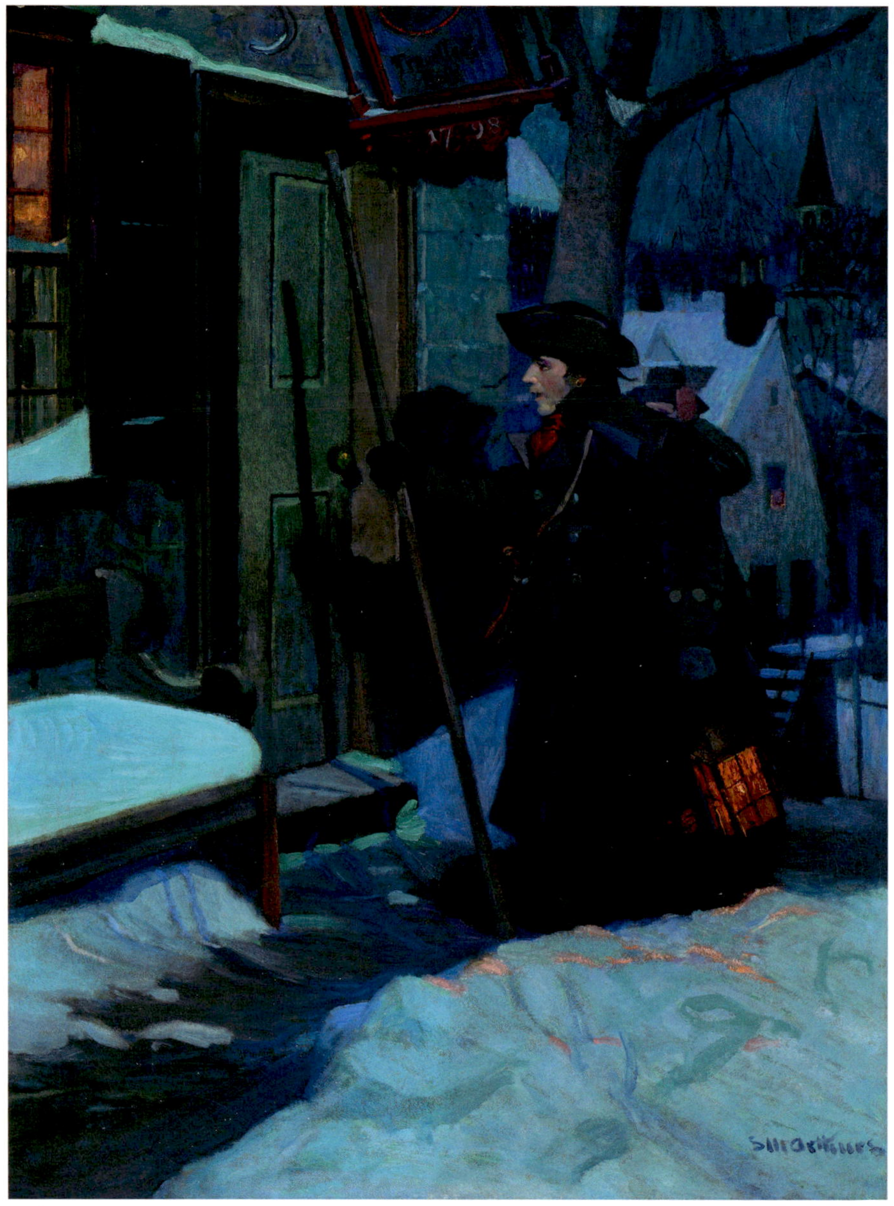

Fig. 59 Stanley Arthurs (1877–1950), *New Year's Eve*, for advertising calendar (Brown and Bigelow, 1928). Oil on canvas, 35½ × 26⅜ in. Delaware Art Museum, Louisa du Pont Copeland Memorial Fund, 1930

popular magazines, including *The Saturday Evening Post*. Dunn composed a scene of women waving farewell to whaling ships in a New England harbor. In print, this picture of colonial America was accompanied by text that rather improbably linked this tableau to DuPont's modern innovations: "For years American industry demanded a finish which would hold its lustre under all climatic conditions, a finish which could withstand the blight of oxidation. And for many years du Pont chemists sought the formula of enduring beauty. The result is Duco, a new essential product as different from the old-time finishes as electricity is different from whale oil."[15] DuPont's marketing seems strained today, but Dunn's painterly pictures served to associate the company with a history that Americans were proud of and a recognizable artistic tradition.[16]

As Michele H. Bogart has pointed out, in the early twentieth century, advertisements became "bigger, bolder, and more calculatedly artistic," as corporations and advertising agencies strategically sought to link products to fine art.[17] Headquartered in Pyle's hometown, the in-house advertising department at DuPont located artistic value in the Pyle school of illustration: the Wilmington Society of the Fine Arts had been founded to preserve Pyle's work, and his students dominated the local art scene.[18] Dunn's paintings were a far cry from the modernist aesthetics adopted by some large corporations, but they hit the mark for many readers of *The Saturday Evening Post*, who had grown up with illustrated books by Pyle and Cream of Wheat advertisements by Wyeth. As the twentieth century progressed, even top illustrators took on work beyond books and magazines.

Women's Magazines

During the Jazz Age, illustrators enamored with history also learned to accommodate contemporary subjects. Through a long career, Pyle's student Gayle Hoskins tapped the sense of drama and rich color he learned from his teacher. A specialist in Western subjects, Hoskins illustrated tales of cowboys and Native Americans in the early twentieth century. By the 1920s, however, he found himself depicting the modern West for romance stories as women's magazines became clients.

In 1927 Hoskins illustrated "Roads of Doubt," a tale set in the Rocky Mountains, which allowed him to show off his knowledge of the landscape in a theatrical scene (pl. 52). Dramatic lighting enhances a tense exchange between two men whose clothing registers their differences: a city slicker in a dashing overcoat and scarf wears impractical dress shoes as he faces off against a local in sensible outdoor gear. Behind them, a young woman with bobbed hair, a fur coat, and a stylish evening dress leans against the automobile. To master the depiction of automobiles—a key element in contemporary fiction—Hoskins took dozens of study photographs.[19] New stories required new skills.

This contemporary romance was published in *Woman's Home Companion*, one of a growing number of magazines catering to women. Founded in 1873, *Woman's Home Companion* was well established by the 1920s and would reach its peak circulation of three million readers in the 1930s. Its primary competitors, *Ladies' Home Journal*, *Good Housekeeping*, and *Pictorial Review*, also were read in millions of households in the 1920s and '30s. All featured contemporary fiction, domestic advice, and fashion. Women's magazines generated demand for illustrations with modern domestic settings, and many women found work painting and drawing women and children for them.

Pyle's female students were regular contributors to leading women's magazines. Although Pyle was best known for narrative images, his portrait compositions demonstrate a keen ability to convey character without sacrificing decorative appeal—a skill his female students used to devise clever covers (fig. 60). Jessie Willcox Smith produced every cover for *Good Housekeeping* from 1918 to 1933, creating images that hook the viewer with a hint of narrative while remaining decorative and uncluttered, like

Fig. 60 Howard Pyle (1853–1911), *Kidd on the Deck of the "Adventure Galley,"* for "The True Captain Kidd" by John D. Champlin Jr., *Harper's Monthly Magazine*, December 1902. Crayon and watercolor on illustration board, 16 15/16 × 10 3/4 in. Delaware Art Museum, Museum Purchase, 1912

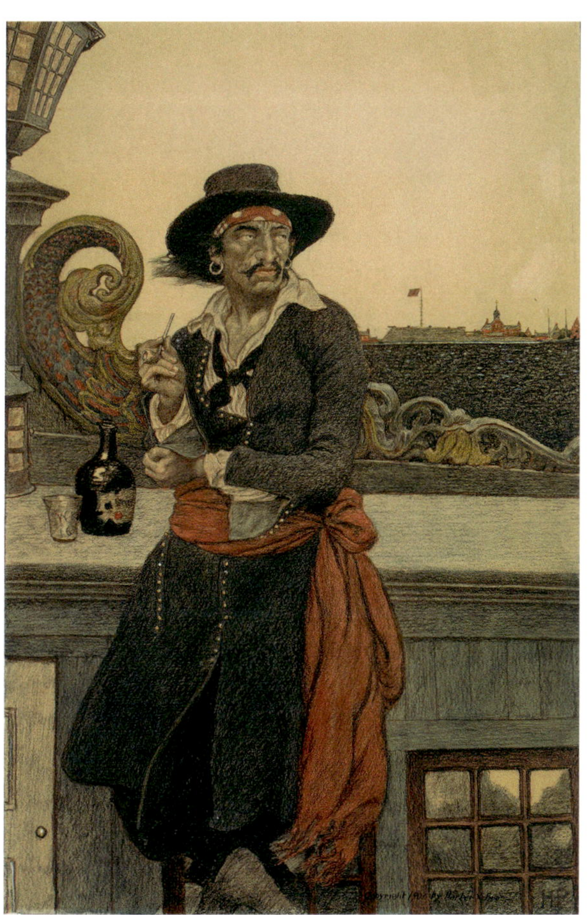

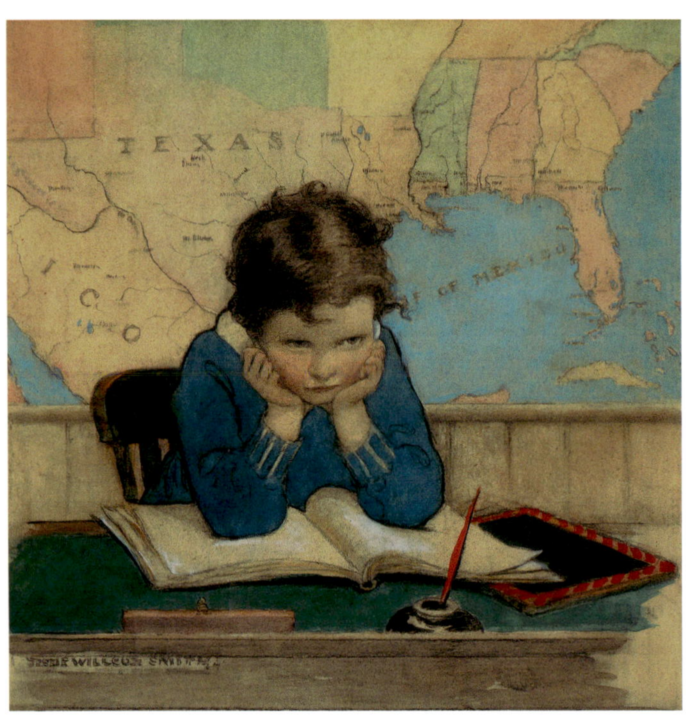

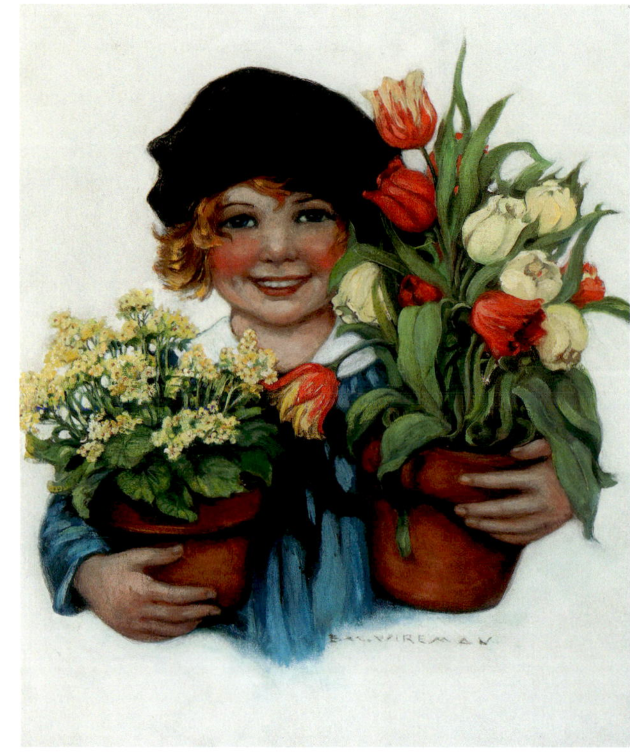

Fig. 61 Jessie Willcox Smith (1863–1935), *School Again!*, cover for *Good Housekeeping*, October 1928. Watercolor and charcoal on paper, 16⅞ × 17⅜ in. Delaware Art Museum, Louisa du Pont Copeland Memorial Fund, 1971

Fig. 62 Eugenie M. Wireman (1874–1961), cover for *Modern Priscilla*, April 1922. Oil on canvas, 20 × 16 in. Delaware Art Museum, Gift of Sharon S. Galm, 2011

School Again! (fig. 61). Similarly, Katharine and Eugenie Wireman illustrated cheery children in bold colors for magazines, including *Modern Priscilla* and *Success*, eliminating background details to create eye-catching designs (pl. 53 and fig. 62).

Not all illustrations for women's magazines focused on family or romance. Pyle's student Douglas Duer produced captivating paintings for "Danger Calling"—a mystery story by Patricia Wentworth for *Pictorial Review*. Duer composed his pictures in two colors, likely because the magazine was economizing on expensive color printing in 1931 (pl. 54 and fig. 63). He worked with an eye toward the relationship of text and image: the white space would have been filled with the story's text. This "vignette style" of illustrating increased in popularity in the early twentieth century, and Duer used it to great effect here, creating sinuous silhouettes for a melodramatic tale with a snake at its center.

As the 1920s progressed, more specialized magazines for women entered the field. With its tagline of "gripping clean love stories," *Love Romances* was one of several pulp magazines that focused on romantic fiction. Named for the coarse wood pulp paper they were printed on, pulps were known for their colorful covers, matched by sensational stories. Pulp publishers did not require famous authors but relied on skilled artists to devise intriguing covers, like this masquerade scene by Clyde Squires (fig. 64). When the publishing industry suffered setbacks during the Depression, the pulps prospered because they did not depend on advertising. During the Depression, Hoskins would find himself illustrating for *Romantic Range*, a pulp focused on Western love stories.

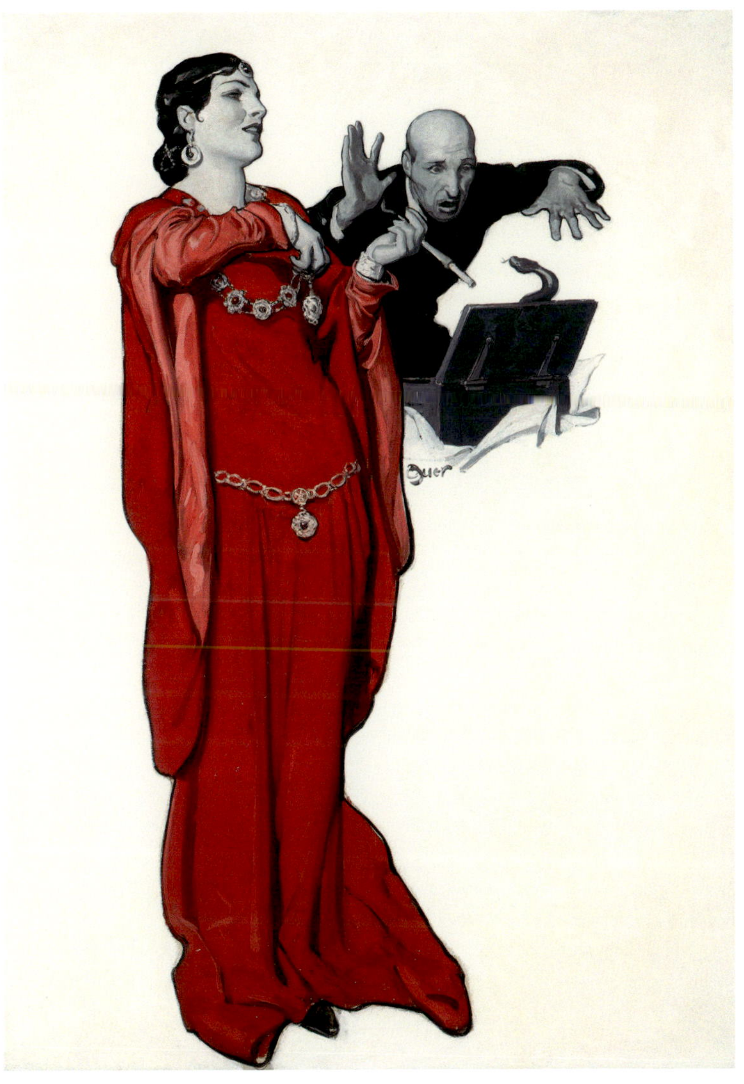

Fig. 63 Douglas Duer (1887–1964), *The waiter dropped the knife upon his foot and leaped back acrobatically*, for "Danger Calling" by Patricia Wentworth, *Pictorial Review*, May 1931. Oil on canvas, 32¾ × 22⅝ in. Delaware Art Museum, Gift of Mrs. Douglas Duer, 1976

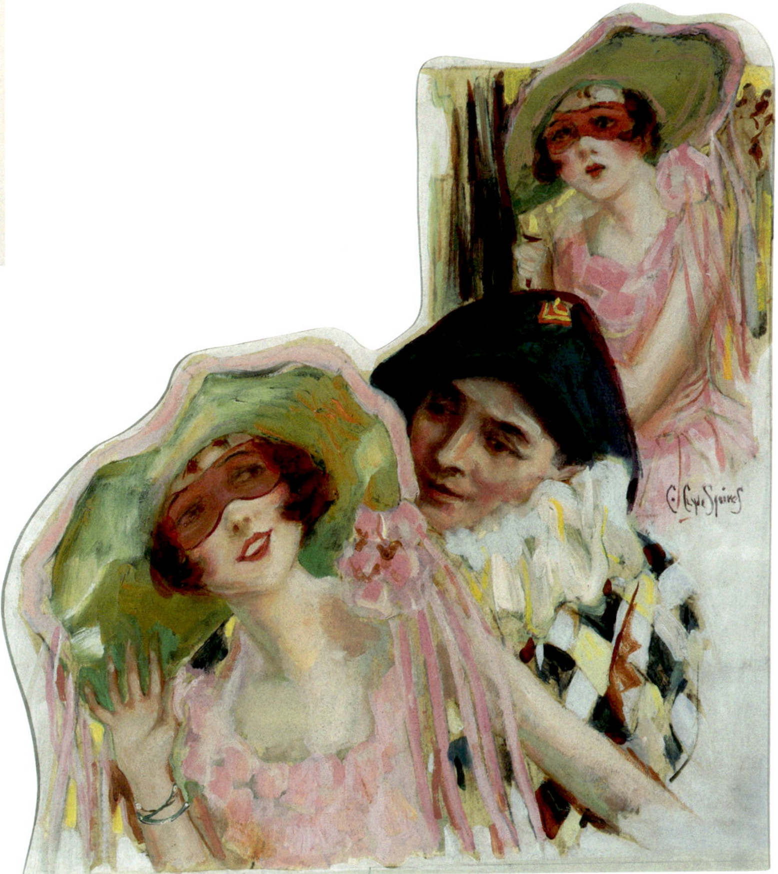

Fig. 64 C. Clyde Squires (1882–1969), cover for *Love Romances*, March ca. 1928. Oil on illustration board, 20 × 17½ in. Delaware Art Museum, Gayle and Alene Hoskins Endowment Fund, 1981

The Next Generation

Several of Pyle's students—including Harvey Dunn, George Harding, and Thornton Oakley—became successful teachers. They connected their own teaching to Pyle's, passing on his aphorisms, advice, and passion for storytelling to a generation of American illustrators who joined the professional ranks during the Jazz Age.

Harvey Dunn began teaching in 1914, founding his own school modeled on Pyle's, and he taught in New York at the Grand Central School of Art and the Art Students League. One of his most successful students was Dean Cornwell, who developed a painterly style and excelled at working in the vignette format, combining figures and just enough background to set the scene (fig. 65). The somber mood of this 1934 painting reflects its sad story and the time of its creation in the depths of the financial crisis. By the time he painted it, Cornwell was working primarily as a muralist—a line of work vital to the careers of Pyle, Arthurs, and Wyeth, among others—although Cornwell occasionally took illustration jobs for additional income.

Fig. 65 Dean Cornwell (1892–1960), *"I'd give you all I have, if I had anything to give," said Sherring*, for "Seven Men Came Back" by Warwick Deeping, *Hearst's International combined with Cosmopolitan*, April 1934. Oil on canvas, 34¼ × 45¼ in. Delaware Art Museum, Gift of Helen Farr Sloan, 1987

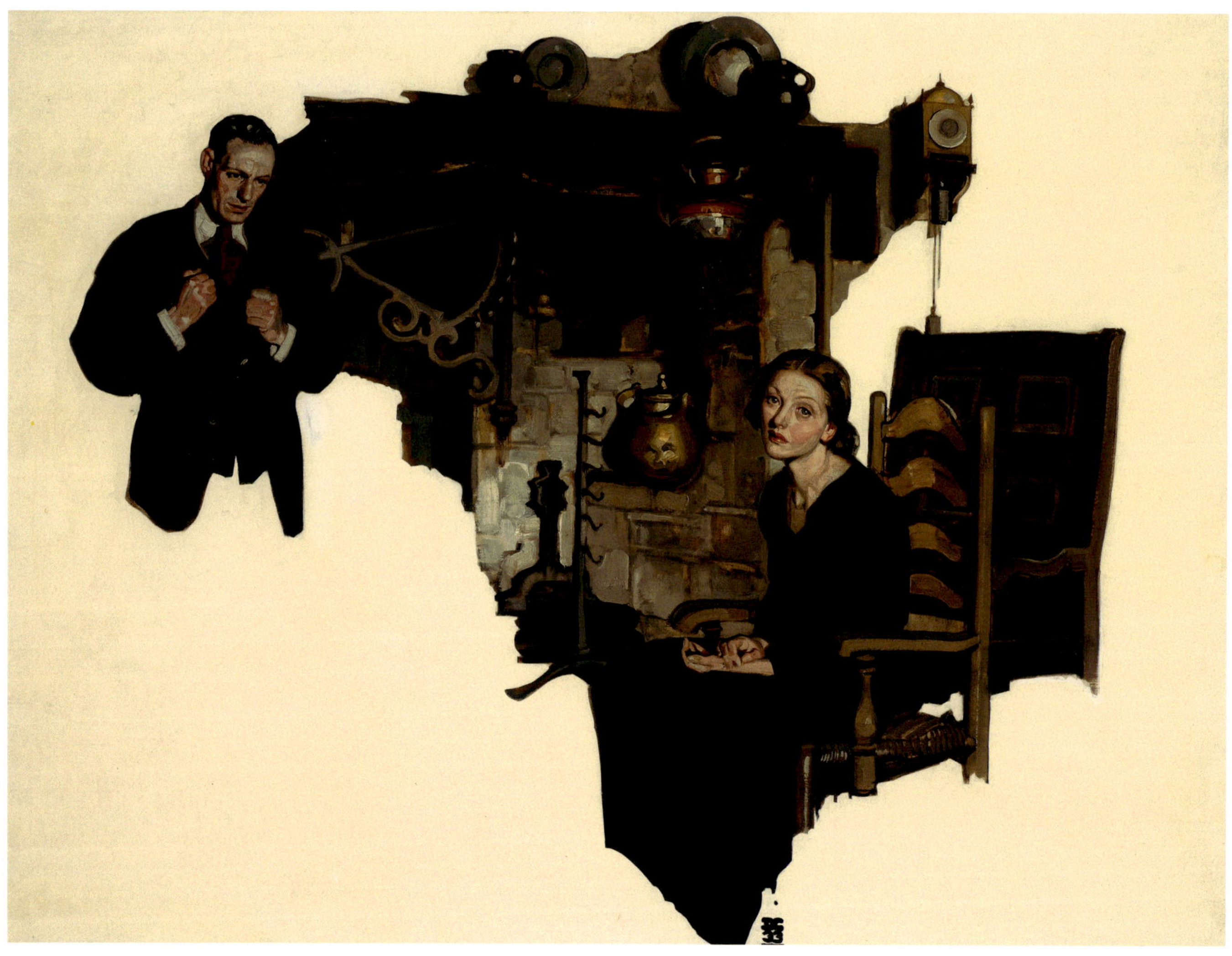

Mead Schaeffer studied with Dunn privately and with Cornwell at the Pratt Institute in Brooklyn. He adopted thick brushwork akin to Cornwell's, applying it to pirates, cavaliers, and adventurers in the Pyle tradition. Schaeffer's illustrations for Alexandre Dumas's *The Three Musketeers* demonstrate his mastery of intense color and bravura brushwork (pl. 55). His broad brushstrokes come through in published images, making it clear that Schaeffer's originals are oil paintings executed in a modern style influenced by postimpressionism. His technique adds a dimension of artistry to the book, which was sold as part of a series of literary classics by the Boston publisher Dodd, Mead and Company.

Publishers found great success selling illustrated classics in the 1910s and '20s, hiring top-shelf artists to create attractive books marketed as series.[20] Pyle was an important inspiration for these projects. He had made his name in the 1880s producing beautiful books for American youth, and in the early twentieth century, he released a four-volume set of Arthurian stories that Wyeth deemed "Pyle's most important contribution to the world of art."[21]

Pyle's pupils and their students also excelled at illustrating quality books for family reading. Leading up to Christmas in 1934, "The Mead Schaeffer Illustrated Classics" were advertised just below "Scribner Illustrated Classics," which included *Drums*, *Treasure Island*, and other titles illustrated by Wyeth.[22] In classic books, as in commercial advertisements, the painterly style of Pyle's followers evoked fine art—a desirable association for a collection of "Fine, Beautifully Illustrated Children's Books—Every One An Enduring Title."[23] In 1933 Scribner's made the homage overt when they issued the Howard Pyle Brandywine Edition, a set of five books originally written and illustrated by Pyle with new color frontispieces and introductory notes contributed by his students Arthurs, Wyeth, Schoonover, Dunn, and W. J. Aylward.[24]

New Media

In the Jazz Age, the visions of adventure crafted by Pyle and his students found a new outlet in movies as filmmakers gleaned lessons in storytelling from their favorite illustrated books. The influence of illustration on films of the 1920s might best be seen in the work of Douglas Fairbanks, who made movies based on literary characters, including pirates, the Three Musketeers, and Robin Hood, and befriended N. C. Wyeth in the process.

Early in his career, Pyle compiled and illustrated *The Merry Adventures of Robin Hood of Great Renown, in Nottinghamshire*, published by Scribner's in 1883. This book crystallized the narrative of Robin Hood for American audiences and raised Pyle to the top tier of professional illustrators. In 1912 Harper & Brothers released a version written and illustrated by Louis Rhead with a color frontispiece and cover by Schoonover. Five years later, Philadelphia publisher David McKay issued Paul Creswick's retelling of *Robin Hood* with Wyeth's full-color paintings. And in 1933 Wyeth provided the frontispiece and forward for the Howard Pyle Brandywine Edition of *The Merry Adventures of Robin Hood*. Heavy on action and not reliant on dialogue, Robin Hood translated well to silent film. The popular story inspired five movies before 1914, and in 1922 *Douglas Fairbanks in Robin Hood* was widely released in the United States.[25] The sets, costumes, and character of the protagonist in Fairbanks's version demonstrated the impact of popular illustration, and years later Errol Flynn built on the work of Fairbanks, Wyeth, and Pyle to create his memorable take on the character.

In 1921 Merle Johnson collaborated with Harper & Brothers to publish *Howard Pyle's Book of Pirates*, a large and richly illustrated volume that brought Pyle's work directly to another generation. That book inspired Fairbanks to produce, coauthor, and star in the 1926 film *The Black Pirate*, which kicked off what David Lubin has termed "The Golden Age of Pirate Movies" (fig. 66).[26] After seeing the film alongside Fairbanks and his wife Mary Pickford, Wyeth gushed in a letter to his father about the "gorgeous and stirring spectacle of pirate life (in full and glorious color—a perfect monument to the legends and traditions of pirates)."[27] According to Wyeth biographer David Michaelis, filmmakers found direct inspiration in Wyeth's pictures, but the artist refused repeated offers from Fairbanks and Pickford to direct pirate movies.[28]

Thanks in part to Wyeth's and Fairbanks's enthusiasm for Pyle's work during the Jazz Age, the artist's legacy continues in popular culture, especially in the realm of pirates. Disney's *Pirates of the Caribbean* series is replete with images rooted in Pyle's paintings. Enthusiasts and illustrators continue to discover Pyle's vision through his books, the art of illustrators he taught and influenced, and his original paintings and drawings, many of which are on view in his hometown at the Delaware Art Museum.

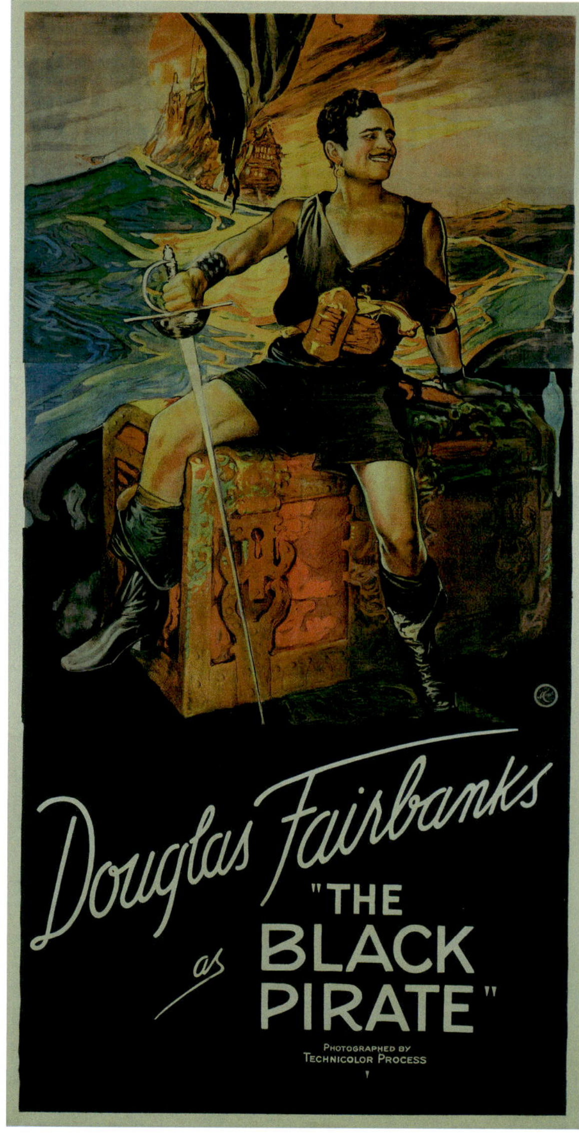

Fig. 66 H. C. Minor Litho Co., New York, three-sheet poster for *The Black Pirate*, 1926. Stone lithograph, 81 × 41 in. Margaret Herrick Library, Beverly Hills

ENDNOTES

1. Ethel Pennewill Brown and Olive Rush, "Notes from Howard Pyle's Monday Night Lectures, 1904–1906," June 27, 1904, 9. Howard Pyle Manuscript Collection, box 3, folder 2, Helen Farr Sloan Library and Archives, Delaware Art Museum.

2. Joyce K. Schiller, "Teaching Storytelling," in *Howard Pyle: American Master Rediscovered*, ed. Heather Campbell Coyle (Wilmington: Delaware Art Museum and Penn Press, 2011), 135.

3. For a more in-depth discussion of the careers of Pyle's students, see Virginia O'Hara, "Inspiring Minds: Howard Pyle and His Students," in Coyle, *Howard Pyle: American Master Rediscovered*, 139–55. For biographies of Pyle students, see Rowland Elzea and Elizabeth Hawkes, eds., *A Small School of Art: The Students of Howard Pyle* (Wilmington: Delaware Art Museum, 1980).

4. "Howard Pyle Dies in Italy," *New York Times*, November 10, 1911, 11.

5. Notebook of Allen Tupper True, quoted in Richard Wayne Lykes, "Howard Pyle, Teacher of Illustration," *Pennsylvania Magazine of History and Biography* 80 (July 1956): 363.

6. On pirates by Pyle and Schoonover, see Anne M. Loechle, "Gunpowder Smoke and Buried Dubloons: Adventure and Lawlessness in Howard Pyle's Piratical World," in Coyle, *Howard Pyle: American Master Rediscovered*, 59–71.

7. That same year N. C. Wyeth illustrated Kingsley's *Westward Ho!* for Scribner's Illustrated Classics.

8. On Pyle's approach to history subjects, see Heather Campbell Coyle, "Composing American History: Howard Pyle's Illustrations for Henry Cabot Lodge's 'The Story of the Revolution,'" in Coyle, *Howard Pyle: American Master Rediscovered*, 73–85.

9. Christine B. Podmaniczky, *N. C. Wyeth: Catalogue Raisonné of Paintings, Volume Two* (Chadds Ford, PA: Brandywine River Museum, 2008), 501.

10. Wyeth would never be satisfied with his career as an illustrator, writing as early as 1907 of his desire to be "a painter" and lamenting the superficiality of illustration. The space he gave to landscape—two-thirds of the canvas—and the impressionist palette of this painting may reflect this desire. See Michele H. Bogart, *Artists, Advertising, and the Borders of Art* (Chicago: University of Chicago Press, 1995), 56–58.

11. N. C. Wyeth to Andrew Newell Wyeth, January 27, 1928, Wyeth Family Archives. Quoted in Podmaniczky, 501.

12. On women taking up needlework in the 1920s, see Beverly Gordon, "Spinning Wheels, Samplers, and the Modern Priscilla: The Images and Paradoxes of Colonial Revival Needlework," *Winterthur Portfolio* 33 (Spring–Summer 1998): 163–94.

13. Mary Miley Theobald, "The Colonial Revival: The Past That Never Dies," *Colonial Williamsburg Journal* (Summer 2002): https://research.colonialwilliamsburg.org/Foundation/journal/Summer02/revival.cfm. Accessed September 26, 2023.

14. This illustration appeared with different titles in two books edited by Oliver G. Swan: *Deepwater Days* (Philadelphia: McCrae, Smith and Co., 1929) and *Anchors Aweigh! Tales of Wooden Ship Days* (New York: Grosset and Dunlop, 1929).

15. The advertisement for Duco Paint appeared in *The Saturday Evening Post*, September 22, 1928, 44.

16. Bogart, *Artists, Advertising, and the Borders of Art*, 125–70. Bogart examines the appeal of modernist art for advertising. Dunn's canvasses were retained by the DuPont Company and tagged as property of the advertising department.

17. Bogart, *Artists, Advertising, and the Borders of Art*, 25.

18. The Wilmington Society of the Fine Arts was founded by community members in 1912 to preserve and display Pyle's work. The Society hosted annual exhibitions of art by Pyle, his students, and Delaware artists. Pyle's students Stanley Arthurs, Gayle Hoskins, Violet Oakley, Frank E. Schoonover, and N. C. Wyeth lived in the region, taught locally, exhibited work, and served on committees at the Society, which eventually became the Delaware Art Museum. Artists in Wilmington continue to occupy studios constructed by Pyle and Schoonover.

19. Hoskins's photographs are in the Gayle Porter Hoskins Manuscript Collection, box 14, Helen Farr Sloan Library and Archives, Delaware Art Museum.

20. On the classics series, see Rebecca Rego Barry, "The Neo-Classics: (Re) Publishing the 'Great Books' in the United States in the 1990s," *Book History* 6 (2003): esp. 255–56. See also Jean C. Roos, "Books and Books," *The Elementary English Review* 6 (April 1929): 109. Published in 1928, *Drums* was the fifteenth book Wyeth completed for Scribner's Illustrated Classics—a series that encompassed some of the artist's most famous books, including Robert Louis Stevenson's *Treasure Island* (1911) and Jules Verne's *The Mysterious Island* (1918). Mead Schaeffer illustrated more than a dozen classics for Dodd, Mead.

21. N. C. Wyeth, "Introduction," in Charles D. Abbott, *Howard Pyle: A Chronicle* (New York: Harper & Brothers, 1925), xiv.

22. See, for example, the advertisements in *Reading Times* (Reading, PA), December 20, 1934, 4.

23. This was especially true in the 1920s when most illustrators were working in ink and watercolor on smooth illustration board—a method better suited to the abbreviated timelines of the magazine industry.

24. "Howard Pyle Honored with Memorial Edition," *News Journal* (Wilmington, DE), October 28, 1933, 8.

25. Valerie B. Johnson, "Robin Hood," for *The Robin Hood Project* (University of Rochester): https://d.lib.rochester.edu/robin-hood/theme/robin-hood. Accessed November 28, 2023.

26. David Lubin, "The Persistence of Pirates: Pyle, Piracy, and the Silver Screen," in Coyle, *Howard Pyle: American Master Rediscovered*, 167–70.

27. N. C. Wyeth to Andrew Newell Wyeth II, March 24, 1926. Quoted in *The Wyeths: The Letters of N. C. Wyeth, 1901–1945*, ed. Betsy James Wyeth (Boston: Gambit, 1971), 718.

28. David Michaelis, *N. C. Wyeth: A Biography* (New York: Alfred A. Knopf, 1998), 274.

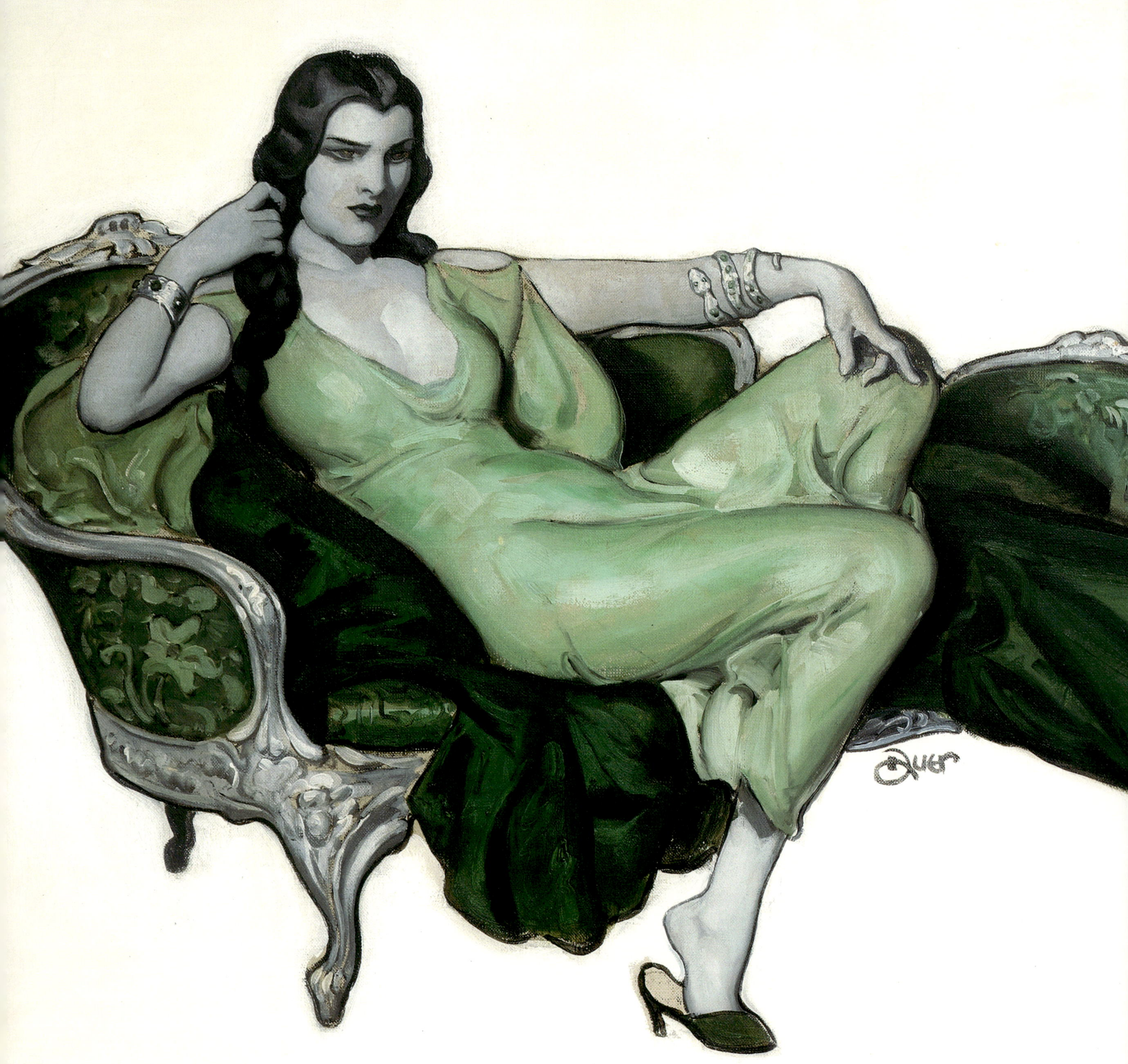

Plates

45–55

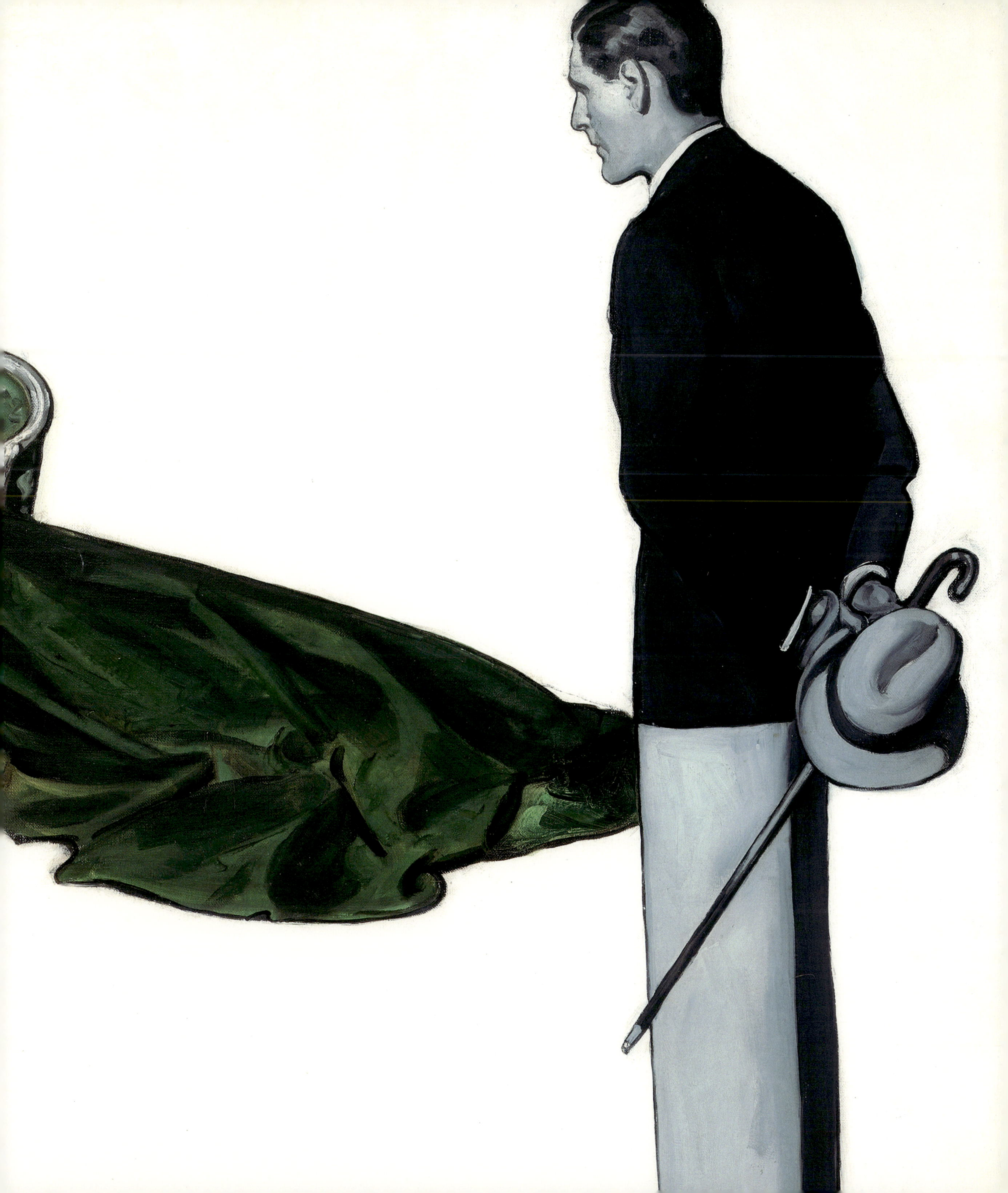

45

Jay Jackson (1905–1954)

Etta Moten Barnett Singing, ca. 1940

Watercolor, ink, and charcoal on paper, 12⅝ × 9$\frac{9}{16}$ in.
Delaware Art Museum, Acquisition Fund, 2022

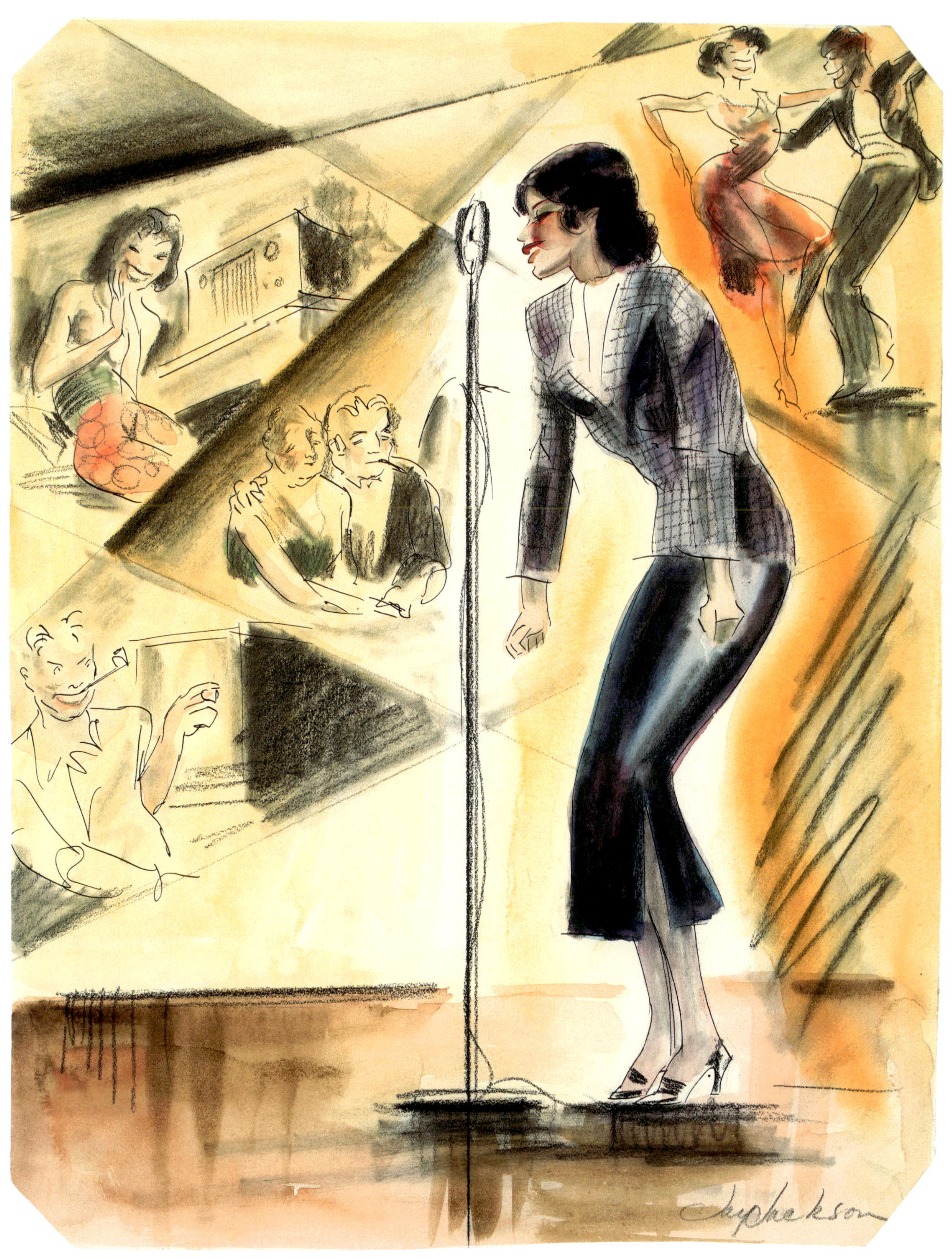

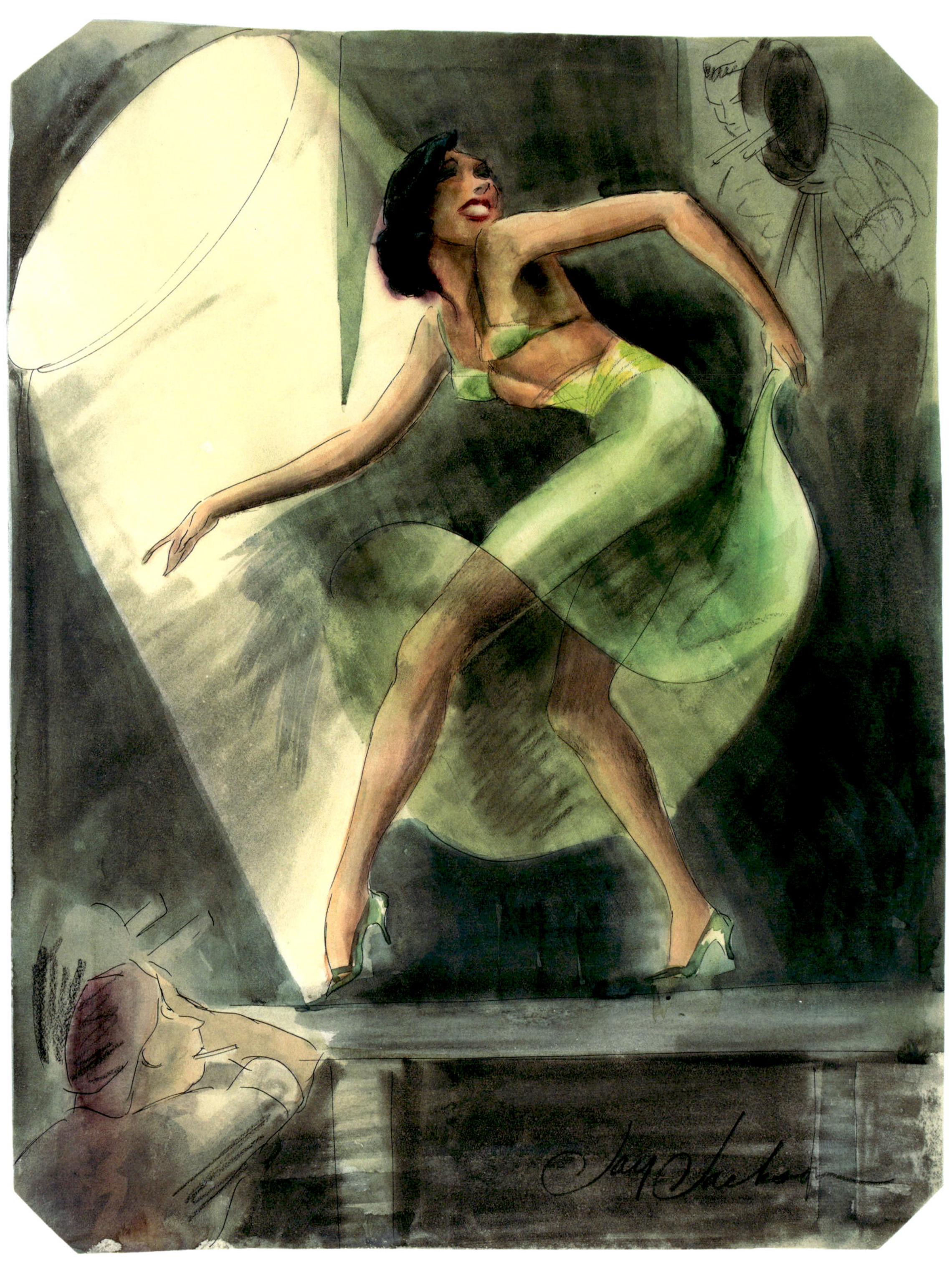

46

Jay Jackson (1905–1954)

Etta Moten Barnett Dancing, ca. 1940

Watercolor, ink, and charcoal on paper, 12⅝ × 9⅝ in.
Delaware Art Museum, Acquisition Fund, 2022

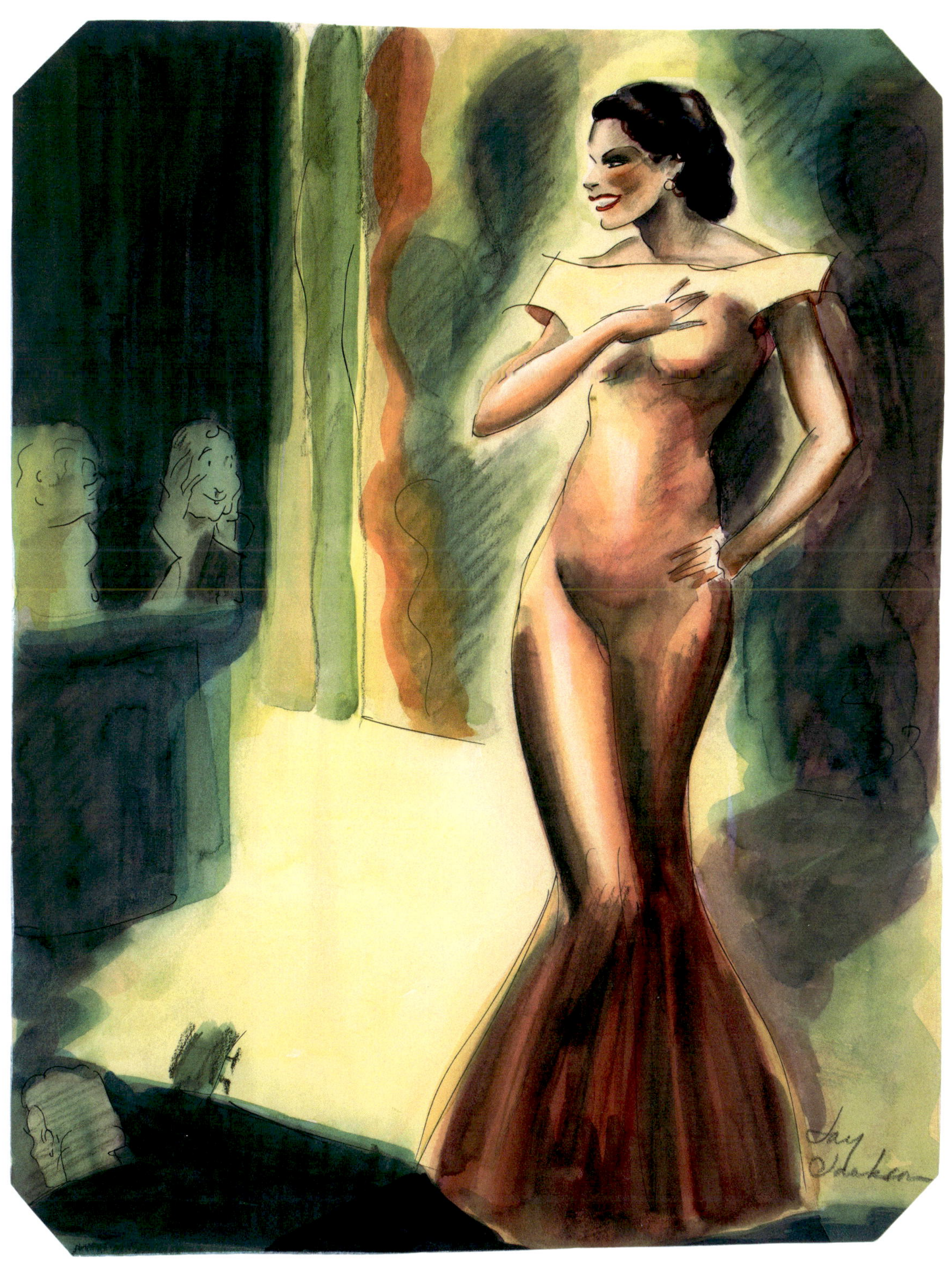

47

Jay Jackson (1905–1954)

Etta Moten Barnett on Stage, ca. 1940

Watercolor, ink, and charcoal on paper, 12¾ × 9¹¹⁄₁₆ in.
Delaware Art Museum, Acquisition Fund, 2022

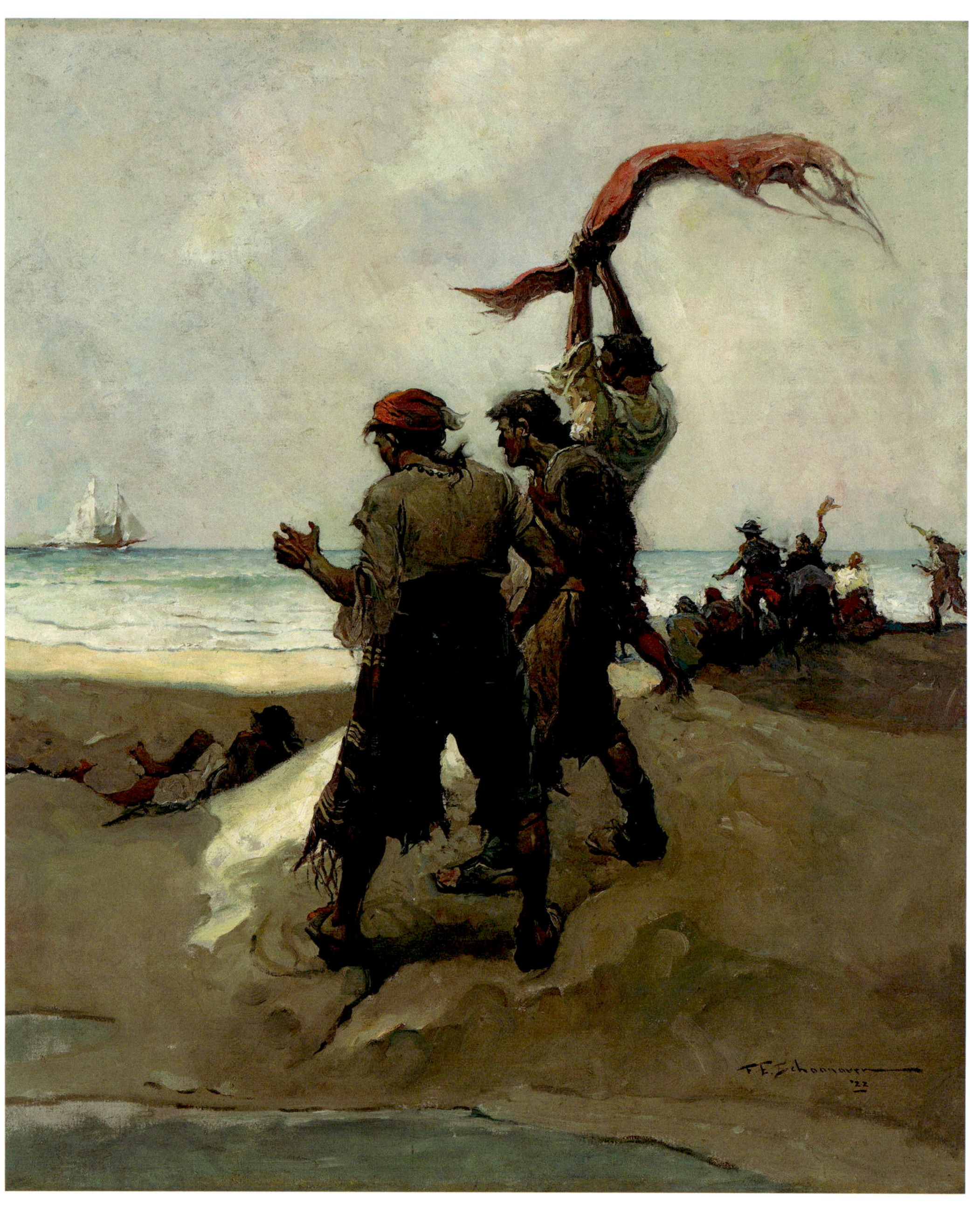

48

Frank E. Schoonover (1877–1972)

Ned Rackham espied the derelict score of captives on the cay, for "Blackbeard the Buccaneer" by Ralph D. Paine, *The American Boy*, July 1922

Oil on canvas, 36¼ × 30¼ in.
Delaware Art Museum, Bequest of Frank H. Mackie, Jr., 1992

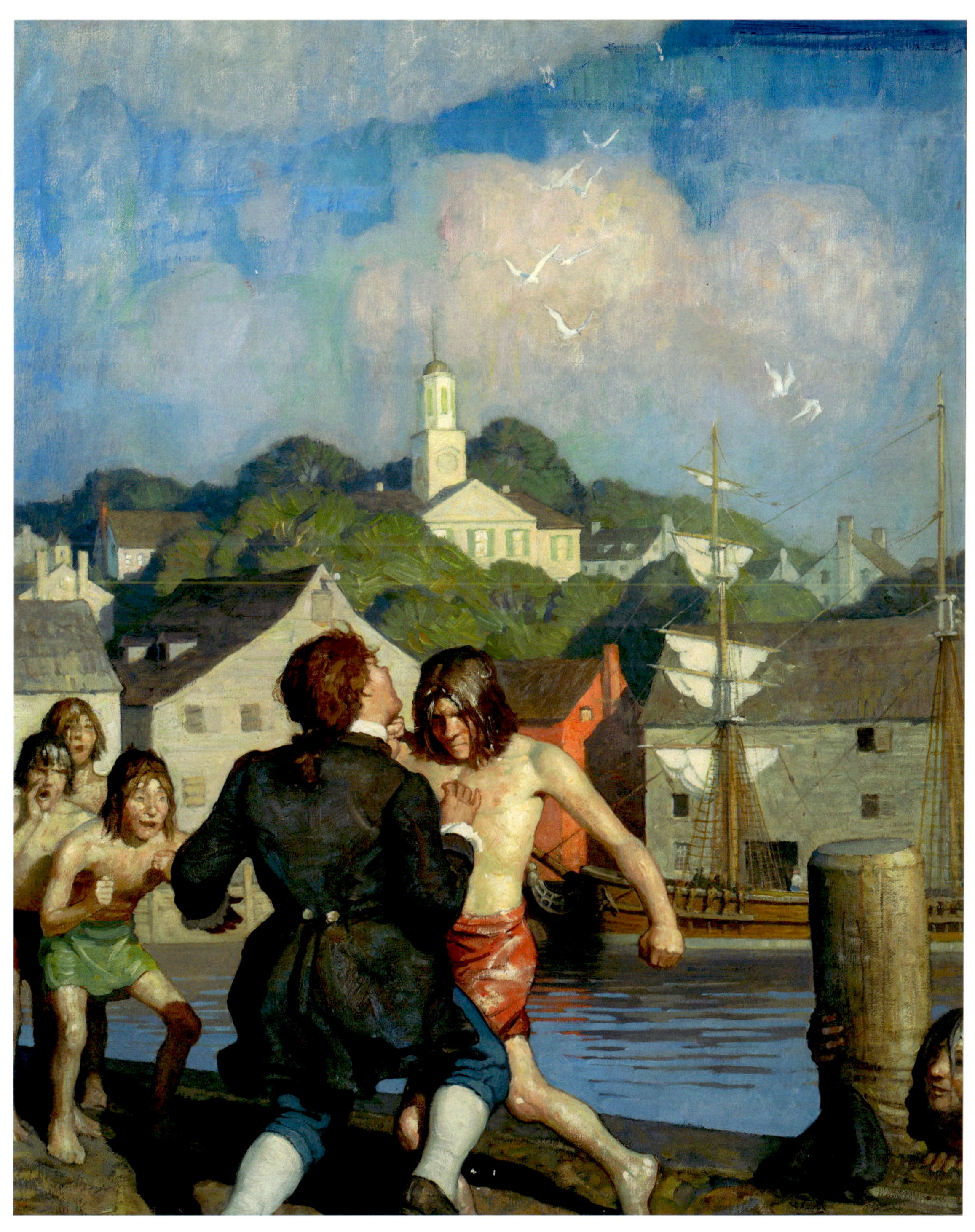

49

N. C. Wyeth (1882–1945)
Johnny's Fight with Cherry, for *Drums* by James W. Boyd
(New York: Charles Scribner's Sons, 1928)

Oil on canvas, 40 × 32 in.
Delaware Art Museum, Gift of Willis du Pont, 1960

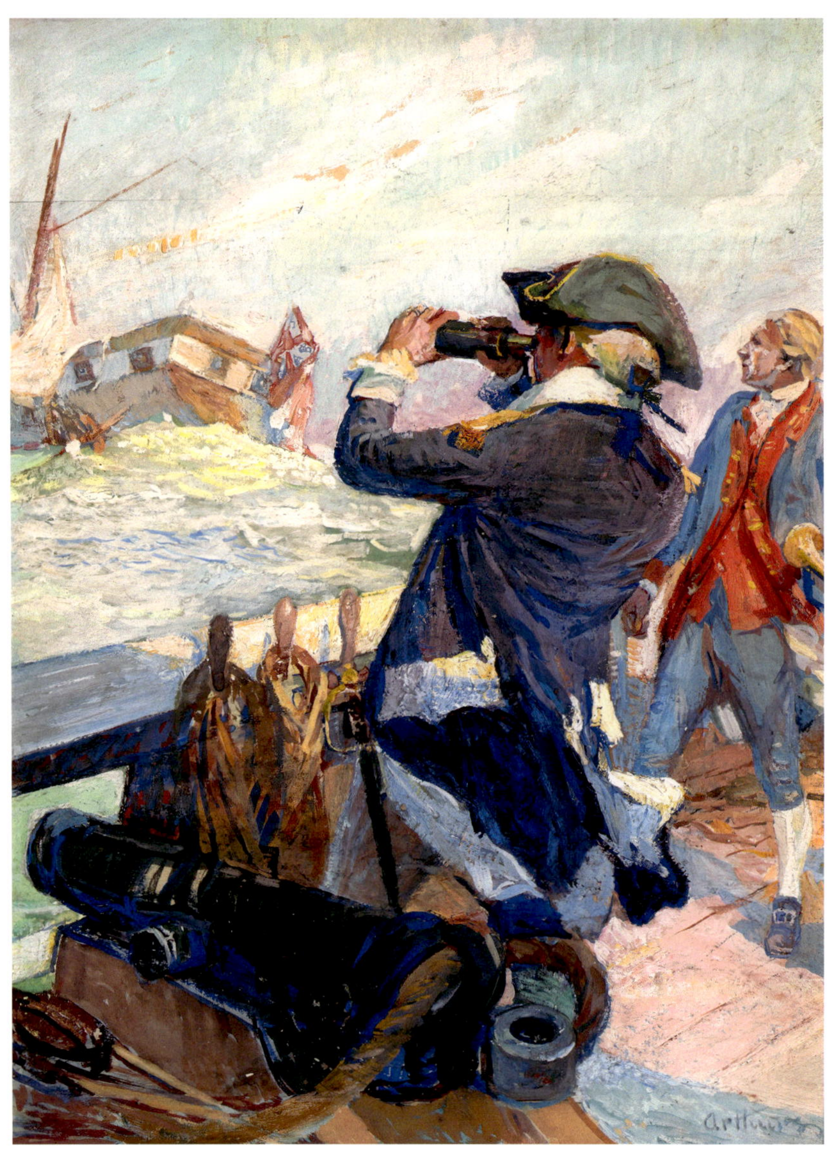

50

Stanley Arthurs (1877–1950)

Captain Barry ordered them to haul down their colors, which, not being complied with, a warm engagement immediately followed, for an advertising calendar (Ketterlinus Lithographic Company, 1924)

Oil on board, 13½ × 10⅝ in.
Biggs Museum of American Art, Sewell C. Biggs Bequest, 2004.419

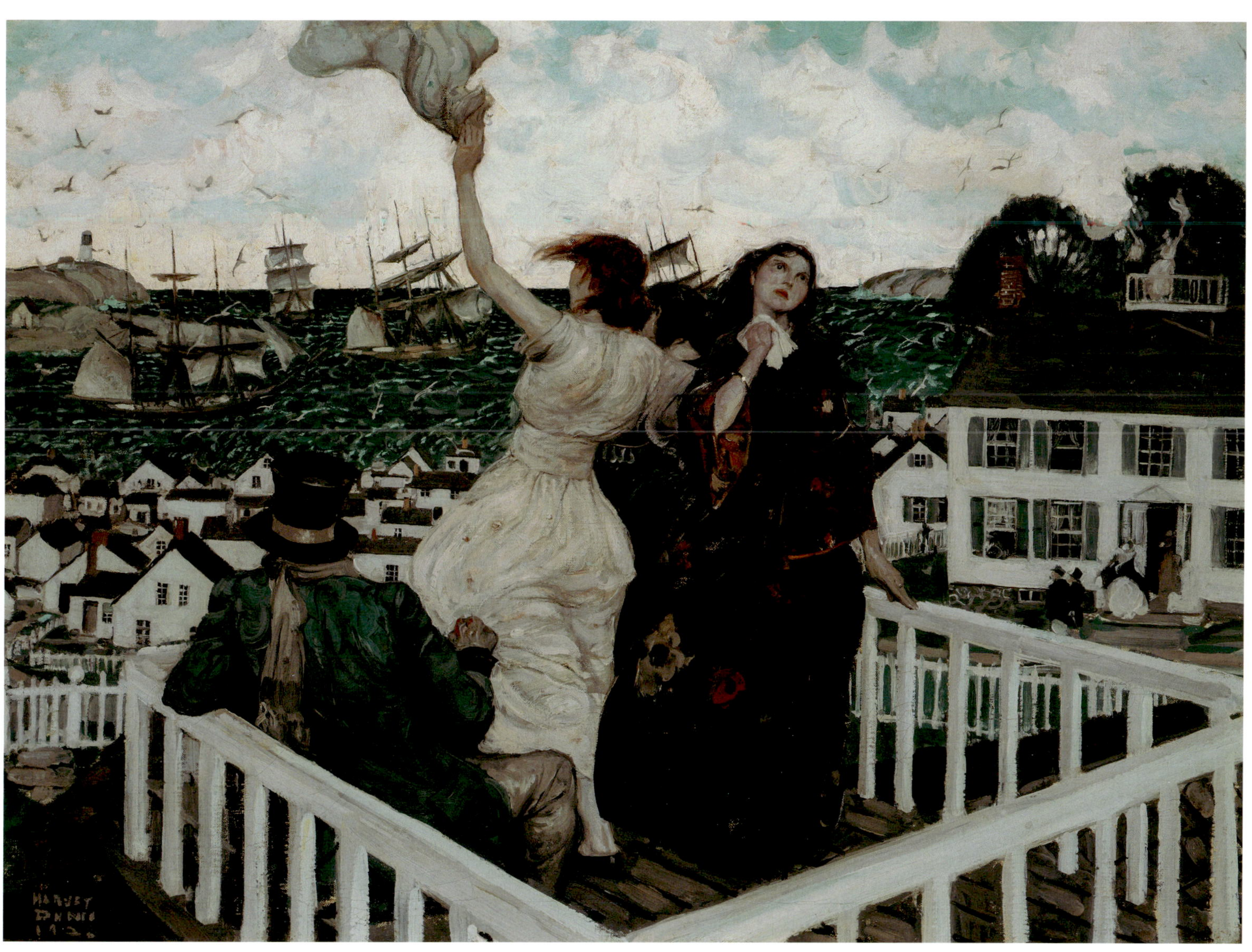

51

Harvey Dunn (1884–1952)

When the Whaling Fleet Cleared for the Caribes, advertisement for Duco Paint, *The Saturday Evening Post*, September 22, 1928

Oil on canvas, 30 × 40 in.

Delaware Art Museum, Gift of E. I. du Pont de Nemours and Company, 2017

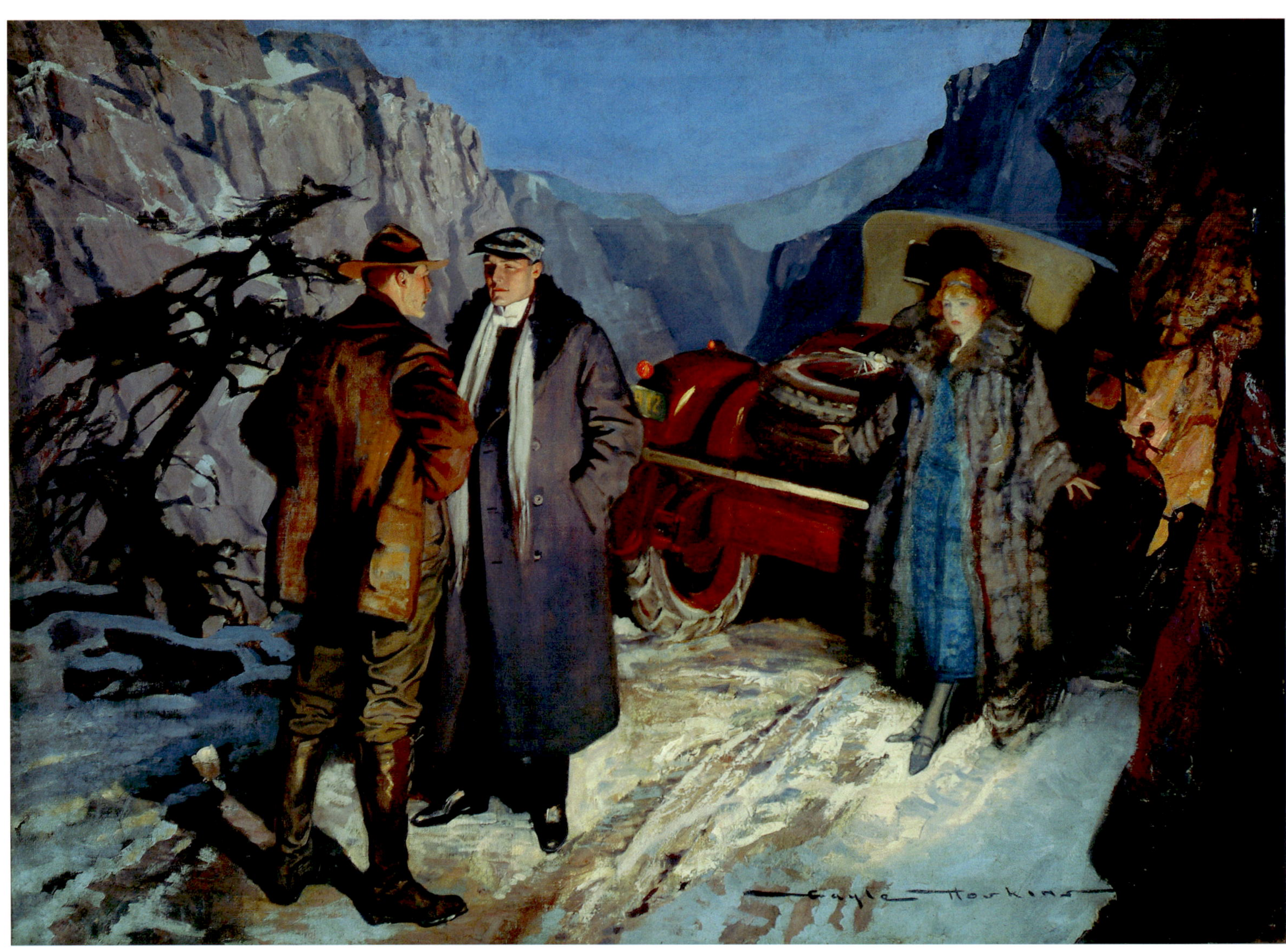

52

Gayle Porter Hoskins (1887–1962)

You can't leave her here to suffer. Whether you want to or not, you'll have to do it, for "Roads of Doubt" by William MacLeon Raine, *Woman's Home Companion*, February 1925

Oil on canvas, 26 × 36 in.

Delaware Art Museum, Gayle and Alene Hoskins Endowment Fund, 1979

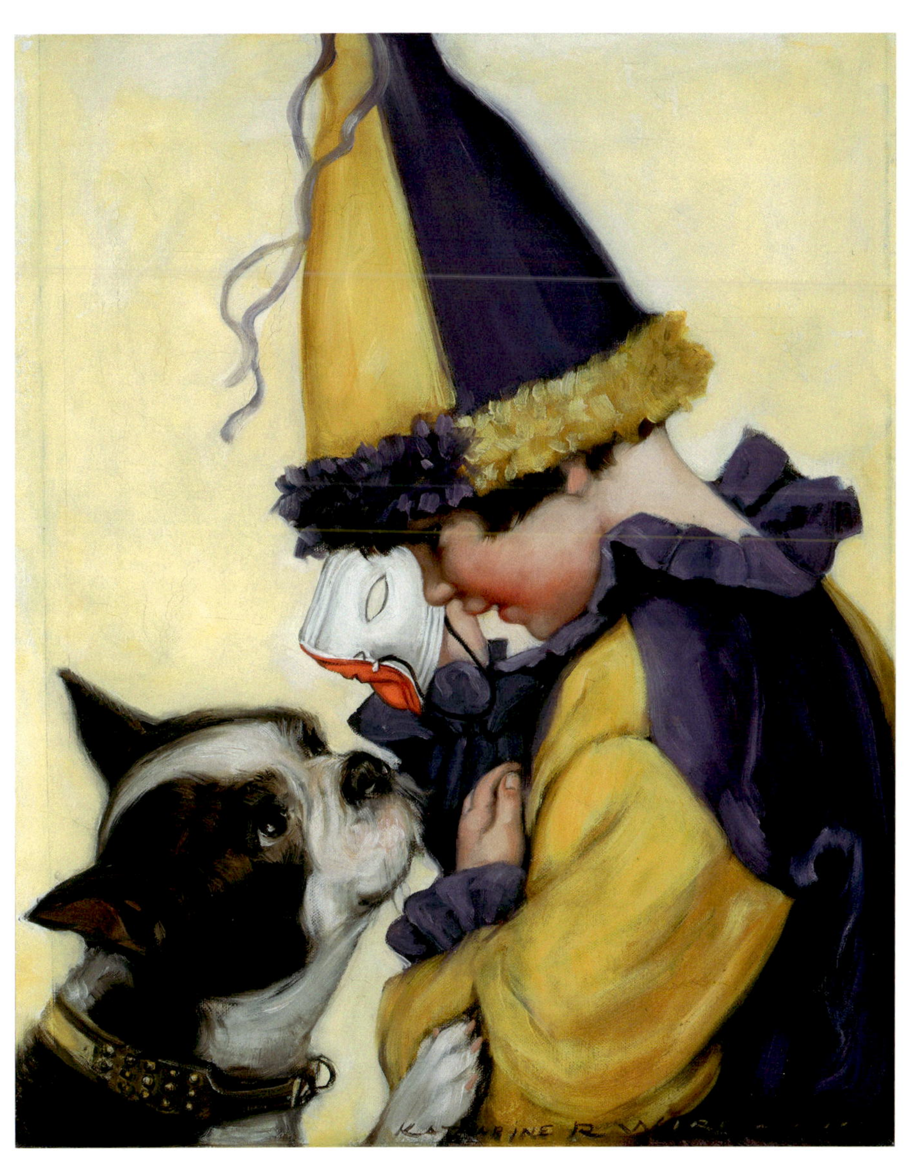

53

Katharine Richardson Wireman (1878–1966)

Cover, 1925, for *Success*, April 1926

Oil on canvas, 20¼ × 16¼ in.

Delaware Art Museum, Gift of Henrietta Wireman Shuttleworth, 2017

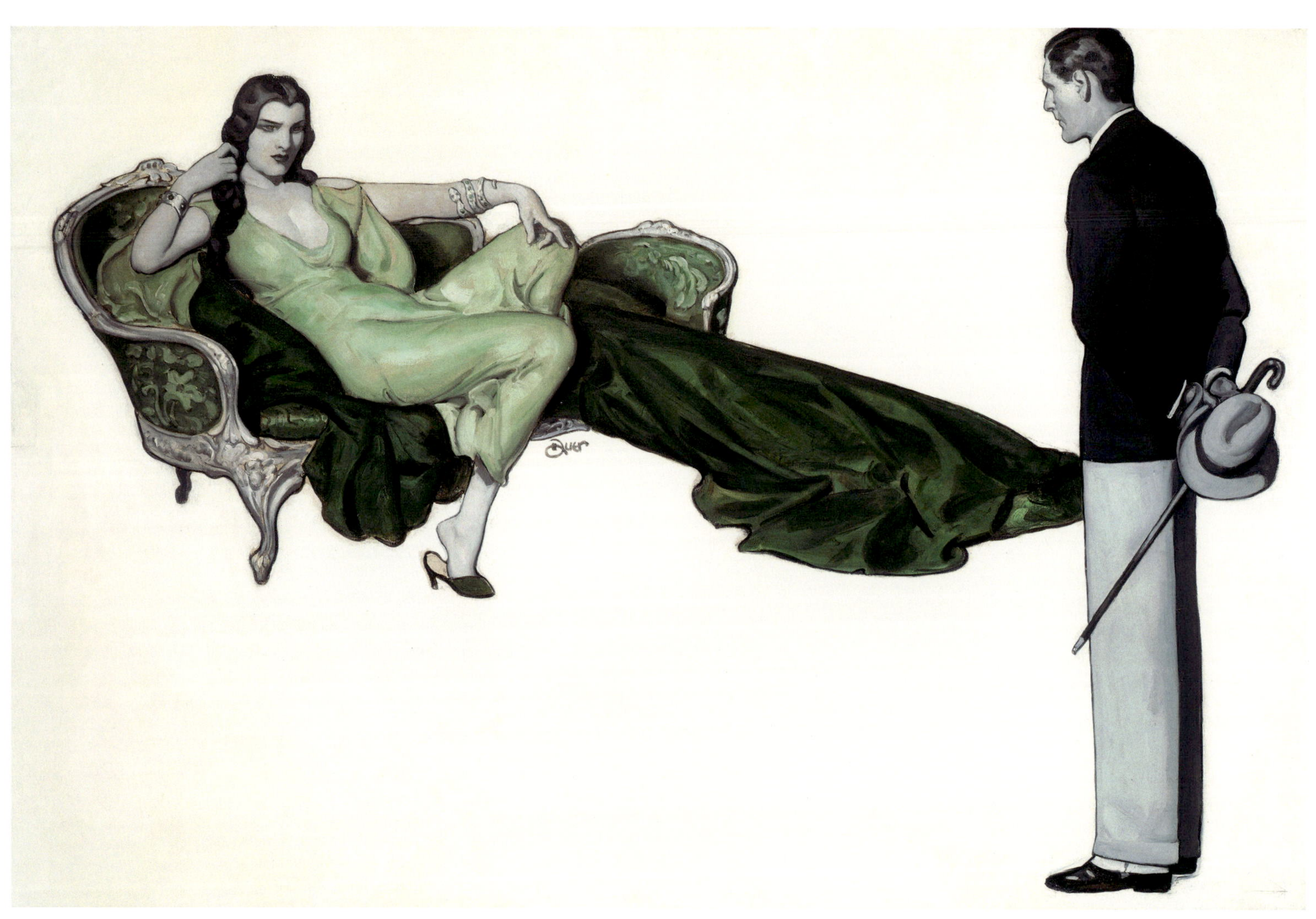

54

Douglas Duer (1887–1964)

I'm billed all over Paris to appear with two lions and a tiger, for "Danger Calling" by Patricia Wentworth, *Pictorial Review*, April 1931

Oil on canvas, 29¾ × 43⅝ in.
Delaware Art Museum, Gift of Mrs. Douglas Duer, 1976

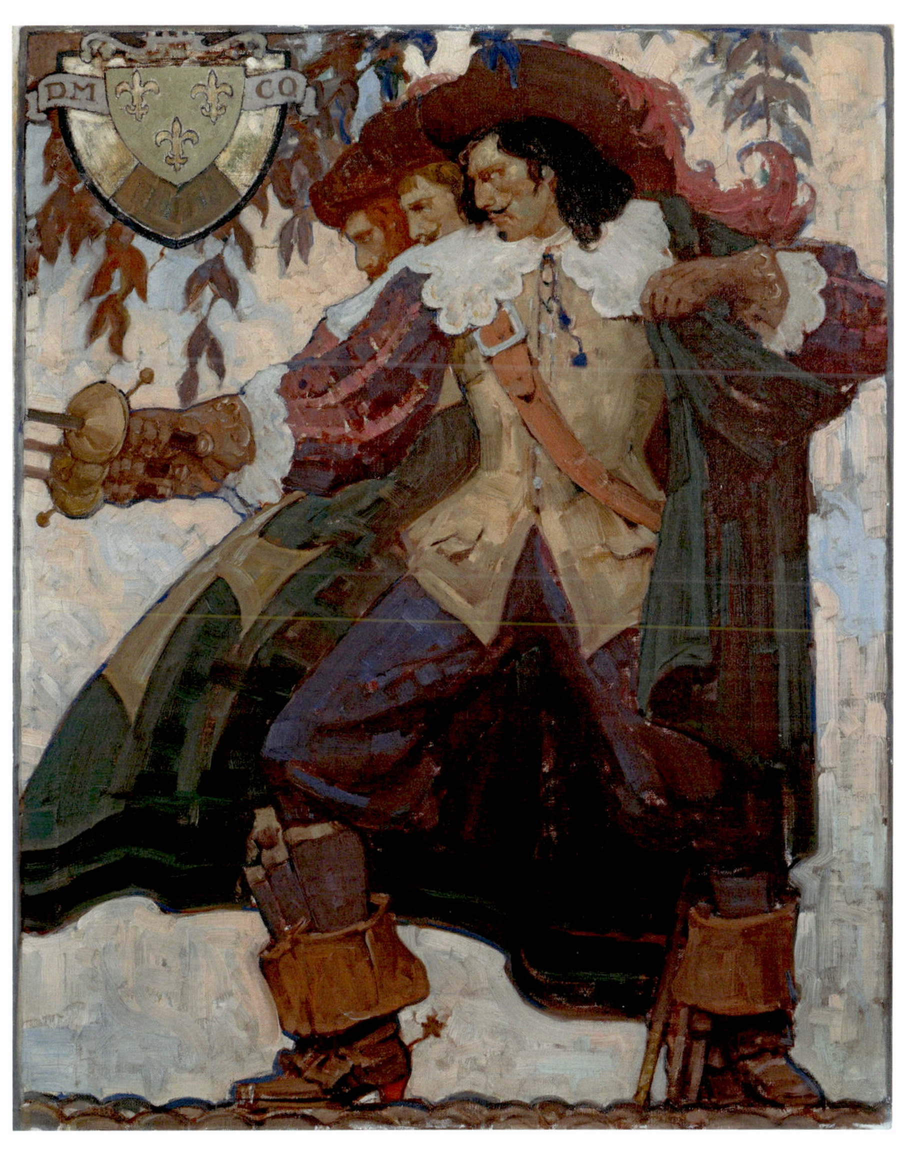

55

Mead Schaeffer (1898–1980)
Cover for *The Three Musketeers* by Alexandre Dumas
(Boston: Dodd, Mead and Company, 1929)

Oil on canvas, 32 × 26 in.
Collection of Brock and Yvonne Vinton

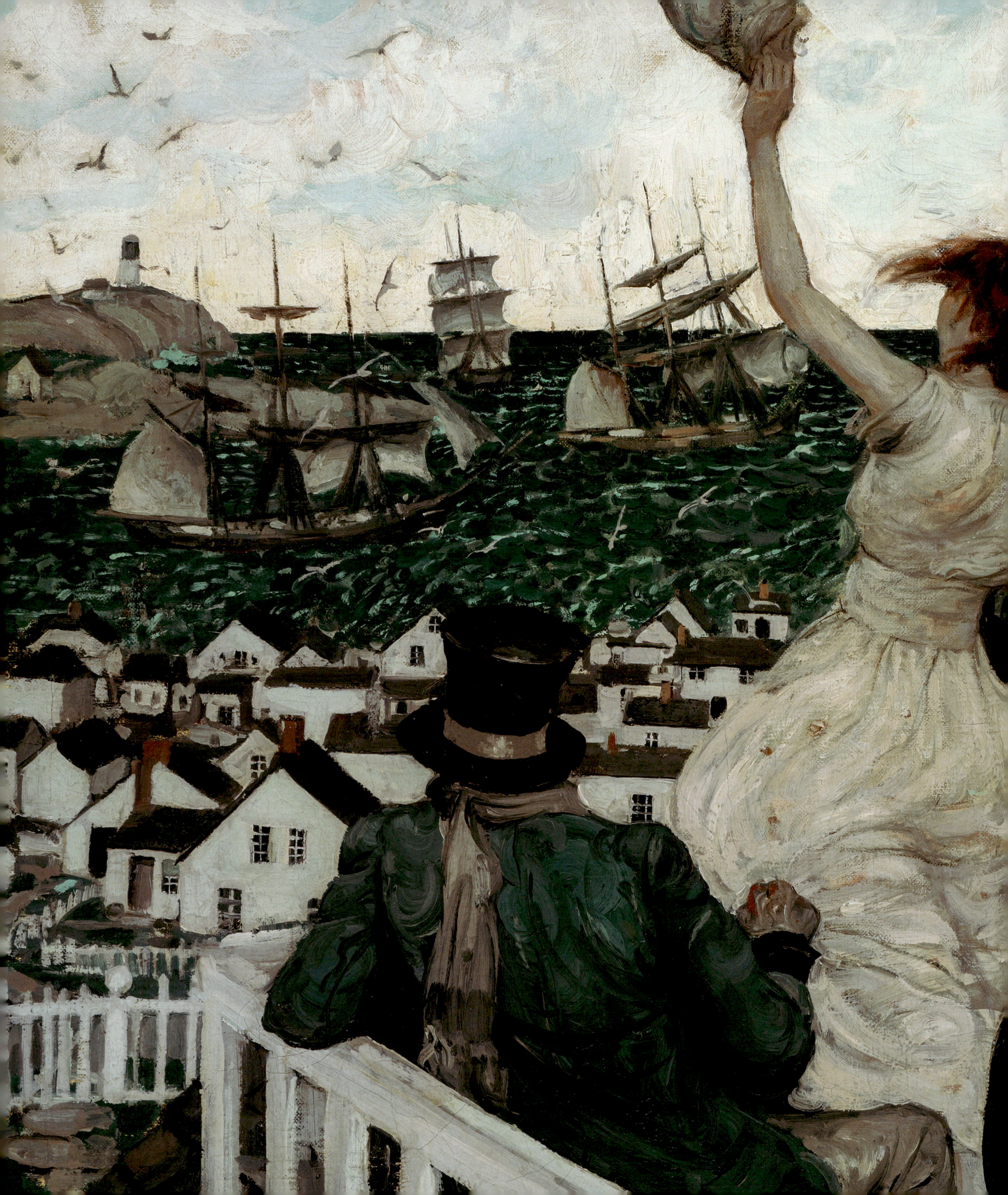

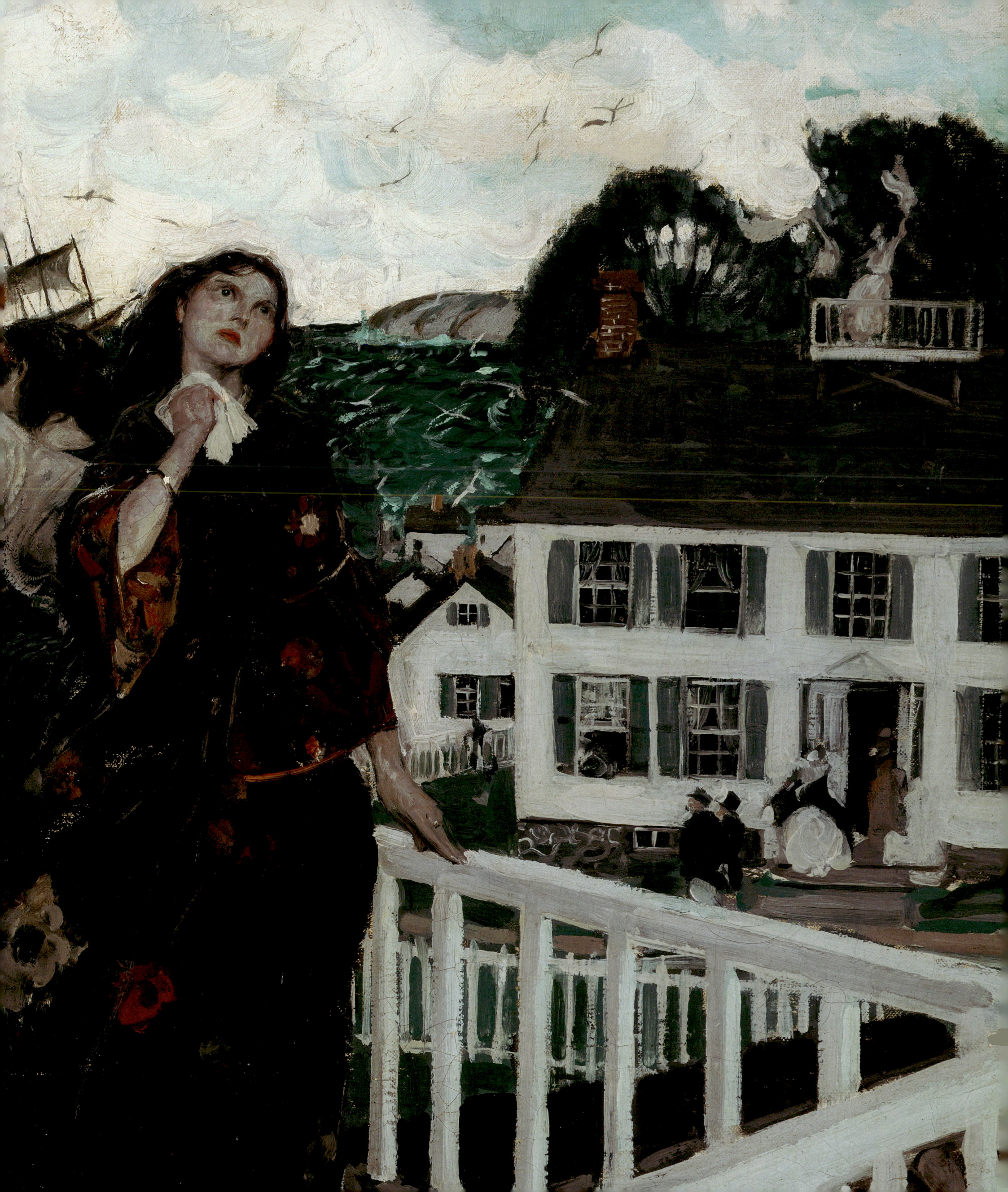

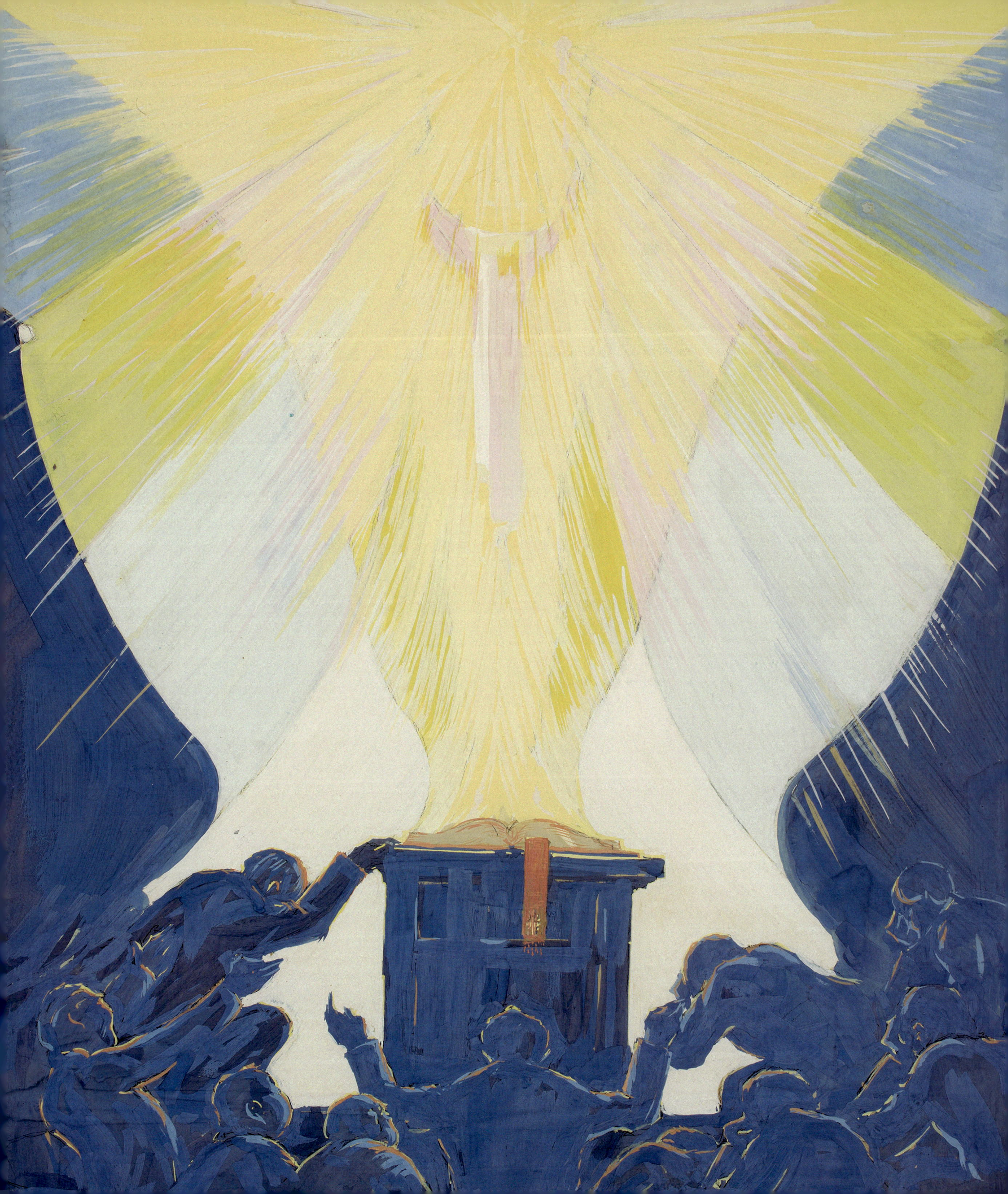

Contributors

Heather Campbell Coyle is curator of American art at the Delaware Art Museum. She is the editor and lead author of *Howard Pyle: American Master Rediscovered* (2011), *Fashion, Circus, Spectacle: Photographs by Scott Heiser* (2014), and *An American Journey: The Art of John Sloan* (2017), and co-editor and co-author of *John Sloan's New York* (2007). She has also published and curated exhibitions on William Glackens, Gertrude Käsebier, George Luks, Everett Shinn, and the Society of Independent Artists.

Anne Strachan Cross is a teaching assistant professor in American art at Pennsylvania State University. She is a specialist in nineteenth- and early twentieth-century American visual culture, with a focus on the histories of photography and illustrated journalism. Her research considers the relationship between the circulation of images as objects and the illustration of the news, especially in regard to issues of race and representation. Her work has appeared in *Panorama* and *History of Photography*.

Chris Dingwall is assistant professor of design history in the Sam Fox School of Design & Visual Arts at Washington University in St. Louis. He is co-editor and contributing writer to *Black Designers in Chicago*, a forthcoming volume from University of Chicago Press about the history of African American craftspeople, commercial artists, and art educators in the making of modern design.

Colette Gaiter is a professor in the departments of Africana Studies and Art & Design at the University of Delaware. Her visual work, exhibited internationally, covers a range of media and forms, including artist books. Since 2005 she has written about art and design, particularly the work of former Black Panther artist Emory Douglas. Her essays appear in *Black Panther: The Revolutionary Art of Emory Douglas*, the Norman Rockwell Museum's book *Imprinted: Illustrating Race*, and *Wonder City of the World: New York City Travel Posters*.

Molly Giordano is Executive Director of the Delaware Art Museum.

Victoria Rose Pass is an associate professor at the Maryland Institute College of Art. Her essay, "Racial Masquerades in the Magazines: Defining White Femininity Between the Wars," was published in the *Journal of Modern Periodical Studies* in 2020. She has co-edited two books, *Design History Beyond the Canon* with Jennifer Kaufmann-Buhler and Christopher Wilson (Bloomsbury, 2019) and *Women's Magazines in Print and New Media* with Noliwe Rooks and Ayana Weekley (Routledge, 2016).

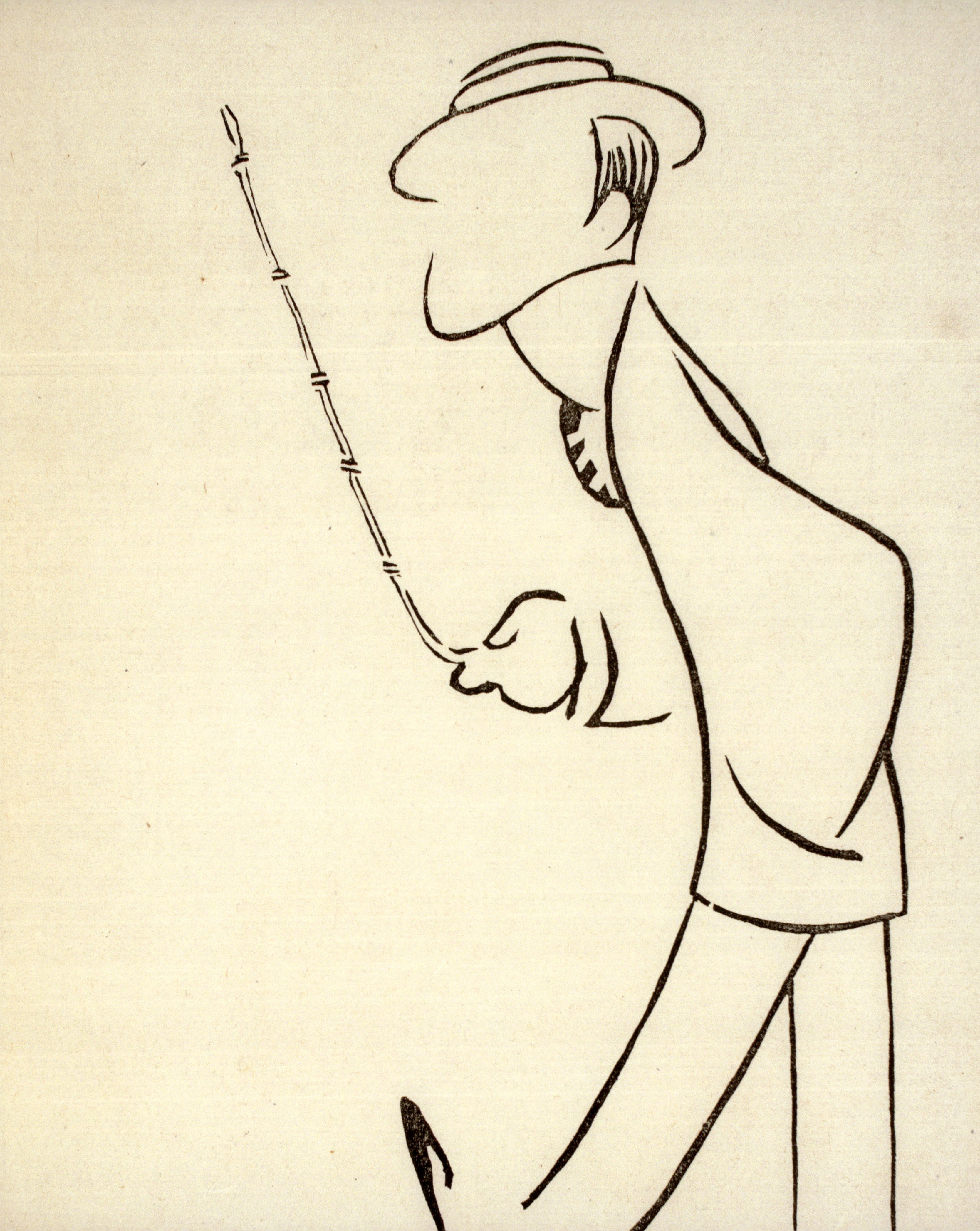

Index

Exhibition pieces are indicated by italicized page numbers.
Figures are indicated by "f" following the page numbers.

C

D

E

F

G

H

I

J

K

Y

Jazz Age Illustration is published in conjunction with an exhibition of the same name.

Delaware Art Museum, Wilmington, DE: October 5, 2024–January 26, 2025
Biggs Museum of American Art, Dover, DE: Spring–Summer 2025
Norman Rockwell Museum, Stockbridge, MA: Fall–Winter 2025–26

Jazz Age Illustration is made possible thanks to the following sponsors:

Lead funding for the exhibition is provided by the Henry Luce Foundation.

Catalogue support is provided by the Wyeth Foundation for American Art.

Major support is provided by the Richard C. Von Hess Foundation; the Rock Oak Foundation, in memory of Thomas Brokaw; and the Roger and Sarah Bancroft Clark Foundation.

Copyright © 2024 Delaware Art Museum
All rights reserved. No part of this publication may be reproduced or transmitted in any form or by any means, electronic or mechanical, including photocopy, recording, or any information storage or retrieval system, without permission in writing from the publisher.

Library of Congress Control Number: 2024934692
ISBN: 978-0-300-27881-1

Published by Delaware Art Museum
2301 Kentmere Parkway
Wilmington, DE 19806
delart.org

Distributed by Yale University Press
302 Temple Street
P.O. Box 209040
New Haven, CT 06520-9040
yalebooks.com/art

Produced by Marquand Books, Seattle
marquandbooks.com

Edited by Melissa Duffes
Designed by Thomas Eykemans
Typeset in Jubilat and Halyard by Tina Henderson, Miko McGinty Inc.
Proofread by Emily Holt
Index by Enid Zafran
Color management by I/O Color, Seattle
Printed and bound in China by Artron Art Group

Details:

Front cover: Jay Jackson, *Etta Moten Barnett Dancing*, ca. 1940 (cat. 46)

Back cover: E. Simms Campbell, *A Night-Club Map of Harlem*, 1932 (fig. 11)

End papers: Loïs Mailou Jones, *Heritage: Illustration for Important Events and Dates in Negro History*, 1936 (fig. 28)

pp. 2–3: Nicolai Remisoff, cover for *Vanity Fair*, March 1923 (cat. 26)

p. 4: Witold Gordon, *Amoré*, for *The Travels of Sindbad*, unpublished, 1932 (cat. 11)

p. 6: Beatrice Anderson, design for an advertisement for Parfums Luyna, ca. 1925 (cat. 12)

p. 10: George W. Gage, dust jacket for *The Door of the Double Dragon: A Romance of the China of Yesterday and To-Day* by Hector Blanding (New York: W. J. Watt and Co., 1920) (cat. 33)

pp. 14–15: Michael Dolas, *Edie's love life was a revolving door*, for "I Wonder What Happened to Tony" by Corey Ford, *Hearst's International Combined with Cosmopolitan*, July 1938 (cat. 6)

pp. 52–53: Helen Dryden, cover for *Vogue*, December 15, 1922 (cat. 27)

pp. 88–89: Francis Cugat, *Celestial Eyes*, cover for *The Great Gatsby* by F. Scott Fitzgerald (New York: Charles Scribner's Sons, 1925) (cat. 32)

pp. 116–17: Neysa McMein, *The Admirable Hostess*, advertisement for Wallace Silver, *The Saturday Evening Post*, January 8, 1921 (cat. 43)

pp. 128–29: J. C. Leyendecker, *End of Vacation*, cover for *The Saturday Evening Post*, September 15, 1934 (cat. 19)

pp. 150–51: Douglas Duer, *I'm billed all over Paris to appear with two lions and a tiger*, for "Danger Calling" by Patricia Wentworth, *Pictorial Review*, April 1931 (cat. 54)

pp. 164–65: Harvey Dunn, *When the Whaling Fleet Cleared for the Caribes*, advertisement for Duco Paint, *The Saturday Evening Post*, September 22, 1928 (cat. 51)

p. 166: Frederick C. Alston, *Light of the World*, 1929 (cat. 4)

p. 168: Al Frueh, *George M. Cohan*, for *Stage Folk: A Book of Caricatures* by Alfred J. Frueh (New York: Lieber & Lewis, 1922) (fig. 10)